TO PAY FOR THE CROSSING

OTHER TITLES BY KIM GRAVELL

The Demon's Call

Child of the Covenant

TO PAY FOR THE CROSSING

Kim Gravell

Matador
Unit E2 Airfield Business Park,
Harrison Road, Market Harborough,
Leicestershire. LE16 7UL
Tel: 0116 2792299
Email: books@troubador.co.uk
Web: www.troubador.co.uk/matador
Twitter: @matadorbooks

ISBN 978 1916324 701

British Library Cataloguing in Publication Data.
A catalogue record for this book is available from the British Library.

Printed and bound in Great Britain by CMP UK
Typeset in 10.5pt Adobe Garamond Pro by Troubador Publishing Ltd, Leicester, UK

Matador is an imprint of Troubador Publishing Ltd

For the Coven.

CHAPTER 1

The demon was gone.

Kneeling in the middle of his living room, Marcus Eldritch knew that he had won. Yet the thought gave him no satisfaction. What he had achieved felt more like defeat than victory.

Helen was dead.

It scarcely mattered that she had been dead since the moment the demon had possessed her, her body reduced to a shell in which the demon could exist in the Mortal World. While it had occupied her there had been the chance to pretend that the woman he loved was still alive. Even after he had realised the truth, when he knew he was only deceiving himself, still there had been times when he would glance at her and, just for a moment, let himself believe he was wrong. She had been his soulmate, his other half. How could she be dead when he could see her there in front of him? But he knew the truth, and, with that realisation, there was no going back.

So, he had armoured himself for the battle he knew was inevitable. There had been no place for grief, no time to mourn for all he had lost. He had locked his emotions away behind a façade and played the demon at its own game. All he allowed himself to feel was a cold, focused anger that sustained him, carried him through as he laid his plans, kept him going until the molten fire of battle took over. Now, even that was gone. He felt as hollow as the shell the demon had left behind, reamed out and empty. The demon was dead. Helen was dead. Now his task was finished, and he could die too.

Eldritch lifted his head and looked at his wife's body. Stretched beside him, her face peaceful, Helen might have been sleeping. The final welter of Levin bolts that had driven the demon from her had left no mark on her body. She looked as though she might wake at the slightest touch. Without conscious thought, Eldritch stretched his fingers towards her cheek, where a blush of colour still warmed the skin, and froze. His breath seemed to congeal in his lungs. Surely the universe could have spared him this? His gut twisted and bile rose in his throat. He had thought he had reached the nadir of his despair, but it seemed there was a wealth of pain yet awaiting him. Helen was still breathing.

A man unfamiliar with demonic possession might have rejoiced, but Eldritch was a wizard and he knew the bitter truth. Those who had been possessed did not recover. Usually, a host's body would die when the possessing demon was driven out, but not always. Sometimes the body continued – an empty shell that went on functioning, devoid of the spirit that had lived within it, purposeless and without hope of recovery. It was the cruellest twist; Helen was dead even though her body still lived.

Eldritch wasn't sure how long he knelt there. His hands tangled in Helen's hair, running the corn-silk fineness of it through his fingers like a man praying over the beads of a rosary, while his mind stalled, caught in a maelstrom of images of all he had lost. When he came back to himself the light had faded from the windows and the room was sunk into shadows, but he knew what he would do.

He pulled Helen's body into his arms, cradling the warm weight of her against his chest. He inhaled her scent, felt the slow rise and fall of her breath, and his heart broke anew. 'Forgive me.'

His muscles cried out in protest as he lurched upright and carried her to the settee, lowering her down carefully onto the cream leather and positioning a cushion beneath her head, as though such niceties could make a difference now.

Moving mechanically, he circled the room, drawing the curtains and switching on a table lamp to hold back the dusk. He chose a favourite CD and slid it into the player. Finally, as the first notes of the piano tumbled into the air, he knelt and lit the gas fire. For several heartbeats he stared into the flames, letting that ancient practice steady him. Then, calling his power to him, he reached out and blocked the fire's air intake. The flames trembled then steadied, their colour shifting from blue to an orangey yellow. Eldritch watched them until he was certain the fire would continue to burn. There would be no explosion to endanger anyone else. Even now that was important to him. All he wanted was the slow build-up of carbon monoxide wrapping around him and Helen, ensuring that they would sleep forever in each other's arms.

Returning to the settee, he knelt once more beside his wife's still form. Helen's lips were slightly parted as if she might whisper to him, but her periwinkle blue eyes were closed and they would never open again. Tenderly, Eldritch kissed those closed lids. He brushed the hair back from her forehead and kissed her once more, cupping her cheeks and staring down at her, filling his mind with her image.

'I love you,' he whispered. 'Wait for me.'

Then he lay down, wrapping his arms around her and drawing her body close. Closing his eyes, he waited for death to claim him.

CHAPTER 2

Bob Finch cast an appraising eye around the small subterranean room he had dubbed the under-cellar. It was surprisingly dry, given that it was underground and had been unmaintained for lord alone knew how many years. Unmaintained? He laughed silently at himself, gently amused. Heavens, no one at the Greenman Clinic had even known the room existed. It was only when he and Terry had been tasked with emptying the adjoining storeroom, clearing out the accumulated detritus of long years of the clinic's history, that they had noticed the door set in a depression in the wall in the farthest corner of the room. Even had the place not been crammed full of rubbish, the natural fall of shadows would have made it difficult to spot. Barely five feet high, the thick oak door opened onto a flight of narrow stone stairs that led down through the darkness to this.

Curiously, unlike the storeroom above it, the under-cellar had been completely empty. Worn marks on the tiled floor suggested there had once been some sort of furniture – perhaps benches or tables – arrayed around the small space, and soot marks on the ceiling hinted at the one-time presence of oil lamps, or perhaps even candles, but nothing remained in place to show the purpose of the room. Some of the staff had come down to see for themselves the rough plaster walls and the unusual curved brickwork of the ceiling, but most were incurious. A long-forgotten storeroom was the general consensus, although to

Bob's mind that made little sense, not with the narrow access and the stairs. Not that it mattered to him. After viewing the find, Doctor Ashwood had decreed that the walls should be given a coat of paint to clean them up and make the place useable again, and that was as much as Bob needed to know.

'Hey, boss. What do you make of these?' Terry, Bob's apprentice, peered at the wall he had been about to paint. 'Someone's been drawing on this plaster. Look.'

He angled the nearest work light the better to illuminate the grubby surface.

Bob snorted with amusement. 'It's not exactly a Roman fresco, is it?'

Even with the halogen bulb shining on them, the crudely drawn images were hard to make out. Odd symbols and squiggles, faded and half hidden by years of grime and dirt – no wonder no one had noticed them before. There were letters there too, scripted in an odd, spikey calligraphy. Bob squinted at them, but he couldn't make sense of the words they spelled, if indeed they did spell anything meaningful.

'Probably some kids have got in here at some time, playing games.'

The letters could have been some sort of code or made-up names. Kids would write anything on a blank wall.

'You don't think we should leave them? Maybe get someone to take a look?'

Bob sighed. Terry had a romantic streak. He dreamed of unearthing treasure or uncovering some long-lost relic every time they worked on an old property. His eyes had positively lit up when he'd heard they would be working in a vault under the clinic.

'No, Terry, I don't. If there was anything of value down here, I'm sure Doctor Ashwood would have known about it.'

'But it's been blocked up for years.'

'That's as may be, and now we're going to clean it up. Get some paint on it, lad. We haven't got all day.'

Terry did as he was told. He was a good lad and a willing worker. Bob nodded approvingly as the first brushstrokes obliterated the curious little squiggles and symbols. The room wasn't that large. They could have the first coat finished in half an hour. He picked up his own brush ready to start work on the second wall but paused when Terry spoke again.

'Tell you what, boss, I hadn't noticed it was so cold down here. Look.' To illustrate his point Terry blew out a long breath. It hung like smoke in the air. 'It's flippin' freezing.'

He shivered theatrically, rubbing his free hand up and down his arm. Bob frowned at this new disruption, but the lad was right; it did seem cold down here. Still, there was an easy cure for that.

'Put your back into your painting, lad. That'll soon warm you up.'

Bob took his own advice and started brushing paint onto the wall, working in the opposite direction from his apprentice. The sooner they got the first coat finished, the sooner they would be out in the sunlight. For no reason he could think of, that seemed important now.

Bob moved along the wall, watching with satisfaction as his brushstrokes swiftly transformed the dingy, greying plaster, covering it with fresh white emulsion. As he did so he became aware of a strange sound, just on the edge of his hearing. He stopped for a moment, trying to identify what it was. Though barely audible, it grated on his nerves like nails scraping down a blackboard.

'If that's you lad you can stop it right now.'

Yet even as he spoke, Bob realised the sound wasn't coming from Terry. Indeed, it wasn't like any noise he had heard made by a human throat. It held a strange resonance that made his flesh creep and had him wanting to look over his shoulder to see what was edging up behind him. It was the sort of sound that a hive of angry bees might make if they were locked in a large and echoey room.

'It's not me, boss.' Terry had lowered his paintbrush and was eyeing the corners of the room anxiously.

'You can hear it too?'

Terry nodded, looking from Bob to the walls and back again. His eyes were wide in the lamplight, and he licked his lips nervously. 'I thought it was you.'

Bob's ears popped as though the pressure in the room had increased. Beside him Terry yelped and put a hand up to rub the side of his head.

'What in heaven's name is going on?' Bob turned in a circle, but he could see nothing untoward. He looked back at Terry, ready to tell him there was nothing to worry about, but the words of reassurance died unspoken. He took a cautious breath and then sniffed again just to be sure. Mingling with the comfortingly familiar smell of fresh paint was something else. This new scent was sweet, but not in a pleasant way. It smelled like the remnants of a strong perfume, something that had been trapped in a fabric long folded away; the sort of thing that had been put into storage on the day its owner had died.

'Boss …' Terry's voice was a nervous whine.

Every hair on the back of Bob's neck stood on end. Some primitive part of his brain screamed at him to run, but it was too late. The bulbs in the four work lights fizzed briefly within their wire cages and then exploded, plunging the cellar into darkness. Beside him Bob heard Terry cry out and then something cold wrapped itself around him, engulfing his face and head. He managed to scream once and then it was over.

The grieve looked out through Bob's eyes. It could remember the world as it had been when it had been imprisoned but, as it slowly assimilated the information from its new host's brain, it realised that that world had changed. How many years had it been locked away? Oh, but the world would pay for that. Red rage coiled and twisted within the grieve's consciousness. For a moment it burned, all-consuming and powerful, but then it was pushed back down, the fires of that anger banked and contained. There would be a reckoning, oh yes, but in its own good time. The grieve was not a slave to its desires. The long years of its incarceration had taught it cunning and caution. First it would learn. So, this body had belonged to Bob. It could understand some of the basic skills of Bob's profession. Others made no sense at the moment but the grieve knew that understanding would come. It sank its consciousness into the fabric of Bob's brain, absorbing and consuming everything within, right up until the last seconds of life. The grieve paused in its process of absorption. Woven around those memories was the terror this man had experienced in those final moments. The grieve chuckled as it savoured that emotion. It tasted delightful.

Finally, when it was satisfied, it turned towards its companion. This was the young man Bob had known as Terry. An apprentice, yes. He sensed the bond that had been shared between the two men. That one was a lower status individual because he was younger and was learning his trade, but Bob had respected the youngster. The grieve could understand that. Now Terry was a host to its mate. The grieve looked towards the other man.

'We are free,' its mate said.

'Yes.'

'We will feast again.'

'Soon. But first we must learn more about this world that we now enter. This man's memories are strange to me. Come, let us go and find out what awaits us.'

CHAPTER 3

The work light in the stairway still functioned, illuminating the worn stone steps and the ancient brickwork of the narrow passageway. Terry paused as they passed beneath its glare, holding his hand towards it and sending shadows grasping across the walls.

'Curious,' he murmured, 'this light without flame.'

'Electricity.' Bob's mind held the knowledge of this tame lightning and its use as a power source. The grieve accepted its function as Bob had, without needing to understand it. 'Leave it.'

It looked around curiously. The last time it had been in this passage the way had been lit by the torches its captors carried, the flames illuminating their faces, fierce and determined, their mouths grim, their eyes dark in the flickering, ruddy light. There had been six of them, it remembered. The woman, Melindra, had led the way, tall and imperious, her iron-grey hair cropped close to her skull like a warrior's. The torchlight had lent it glints of rusty brown. After her had come the guards, four burly men who half carried, half dragged the bodies of the two hosts between them, paralysed with drugs and bound with magic, their mouths stopped with cloth and wax so they could utter no sound. Despite the fact that they were unable to move, their hands were manacled and chained behind them as additional protection. Their captors were taking no chances.

Even now the grieve remembered the indignity of that manhandling and fury burned through it again. The guards had pulled the two hosts down the steps, careless of the way their feet bumped and jarred across the stones. And behind this motley procession came the wizard, Gwydion, bringing up the rear. Thus, they had come to the Chapel of the Maiden. In Bob's body the grieve stiffened as it recalled the prickling touch of magic within these walls. That magic had long since faded, eroded by time and the constant wear of life energies brushing against it. The little that had remained within the chapel itself had been nullified by the workmen painting over the sigils of ward and closure. It laughed at the irony of what its new host had done.

The storeroom at the top of the stairs was empty, devoid of any distraction, and the two grieves passed through it, crossing to the outer door which opened onto one end of a wide corridor. The pair stood for a moment considering their options. It would be several minutes before either had fully merged with their new host and was able to access the man's memories effortlessly, as though they had lived them. Until then, information had to be sought. It would be safer to stay hidden until the process was complete. Yet it had been so very long since they had been free. The two looked at each other, recognising that common desire. As one they turned and walked forward.

On either side of the corridor were doors set at regular intervals in the green-painted walls. The grieve within Bob ignored them. It wanted to get out of the building, to see the sky and feel the warmth of the sun on its skin. Bob's memories told it that this was the correct way to go; further details were unnecessary for now. Its mate was with it. They would deal with whatever they encountered.

Then he felt it. Bob's head came up sharply and he looked around. Just for a moment he thought he had sensed something – magic! Like a snatch of music and laughter when the door to a great hall was opened, revealing the revelry within. The next instant it was gone, as though that door had been slammed shut in his face.

'Did you feel that?'

His companion shook his head, but his eyes were wary. 'What?'

'I thought—' Bob stopped at the sound of voices. The speakers were blocked from view by the turn of the corridor but Bob recognised one of the voices. It was the physic: of course, this place was a hospital of sorts. A physic – the term now was *doctor*, he remembered. This was bad. The witch Melindra had been a healer. That calling was sometimes linked to those of power, though the wizard, Gwydion, had not had the skill. It had been Melindra who had administered the potions that had paralysed him and his mate. Anger flared again at the memory, but with it came caution. If the doctor did have power this was not the place to confront him. The voices were coming closer. In a moment the speakers would turn the corner and they would be discovered. There was no time to retreat to the storeroom or the chapel beyond it.

Quickly he made his decision. 'In here.'

The room the grieves entered was simply furnished but cheerful, with walls the colour of primroses and the window draped in bright fabric covered in stylised flowers in orange and green. A wooden-framed chair stood in one corner, its seat padded with the same fabric, and in the other a plain cabinet made of a pale wood. Above it a thin, rectangular box was mounted on the wall. *Television*, Bob's memories supplied. But the main feature of the room was the bed. Bob stared. There was a woman asleep in the bed.

A halo of blonde hair spread out across the pillow, surrounding a pale face with fine, delicate features. Terry took a step closer to the bed, his eyes fixed on the woman. His lips parted and he turned to his companion with a grin. Desire surged through Bob, all thought of the doctor forgotten. He nodded his agreement.

Terry stepped forward eagerly but, as he reached out to pull the covers from the bed, he hissed and jerked his hand away. His face contorted with rage. 'Witch!' he snarled.

His hand drew back to strike the sleeping woman, but Bob caught his wrist. Terry twisted in his grip like a snake, turning to strike at his partner instead.

'Peace, mate of mine.' Bob fielded the blow easily. 'She cannot hurt us. She is not asleep.'

Bob dropped Terry's wrist and turned to look at the woman more closely. 'She breathes still, yet her spirit is gone.'

A patient.

'How? What kind of sorcery is this?'

Bob shrugged. 'I know not.'

Now he was closer he felt the residue of power in the woman's flesh. So, this was the source of what he had sensed, not the doctor after all.

Interesting.

A new idea was forming, displacing the physical lust with a stronger urge.

'We could still have her.' Terry traced his fingers across the woman's face, exploring the sensual contours of her lips, running them over her chin and down the slender column of her throat. 'It would still be … rewarding.' Terry leered at Bob but made no further move. It was almost as though he was waiting for permission.

Bob watched Terry's hand toying with the neck of the woman's gown. He could imagine his own fingers slipping beneath the loose fabric, digging into the soft mound of her breast, sliding further down, her body pliant and unresisting beneath his caress. Lust rose in him again with the image, hot and sweet and powerful. His body throbbed with it.

Yes.

It had been so long since he had had flesh to enjoy such pleasures. The sensation was intoxicating, heating his blood like a deep rich wine. He allowed himself to savour the ache and the longing before he reined it in. Oh, but there would be time to indulge, to feast on such things, but not yet.

He smiled at his partner. 'No. I have a better idea. I fancy a host with power.'

Terry's eyes narrowed. He scowled at the older man. 'What madness are you suggesting? Her shields are gone so you could possess her, yes, but what if her body is defective and she cannot rise from her sickbed? That body you inhabit now will die when you leave it.'

'Then you will bring me another.' The tone was curt and brooked no further argument. 'Yes, I like this.'

'You will be a woman.' Terry's contempt was palpable.

'A woman, true. They are lesser creatures. But a woman with power? That is a different matter. Have you forgotten the witch that bound us? We underestimated her.'

'The crone was abnormal.'

'I agree. She was old. This one is not.' He studied the unresponsive form in the bed, liking what he saw. 'She is ripe. I might enjoy a woman's body for a change. We might enjoy it.'

He reached out and ran his fingers across the other man's face.

Terry twisted away. 'I do not like this.'

'It is not your decision. Enough. I have made up my mind. I will—'

The two men started as the door behind them opened.

'What are you doing in here?'

They spun round. A tall man with reddish brown hair was standing in the doorway. He wore a white tunic and dark breeches. *Trousers*, Bob corrected himself.

'Oh, it's you, Bob.' The newcomer's face relaxed. 'And Terry, isn't it? You gave me quite a surprise. Even so, you shouldn't be coming into the patients' rooms. What are you doing in here?'

Terry cast a sidelong glance at Bob.

'We were walking down the corridor. I thought I heard someone call out.' Carefully, the grieve slid into Bob's mannerisms, deferring to the man he recognised as the head of the clinic. 'There wasn't anyone around, so I came in to check.' He cast a concerned look towards the woman in the bed and then stepped back, motioning Terry to do the same. 'I suppose I must have been mistaken, but I could have sworn I heard something.'

'Hmm …' The doctor stepped up to the bed. With his thumb he raised one of the woman's eyelids, peering briefly into her eye before letting the lid slip closed again and then feeling the pulse in her neck. With a sigh he straightened up. 'I don't know what you heard, Bob, but I'm afraid it wasn't Helen. She was diagnosed as suffering from UWS two years ago.'

'UWS?' The grieve found no explanation in Bob's memory.

The doctor treated Bob to a gently condescending smile. 'It stands for Unresponsive Wakefulness Syndrome. Less enlightened institutions might still refer to it as a permanent vegetative state.' Now the physician's lips tightened as though he were tasting something unpleasant. 'That's not a term we consider to be appropriate here. Nevertheless, it is highly unlikely she's ever going to wake up.'

Bob looked at the woman in the bed. 'What happened to her?'

'Really, Bob. It's hardly proper for me to be discussing a patient's medical history with you.'

'No, of course not, Doctor Ashwood.' The grieve bit back its irritation at being denied information. 'I didn't mean it like that. It just seems such a shame, that's all. A beautiful young woman, cut down in her prime.'

'And no family with her?' Terry added, managing to convey sympathy rather than sounding as though he was probing for information.

'People often find it difficult to cope when a loved one is struck down with something like UWS, Terry. We all have different ethics and Helen's husband was against her continued treatment.' Again, the little tightening of the doctor's mouth suggested his disapproval. 'He was insistent that she had no hope of recovery. Fortunately, a cousin was of a different opinion and it was he who arranged for her referral here. Despite his reservations, Mister Eldritch did visit in the early days, but he hasn't been for some time. And now, I have to get on with my rounds. I'm sure you gentlemen have other things to do, too.'

Doctor Ashwood gestured towards the door.

The handyman's storeroom was located in the clinic's east wing, well away from the public parts of the building or the patients' rooms and the state-of-the-art treatment areas. The two grieves retreated there to take stock of their situation. Bob sat on the one battered chair while Terry prowled the small space, edgy as a cornered animal.

'I will take her tonight.' Bob leaned back, his legs crossed, his hands folded on his knee. 'We will go back to her room. If the physician returns before I take her, we will say we were saddened by her plight and thought to visit her.'

At Bob's mention of the doctor Terry stopped his restless pacing. His thin face lit with interest. 'Doctor Ashwood. I could take him. He has authority here.'

The low status of his new host was galling. His previous host – the fool who had conjured them, opening a portal from the Unseen Realm through which he and his mate had entered this world – had commanded respect and obedience and Terry had enjoyed the power that gave him immensely. There had been servants only too eager to do his bidding or too terrified to refuse him. To Terry it was one and the same. He felt his new body stiffen at the memories.

'Perhaps.' Bob's response cut across Terry's fantasies. 'But first let us see what we can learn from the woman. There may be others of power she knows. The physician mentioned her husband. If he is a wizard …' Bob smiled slyly as he contemplated this new scenario. 'Now, that would be interesting.'

Terry hissed. 'This is a dangerous game.'

'But it is one with great possibilities. What would you do if you could wield a wizard's power, my mate? Think of it. Think of the mortals we could bind to us, their willing, eager bodies. Or those we bind against their will and force to serve us.' He stood in one swift, predatory movement and seized the other man by the shoulders. 'Think of it.' He pulled Terry closer, leaning in until their foreheads touched. His hands slid to the other's biceps, his fingers digging in to squeeze muscle against bone. 'Feel how sweet their struggles will taste. The witch's powers will render us magnificent. But a wizard's?' He gave a low croon of pleasure, deep in his throat. 'Ah, with a wizard's powers we will be invincible.'

CHAPTER 4

'Don't fuss over him, Gwyn. You'll only encourage him.'

'I don't think she's fussing,' Aidan protested as he batted Gwyn's hands away from his face. 'More like admiring your handiwork.'

'Well, it's not everyone whose girlfriend can give them quite so spectacular a black eye.'

There was more approval in Gwyn's tone than Aidan thought was appropriate, especially given the dull throb emanating from his cheekbone, not that he was about to admit that to anyone. Gwyn ignored the scowl he sent her and ruffled his hair affectionately – he knew it was a sign of affection because she did the same thing to her cats – before settling back down, cross-legged, on the rug.

The girlfriend in question made a little humming noise. 'He's lucky it was me who hit him and not Sensei,' Jane said darkly.

'Well, whoever did the hitting, they certainly did a good job of it.' At least Eldritch sounded sympathetic as he came back into the room. He handed Aidan a pack of frozen peas wrapped in a tea towel. 'This is the best I can do for the moment. If I'd known the pair of you were going to be fighting before you came for dinner I'd have made a point of getting in some first-aid supplies. What on earth were you doing, anyway?'

Aidan shared a look with Jane over the impromptu icepack. *Civilians!* 'Er … it's called training.'

'Yes, alright, I get that. But I didn't think you were actually meant to hit each other. What happened to pulling your punches?'

'That's for the juniors,' said Aidan.

'And for people who aren't trying to jazz up their freestyle technique by throwing psychic energy,' Jane added. She shot Aidan a complicated look which he pretended not to notice.

Gwyn raised an eyebrow. 'Tell me you didn't.' She sounded disappointed.

Aidan rolled his eyes at Jane. 'You really had to say that, didn't you?' he muttered. He had hoped that aspect of the afternoon's training session wouldn't get mentioned. 'It's not what you think, Gwyn. It wasn't as though I was trying to use it to do anyone any real damage.'

If he had hoped this would be sufficient to appease Gwyn, he was mistaken. She tilted her head to one side and eyed him dubiously, but said nothing, clearly waiting for him to continue. Aidan thought about brazening it out and letting her wait, but he knew when he was outgunned. 'It was an experiment.' He settled the tea-towel-wrapped bundle a little higher on his cheek, allowing himself a brief moment to appreciate the soothing properties of a bag of frozen vegetables. 'I wanted to see if I could use a Levin bolt – a really tiny one,' he qualified quickly, 'as a distraction technique. You know, give someone a little tap on the side of the head to take their attention away from the punch coming in from the other direction. It was working, too.'

His grin at the memory was cut short as Gwyn leaned forward and flicked him on the ear.

'Ow! What was that for?' He glared at her around the peas.

'The last time we worked on it you said I'd got the hang of throwing consistent amounts of power.'

'I did, and given how little training you've had so far you're doing very well, but that doesn't mean you're safe to go around using it on people. Sweet Lady, Aidan! I've been doing it all my life and you don't see me going around throwing psychic bolts at people for fun.'

'It seems to me that you could have done with throwing a few more psychic bolts at people,' Eldritch interjected. 'If you'd thought to do that last October it might have saved you from Griff Howell. And me and Aidan from a demon.' Unconsciously his fingers strayed to rub the crescent-shaped scar on his cheek.

'You stay out of this, wizard.' Gwyn shot Eldritch a warning look and returned her scrutiny to Aidan.

'I wasn't doing it for a laugh, Gwyn. I was testing it out as a fighting technique. That's how you learn if something works. Hell, you've had me throwing energy bolts at you for months now. What have we been doing all this time if not practising so I can throw them at other people?'

'What we've been doing has been controlled. We've been working in a circle, and you and I were both aware of what was happening, unlike the people you were testing your skills out on today. They weren't willing participants, Aidan. They didn't know what you were doing and – more to the point – you couldn't tell them.' Gwyn frowned. 'It's not the amount of energy you were using. Yes, your control is coming along well, so I'll accept that you weren't throwing enough to do any damage, but what if someone had noticed? Had you thought what you'd say if someone had asked you what you were doing or how you were doing it?'

'I have to say I side with Aidan on this one,' Jane commented before Aidan could respond. 'If there's a chance you're going to use something like that in a fight then you should try it out in the dojo first. At least there no one's seriously trying to hurt you. Mostly.' She smiled sweetly at Aidan and fluttered her eyelashes. 'But, back to your point, Gwyn, someone did notice. That's why he's got the black eye. When he throws a bolt he curls the fingers on his right hand. It's only a small movement but I noticed him doing it. So did Sensei. She didn't know what he was doing, or at least she didn't say she knew what he was doing. She just told me to take the next fight and if he tried it on me to hit him. So I did.'

Jane's tone made it clear she thought the instruction had been reasonable and Aidan agreed with her, despite the resulting bruise. There was a moment of quiet while the two non-combatants in the room considered this.

After a moment Eldritch asked curiously, 'But if Aidan threw a Levin bolt at you when you were fighting, why didn't it distract you?'

Jane shrugged. 'I didn't feel anything. The moment I saw him make that little twitchy move with his hand I threw a uraken at him. That's a back-knuckle strike,' she explained in response to Eldritch's blank look, adding a demonstration for effect. Eldritch jerked his head back as Jane's knuckles stopped just above the bridge of his nose. Jane gave him a knowing smile. 'He wasn't expecting it either,' she said, sounding pleased.

'I do wish the pair of you wouldn't do that.'

Aidan smothered a grin, both at Jane's uraken – it had been beautifully judged – and at the wizard's reaction. 'It is weird though, Jay, the fact that you didn't feel anything.' He considered their earlier fight. 'When you said you'd twigged about the hand movement – and I'm really going to have to work on that – I figured that put you on your guard so the bolt hitting you didn't work as a distraction. But you reckon you didn't feel it?'

'Nope. Sorry, Tarzan, not a thing.'

'Huh! I always said you were thick skinned.'

'Better than being a delicate little thing like you.' Jane pushed the icepack down and kissed Aidan on his bruised cheekbone. Her lips lingered just long enough to let him know that, had they been alone, it might have led to other things. Aidan appreciated the sentiment but for now he could satisfy only his curiosity.

'So, how does that work? How come Jay didn't feel the bolt I threw at her?' Aidan looked first at Eldritch and then at Gwyn for an explanation.

'Maybe you didn't throw it as hard as you thought you did,' suggested Eldritch.

Aidan shook his head. 'I'm pretty certain I threw as much energy at her as I did at Keith or Tigger. Maybe even a bit more. Purely because you're a higher grade and not so easily distracted,' he added quickly before Jane could take offence.

'Hmm.' She gave him a mock glare. 'Correct answer. You can live for now.'

'Maybe Jane's a null.' Gwyn's voice was teasing and Eldritch laughed as though she had said something funny.

'That would be a first.'

If Gwyn's suggestion had been a joke, it was one that Aidan didn't understand. He shrugged helplessly when Jane turned to him for an explanation.

'What's a null?' Jane eyed Gwyn and Eldritch curiously.

'A null is someone who's totally unaffected by magic. Immune to it, if you like,' Gwyn supplied.

'Really?' Aidan was intrigued. He was still very much a novice where magic – otherwise known as the use of psychic power – was concerned, but the idea didn't seem unreasonable. He could tell from the look on Jane's face as she thought this through that she rather liked the idea. Given what he'd been trying in the dojo she probably viewed it as an advantage. And that was not a concept he would ever have imagined ten months ago. It was incredible how one's world view could shift in such a short space of time.

'Cute.' Jane gave a little nod of approval. 'I like the sound of that. A null, eh? Can we prove it?'

This time it was Gwyn who laughed. 'Well, Eldritch and I could always throw a few Levin bolts at you and see what happens. You could be certain we wouldn't pull our punches. But I don't think we need bother. Nulls are more a theory than a reality. I'm not entirely sure they exist.'

'Me neither,' confirmed Eldritch. 'I've never met one and I don't know of anyone who has. Everyone's affected by magic. Your natural shielding might be quite high but you're not going to be immune. No one is.'

'Oh.' For a moment Jane looked crestfallen. 'That's a pity. Still, I don't think anyone's going to be using magic in the dojo again.'

Jane directed a knowing look at Aidan. He pulled a face but didn't argue with her.

'Why? What did Sensei have to say?' Gwyn was happy to move the discussion from the possibility of there being nulls back to the fallout from her ex-ward's experiment with magic. 'Aidan?'

Aidan sighed. It was all rather embarrassing, but he supposed Gwyn wouldn't let it drop until she had all the details.

'She didn't say anything, or at least not until after the lesson. Then she took me to one side and suggested that whatever I thought I was doing it had better stop. She reminded me in no uncertain terms that her dojo is a place for learning traditional karate skills and that's what I should be focusing on, not relying on some trick to get the better of my opponents, especially as she'd proven that the trick didn't always work.' Aidan reached out and squeezed Jane's hand. 'Mind you,' he added more cheerfully, 'she did say she had no issues with me using it on the street if I ever needed to. Or in any inter-club competitions.'

Gwyn laughed appreciatively. 'I've always said that woman was a pragmatist.' Her good humour restored, she added, 'It's unlikely you'll have to worry about someone from another club throwing a Levin bolt at you during a competition. Those of us who can do it are few and far between.'

'Not strictly true, given that you've got three of those people in this room,' Eldritch pointed out, with an all too innocent smile.

Gwyn made a growling noise deep in her throat like an angry cat. 'That's not the point.'

Aidan stifled a grin. It amused him how much Gwyn and Eldritch could wind each other up. He was waiting to see how Eldritch would respond, but the next moment a strident beeping sounded from the kitchen.

'Saved by the bell,' he whispered to Jane.

'If you'll excuse me for a minute.' Eldritch opted for a tactical withdrawal and headed for the doorway leading into the kitchen. Moments later, the beeping ceased and was replaced by the clatter of crockery and cutlery before Eldritch reappeared in the doorway. 'I hope your fighting didn't spoil your appetites. Dinner's ready.'

Aidan and Jane were on their feet in an instant.

Jane sniffed the air appreciatively as they filed past Eldritch into the kitchen. 'Mmm … whatever that is, it smells great. And if it's anywhere near as good as your pot roast chicken, then I want the recipe.'

'That was one of my grandma's favourites. This one's a bit different – it's a vegetable chilli. It is quite hot though. I hope that won't cause anyone any problems.'

'Not me. The hotter the better as far as I'm concerned.'

'Gwyn?'

'You know me. I've got the stomach of a small goat.'

'Yeah, I've seen it,' Aidan confirmed. 'She keeps it pickled in a jar of formalin in the larder.' He ducked into the kitchen before Gwyn could respond leaving Eldritch to disguise his chuckle with a hasty cough. Given the things that Gwyn did keep in her larder, Aidan knew his suggestion wasn't beyond the realms of possibility. He suspected the wizard recognised that too. Certainly, Eldritch was still smiling when they sat down at the table.

CHAPTER 5

Bob leaned across the unconscious woman's body. He raised his eyes to his mate, who was standing on the other side of the bed, and smiled lasciviously. 'Wait for me. We will enjoy this one.' He thought for a second and then added, 'If she does not wake, bring the physician to me.'

Not waiting for an answer, he bent forward. Placing his hands on either side of Helen's face, as though to hold the unresisting woman still, he kissed her firmly. His fingers tightened briefly as if in passion, clenching in her hair, and then his body slumped heavily across hers. As his knees buckled, he slowly slid down the bed to drop, limp and lifeless, to the floor.

Terry paid no attention to his colleague's collapse, nor did he spare a glance at the crumpled body. His gaze remained fixed on the woman in the bed. Her lips were slightly parted after the kiss but beyond that her appearance seemed unaltered. Terry leaned closer, scrutinising her. Beneath his gaze the slow rise and fall of her chest continued in the same, steady rhythm. Then her body jerked sharply, her eyes darting beneath the pale lids. Terry jerked too. He caught Helen's face in his hands, his splayed fingers pressing against her cheekbones and her jaw and against the fine ridges of her orbits. Urgently his fingertips absorbed the sensations, exploring the suppleness of her skin, the rapid motion of the eyeballs in their sockets, feeling the warm exhalation of air on his palm as her breathing deepened.

His own breath quickened. He ran his hand down, his fingers tracing either side of the fine prominence of her nose and over her parted lips, rolling the flesh back, exposing the moist, tender pinkness of her mouth. Terry moaned as Helen's head moved under his hand, the firm smoothness of her teeth sliding against his fingertips. He shuddered, leaning closer, pressing his chest against the blankets, feeling the rounded firmness of the woman's flesh beneath them, imagining the heat and the softness there, waiting to be uncovered. No longer thinking of the consequences of being discovered, Terry reared back from the bed. In a single, convulsive move he tore the bedclothes away. A short cotton gown covered the woman's body from throat to knees. Beneath it her legs were bare, the skin pale and smooth. Terry groaned. Fumbling one handed with his own clothes he pushed the gown up over her flesh, his fingers impatient on her thighs as he parted them.

A hand clamped around his wrist.

'No.'

Had it been the scream of a desperate woman it would only have added to his pleasure, but the single word held the snap of command and more besides. Terry froze, and in that moment the frenzied tension drained from him. Unresisting, he looked into his prospective victim's face. His fellow grieve stared out at him through the woman's eyes.

Terry's head dipped in unconscious submission. 'Mate of mine,' he acknowledged. 'You have returned.'

'Yes.' There was a wealth of satisfaction within that single word.

Slowly, the woman sat up. She made no move to cover herself but sat on the side of the bed, her bare legs exposed and the cotton gown tangled over her hips as she twisted carefully from side to side, moving her limbs and her head, the grieve judging the feel of this new body.

Terry watched the process of assimilation avidly.

He wetted his lips. 'Do you have her power?' His tone was greedy and demanding.

Helen's eyes narrowed. She made a sharp gesture with her right hand and Terry was flung backwards. He hit the wall, not hard enough to stun, but with enough force to shock.

'Does that answer you?'

Terry pulled himself upright, his face thunderous. 'And what of any wizard?' he snarled as he stepped back to the bed.

Helen smiled, amused by her mate's impatience. Almost languorously she closed her eyes, consciously submerging herself in her new host's memories like a swimmer diving down through layers of dark water, combing through them for any trace of the knowledge she sought.

When she found it she spoke. 'There was a wizard. One of great power.' The picture in her mind was of a tall, dark-haired man. 'This one fought him. And lost.'

The host's final memories were of being forced to the floor by a welter of Levin fire, of layer after layer of magic binding her body. The man had towered over her as she fought and spat and sobbed to be released – all to no avail. And then there was nothing.

Curious.

Helen opened her eyes. 'That is the last she remembers. The physician said this one had been here for two years. I believe it was as a result of that fight. Yet her memories are muddy – tainted – in a way I have not come across before. Something happened prior to that encounter, something important.'

'And what of the husband?'

The abruptness of Terry's question made it clear he cared little for how this new host had ended up here or the quality of her memories. His interest lay in the potential for acquiring another host – a man this time, not some feeble woman – and maybe one with power.

Helen slid back into the stream of memories. 'Ah, yes. The wizard who defeated her – he was her husband.'

Now *that* was interesting.

There were other memories there, layers of them, buried deeper than those of the host's last moments. And these were clear, not the odd, sepia-tinged images of those more recent events.

She pictured dark hair falling across storm-grey eyes, a sharp, almost angular face.

Strong, she thought and remembered other things – the feel of lips moulding to her own, the sensation as she ran her tongue over taut muscles outlined under pale skin. Lean hips and a flat belly. Her hands tracing down the lines of him. His hands on her and in her. Their sweat mingling, skin hot, almost liquid with passion.

Helen shifted restlessly. The sensations the memories conjured were deliciously strong and the temptation to indulge in them was all but overwhelming. She looked at Terry appraisingly. Her mate's new host was tall with the lean, almost thin, look of youth. His hair was a light, sandy brown and curly. Not unpleasing to the eye, she decided. Her husband – the thought amused the grieve – had been very well made. She would enjoy finding out how Terry's body compared with his. He would have stamina, she decided, though she doubted he would have much experience. No matter. She and her mate knew plenty. She made a low, crooning noise in her throat. Maybe … but no. There was more to be done before such indulgences.

She raised her hand as Terry moved towards her, an expression of eager anticipation on his face.

'No. Not yet. We need to know more.'

'What more do we need to know? Her husband is a wizard. It is enough. He is strong.' Terry's expression shifted, becoming sly. 'Stronger than you,' he added.

'Stronger than this host, you mean, mate of mine. Never stronger than me. You might do well to remember that.'

When Terry bristled, she smiled at him.

'Patience, my mate. He will be ours. Let me understand what has happened and we will set such a lure that he will be unable to resist.'

She plumped the pillows up behind her and settled back against the headboard of the bed. Closing her eyes once more she delved further back.

The woman's memories were curious. In the months before that final fight she had delighted in needling her husband, savouring the small hurts she inflicted, revelling in the man's pain. The grieve could understand the amusement gained from such acts, yet it was at odds with what she had sensed in those deeper memories. There had been love there – *a very human emotion,* she thought dismissively – bound inextricably with the passion she had sensed, yet in the more recent memories the accompanying emotions were of loathing and contempt.

And there was another man.

'There was a brother too.'

'Was?'

'This one killed him. A shame. He was also a wizard, though not as powerful as her husband.'

Terry made a small, irritated noise, which Helen ignored.

'Ah, now it makes sense. The three of them fought a demon. They thought they had vanquished it but instead this one was possessed. The two men did not realise.' She felt the satisfaction and the greedy longing for what was to come, recognising it now as the demon's memory. 'Not until it was too late.' She opened her eyes again. 'Now we know.'

'We can find the husband. You know where they lived?'

Helen flicked through her memories. The more time she spent in a host's body the easier it became to access such things. 'I do. But, if it has been two years, he may not be there. Better to have the physician summon him. I believe he will be pleased to be reunited with his wife.'

She chuckled and Terry laughed with her.

'We will be the ones pleasured by that reunion.'

'Indeed. Yes, this was a good choice of host. Much better than the man.' She glanced dismissively at Bob's body, lying abandoned beside the bed. 'You will have to get rid of him. There will be too many questions if his body is found in this room, and obviously I cannot do it.'

'Where should I take him? The storeroom is too far to carry him without someone seeing.'

'It should be somewhere he won't be found for a few hours.' Helen considered the possibilities. This new host had no knowledge of the clinic but her experience of it while in Bob's body – brief though that time had been – provided the answer.

'The atrium at the end of this corridor. There are toilets there. Leave him in one of the cubicles.'

Terry considered this for a moment, then he nodded, his expression turning sly as he added the knowledge gleaned from his own host's memories.

'The cleaners will find him in the morning. If anyone asks, I will say he complained of feeling ill and that I thought he had left. They will think he went in there before he succumbed.'

'Good. Once you have done that you will fetch Doctor Ashwood,' Helen commanded. 'I want to see my husband. But first …' She smiled at Terry. Hitching the hospital gown up around her waist she lay back on the bed and spread her thighs. 'Come to me.'

CHAPTER 6

'That,' said Jane, pushing her empty plate away and leaning back in her chair with an appreciative sigh, 'was lush. What did you put in it? You don't make something that good with just run-of-the-mill chilli powder.'

'It's the chocolate. Seriously,' Eldritch said as Jane eyed him sceptically. 'It's what adds that hint of richness.'

Jane huffed out an amused breath. 'Well, that's another recipe I want from you. You know, you should write a cookbook. It would be a bestseller.'

Eldritch made a deprecating noise but, watching his friend from the other end of the table, Aidan thought he looked pleased with the compliment. Who would have thought that the wizard would turn out to have a flair for cooking?

'Talking of books, how's the Welsh ghost stories one coming along?' he asked.

'Pretty well, thanks. The final proofs are in and it's due to be published next month.' There was a degree of quiet satisfaction in Eldritch's response, of pleasure at a job well done. 'Maybe I'll do the cookbook next,' he added with a smile at Jane. Then his smile slipped. 'Rowan wants me to do a book signing at the Gaia centre. She says she'd have asked me anyway but she's especially keen now that I'm a local author.'

Aidan smirked. 'That's not all Rowan wants you for,' he pointed out, underlining his comment with a suggestive leer, and was amused to see Eldritch blush. The man who faced down demons had considerably more difficulty dealing with the flame-haired doyen of Llancathan's alternative healing community.

'I can't see anyone paying the book that much interest,' Eldritch continued, resolutely addressing the issue of the book signing rather than the centre's matchmaking owner. He sounded as though he was trying to convince himself.

Aidan's grin grew wider. 'That's what you think. It's not your mind, it's your body they're after.'

He looked appraisingly at Eldritch. The wizard had put on a little weight since last autumn. Not that his face would ever be less than angular, but it had lost something of the sharpness that had marked it before. The edgy, dangerous look was mostly gone, surfacing only in a wolfish smile that, for reasons Aidan could never quite fathom, seemed to have most of the women it fell upon eating out of his hand.

Even Jane – who for all her easy-going surface charm was as cautious as a feral cat when it came to actual friendships, something she claimed was an inevitable consequence of working in the perennially suspicious world of security – had taken to the tall wizard as soon as they had been introduced. And that, thought Aidan, had been before they had found out about Eldritch's cooking skills.

In fact, one of the few women who seemed immune to the wizard's charm was Gwyn. The very idea of her fawning over Eldritch was so ridiculous it was laughable. Though they were friends, put Gwyn and Eldritch in the same room and it was a safe bet that they would be squabbling within half an hour.

As if the thought of her name had intruded on Eldritch's mind, the tall man looked over at Gwyn.

'You did all the copy-editing for me. Hell, you practically co-wrote half of the book. You should come along and take some of the credit.'

'Oh, no.' Gwyn crossed her arms and did her best to look stern. 'You can look elsewhere for your chaperone. I've told you before, the last thing I need is to be associated with ghost stories and the paranormal. If any of my editors spotted something like that, bang would go all my professional credibility. No, thank you very much. You'll have to face Rowan and your legions of adoring fans on your own.'

'I could protect you,' offered Jane. 'Of course, you'd have to swear to be my kitchen slave for the rest of your natural life but, given the alternative, it's probably worth it.' She gave Eldritch a knowing look. 'It's not the cooker that Rowan wants to chain you to.'

Eldritch winced and his blush deepened. 'I think Aidan might have something to say about that,' he demurred.

'Do you, Tarzan?' Jane looked quizzically at her lover.

'That depends. Do I get to share the food?'

Jane tapped her lip thoughtfully as she considered this. 'Given that I wouldn't be the one having to cook it, I don't see why not.'

'In that case, done.' Aidan turned back to Eldritch. 'There you are, then. Consider yourself protected.'

Eldritch looked down at the table and shook his head and Aidan smirked. While the wizard habitually used humour to mask his own feelings, he was less sure how to react when he was the one being teased. Now it seemed he would opt for pretending the conversation hadn't happened.

'I think I'll make coffee,' he said.

The small talk turned to other things while Eldritch busied himself with the kettle and the cafetière. Jane described how she had talked her way into the London offices of a major bank with nothing more than a clipboard and a faked letter from the personnel director, and Aidan followed that with the story of a lost hiker he had helped to rescue who had thought flip-flops were reasonable footwear for the slopes of Plynlimon.

'He even told us that he'd bought them that morning from the outdoor leisure store in Llancathan so he knew they were okay. I thought Hazel was going to choke.'

The sound of the phone ringing cut over Gwyn's suggestion that it was more likely that the leader of the Plynlimon Mountain Rescue Team would have choked the unfortunate hiker. She glanced over to Eldritch who was spooning coffee into the cafetière.

'Do you want me to get that for you?'

'No, just leave it. It's probably another one of those PC support scams. It'll go through to the answerphone in a moment. If it's someone genuine I'll call them back later.'

Aidan hadn't intended to eavesdrop, and he was sure Gwyn and Jane hadn't either, but somehow the conversation hadn't started again when the recording of Eldritch's voice finished exhorting the caller to leave a message after the tone.

'Oh, er … hello, Mister Eldritch. It's Doctor Ashwood here, from the Greenman Clinic. I … well, I don't think this is something I should say to an answering machine. If you could give me a call back as soon as possible please, I'd much appreciate it.'

The canister jerked in Eldritch's hand, sending a cascade of coffee grounds arcing across the worksurface.

Aidan took one look at his friend's face and all thoughts of coffee vanished. He was on his feet and across the room before he was consciously aware of what he was doing. 'What's wrong?'

Under his hands, Eldritch's shoulders were rigid. The wizard's mouth was open but he made no attempt to speak. His face held little more colour than the white china mugs lined up along the counter.

'Eldritch?' Aidan gave those rigid shoulders a shake but there was no response. 'Come on, talk to me! What is it? What's going on?'

He stopped, realising his panicky barrage of questions wasn't helping, and forced himself to take a steadying breath. He had learned from bitter experience that unexpected phone calls from doctors rarely meant good news. His mother's cancer had taught him that. But that was no reason to think that Eldritch had been keeping quiet about a serious illness. And yet, a small and frightened part of his mind argued, what other reason could there be for Eldritch's reaction? Feeling awkward and concerned in equal measures, Aidan loosened his death grip on his friend's shoulders.

In a carefully controlled voice he asked, 'Are you ill?'

The question seemed to bring Eldritch back from whatever private hell he had been facing. 'Ah …'

He reached up to squeeze Aidan's hands, his long fingers clenching convulsively over Aidan's, offering reassurance or taking it – Aidan wasn't sure which – before he shook his head. 'No. No, it's not me. Don't worry, Aidan.'

Aidan wasn't convinced by this reassurance, nor by the fraction of a smile that Eldritch sent his way, but the wizard merely turned and walked back to his chair. No one else moved or spoke as Eldritch sat down, carefully avoiding eye contact with any of them. An awkward silence settled over the room.

Finally Eldritch lifted his head. 'It's about Helen …' He swallowed heavily, losing the end of the sentence. In a voice that was barely audible he added, 'My wife.'

'Your wife?'

'But I thought—' Jane and Aidan spoke together.

'She survived, didn't she?' It was Gwyn. Her voice held a wealth of sympathy and understanding tangled around that simple question that was, somehow, a statement. Eldritch's eyes sought hers. Wordlessly he nodded.

This made no sense to Aidan. He thought he knew what had happened to Eldritch's wife. After all, it had been Eldritch himself who had told him. Helen had made a fatal mistake while fighting a demon. Her brother had been injured and she had dropped her shields to heal him. The demon had possessed her even as she saved her brother's life.

Aidan looked from Eldritch to Gwyn and back again. 'You mean she's been alive all this time?'

'No!' Eldritch jerked upright, horror and outrage in his eyes, then sagged back into the chair. 'No. She died the moment the demon took her.' There was absolute certainty in his voice. 'But her body—'

He broke off, his teeth clenching on his lips as he fought down the emotions that came rushing in with those words, threatening to swamp him. 'After I drove the demon out of her … her body was still alive.' He swallowed as if the memories of that day had lodged in his throat so that he had to force the words out through them. 'She kept breathing.'

His whole body grew still, seeming to shrink in on itself. He didn't look at any of them as he spoke, just stared across the room, and it was obvious that it wasn't the little kitchen that he was seeing. Without a word Gwyn got up and fetched a bottle of brandy from the cupboard. Snagging one of the mugs from the worktop, she poured a generous measure and thrust it into Eldritch's hand. The wizard took it without looking at her.

'They made her a ward of the court after—'

His words choked off, his free hand stealing up to cover his mouth as though the very thought of what he had been about to say made him sick.

'It's alright, you don't have to explain.' Gwyn put her arm around the wizard's shoulders. She leaned her head against his. 'I know.'

For several breaths Eldritch was motionless, taking comfort from that non-judgemental closeness, but then he shifted away. He took a long swallow of brandy. 'No. No, you don't.' He looked down at the remaining liquid in the mug, swirling it around the sides and then raising it to his lips. He drained it in one long swallow, then he put the mug down on the table with an audible click, like the determined gesture of a chess master moving a piece into check. He sat back and looked at each of his audience in turn before he spoke. 'It's not as though it matters now. You might as well know what happened.'

He sounded at once weary and defiant, like a man finally putting down a burden he had carried unwillingly for years, unsure what reaction it would cause but doing so regardless. 'When I realised, I tried to kill us both. I didn't want anyone else to be hurt so I rigged our gas fire … carbon monoxide.' He studied his hands where they lay in his lap, as though he could read something in the closely clenched fingers and whitening knuckles. After a moment he continued without looking up. 'I didn't know what else to do. I couldn't bear the thought of living without her.'

Slowly he raised his head as though the effort to do so cost him dearly. With a laugh that was more like a sob he added, 'As you can see, I wasn't successful.'

'Someone found you.' Her voice gentle, Gwyn filled in the pieces.

'Steve, a close friend. He'd called round to see us unexpectedly. When he didn't get an answer, he tried the door. I hadn't locked it.' Eldritch shook his head as though deriding his own foolhardiness. His fingers played with the copper bracelet he wore on his right wrist, turning it round and round like a worry bead. 'He dragged us both out and called an ambulance. I came round in hospital the next day. Of course, Helen didn't. They classed her as being in a permanent vegetative state. I wanted them to stop treatment. I knew there was no point, but her cousin forced the issue.'

'But you were next of kin. Surely they should have listened to you?' Aidan heard the bitterness in his own voice at the suffering inflicted on his friend.

Eldritch's lips twitched in the briefest of smiles at this show of solidarity. 'There were questions raised about the circumstances, whether it was an accident or a suicide pact. Or even attempted murder.' Eldritch stumbled a little on the word. 'Laurence insisted Helen should be treated. The judges agreed. Maybe I should have fought harder, taken it to appeal.' Eldritch shook his head, a small, tired motion. 'I couldn't do it.'

His shrug barely moved the fabric of his shirt. 'Laurence had contacts and once she'd been made a ward of the court he had her referred to a private hospital in London, the Greenman Clinic. It specialises in the treatment of neurological conditions. They have all sorts of fancy treatments – electronic muscle stimulation, deep tissue manipulation …' Eldritch sighed. 'The aim is to keep the body in peak physical condition until the brain recovers and the patient wakes up. Maybe that's a realistic goal in the case of their other patients, I don't know. Of course, when you're dealing with the aftermath of possession, there's no hope of that ever happening. All you're doing is keeping a corpse out of the grave. Not that that's something you can tell the doctors.'

Silence descended on the room as Eldritch stopped speaking. Gwyn and Aidan had been aware of some of the circumstances around Helen's demise, but this new revelation left them both speechless. Jane simply looked stunned.

Before any of them could think of anything to say, Eldritch started speaking again. His tone was reflective as though he were relating events that had happened many years ago or even to another man.

'If Paul … he was Helen's brother,' he added looking at Jane. 'If he hadn't been Best Man at our wedding then it would have been Steve. That's how close we were. How do you tell someone like that that you wish they'd minded their own business and left you to die?'

'They're probably the only ones who would understand,' Jane said quietly.

Eldritch continued almost as though he hadn't heard her. 'I couldn't face him afterwards. He must have thought it was because of Helen. I know he blamed himself for not getting us out in time. How could he know that there was never any chance for her? But all he knew was that he hadn't saved her and that I hated him for saving me.'

'You could always get back in touch. Apologise to him. Even if he doesn't accept it, it's never too late to set the record straight.' If life had taught Aidan anything it was that.

Eldritch shook his head sadly. 'It's too late for Steve,' he said, and his voice was bitter as ashes. 'One of the reasons he'd come to see us that night was to tell us he was off. He'd done a stint in the TA as a mechanic of all things. He was a doctor, but he said he might as well learn something new from it. They called him up. He was on his way to Helmand Province, in Afghanistan. Two months later – roadside bomb.' His hands mimed a grisly parody of an explosion. 'They brought him home in a box.' His voice trailed off.

What could you say in response to something like that? Aidan did the only thing he could think of. 'It seems that being your friend is a dangerous occupation,' he joked. 'Do you have any left?'

Eldritch looked back at him, a wealth of tangled emotions on his face. 'A few,' he said, mirroring Aidan's tone, though his eyes were suspiciously bright. 'And despite everything I do to the contrary to try and keep them safe they insist on getting involved. I'm surprised I still have them.'

'So, why would this Doctor Ashwood be calling you?' Gwyn asked, pushing back against the maudlin atmosphere with a practical question.

'This will be the phone call I've been waiting for, ever since that day. The one to tell me that she's finally slipped away.'

Gwyn took Eldritch's hands in her own. 'I'm so sorry. It's still a shock, isn't it? Even when you know they're long gone in spirit.'

Eldritch's hands tightened on hers. 'Thank you.'

Aidan could think of nothing to say that didn't seem trite or trivial. He had his own experience of losing loved ones, but he couldn't begin to guess how Eldritch was feeling. Self-consciously, he put his hand on the other man's shoulder and hoped that Eldritch would understand.

Only Jane made no move to offer comfort. Instead, she regarded the phone thoughtfully. 'You know, this might seem crazy – and I don't know this Doctor Ashwood from Adam – but he didn't sound like a man phoning to give you bad news. Are you sure there's no way that your wife could have recovered?'

CHAPTER 7

A chorus of denial answered Jane's question.

'People don't recover from demonic possession, Jane,' Gwyn said firmly. She seemed to be speaking in order to spare Eldritch the burden of doing so. 'It's not something you get over. The demon drives out the soul when it enters the body. Though the body itself survives for the demon to use, whoever has been possessed is dead from that moment.'

Jane digested this silently. A little crease formed between her brows as she worked through the implications of this new knowledge, then she looked at Gwyn quizzically. 'How do you know? I mean, I hear what you're saying about how the demon kills the person it possesses. And, if that's the case, it makes sense that the body usually dies when a demon is driven out. I get that. But, when that doesn't happen, in those rare instances when the body doesn't die, how do you know the possessed person can't recover? Has anyone tried keeping an ex-host alive to find out?'

Aidan raised an eyebrow, surprised, but also a little intrigued, by the suggestion. His knowledge of possession was limited. Neither Gwyn nor Eldritch had spoken much about it and on the rare occasions when it had been mentioned it had never occurred to him to doubt the truth of what they said. It was just typical of Jane that she would ask such a question.

From the look on Gwyn's face it was clear she wasn't viewing Jane's question in such a kindly light. Very little tended to shock her, but it seemed this had. She glared at the younger woman as though she suspected her of being deliberately hurtful.

Surprisingly it was Eldritch who answered. 'There are records of it having been tried. Once.'

'And?'

'The ex-host survived for two weeks before …' Eldritch broke off.

Hearing the pain lurking beneath that flat response Aidan would have let the matter go, but Jane was as focused as a terrier with a rat.

'Before what?'

Eldritch looked faintly sick. 'Before she was killed by the people caring for her. Her husband and daughter, I believe.'

He gave a small shrug as though dismissing any similarity between this and his own circumstances. 'It was a long time ago. If anyone has tried since it hasn't been recorded.'

'Which would suggest that, even if it has been tried, the outcome was no different,' Gwyn added. Her lips pressed together into a thin line suggesting the conversation should end there.

'Hmm … medical science has come on—' Jane stopped as if only just sensing the tension in the room. She raised her hands. 'I'm sorry. This isn't my area of expertise and I really didn't mean to hurt. I am sorry.' She held Eldritch's eye, waiting until he had nodded, acknowledging her apology even if he might choose not to accept it. 'But I still say your Doctor Ashwood didn't sound like a man delivering bad news.'

Instead of answering her directly, Eldritch got up. 'There's a very simple way to find out. No, it's okay,' he brushed off Gwyn's half-formed protest. 'There's no point putting it off. I need to call the man back.' He lifted the phone from its cradle. 'If you'll excuse me for a moment.'

'Of course.'

'We'll sort the coffee,' suggested Aidan.

The three of them were sitting at the table, coffee untouched in the mugs in front of them, when Eldritch came back. Knowing his friend, Aidan had expected a stoic expression to be hiding the grief he was sure the wizard must be feeling. Instead, Eldritch was wearing an oddly dazed look, rather as if someone had hit him over the head with a piece of four-by-four timber. No one spoke as he returned the phone to its cradle, moving like a man functioning on autopilot. For several moments he stood there, studying the phone as though he wasn't quite sure what else he should do.

Aidan was steeling himself to ask the obvious question when the wizard turned to look at them.

'Well?' he asked as gently as he could.

'Helen … I … she's come out of her coma.'

'What?'

'She woke up earlier this evening. She's regained consciousness and she was asking for me.' Eldritch made a sound somewhere between a sob and a haunted laugh.

'Sweet Lady!' Gwyn looked as stunned as Eldritch. 'But that's—'

'Impossible,' Eldritch continued for her. 'I know.'

He sat down heavily, like a man who no longer had the strength to stand, and one long-fingered hand crept up to cover his mouth as if to hold back a tangled roil of words and emotions. Aidan stayed silent, uncomfortably certain that there was nothing he could say that would help and afraid that any comment he did offer would only make things worse.

Yet it seemed that Jane had no such reservations. 'Whether you think it's possible or not doesn't matter. Clearly it must be because it's happened.'

'Jane.' Gwyn's voice held a note of warning.

Jane deflected it with rolled eyes. 'Yeah, I understand, it's never happened before. I get that.' Her brows quirked down into a puzzled frown that only got deeper as she looked from Eldritch to Gwyn and then to Aidan. 'But it's happened now.' An edge of exasperation tinged her voice as though she was baffled by their reluctance to accept that simple fact. 'You should be celebrating, dancing on the table. Why aren't you?'

'Because it can't happen. The human spirit cannot coexist with a demon. The act of possession drives it out and that means death.'

Eldritch sounded as though he was repeating something he had learned by rote.

'But how do you know?' Jane drew a deliberate breath, and her tone became gentler but no less insistent as she continued. 'You said no one's kept a … I don't know what you'd call them – an ex-possessee? – alive for more than a couple of weeks. Now, I don't know about spirits and demons but what if, in some circumstances, the spirit isn't driven out? What if, in the people who keep breathing, it's because their spirit's retreated instead? It's squished itself down inside them, into a tiny part of their brain or wherever it is that your spirit lives, and it's hiding there. Then, once the demon's gone, it can come back but it takes a long time for that to happen. It must have seemed like a lifetime to her family, but a couple of weeks is no time at all when you're talking about someone recovering from severe mental trauma.'

'We're talking two years here, Jay,' Aidan murmured, but no one seemed to hear him.

'Everyone's different when it comes to recovery times.' Jane smiled at Eldritch. 'I'll bet your wife was a fighter. Maybe it's the case that if you keep someone alive for long enough – and medical care's come on sufficiently that we can do that now – their spirit has a chance to find its way back and they can get better.'

For several moments no one spoke. Jane sat back in her chair and waited.

Eldritch ran his tongue over his lips. He looked at Gwyn. 'Could it be?' His voice was hesitant as though he wasn't quite sure what he was asking.

'I ...' Gwyn seemed equally unsure but gradually her expression changed. 'It doesn't matter, does it? Jane's right. Whether we think it's possible or not isn't the point – it's happened. It's actually happened. Sweet Lady!' She reached out and gripped Eldritch's hand and then, before he could react, she was out of her chair and pulling him into a hug. 'I don't believe it! But who cares? Oh Lady, that's wonderful!'

Aidan turned to Jane. 'You knew,' he said. 'When the doctor phoned, you knew. But how?'

Jane tore her eyes away from the spectacle of Gwyn all but smothering an unresisting Eldritch and grinned at him. 'It was his tone of voice. It's a dead giveaway.' She laughed when that statement elicited nothing but bafflement. 'When you're trying to bluff your way past someone you learn to pay attention to their body language and their tone of voice as much as to what they're actually saying. It tells you so much more about what's going on in their head. That way you know how to play things, whether you need to be reassuring them or ordering them around.' She shrugged. 'I guess I do it automatically.'

'Cyber ninja, you are awesome!' Aidan kissed her enthusiastically.

'Yes, I am. It's one of my many skills. That and my engaging modesty.' She pulled back from him slightly. 'Not that any of that matters right now.' Together they turned to look at Eldritch who was holding on to Gwyn as though she was the last lifebelt on the *Titanic*. 'How amazing is this?'

'I've got to get to the clinic.'

Abruptly Eldritch stopped hugging Gwyn. His arms dropped back to his sides and he stared around him as though wondering what he was doing in a house in mid-Wales.

Gwyn took a small step backwards. 'Not tonight you don't.' A sideways glance at the brandy bottle made her wince. 'You'll be well over the limit for driving and,' she checked her watch, 'the last train's already gone.'

'I could run you to Shrewsbury,' Jane suggested. 'I'm tonight's designated driver. Someone felt he ought to be the one to have a drink this evening.' She turned and ruffled Aidan's hair. 'It'll be gone midnight by the time you get to London, but it's doable. Just about.'

Eldritch looked sorely tempted but then he sighed and some of the energy seemed to drain out of him, leaving him just a little shell-shocked.

'No. No, it's alright. I don't think they'd thank me for turning up in the middle of the night.' He laughed a little shakily and ran a hand through his hair. 'Doctor Ashwood said she was resting, but she's definitely conscious and she was talking and asking for me.'

Abruptly his face crumpled. 'Oh, dear God! I would have killed her. I tried to kill us both and when that failed I left her alone in that hospital.' His hand moved to cover his mouth as though sickened by the thought of what he had done. Grief tightened his features. In a small voice he continued, 'I scarcely visited. I haven't visited at all this year.'

'Marcus, stop it!' Though the top of her head barely came level with Eldritch's shoulder, Gwyn could be formidable when she chose to be. 'As far as you knew she was dead. Everything you knew, everything you believed, pointed to that being the case. You had no way of knowing that she could survive. Sweet Lady! As far as we know she's the first person ever to have survived demonic possession.' Her voice softened and in an uncharacteristic show of support she put her hand to his cheek. 'Don't beat yourself up over what's in the past. I'm sure Helen wouldn't want you to. Celebrate the fact that you've been given a second chance. They don't come to many of us.'

CHAPTER 8

Doctor Ashwood escorted his visitor through the patients' wing. Normally he would have made small talk about the weather or his guest's journey. Or, if it was someone new to the clinic, he would have pointed out the bold paintings on the walls and remarked on the clinic's deliberate use of colour to create an energised and positive atmosphere in the public spaces. Neither seemed appropriate this morning and as the other man seemed disinclined to offer any conversation himself the pair of them walked in silence.

They passed through a glass-walled atrium filled with sunshine and the glossy greenery of potted palms and strelitzia, and from there into another corridor. Near its end, Doctor Ashwood stopped and gestured to one of the doors. 'Well, this is Helen's room.' He smiled broadly at the tall man beside him. Though the visitor was trying to conceal it he could read both fear and excitement in the man's face mingled with a desperate desire to believe that what was happening was real.

Ashwood could understand the mix of emotions. While he worked diligently for all the patients at the clinic, holding fast to the belief that any one of them could regain consciousness, if he was honest he had never truly expected to have the pleasure of this particular moment.

'I'll … leave you and your wife to get reacquainted. Take all the time you want. If you need me or any of the nursing staff, there's a call button by the bed.'

'Yes, yes. Thank you, doctor.'

On instinct Ashwood reached out and squeezed the man's arm. It was rigid under his fingers. 'She's fine, Mister Eldritch. Honestly.'

He withdrew his hand, not sure the other man had even registered his gesture, and turned away. At the atrium he looked back. Helen's husband was standing motionless beside the door, his head bowed against the frame. Ashwood smiled wryly to himself, recalling the man's adamant belief two years ago that his wife was as good as dead. There was someone who had a lot of adjusting to do. His smile broadened as he carried on walking.

Eldritch waited for the doctor's footsteps to recede down the corridor, grateful for the medical man's tact. It might be cowardly, but he needed these few moments alone to gather himself. He rubbed his fingers over gritty, tired eyes. Sleep had come in brief and troubled snatches, his mind returning again and again to Jane's words.

Whether you think it's possible or not doesn't matter … You should be celebrating, dancing on the table …

And to Gwyn's. … *you've been given a second chance.*

A second chance. Eldritch shook his head – a small negating gesture. He didn't feel worthy but surely, if such things were possible, they wouldn't hinge on whether the recipient thought they were deserved. Eldritch didn't know, but he thought he might go mad before he found an answer. Eventually, finding himself awake once more in the early hours of the morning, he had given up on the idea of sleep and had got up, showered and dressed. He had been on the road at first light.

And now he was here. The moment had arrived and everything he wanted was on the other side of that door. Yet he could scarcely bring himself to touch it, let alone to open it. His palms were sweating, his mouth was dry, and he was aware of his pulse hammering in his throat.

Fool!

Mentally Eldritch revisited everything Doctor Ashwood had told him on his arrival at the clinic, everything the man had said to him on the phone the previous evening.

She's alright. She wanted to see me. It's real. She's alive!

He ran the words through his head like a mantra, as though doing so would ensure it was true. Then, before he could think of any reason not to, in one swift movement he opened the door and stepped inside. His eyes went straight to the bed.

Oh God!

Eldritch froze. It was over a year since he had last seen her. He knew she was beautiful but how could he have forgotten the exact shade of gold of her hair or the pale flush of pink along her cheekbones, the bone china fineness of her nose or the sensual curve of her lips? His breath clogged in his lungs. She looked so fragile. It scarcely seemed that anything had changed since he had last been in this room. Helen had always looked as though she might open her eyes at any moment, but he had known it was impossible. Despite everything that Doctor Ashwood had told him, all the man's reassurances, Eldritch wondered if the consultant had somehow been mistaken. For so long he had believed that Helen could never wake up. The doctor had said she had but perhaps he was wrong. It seemed to Eldritch that he wanted this too much for it to be possible and seeing his wife now, lying motionless in bed, he thought his heart might break. And then Helen opened her eyes.

She looked up at him, her expression sleepy, and a little frown line creased the pale skin between her brows. 'Marcus? Is it really you?'

It was as though the world had stopped turning. For a heartbeat Eldritch was conscious only of the fact that his greatest wish had just been granted. The nightmare of the last two years shattered with the impact of those few words and fell away. Then he was across the room and gathering Helen into his arms, his face buried in her hair, breathing in her scent, and then kissing her and having her kiss him back equally fervently.

'Oh God! You're back. You're really back!'

He held her away from him so he could look at her again and then crushed her back against him as though he would meld their very bones together.

At last he loosened his grip and sat back, looking at her. He dashed one hand over his eyes. The other he kept locked on hers, unwilling to let go of her fully, even for an instant.

Helen seemed almost amused by this possessive display of affection. She smiled and squeezed his hand, her long, slender fingers locking round his own. 'It feels as though I've been asleep forever.'

Eldritch nodded. He had to swallow hard before he found his voice. 'It's been two years.'

'Two years.' There was wonder in her voice though she didn't question the truth of what he said. Rather, she shook her head, dismissing it as irrelevant. Instead, she focused on him. 'It's been hard on you.'

She raised her free hand to touch the crescent-shaped scar on his cheekbone, her fingers tracing the darker skin and the slight puckering around its edges. 'What have you been doing with yourself?'

'This and that.' *Looking for ways to get myself killed, until I found some people who helped me want to live again.* 'Nothing that matters very much. I'll tell you all about it sometime, but not now.'

He looked at her with hunger as though he wanted to imprint every cell of her body in his mind. 'What I've been doing isn't important.' He raised their joined hands to his lips and brushed a kiss over her knuckles. 'What about you? Do you remember anything?'

When she didn't answer immediately he said carefully, 'Paul's dead.'

'Yes, I know.'

The simplicity with which she said it cut Eldritch to the core. The demon had told him what it had done, had taunted him with how it had killed Paul, relishing every moment as it watched him die. Paul might have been one of his closest friends, but he was Helen's brother. If she could remember what the demon had done while in possession of her body, Eldritch hated to think what images might be haunting her.

'It was the demon. You mustn't blame yourself.'

'I don't.'

She shook her head and Eldritch could almost believe she meant it. Not for the first time he marvelled at his wife's bravery, knowing she must be locking the pain away. He gathered her to him again, not wanting his own emotions to shatter her calm determination. He would be there for her when she was ready to mourn, but for now he would choose only to rejoice.

'I love you.' He whispered it to her hair, to the softness of her skin as he brushed his lips over her face, and to her mouth as he kissed her again and again.

Eldritch was still holding Helen, nestled in his arms, when he heard the sound of the door opening behind him. He looked round, expecting to see Doctor Ashwood or a member of the nursing staff, but instead there was a young man in a faded black T-shirt and the white dungarees of a painter or a workman. He stopped abruptly on the threshold when he saw Eldritch, and Eldritch expected him to offer a swift apology for coming into the wrong room and then leave. Instead, he stood in the doorway, staring hard at Eldritch, his expression sullen and resentful, though Eldritch couldn't imagine what he had done to earn the young man's ire. Nor could he have said why, for the briefest moment, he had the inexplicable feeling that this stranger knew not only who he was, but also what. His arms tightened protectively around Helen. Still the young man made no effort to introduce himself.

Eventually, at a loss as to how else to react, Eldritch opted for politeness. 'Can I help you?'

To his amazement it was Helen who spoke next. She shifted in his arms, turning towards the doorway and said brightly, 'Oh, it's you, Terry. I wondered when you'd be back.'

Bemused, Eldritch's attention snapped back to his wife. 'You know each other?'

To the best of his knowledge he had never met the young man before. How could his wife, who had been conscious for less than twenty-four hours, know him?

Helen tilted her head against Eldritch's shoulder and smiled up at him impishly. 'Of course we do. Come in, Terry. Don't be shy.'

For a moment it seemed that Terry would refuse the invitation but then he muttered something under his breath and stepped into the room, letting the door swing shut behind him. He stopped several feet away from the bed and he and Eldritch eyed each other while Helen made the introductions.

'Terry, this is my husband, Marcus.' Her hand rested lightly on Eldritch's forearm as she spoke. She turned to Eldritch. 'Terry works here at the clinic.'

'Hello.'

Terry grunted a response, reminding Eldritch of a story Gwyn had told him once about Aidan as a teenager. The memory eased some of the tension he had been feeling.

'So, how did you and Terry meet?'

'Well, it was Doctor Ashwood who introduced us formally, but Terry has been coming in to see me while I've been unconscious. He'd heard I didn't have any visitors and decided he'd come in and talk to me.'

'No one else was visiting her.'

Terry glared at Eldritch as he spoke.

'Terry,' Helen chided him gently. 'Terry was with me last night when I woke up. I suppose you'll think I'm silly but having him there made everything seem so much easier. Now I feel like he's an old friend.'

'I don't think that's silly at all.'

Eldritch could only berate himself that it had been a stranger's kindness that had eased her awakening. But for this young man Helen would have awoken alone, with no one to comfort or reassure her.

He stood up and offered his hand to Terry. 'I want to thank you for being there for my wife.'

The young workman eyed the outstretched hand but made no move to take it.

'Doctor Ashwood said that having someone talk to them helps the patients recover.'

The words could have been barbs aimed at Eldritch's heart but his joy at Helen's recovery was sufficient to cushion him for now.

'Whether that's true or not, I still want to thank you.'

'I did it for her, not for you.' Terry took Eldritch's hand in the briefest of shakes.

'Understood.'

And if Eldritch felt the young workman's attitude towards his wife was unusually possessive he was too grateful for any part that Terry might have played in her recovery to take offence.

CHAPTER 9

'Stop the car.'

Helen's sharp command had Eldritch reacting with alarm. 'What's wrong? Are you feeling sick?' Even as he spoke he was pulling into the side of the road, unheeding of the angry blare of horns behind them.

'I need to get out.'

Helen had the door open almost before the car had stopped. Then she was out and running across the softly sloping grass verge. Eldritch bit back a curse and dived after her. He caught up with her as she stopped under one of the graceful old chestnut trees that lined the park road. There she stood, her face upturned to the wide, spreading branches and to the sky. A look of intense pleasure suffused her face as she flung her arms out and took a deep breath. Eldritch watched her closely, his feelings a mixture of concern and puzzlement. The shafts of sunlight coming through the leaves lit her as though she were on a stage, brightening the pale blues and lemons of her dress and threading her hair with molten gold. Even the pallor of her skin was transformed, turned to ivory with the palest flush of rose along her cheeks and on her lips.

'You can't realise how good it feels to have the sun on your face after being imprisoned for so long.'

It was an odd way to describe her time lying unconscious in the hospital but Eldritch felt he understood. He relaxed, his smile returning as he watched his wife turn in a circle, her arms outstretched as though she would gather in the trees, the grass, the cloudless blue of the sky; everything around her. She looked like Titania dancing in a woodland bower, a fairy queen surrounded by a shimmering haze of sunshine.

'I could get drunk on the smell of the air.' Helen turned to look at him, her expression suddenly fierce. 'Never take these things for granted.'

'I'll never take you for granted again.'

Eldritch opened his arms and she came back to him, mortal once more, and let him enfold her. 'To hell with the fresh air,' he said, pressing his face to the top of her head. 'You smell wonderful.' He ran his hands through the silky fineness of her hair, catching the blonde strands around his fingers as he had always loved to do. It was much longer now than it had been when she had been taken into the clinic. And because he was holding his wife in his arms on a glorious summer afternoon that small detail made him smile rather than despair. 'I like your hair like this.'

'I like you like this, my love.' Helen tipped her head up. Her hands slid from his back to pull his head down towards hers and she kissed him hungrily. 'Take me home.'

The narrow mews was quiet as Eldritch pulled the car up outside their house; their neighbours were out at work or off enjoying themselves. Eldritch was grateful for the privacy it afforded them. He wasn't ready to share Helen with anyone. He glanced over at the passenger seat and his wife's sleeping form. Doctor Ashwood had told him that she would tire easily at first, but that it was nothing to be concerned about. Eldritch accepted the doctor's words and yet this sense of fragility still worried him. He was uncertain as to how to deal with it. All he knew was that having lost Helen once he would do nothing now that would endanger her. If need be he would protect her with his life.

Eldritch pulled himself back from that line of thought. He had no reason to think there was anything wrong with Helen. The important thing now was to ensure he didn't let his own dark thoughts mar this new life. Conscious of the gift he had been given, he reached across and gently shook Helen's shoulder. His heart lifted anew as she opened her eyes and turned her head towards him. Eldritch thought he would never get over the joy of watching her wake up. Each time it felt like a new miracle.

'We're home.' He brushed the strands of hair back from her face, smiling a little as she scowled at him.

'You shouldn't have let me sleep.'

'Why not? Doctor Ashwood said you'd need to. This way I get to watch you wake up all over again.'

Helen pouted. 'I've slept for long enough.'

'For far too long,' Eldritch agreed, but he couldn't keep the smile from his voice. 'But you'll soon be back to normal. You just need to give it a few days. Don't be so impatient.'

Somehow his fingers had found their way from her hair to her cheek. He cupped his hand against it and his smile spread as she sighed and leaned her head into his caress. The warmth of her skin against his palm was like a blessing.

'I feel I should be carrying you over the threshold.'

Helen raised her head and looked at him, eyes twinkling with mischief. 'Maybe you should.'

Helen reclined against the cushions, regal as a queen. Having carried her through the house, her husband had lowered her onto the cream leather settee as carefully as though she were a china doll, tucking the jewel-bright silk cushions around her. Now he stood over her, trying for normality but coming across as curiously formal and reserved.

'I'll make us a drink. Tea?'

'In a minute. Just sit with me for a while.'

She reached for his hand and guided him down beside her. As he sat, she moved over and snuggled up against his side. She felt him tense momentarily as she did so but then he relaxed and put his arm around her. The feel of the solid warmth of him brought a little hum of pleasure to her throat. She leaned into him, turning so that her breast rubbed against his hand, the nipple stiffening under the thin silk of her dress, pleasuring her. The wizard was certain to have felt it, but he made no attempt to take advantage of the contact. The grieve was surprised. Apparently her husband was a gentleman. Helen smiled inwardly, amused by the idea. She would enjoy making the first move.

She turned slightly in his arms. 'No, stay there,' she reassured him as he started to shift to allow her more space. Keeping her body close to his, she brought her hand to his chest. The white cotton of his shirt felt smooth and inviting beneath her palm as she toyed with the buttons, her fingers flirting with them before she let one slip through the fabric. Slowly, deliberately, she slid her hand inside. She traced it over the firm pectoral muscle, enjoying the sensations as she pressed her fingertips into his skin and relishing the catch of his breath as she rubbed her palm over the nipple. The wizard stiffened, holding himself rigid as though he didn't quite trust himself to move. She felt the fine tremble in his muscles and smiled.

He wants me.

Helen didn't need to feel the spiking heartbeat or to hear the quickening of his breath to know that.

But he doesn't think he should. He's scared in case he might hurt me.

The thought of her husband's conflicting emotions excited her all the more. She dragged her nails lightly across his skin and felt him twitch under her hand, fighting for control. The realisation was unbearably arousing. This was power. It was very different from her experience in previous hosts. She had seduced before but there had always been the knowledge that she could back up her desires with force if her chosen partner resisted. That too was arousing, but this? This was delicious. Who would have thought that a woman could wield such control? She laughed, her breath catching, and undid another button. Slowly she walked her fingers up his chest, toying briefly with the gold chain that lay across his collarbone, and the ring suspended from it, and withdrew her hand once more.

She nipped her bottom lip between her teeth, enjoying the little frisson of pain, and caught his eye. 'I want to see you.'

The wizard watched her, his eyes wide and slightly dazed. He made no attempt to stop her as she worked her way down his shirt, slowly undoing the remaining buttons. At his waist she slipped her hands under the fabric, sliding them up the length of him as she pushed his shirt back.

'Mmm.' Helen made a little crooning noise in the back of her throat. Her memories had not misled her; her husband's body was lean and strong, the firm lines of his muscles clearly defined under pale skin decorated with a patina of scars – a visible record of his past. Helen found them fascinating. Her fingers itched to trace them, to relearn the shapes of those she recalled and to explore those others that were new. She wanted to see them slick with sweat as his body bucked beneath hers, driven mindless with passion. Her lips parted and she groaned, torturing herself with the deliciousness of the image, relishing the way her own skin heated and throbbed. Yes, she would savour the knowledge of every inch of him – his taste and his feel and his scent – but she knew also the delight of anticipation so for the moment she satisfied herself by feasting with her eyes. The majority of the marks on his chest and shoulders were pale as nacre and silvery with age but some – like the ones over his ribs – were newer.

She remembered those, but not as scars. 'I did this.'

'The demon did it.' Eldritch's voice was flat. Bitterness and confusion flooded his eyes as he moved to tug his shirt closed and Helen reacted swiftly before the moment was lost in the change of mood. As he started to sit up she shifted, slipping onto his lap, her hands spread on his chest. He froze, unwilling to fight her.

'Don't,' she said. She pressed him backwards, her hands easing him down as he gradually surrendered to that gentle insistence. 'Good.'

He offered no resistance, his arms staying limp at his sides, as she pushed his shirt open once more. Leaning close Helen traced her hands up over his ribs, her fingertips following the lines her nails had once gouged in his skin. She moved slowly, feeling the difference in texture, the slightest of ridges that separated scar from unblemished skin. Once she had completed that exploration with her hands she lowered her head, inhaling the scent of him, following her fingers with her lips and then with her tongue, tasting him. Eldritch shifted unconsciously, lying back fully on the pale leather. Helen smiled and pressed herself closer, gliding the silky fabric of her dress over his chest. His hands fisted in the cushions as hers roamed down his body. She felt him rigid beneath the dark denim of his jeans.

Very good.

She increased the pressure of her touch. His body strained against her, pushing up into her hands, but still he didn't reach for her.

'Don't you want me?' Helen's voice was husky, teasing and tormenting. Her hands were insistent, demanding.

Eldritch bit back a moan. 'We can't. I'll hurt you. I might—'

Whatever else he would have said was lost as Helen covered his mouth with hers, the kiss greedy and urgent. When he responded she went deeper then pulled back, looking into his eyes, challenging, fierce and hungry. She held him, her hands on either side of his face, watching as she shifted so that she was kneeling astride him, the pale silk of her skirt hitched around her thighs. Her head dived towards him and she plunged them both back into a devouring kiss, rubbing herself over him, teasing and tantalising herself with the feel of him beneath her, delighting in the building sensation of liquid heat between her thighs.

'I want you.' Her hands released his head and fumbled urgently with his jeans. 'Now!'

At last he moved to help, lifting his hips so she could free him. Then it was Helen's turn to gasp as he caught her by the hips. His fingers slipped under the thin triangle of lace between her thighs, pulling it aside. She moaned as he caressed her, arching up and back as his fingers slid into her. Aching and liquid she opened further for him, her own fingers working, urgent and insistent. Breath mingled in hot, panting gasps as they drove each other onwards, frantic and demanding.

The wave was building inside her, the throbbing, aching need of it overpowering her, turning her mindless and craving and desperate. Helen screamed as she came and then cried out again as Eldritch drove into her. Shuddering with passion, she tightened around him like a hot, wet fist and rode him, driving her hips against him, filling herself with him as she matched his frenzied movements thrust for thrust. In a wild ecstasy they climbed, bodies joined, sweat running. They rose, their cries merging as they shattered and fell together.

After an eternity, Eldritch found the strength to clear his throat. 'About that drink.'

'Mmm?'

'It's going to have to wait for a while. Possibly for a year or two. While my bones re-solidify.'

Helen snuggled closer against his chest but made no other response.

Holding her with one arm he reached up and dragged the woollen throw from the back of the settee. One handed, he draped it over her. 'Can't have you getting cold.'

He stroked his hand through the tangle of her hair and then down her back, under the blanket, fingers playing with the rumpled silk of her dress. Helen shifted against his chest, moving into the caress like a cat. She lifted her head enough to look at him and chuckled, the sound deep and throaty.

'I'm sure I can rely on you to warm me up if I do.'

Helen looked down at her sleeping husband. Eldritch lay on his back, his body sprawled across the settee in an attitude of reckless abandon. One arm was draped across his belly, long, competent fingers splayed as though holding something against him; the other was thrown out to the side. He was too tall for the length of him to fit comfortably on the cushions so his left leg was bent, the knee propped against the back of the settee, while his right leg stretched out, calf and foot dangling in space. The white shirt he had been wearing earlier was just visible, crumpled beneath his thighs. The rest of his clothes were scattered over the floor. The sight of them made Helen smile. There had been little finesse involved in their removal. Her own clothes lay where they had been thrown, the silk dress tossed aside like a rag, her discarded bra hanging down wantonly from one corner of the glass and chrome coffee table in a cascade of sherbet-coloured lace. It amused her that she couldn't recall what had happened to the matching briefs.

The room was dark save for the pale glow of moonlight filtering through the thin voile that curtained the windows. In that washed out, cool silver the wizard's face looked younger despite the shadowing of stubble that darkened his jaw. There was a softness to his sleeping body, a vulnerability at odds with the muscled leanness of his frame. A slight smile curved his lips as though he dreamed of some impossible sweetness. Helen's own smile widened, turning proprietary. Her husband. Fate had already bound him to her to do with as she pleased. She intended to enjoy him before she turned him over to her mate.

It had been no hardship to make love to him until they had both been fully sated. She stretched languorously, turning away from the sleeping man for a moment to admire the play of moonlight over her own body, running her hands over her arms and across her breasts in a slow, unhurried caress, feeling the contours and lines, the soft, rounded curves underlain with the strength of muscles beneath. This woman's body had been a good choice after all. She had delighted in taking pleasure from it and had used her husband to the full to satisfy herself. Only in one respect had the experience been disappointing. Even in the final throes of ecstasy, the wizard had not dropped his shields. The thought turned Helen's smile into a little moue of discontent. The first time she had taken him to that peak she too had been lost in the frenzy of their mating, mindless and driven and unable to think beyond the aching desperate need that had consumed her body. That she had lost all control, recklessly abandoning herself to that flood of sensations had both shocked and delighted her. She had not anticipated the strength of her body's reactions. The second time she had been more careful, holding back enough so that she retained the awareness to test him. But, though his outer shields had softened, the deepest layers had remained strong and unassailable.

Helen bit her lip. The most she had been able to do was to use a little power to nudge him towards sleep, but that was all. It would take more than that to overwhelm his shields so that he could be taken as a host. She pouted a little at the thought of her mate's current host body. Their one coupling had been enjoyable for both of them, but it had been brief. She had not experienced the heights of sensation her husband's skills had aroused in her. Nor had she realised how much she would relish her ability to drive her husband into reckless abandonment. She felt herself growing wet thinking of how he had arched under her, their frantic coupling when his control had finally splintered and he had driven into her. Helen purred with pleasure as she turned back to the sleeping wizard. It would be an enjoyable task to keep testing his shields. Her mate might have to wait to claim his new host.

Reaching out, she ran a hand slowly down her husband's body, following the touch with a lazy tendril of suggestion. Though his shields remained impenetrable, even when sleeping, the surface of his dreaming mind was open to her. Helen added the image of a willing and compliant wife stretched out alongside him, twining his limbs with her own and laughed as she watched him stiffen.

Sweet dreams, my darling.

Naked and glorious in the moonlight, she stalked across the room and picked up the phone.

CHAPTER 10

Eldritch stopped in the kitchen doorway to stare at his wife, spellbound by the living beauty of her and by the sheer delight of having her back. This morning she was wearing a simple shift dress that shaded from the palest shell pink at her throat to a deep rose at the hem. It fell straight from her shoulders, skimming her breasts and flaring slightly over her hips so that the gauzy material swirled around her calves as she moved. Her feet were bare and her toenails were painted a pretty blush shade. She looked slim and elegant against the pale limestone tiles of the kitchen, her hair lit by the sunshine flooding in through the roof light as she stood at the kitchen's central island. She was grinding something in the large granite mortar that had stood unused on the counter since the coming of the demon. Whatever she was preparing, she seemed to be enjoying herself for she was humming softly and swaying a little from side to side as she worked. A cafetière of coffee stood on the counter along with two mugs.

Though Helen had seemed engrossed in her work, maybe she had heard him or sensed him watching her, for at that moment she put down the pestle and turned. Eldritch wondered if his heart would stop through sheer happiness as she smiled at him.

'Good morning.'

For a moment he stayed where he was, drinking in the sight of her.

'I didn't hear you get up.'

He crossed the room and she stepped into his arms. He toyed with her hair and ran his hands down her back, reassuring himself that she was real. He remembered waking in the small hours of the morning with her curled beside him on the settee and carrying her, still sleeping, upstairs to their bedroom. But when he had woken alone, the bed beside him cold and empty, he had feared for one awful, heart-stopping moment that that and everything else that had happened in the last two days had been a dream. Even now, holding his very real and vibrantly alive wife in his arms, Eldritch shuddered at the memory. The fear had left him panicky and breathless, uncertain that he had the strength to pick up the pieces of his life once more and carry on. Then he had heard her moving downstairs and had smelled the aroma of brewing coffee.

'You should have woken me,' he murmured, running his lips over her hair. 'I'd have got up and made you coffee.'

'The sun woke me. It was early and I didn't want to disturb you, you looked so comfortable. Just because I couldn't sleep there was no reason you had to be up.' She sighed and leaned her head on his chest. 'I think it's going to be a while before I enjoy lying in bed when I'm awake.'

'I can think of other things to do in bed.'

Eldritch hadn't come downstairs with the intention of seducing her, but the feel of Helen's body through the thin shift was arousing. Mischievously he rubbed his hands over her breasts and felt the nipples stiffen. His muscles clenched when she gasped and raised her arms, linking her hands around his neck, and he realised that beneath her dress she was naked.

'Why don't you tell me?' she suggested. Her smile grew wicked and she nipped the skin of his neck between her teeth as she pressed against him.

'Maybe I'll just show you.'

Eldritch dropped his head, grazing his lips over the slender column of her throat, down over her collarbones to the soft swell of her breasts.

'Ahh,' Helen breathed, her head falling back as she arched under him. She leaned back, steadying herself against the marble counter. His fingers caressed her through the gauzy fabric of her dress.

'God, you're beautiful.' Eldritch stared at his wife as he ran his hands up and down her body, cupping the soft material of the dress against her skin. 'I don't think I can get enough of you,' he murmured. 'You've bewitched me and I don't ever want to wake up.'

Helen laughed delightedly, a low, husky sound, but when she straightened and reached for the waistband of his sweatpants, he caught her wrists, gently holding her hands away from him. 'No, not this time. This time I want to please you.'

'You pleased me last night,' she reminded him, but she didn't resist. Instead, she kept her eyes on him and, when he released her wrists, she let her arms drop limply to her sides. It was an act of conscious surrender and one of the most powerfully erotic things Eldritch had ever witnessed. His dreams had been full of her but to have her stand in front of him, to see that willing submission to whatever he intended to do to her, was almost unbearably arousing. Eldritch fought down the animal urge to lift her against the counter and take her there and then. He wanted her desperately but he intended to tantalise them both.

Slowly he undid the tiny shell buttons that fastened the front of her dress, taking his time, his lips following the fabric as it parted. He drew in the scent of her, the petal softness of her skin. Finally he parted the dress, revealing her long slender legs and the pale gold triangle of hair at the point of her thighs. The skin around it was pink and already flushed with desire. Seeing it, Eldritch groaned in anticipation. He traced his hands up along her legs, delighting in the tremble of her muscles and the catch of her breath as his thumbs skimmed the inside of her thighs. They parted for him, but he ignored the invitation, though he could feel his own blood pounding, his body aching with the need to bury himself deep within her. Instead he ran his hands back down to those slender ankles. He nudged her feet further apart so he could kneel between them. Looking up, he caught her eye.

'Do you like what you see?' Helen's tone was at once both brazenly wanton and yet curiously shy, as though she genuinely wanted his approval. Like her gesture of submission, that hint of innocence, that handing of control to him sent a bolt of lust through Eldritch's gut.

'What do you think?' His tongue felt thick and his mouth dry. He thought he would go mad if he didn't take her soon, yet the desire to prolong this delicious torment of anticipation was even stronger. He lowered his head to her thighs, feeling the flushed warmth of her skin. Helen's breath caught as he slowly parted her further. She gasped as he ran his tongue over her moist inner skin and sobbed as his fingers followed.

Delighting in his wife's obvious arousal, Eldritch continued to caress her until she was trembling, her body spread above him, her breath coming fast and frantic. His own heart was pounding to the same rhythm as he stroked and teased, his body hard and desperate for release. He could take her now, pull her down with him to the floor and be inside her in moments, driving them both to a hard, fast climax. It would take so little to push them both over the edge. Eldritch panted; the knowledge of how it would feel to take her as she shuddered and bucked under him, to have her clenching around him as her climax overtook her, was almost enough to have him doing just that. Dear God, he wanted her! Yet he held himself back. Though it felt like torture to do so, he pushed himself away from his wife's body. Helen gave a half-voiced sob of protest as he withdrew, sagging against the kitchen unit.

In one swift movement Eldritch stood, scooping her up in his arms. 'I think we'll continue this upstairs, in bed.'

The phone rang as he carried her across the landing.

'To hell with whoever that is,' he muttered. 'We've got more urgent things to attend to.'

'Very urgent.' Helen shifted in his arms, her hand reaching once more for the waistband of his sweatpants. 'If I don't have you inside me soon, I'm going to go mad.'

Eldritch hitched her a little higher in his arms, keeping himself tantalisingly out of her reach.

'We wouldn't want that, now would we?' He dropped his head and nipped gently at the soft skin of her throat. 'Although it might be quite entertaining,' he murmured. He shifted his grip so he could caress her again.

'Oh!' Helen shuddered in his arms, her head falling back against his shoulder. 'Don't stop!'

Her breath hitched and she stared at him, her eyes wide and dark with pleasure. Eldritch smiled wickedly and stopped the slow movement of his fingers.

Helen squirmed in his arms. 'Please!'

'All in good time.'

He shoved the bedroom door open and laid her down on the bed. Spreading her thighs open, he knelt between them. When Helen tried to sit up and reach for him he cuffed her wrists with his hands, pushing her back onto the bed. Gently he guided her hands to the ornate wrought-iron bedstead, wrapping her fingers around the curling scrollwork. 'Hold on tight.'

Helen gazed at him, her blue eyes almost violet, wide and drugged with passion. For a moment he thought she would protest but then, very deliberately, she closed her eyes, surrendering herself to him once more, just as she had done in the kitchen. Tantalising them both, Eldritch traced a line of kisses down her body, down over her breasts and the smooth soft skin of her belly, down further to the hot, wet centre of her desire.

He teased her first with his tongue, slowly gliding it over her, and then with his fingers.

Helen twisted on the sheets, her hands clenched around the bedstead, her skin flushed, her lips parted. 'I want you.'

He raised his head but continued to stroke her with his fingers. 'I like the sound of that. Tell me again.' Still caressing her he pushed his sweatpants down with his other hand and tossed them aside.

'I want you inside me.' She moaned as his fingers slid a little way in, tormenting her. She opened wider, her body quivering with desire.

'Tell me again. What do you want?'

'I want to feel you pushing into me, thick and hard and strong.' Helen's head tossed from side to side and her hips bucked under his probing hand. 'I want you to take me hard and fast until I explode around you.'

Her back arched as he continued to caress her, holding her just short of her peak. 'I want to feel you. Now! Please!'

'Why didn't you say so?' Eldritch lowered himself over her, catching her hands in his own. Still he held himself back, poised on the very brink of entry, feeling the heat of her ready to envelop him and the answering surge of desire building irresistibly within him. 'All you had to do was ask.'

With a cry of release, he thrust into her and the world exploded around them.

CHAPTER 11

With Helen nestled in the curve of his arm, Eldritch decided he could happily stay where he was forever. Earlier, he had feared the events of the previous two days had been a dream. Now he wondered if it was the last two years that had been a nightmare. The warm softness of Helen's body lying against his felt so normal he could almost believe they had never been apart. He turned his head to look at her and, for no better reason than because he could, he dropped a sleepy, sated kiss on the tip of her nose.

Helen opened her eyes and regarded him lazily.

'Feeling any better about being awake in bed?'

'Hmm …' She pursed her lips, considering the matter. 'I do believe I am. It might take a while to fully convince me though.'

Eldritch laughed. 'God! You're insatiable. I love you.'

'I'm growing quite fond of you, too,' she said with a teasing smile.

Eldritch's own smile grew wolfish in response. 'Feel free to demonstrate just how fond of me you are.'

'Ha ha. Now who's insatiable?' She leaned over and nipped his ear but pulled back before he could respond with a proper kiss. 'I started blending one of my special teas. I'll make it for you later … if I don't get interrupted again.'

'You didn't seem to mind too much.' Eldritch smirked.

'Maybe not.' Helen propped herself up on her elbow and studied him. 'But we can't spend the rest of our lives in bed, delicious though that thought might be. Tell me, my love, what did you do with yourself while I was asleep?'

'I thought I was the one who had a lie in this— Ah. You're not talking about this morning, are you?'

'No.' Helen walked her fingers along his forearm. 'I want to know what you've been up to. What have I missed out on?'

Her tone remained light as though she understood this might be difficult for him. It was, but that didn't mean he didn't want to share this part of his life with her.

Eldritch rolled onto his back and stared up at the ceiling, wondering where to start. After a minute he said, 'I've written a new book.'

Helen's fingers moved from his elbow to his shoulder. She traced the tip of her index finger over the scars there. 'You didn't get these writing a book.'

'No.' Eldritch smiled ruefully. 'No, I didn't. There were more demons.' Eldritch found he couldn't bring himself to look at her. 'After what happened with you and Paul … after I—'

'Stop it, Marcus.' Helen poked him in the ribs. It wasn't a painful dig but it wasn't all that gentle, either. 'What happened with the demon wasn't your fault. Nor was what you did afterwards. For what it's worth, I would have done exactly the same thing if it had been you.'

'Would you really?'

'In an instant.'

Eldritch couldn't help but laugh at the fierce expression on his wife's face and the vehemence with which she spoke. 'Thank you. I think.' He sobered a little. 'I've missed you so much.'

He ran his hand along her arm, not seducing this time but simply pleasing himself with the reassuring feel of her there, beside him. Somehow, he had forgotten how easy it was – how easy it had always been – for them to talk, how little explanation they needed to understand each other. It felt so natural, so normal. He sighed and something settled within him. With the solid reality of her in his arms the guilt he had carried for the past two years fell away.

'You were telling me about the demons,' Helen prompted after he had been silent for several minutes.

'Hmm, yes. I've killed three more.'

'Three?'

Eldritch chuckled. 'Not all at once. The first two weren't a big deal – they were both relatively minor. Neither of them was strong enough to punch a hole in the boundary on their own, but there was a ripple left over from Nigel Granger.'

Not 'from your demon'. In his mind that entity was now solidly bound to the ill-fated hedge fund manager who had been its first host. It no longer had any connection with Helen.

'They used that to get through. Neither of them got to take a host.' There was fierce satisfaction in his voice as he said it. No one had had to die. 'The third one was different. That's where I got these.' He shrugged his scarred shoulder. 'It had created an avatar.'

'An ava—' Helen stopped short, her eyes widening. 'Really?' She regarded her husband with undisguised amazement. 'But you were able to destroy it?'

'Eventually.' Eldritch shrugged again, trying for nonchalance, although he was both pleased and embarrassed by Helen's reaction. 'I had some help.'

'Tell me more.' Helen plumped up the pillow under her head and settled back to be entertained. 'Was it anyone I know?'

'No.' Eldritch shook his head. 'You've never met. She's a Welsh witch by the name of Gwyn. That's Gwyn with a Y, not an E, by the way.'

'And that's significant?'

'Apparently, but you'd need a deep interest in Welsh to understand why. Quite,' he added with a laugh as Helen wrinkled her nose in response. 'But it rather sums her up. She's …' As so often when dealing with Gwyn, Eldritch found himself at a loss as to what to say. 'I think I'd have to say she's unique. She's small and she has this crazy mass of hair – jet black, or at least it used to be. Now it's got this one white streak in it.' He gestured vaguely, trying to convey the impression of Gwyn's wild mane. 'A bit like Medusa but without the snakes.' Although sometimes he wasn't absolutely sure about that; maybe she just kept them well hidden. He smothered a grin at the thought. 'Think cats and crystals. Oh, and she has a temper like a harpy. You'll like her.'

This time he allowed his grin to break through. He was looking forward to introducing the pair of them.

'You seem quite taken with her.' Helen sounded amused. She raised her head from the pillow and regarded him levelly. 'Have you slept with her?'

'What? No!' Eldritch reacted with horror, genuinely appalled by the suggestion. 'No, she's a good friend, but that's all.'

'She could be a good friend with benefits,' Helen countered lightly. She seemed surprisingly unbothered by the scenario she had proposed, much less so than Eldritch. 'You thought I was dead. To all intents and purposes, I was dead. I wouldn't hold it against you if you had.'

Whether or not that was true, Eldritch didn't care; he wanted to set the record straight. He reached over and cupped Helen's cheek in his hand.

'No,' he said, firmly. 'I haven't slept with Gwyn and I haven't slept with anyone else, either.' He looked directly into her eyes, knowing he had no secrets to hide from her, hoping she would accept the truth of what he was saying. 'There's been no one but you, Helen. After I lost you I didn't want anyone else, and I haven't wanted anyone since then. Just you.'

Helen turned her head so that her lips brushed his palm. 'Thank you,' she whispered. She touched his cheek, mirroring his gesture to her. 'I believe you. But I wouldn't have blamed you if there had been someone.' Before he could respond her expression changed, becoming impish. 'To be honest with you, I'm rather disappointed. I might have liked being part of a ménage à trois with you and a Welsh witch.'

Eldritch nearly choked at the image that conjured. 'Gwyn's a good friend,' he repeated, as much to reassure himself as his wife. Resolutely he pushed away the recollection of the one occasion when Gwyn had undressed him. It had been after his first ill-fated encounter with the avatar, and she had just spent what had seemed like an eternity cleaning and binding the wounds its teeth had left in his shoulder. For goodness' sake, he had been barely conscious at the time! There had been nothing even remotely sexual involved. *Had there?* No, he was not going to think about it and – please God! – Gwyn never gave it a moment's thought either. 'When you meet her, you'll realise that's all she is.'

Helen pouted theatrically. 'What a pity.'

Eldritch decided it was time to steer the conversation back to safer ground. 'She saved my life.' *And not just after the avatar.* He owed Gwyn too much to risk their friendship by starting to think about her in any other way.

'She's powerful, then?' Helen cocked her head to one side, considering.

'She is, yes, although I don't think she'd say so if you asked her. She burned herself a long time ago, tangling with wild magic unshielded. The fact she survived gives you some indication as to how powerful she was. I reckon she still has that ability, but sourcing power's difficult for her now. She has to eke out what little she can access, but she can still handle it.

'Then there's Aidan.' Eldritch smiled at the thought of the young man who, against expectations, had turned into a firm friend. 'Gwyn was his guardian after his mother died,' he added by way of explanation of that complex relationship. 'Now she's training him. They're the reason I stayed in Wales after we'd got rid of the demon. I've been renting a small house there for a few months, a cottage really – except that makes it sound quaint and it's not. I was thinking of moving there permanently.' He fell silent for a moment. 'There wasn't much left for me here.' Pushing away the black mood that loomed in the wake of those words he said, 'I really should give them a call. They'll want to know that everything's okay.'

'Don't!'

For a second Helen froze, as if taken aback by the sharpness of her own response, but then she smiled ruefully. 'I don't want to share you,' she said. She ducked her head, shyly. 'Not yet.

Not even with good friends.' She glanced up at him to see if he understood. 'I'm sure they'll forgive you.'

Eldritch had forgotten how pleasant it could be to spend a day doing very little. Though he and Helen had migrated from bedroom to lounge – via the kitchen where he had made them both a light lunch – he felt no desire to do anything beyond sprawl on the settee with Helen stretched beside him, her head resting on his thigh. She had dozed and he had read, something else he had had little time for recently while he had been working on the final proofs for his book. When the doorbell rang he had little inclination to get up and answer it.

Helen lifted her head from his thigh. 'You should get that.'

The bell rang again, supporting her suggestion. The chime pealed for longer this time, as though whoever stood on their doorstep had grown impatient.

Helen poked him in the ribs. 'Go on. It might be important.' She sat up and ran her hands down her shirt, smoothing the creases from the fabric. 'And we are decent for receiving visitors.'

Eldritch grunted. 'We're dressed,' he conceded, getting to his feet. 'But I wouldn't go so far as decent. Thankfully.' He smiled wolfishly and was pleased by the look Helen sent him in return. Grinning to himself, he went to the front door.

'Hang on, I'm coming,' he yelled as the doorbell rang a third time. 'I'll bet you it's only Carol from next door,' he added over his shoulder to Helen. 'She'll have noticed we're home and be wanting to rope us into her latest community improvement scheme.'

Perhaps he should have read the flyer that had been pushed through the letter box the previous day. Well, it was too late now. He was rehearsing his excuses even as he opened the door, so it took him a moment to process the fact that it wasn't Carol standing on the doorstep.

'Oh, hello.' Eldritch shook himself mentally and readjusted his thoughts. The young man was wearing jeans and a scuffed leather jacket, rather than painter's dungarees, but there was no mistaking the lanky frame or the sour look he got in response to the greeting. 'It's Terry, isn't it?'

Terry sniffed disdainfully. 'I've come to see her.' His tone suggested he begrudged sharing even that little information with Eldritch.

Eldritch's eyebrows rose. He couldn't help it. He had been puzzled by the younger man's odd attitude when they had met at the clinic but had dismissed it as unimportant. He hadn't expected to see Terry ever again. Now, having him turn up uninvited on the doorstep, he felt that some attempt at courtesy would have been appropriate. Certainly, his grandmother would have boxed his ears if he had ever spoken to anyone like that. And that thought made him feel rather old and uncomfortably strait-laced, so he throttled back his initial impulse to respond by shutting the door in the younger man's face and contented himself with a bland look instead.

'I'm sorry?'

'Helen. I've come to see her.'

'Of course you have.'

Eldritch might have said more but, at that moment, the lady herself called out from the lounge.

'Who is it, my love?'

'It's Terry, from the clinic.' Eldritch kept his arm across the doorway as he turned to answer her.

'How lovely. Well, don't leave him standing on the doorstep. Ask him in.'

Eldritch let out a huff of breath, partly amused and partly bemused by the instruction. He couldn't understand why Helen had taken a shine to the young man, but it seemed that she had. Maybe it was as she said, that it was because he had been there when she had first recovered consciousness. And that, Eldritch reminded himself, had been an act of pure kindness on Terry's part. Regardless of how socially inept Terry seemed around him, the fact remained that he had been moved by the thought of an unconscious woman lying alone in the clinic and had felt strongly enough about it that he had visited her. For that alone Eldritch felt he should make an effort to be nice. He nodded at the small package Terry held in one hand. It was wrapped in plain brown paper and tied with rough string. If this was a courting gift it was as gauche as its bearer.

'Chocolates?' he enquired. 'I should warn you that she doesn't have a very sweet tooth.'

'It's not chocolates.'

Terry's look implied that Eldritch was stupid for suggesting such a thing. Eldritch took a breath and let it slide over him.

'Fair enough. Well, you heard the lady.' Eldritch tried a final smile which Terry ignored. 'Come on in.' He stepped aside to let Terry go past him. 'She's in the lounge. It's the door on your right.'

'Hello, Terry.' Helen rose from the settee to greet her visitor. She took his hand, leaning in briefly to kiss his cheek.

Terry stiffened as though uncertain how to respond. Helen stepped away before he could decide and settled herself back down on the cream leather, tucking her legs up underneath her.

'Why don't we have a drink?' She looked over at Eldritch who had stopped in the doorway, watching the exchange, and smiled winningly. 'Would you mind making some tea, my love? Doctor Ashwood did say I needed to make sure I was getting sufficient fluids.'

'Are you feeling okay?'

She didn't look ill; in fact Eldritch thought she looked radiant; slender and sophisticated in her tunic-style shirt and those wide-legged linen trousers, the colour of crushed raspberries, that made her legs look as though they went on forever. But looks could be deceptive and he wasn't about to take such things for granted. He came to stand beside the settee, looking her over with concern.

'Of course I am.' She reached a hand to him. 'But it's not often one gets the chance to be waited on, on doctor's orders, so I'm going to make the most of it.' She let her fingers trail down his arm. 'I'm saving my energy for later,' she added in a low whisper.

'Good idea.' Eldritch cleared his throat, both embarrassed and delighted that his wife was flirting with him in front of their visitor. 'Lapsang?'

'Mmm, you know me too well.' Her eyes met his, adding a wealth of additional meaning to the words. 'Yes please. Warm the pot first though and make sure you let it brew for five minutes – no more, no less.'

Eldritch smiled indulgently. 'I'll watch it like a hawk,' he promised. 'Would you prefer normal tea, Terry? Or coffee?'

Terry hadn't moved from the spot where Helen had greeted him. He turned his head to stare at Eldritch. 'Whatever you're making.'

'Fine. Tea it is then. I'll leave the pair of you to catch up for a few minutes.'

He squeezed Helen's fingers and then brushed a kiss over her knuckles, aware that Terry was watching him. 'Love you,' he murmured.

'I know.'

Helen watched Eldritch, a dreamy smile on her face, but as soon as he had left the room her expression turned hard and cold. 'Behave yourself,' she hissed, turning on Terry. Temper flashed in her eyes. 'Or have you forgotten that he is a wizard?'

Terry bristled angrily. 'I know what he is.' In two strides he was looming over her. He dropped the parcel he had been carrying and caught her chin in his hand. 'You said you were stronger than him.'

Helen slapped his hand away, backing up the gesture with a little flare of power. 'And so I am. But better yet if it does not come to such a contest. Would you have it that I must destroy him?'

The look that flashed across Terry's face suggested he would like that very much indeed.

Helen snorted in disgust. 'If I do, you will not have a host with power.'

Terry snarled. 'I do not want you and him together.'

Helen was on her feet in an instant, facing him down. 'What you want is immaterial. I decide what I will and will not do with this body. If I want to take the wizard then I will take him. Besides,' she added slyly, 'he is my husband. It is his right to have me.'

She stretched, lithe and sensual as a cat, arching her back so her breasts pushed against the fabric of her shirt. Keeping her eyes on Terry she ran her hands from her collarbones to her waist, moulding the cloth provocatively against her body.

'Are you jealous of him, oh my mate? Or is it the thought of my enjoying someone else that displeases you?'

Terry said nothing but his expression hardened.

'And what of the woman, Joanne?' Helen kept her voice low but her tone was deadly. 'Or had you forgotten that Bob knew of Terry's girlfriend and so I know of her too? Can you tell me that you have not seen her, that you have not been enjoying her these past days, mate of mine? Have you not worked on her body until she begged you to enter her? Has she not kissed you and caressed you, heating your blood until you could think of nothing but the need to spend yourself between her thighs?'

Though Terry stayed silent Helen nodded, reading her answer in the stiffening of his muscles and the quickening of his breath.

'Then call me not for enjoying the wizard.'

In the next instant she softened, her eyes becoming warm and languid. 'Wait until you have taken his body,' she promised, stepping closer. She cupped one hand around the back of his head, fingers tangling in his hair as she drew his head down to hers. Her other hand pressed against his jeans and Terry gasped as her fingers found what they sought through the denim.

'We will both enjoy his body then, mate of mine,' Helen whispered. 'There is no need for jealousy. He will be yours as the woman, Helen, is mine, and you and I will be together.'

As suddenly as she had caught him she released him and stepped away, imperious and regal. 'Now, have you brought me what I asked for?'

With a frustrated snarl, Terry retrieved the parcel he had brought with him and thrust it into her hands.

'Good.' Helen stroked her fingers over the paper before putting the package down beside the settee. 'I have already started the preparation. Now I have these I can make the tincture that will block his power. Then we will be able to break his shields.'

'And take him.' For the first time Terry's expression showed approval. 'When?'

'Three days.' Helen raised a hand to forestall any protest. 'The drug must be administered in stages. Too much at once and it will surely kill him, strong though he is.'

'And you are sure this will work?'

Helen smiled. 'Oh yes. This host was most skilled as a herb wife. I will bind him just as the crone, Melindra, bound us. He will be yours, my mate, I promise it, in three days' time. In the meantime, come to me tonight, when I call you.'

'And the wizard?' Terry cast a wary glance at the lounge door.

'I will take care of him. By tonight it will already be too late.'

CHAPTER 12

Eldritch looked around the lounge and then at his wife, curled against the cushions of the settee. There was no sign of her visitor.

'Where's Terry?'

Helen lifted one shoulder dismissively. 'He decided he didn't want to stay.'

'Oh.' Eldritch glanced at the three mugs he held. 'Fair enough.' He couldn't say he was upset by this development.

Helen looked at him apologetically. 'He is a rather strange young man,' she conceded.

Eldritch set the mugs on the coffee table. 'I'm glad you said that. I know he's your friend.' He wasn't certain if that was the right word for Terry, but it would do for now. 'But he strikes me as a bit odd. Sorry,' he added, with a shrug that acknowledged his words might cause his wife offence. 'I don't think he likes me much, either.'

'I'm sure that's not true, but I'll admit he is a little lacking in the social graces.'

Helen unfolded her legs, stood up and stretched, then took the mug Eldritch reached over to pass her. 'Unlike you, my love. Thank you.'

'So, if he didn't want to chat, why did he come round?' Eldritch spotted the brown paper parcel on the floor by the end of the settee. 'Oh yes.' He eyed it curiously. As far as he could tell it hadn't been unwrapped. He turned his gaze back to Helen. 'Please tell me he's not courting you.' He was only half-joking.

Helen chuckled, a deliciously throaty sound. 'What a delightfully old-fashioned idea.' She batted her eyelashes flirtatiously at him over the rim of her mug. 'Are you worried?'

'Only about what I'd do to him if he tried anything inappropriate.' Then, playing along, he narrowed his eyes. 'Why, should I be?'

Helen pretended to consider this. 'Two handsome men fighting for my hand. What more could a woman ask for?' Her smile was arch and vampish, matching her words, but then it faded. She took a sip of her tea and shook her head. 'No, he's not courting me.'

'So, why did he come? And what's in the parcel?'

'He came because I asked him to. He brought me the herbs I need.'

'Herbs? I don't understand.'

Helen set her mug down. For a moment she studied it as though it had become the most fascinating thing in her world. When she looked up at Eldritch her expression was serious. 'I want to mix a potion.' All the teasing had gone from her voice. 'Something to strengthen my shields. What happened before, with …' She hesitated, catching her lower lip between her teeth. The words 'the demon' hung unspoken between them. 'I couldn't … that is, I don't …' Helen shook her head as if doing so could unblock the words from her throat. Eventually, in a voice that was little more than a broken whisper, she said, 'I never want that to happen again.'

She reached out towards him as though grasping for something to steady herself.

Eldritch took her hand and pulled her into his arms. 'Sshh.' He smoothed the hair back from her face. Her eyes seemed large and dark as lapis against the sudden pallor of her cheeks. He held her closer still as he realised she was trembling.

'It's not going to happen again, Helen. I promise. I won't let anything happen to you. I'd rather die first, you know that.'

With her head pressed against his chest, Eldritch couldn't hear Helen's answer but he felt the small movement as she nodded. He continued to hold her, willing to offer the reassurance of his arms for as long as she needed it while wishing he knew what else he could do to help. Once he had thought of them as invincible – him, Helen and Paul. They tracked, fought and destroyed demons; it was what they did. But the last one had shown that they too were vulnerable. Paul dead, Helen possessed, and him, victorious in the end, yes, but broken apart by what that victory had cost. Unconsciously Eldritch's arms tightened around his wife and Helen nestled a little closer against him, her right hand resting softly over the place where her nails had once scarred his chest. No, none of them had escaped unscathed from that last encounter with the Unseen Realm.

They stood for a minute more, Helen huddled against him while Eldritch rested his cheek on the crown of her head, but then Helen straightened and looked up. The colour had returned to her face but Eldritch thought she looked fragile, even brittle.

'I don't want to be a burden for you to protect. It wouldn't be fair. There are things I can do to make sure that what happened could never happen again.' She sounded both fierce and frightened.

'So you asked Terry to get you the herbs you needed.'

'I don't want to go out, not until I've strengthened my shields.' There was defiance in her tone, but she wouldn't look at him.

Eldritch tipped her head up with a finger under her jaw. 'I would have gone and got you whatever you wanted.' He tried to keep his tone reasonable, but he couldn't help the trace of bitterness that slipped into it at the thought that she had turned to a stranger for help, rather than to him. That one fact hurt more than any demon-inflicted wound ever could.

Helen made a small keening noise. 'I know you would.' She blinked and her eyes looked suspiciously bright as though, for all her earlier brave words, she was fighting back tears. 'But I don't want to be left alone.' Still within the circle of his arms, she turned away from him. 'Not yet.' In a voice bleak with self-recrimination she added, 'I suppose you think I'm pathetic.'

Eldritch wondered if his heart might break anew at the sound of the raw misery in his wife's voice. He closed his eyes and concentrated on the feel of her living, breathing body under his hands, using that to steady himself. How could he have been so blind? He had so wanted to believe that she was alright that he had let himself be taken in by the brave face she had put on for him, not even thinking to question the reality of what was happening, because he desperately wanted it to be true. But of course, it wasn't. How could it be? It was unreasonable to think that Helen could get over what had happened to her so quickly.

Unreasonable and unkind, he berated himself. *And then you have the gall to feel slighted because she asks a favour of someone else rather than you.*

There were times when Marcus Eldritch could hate himself, but he could also realise when he had been given a second chance. He would beat himself up for his lack of sense some other time, but now he needed to be there for Helen. Whatever she needed from him, big or small, and no matter how unnecessary it seemed to him, he would do it – anything to bring her peace of mind. It was the least he could do.

Very gently he raised his hands to her shoulders and turned her back to face him. 'I don't think that's pathetic at all.'

Not waiting for a response he kissed her forehead, then the bridge of her nose and then, very tenderly, he kissed her lips.

At first Helen stood rigid under his touch but then she sighed and the tension eased out of her. 'You're very good to me, my love. I'm sorry, bits of what happened keep coming back to me. I suppose it's going to take me a while to get over it.' She looked at him ruefully. 'I'll bet your Welsh witch wouldn't be as silly about it all as I'm being.'

She made as if to pull away from him but Eldritch wouldn't release her, enfolding her in a hug instead.

'You'd be surprised by just how silly Gwyn can be,' he said dryly. Then, seeing his wife's expression he added, 'And she's not my Welsh anything. You don't have to compare yourself to her, Helen. I promise you, there's nothing but friendship between us and there's certainly no reason to be jealous.'

He cupped her cheeks in his hands, studying her face. 'I can't change what's happened, but we don't have to go back to it,' he murmured, giving voice to the thought that had been slowly taking shape in his head. 'We never said we were going to dedicate our lives to demon hunting.'

'But it's what we've always done.' Helen seemed genuinely taken aback by his words.

'I know, but it doesn't have to be. This is our chance to start afresh, to do something different.'

'We could.' Helen didn't sound entirely convinced. 'But what would we do?'

'We could start by taking a holiday, somewhere nice. Somewhere warm.'

Helen eyed him curiously. 'Why somewhere warm?'

Eldritch pulled out his best wolfish smile. 'Because then I can have the pleasure of watching you wander around in nothing but a tiny scrap of a bikini.'

'Oh, you!' She gave him a little shove, her fists against his chest, but she was laughing, delighting Eldritch. The bleakness had lifted from her eyes.

His voice grew husky, driven by emotion. 'I love you. Whatever you need to get through this we'll do and, whatever it is, I promise I won't think you're being silly. You're my wife. I love you.'

As he held her against him he thought again of the special tea she had said she wanted to make. Now he understood the reasoning behind it.

'I think this potion of yours sounds like an excellent idea. Do you have enough herbs to make it for both of us?'

Later, when Helen handed him a teacup full of a greenish-brown liquid, Eldritch wondered if there was a diplomatic way to renege on that suggestion. Helen had spent the remainder of the afternoon and the early part of the evening in the kitchen, blending and steeping different herbs, a white chef's apron tied over her clothes to protect them and her hair snagged up in a ponytail to keep it from her face. The brew that was the end result of all that work looked considerably less appealing than its creator. 'Pond water' was the term that sprang to Eldritch's mind although he decided to keep the thought to himself. To buy himself time before he committed to tasting it he took a cautious sniff. Unsurprisingly the liquid had a strong herbal smell, but Eldritch had to admit that it wasn't entirely unpleasant. He thought he could detect mint and rosemary and something sharp and slightly almondy, but beyond that the ingredients remained a mystery. Curiously he leaned over to inspect the cup Helen had put to one side for herself. The liquid in it was paler – more water, less pond.

'They look different,' he commented, mentally weighing up whether adding 'yours looks nicer than mine' would earn him a smile or a slap. He decided not to risk it. From the look Helen shot him he wondered if she'd guessed his thought anyway and reckoned he'd made the right decision.

'That's because they are different.'

'Oh? I thought we were both having the same.'

'Same effect,' Helen agreed, as though explaining something he should have known, 'but a different potion. Because I'm a woman,' she added, forestalling his question. 'And you –' she drilled him in the stomach with her index finger '– aren't. Obviously.'

'Obviously.' Eldritch grinned. 'I'm glad you noticed.'

Helen seemed calmer after her hours of concocting and brewing and more settled. Eldritch considered that to be as much a benefit as any arcane protection offered by the resulting elixir. Not that it wasn't an interesting concept – and he had no doubt that the potion would do what Helen claimed – it was just that he had no intention of letting her get anywhere near a demon ever again. But he wasn't going to tell her that. Nor would that get him out of drinking the potion.

Putting off the inevitable for a moment longer, Eldritch commented, 'I had no idea these things made a difference.'

When Helen raised her eyebrows he added, 'To the make-up of a potion, that is.'

That earned him a snort and a toss of her head.

'And that, my love, is exactly why you should stick to cooking and leave healing drafts and potions to me.'

Eldritch smirked. It crossed his mind to suggest Helen would enjoy comparing notes on healing with Gwyn but, given how sensitive she had been about that particular friendship, he decided to leave that idea for another day. For now, he was happy simply to have his wife back.

'I could learn.' With a swift move he snagged Helen round the waist with his free hand and pulled her close. 'How long would it take?'

'About thirty years,' Helen said drily. 'Are you going to drink it or not?'

'All in good time.' He ran his lips over the nape of her neck where a few fine strands of hair had escaped from her ponytail, making her shiver and arch back against him. 'Thirty years is an awfully long time,' he breathed. 'I can think of other things I'd rather be perfecting in that time.'

'I'm sure you can.'

She turned and took the cup from his hand, putting it down next to hers on the counter. 'We'll drink those later.' Her voice was already husky, her eyes dark and full of promises.

She smiled and ran the tip of her tongue over her parted lips, wetting them. 'After you've shown me your area of expertise.'

It felt decidedly wanton – decadent even – to walk through the house naked, even if it was only from the bedroom to the kitchen and back. As he padded across the wooden floor Eldritch smiled at the thought. It occurred to him that he couldn't recall doing so before, not even when he and Helen had first moved here as newly-weds, and certainly not in the months after her possession when he had lived in the house alone. Now he thought he might like to do it more often, especially when Helen was sprawled naked across the bed, glorious and unselfconscious, like a modern-day Venus. He paused, teacup in one hand and two wine glasses and a bottle in the other, and took a moment to savour the sight. Helen's blonde hair was tousled messily over her shoulders, and her lips and cheeks were still flushed in the aftermath of their lovemaking. A little curl of lust tightened his belly as she rolled from her side onto her back and stretched, looking up at him with eyes that were dreamy and sated. Her smile was full of promises and the hint of secret and hidden delights.

'Mmm, I wondered where you'd gone.'

She ran one hand slowly across her lips and down over her chin and throat, trailing her fingers between her breasts and down over her stomach before letting them rest at the top of her thighs. 'I missed you.'

Eldritch bit back a delighted groan. He swallowed, his tongue thick, his mouth dry. 'I thought you might like a drink.' He showed her the wine glasses and the bottle. 'And your potion, of course.' He raised the teacup and added, 'I've already had mine,' because he knew it mattered to her.

Was that a trace of sadness that flashed in her eyes? It was gone in an instant leaving him uncertain what he had seen. Maybe it was the thought of what that potion was meant to guard against. Anxious not to spoil the mood, Eldritch turned and put the cup to one side on the dressing table, out of the way. Helen could have it when she wanted it; there was no rush. They would drink the wine and then taste it a second time, sweet and heavy on each other's lips, as they made love again. Turning back to the bed, Eldritch was shocked when the world lurched sideways under his feet. Staggering, he grabbed for the metal bedstead to steady himself.

'What the—'

He stopped as the room blurred and then, just as suddenly, snapped back into focus. He was aware of Helen getting up from the bed. A small part of his mind registered the fact that she didn't seem at all concerned.

'It's alright, my love.' Her voice was cool and somehow distant. 'Sometimes it provokes a strong reaction. It's nothing to be frightened of.'

'I'm not frightened.'

But he was – just a little.

A sensation of icy cold was spreading rapidly up his legs, racing from his calves to his thighs, up through his groin and into his body. Numbness followed in its wake. When it hit his diaphragm he doubled over, unable to breathe. He was vaguely aware of the wine glasses falling from his hand and shattering on the floor, the bottle following them. Wine spilled out, splashing over the shards of glass, slicking the thin sickle shapes and pooling like blood around his feet. Eldritch saw it but he felt nothing.

As if from a long way away he sensed Helen come towards him. She was speaking but the words were unintelligible over the rush of blood through his ears. He clung to the bedstead, desperately aware that something was awfully – terrifyingly – wrong. He thought he felt a hand on his arm, warm flesh against the icy coldness of his own, as he struggled for breath which refused to come. His chest contracted, the muscles spasming then locking tight though he tried to fight down panic and force himself to relax and breathe. His vision was narrowing, darkness spreading in from the edges to merge with the ice that locked around his organs. Unable to move, unable to speak, Eldritch looked up into Helen's face, expecting to see his own desperate fear mirrored there. He didn't. His last thought, as he slid down into darkness, was that she was smiling.

CHAPTER 13

Eldritch stood in the clotted patchwork of shadows and crystalline moonlight at the foot of the bed. In her dream, Gwyn spoke to him, but the wizard didn't answer. She wasn't sure if that was because he couldn't or because he didn't hear her. Maybe it was both. Though his eyes were open there was no awareness in them and he gave no appearance of seeing her as she sat up in bed and stared at him.

'Eldritch?'

He continued to look at – or possibly through – her, unblinking and unresponsive, and Gwyn noticed how the moonlight had bleached the colour from his skin. Face, limbs, torso – all were rendered in bone-white monochrome against which the dark scrub of his hair stood out like a smear of ink. Gwyn tilted her head to one side and studied him curiously. The scatter of demon-bite scars that patterned Eldritch's chest and shoulders were just visible, like a constellation of faint crescent moons. The darker lines raked across his ribs showed more clearly, though they were less noticeable now than when she had first seen them, while the more recent marks left by the avatar's teeth tracked across his right shoulder and biceps like a brand. If this was an image conjured by her mind, then it was uncannily detailed, but if it was some form of apparition, what exactly was it that she was being shown?

In a voice that echoed her puzzlement she spoke to him again. 'Eldritch?'

But there was no response.

How like a wizard to be enigmatic!

Even in her dreaming state Gwyn huffed in annoyance. Maddening, Machiavellian, manipulative … she had used all those words to describe Marcus Eldritch, and more besides, but it was also true that he was her friend and Gwyn found herself uneasy as she considered what had drawn this apparition to her. If the wizard wouldn't – or couldn't – speak, then how was she to work out what he was trying to tell her?

Putting her misgivings to one side, Gwyn leaned forward, peering towards her silent visitor. Were the shadows around Eldritch denser than they had been just a heartbeat ago? The hairs on the back of her neck prickled, standing on end as she realised she could no longer make out anything in the room beyond where he stood. Where, only moments before, she had been able to see the silhouetted bulk of the wardrobe and the pale blur of moonlight reflected in the old cheval glass, both had now vanished. It was as if the wizard stood in front of a wall of darkness. Or perhaps not a wall but a curtain, for, as Gwyn eyed it, that obscuring blackness seemed to ripple and shift. She swallowed queasily. There was something fell there. All her instincts were shouting it to her, warning her not to get any closer, but whatever the danger that lurked there, she knew she needed to get Eldritch away from it.

Ignoring the little voice that urged her to press herself back against the headboard of the bed and stay as far from that blackness as she could manage, Gwyn reached out towards Eldritch, willing the wizard to see her hand and take it.

You've only got to step forward. Just one step. Come on. Take my hand. That's all you need to do.

Fear of whatever lurked in the darkness stopped her saying the words out loud, but in her head she was shouting them, willing the wizard to respond to her. Her right hand fizzed with the energy of the Levin bolt she planned to throw into that dark curtain as soon as she had pulled the wizard clear. But Eldritch remained motionless, standing like an idol carved from ivory and obsidian, and for all she desperately wanted to, Gwyn could not force her own body to move towards him.

She felt a whimper rise in her throat as the darkness behind Eldritch shifted and something moved within it. It was a woman, or at least it wore a woman's shape. Gwyn couldn't see her properly for she remained behind Eldritch, but she saw her slender limbs emerging from the snaking coils of darkness as though she wore them like some fantastical gown. As Gwyn watched, silent and horrified, the woman wrapped her arms around Eldritch's chest, holding him to her. Gwyn could all but feel the way she pressed herself against the wizard's back, moulding herself against him, lithe and sinuous, and how the heat of that contact spread out across the wizard's skin. Still Eldritch did not move as those long, shapely fingers closed over him, the jewelled nails digging lightly into his flesh.

Mine, that grip seemed to say. *All mine.*

One elegant hand slid up to cup the wizard's jaw, turning Eldritch's face to the side, and still there was no change in that blank expression, no trace of awareness in his eyes. Gwyn watched as the strange woman stepped from behind him. Her face was blurred, the features hidden by darkness, as she turned towards the unresponsive wizard. Unhurriedly she reached up with her other hand, gliding it through his hair and pulling his head down to meet hers while her grip on his jaw tightened, forcing his mouth open.

No!

Eldritch made no sound but Gwyn was certain that he would have resisted had he been able to. She herself wanted to scream – a warning, a protest – anything to stop what was coming next. At the very least she wanted to close her eyes, for above all she did not want to see what she knew was about to happen. But the fabric of her dream held her captive and silent. Trapped within her nightmare and sick with horror, she could only watch as the woman raised her head and took Eldritch's mouth in a long, devouring kiss. And Gwyn knew, with the cold certainty of the dreamer, that when that unknown woman drew back, the man she held in her thrall would no longer be Marcus Eldritch.

Gwyn sat bolt upright in bed, her heart hammering at her ribs. Without conscious direction her eyes went to the foot of the bed and for one awful instant she thought she saw someone standing there. Fear was like a clammy hand tightening around her throat, but even as she was shaping a Levin bolt, the image was gone. The pale wash of moonlight coming in through the open curtains showed nothing but the shadows of her bedroom furniture – the old pine wardrobe, the two mismatched chests of drawers and Nain's old cheval glass standing in the corner like an oval cascade of quicksilver frozen between the wooden barley sugar twists of its frame. There was no one standing at the end of the bed, no curtain of darkness bisecting the room.

'Hah.'

The exhalation came out more like a sob than she cared to admit. Gwyn crossed her arms over her chest, hugging the familiar softness of her old oversized T-shirt around her, and sank back against the carved wooden headboard of the bed. 'Sweet Lady.'

She scrubbed her hands across her face and wished she could wipe away the aftermath of the dream as easily. Her pulse might be slowing but she felt no desire to try to sleep again, not if there were images like that waiting for her. Though the night was mild she shivered. What she had seen had felt too much like reality to dismiss it out of hand. The dreaming mind walked strange paths, some very close to the boundaries of the Unseen Realm, and revelations and warnings were by no means impossible. Then again, though she believed in such premonitions, she had never yet been chased across Tower Bridge by giant spiders. Nor had she ever walked into an important meeting with an editor only to realise that she was stark naked. She smiled ruefully. That was the trouble with dreams; determining what was a warning and what was down to an overactive subconscious was an exercise that all too often was accurate only in hindsight.

So, what was an English wizard doing in her dreams, apart from scaring the life out of her? And why, in the name of the Lady, had he been naked? Eldritch had been in danger, that much seemed obvious, but from what? He had gone back to London to be reunited with his wife. That was scarcely cause for concern and, given those circumstances, she could hardly imagine he would then abandon her to go up against some entity from the Unseen Realm. Even if he had, the idea of him striding into that battle naked like some revenant Norse berserker was ludicrous. The image was so out of character that it startled Gwyn into a chuckle. The tall Englishman was reserved to the point of primness when it came to nudity. The few days he had spent at her house the previous year, while recovering from a violent encounter with a demonic avatar, had taught her that. The knowledge that he had turned up naked in someone's dream – especially hers! – would leave him mortified. Not that Eldritch wasn't attractive. Gwyn wasn't above appreciating the finer details of the naked male form if it was presented to her in her dreams. She chuckled again, this time more wickedly. She would have to ask him if he had been working out when she next spoke to him.

The thought of her friend's likely response made her smile. She wasn't quite ready to dismiss her dream and settle back down to sleep but she felt calmer; uneasy still, but not so much frightened as puzzled. If Eldritch wasn't in danger, what had her dream been about? Could something be wrong with Helen? Yet surely Eldritch would have phoned her if that was the case. Gwyn considered that for a moment.

Ah, there's the nub of it.

She had expected him to phone and let her know everything was alright, and he hadn't. Of course, there was nothing to stop her contacting him, except that she didn't want to intrude. Still, it wasn't unreasonable – was it? – to want to know that he was okay and to hear about Helen. She knew that things would be different now that he had her back, but …

Oh!

The realisation hit her as to what her dream could have been about and the thought made her blush, her sense of unease melting into shame. Eldritch naked and vulnerable – yes, that could be a threat, but the unknown – indeed, faceless

– woman who held him so possessively … Gwyn let her head drop back against the headboard and stared unseeing up at the ceiling.

'Gwynyfa Hughes, you are a sad, pathetic woman.'

She shook her head, heartily embarrassed by what she realised was a more likely explanation for the content of her dream.

'Freud would have a field day,' she muttered. It wouldn't take an expert on dream analysis to dissect what her subconscious had shown her. 'Are you really so scared that your friendship is going to change now that she's back in his life that you transfer that fear to him in your dreams?'

With a disgusted sigh she lay down and reached to pull the rumpled duvet back over her. Her hand encountered the warm curl of a sleeping cat and she stroked her fingers down Kali's soft coat, taking comfort from the cat's presence. It made a horrible kind of sense.

'The man's just got his wife back,' she murmured as Kali opened her eyes and yawned hugely. 'His soulmate. If I was any sort of friend I'd be delighted for him, not worried that he's going to go back to his life in London and I won't see him again. Lady bright! Could I be any more pathetic?'

She recalled the sick dread she had felt as she had watched the unknown woman kissing Eldritch. Angry at herself she tried replaying the images in her mind, but this time she changed them, picturing Eldritch returning his wife's kiss, his features no longer frozen but relaxed and tender as he embraced her. It didn't help; it simply made her feel like a voyeur instead. Gwyn groaned and rolled onto her side. It was bad enough that she had Eldritch featuring in her dreams naked without then turning them into the start of a third-rate porn flick. Hastily she clamped down on an image of Helen dressed as a dominatrix, tying an unresisting Eldritch to a bed. There were times when the ability to visualise was not in the least bit helpful.

The only person Eldritch is in danger from now is you, turning into some kind of crazed stalker, she told herself firmly. *Mind you, it wouldn't hurt if he'd call just to let me know that everything is alright, so I can put my mind at rest.*

She scowled into the darkness.

'Just one little phone call, Marcus Eldritch. Is that really too much to ask for?'

Recognising she was trying to shift the blame did nothing to improve her temper. With an irritated huff she pulled the duvet up under her chin. From the bottom of the bed, Yard Away Cat gave a sleepy yowl of protest while Kali shifted and then resettled so she was leaning against Gwyn's hip.

Crazy cat lady, Gwyn thought as she schooled herself to relax. *It's no wonder Eldritch hasn't phoned now that he's got Helen back.*

CHAPTER 14

'Kali, I can tell you with good authority that you are not starving to death. You've only just been fed.' With practised ease Gwyn blocked the lithe brown form with her elbow and then scooped it off the table. 'And, despite what you may think, the natural food of the Burmese cat is not chicken jalfrezi.'

She kissed the top of the cat's head and deposited her on the floor. On the windowsill Yard Away Cat turned his back and washed a front paw as if distancing himself from such unbecoming behaviour. Outside the sky was alive with the darting shapes of house martins, swooping and diving like dogfighting pilots, chasing flies in the warm dusk. Their high-pitched calls drifted in through the open window along with the scent of the honeysuckle growing rampant along the cottage wall. In an hour or so the twilight would have deepened enough for the birds to give way to bats.

'I think it was Jay's prawns that she had her eye on,' Aidan commented, continuing to dole out rice onto the three plates without so much as a break in the rhythm of what he was doing. He had grown up with the vagaries of eating at Gwyn's house. The cats might have changed over the years, but Gwyn hadn't.

'In that case, the cat must die,' Jane declared matter-of-factly. She squeezed between Aidan and the sink to put a plate of naan bread and poppadoms in the middle of the table. 'You should get a dog, Gwyn. You don't see Sula eyeing up anyone else's dinner.'

The dog in question was stretched like a drowsing sphinx beside the open back door. At the sound of her name she raised her head and gave a hopeful whine.

'No,' Aidan said firmly. Sula subsided with what sounded like a sigh of resignation, her head dropping back to her paws.

Gwyn laughed. 'That's not to say she's not thinking about it, Jane. It's very good of you two to bring a takeaway round this evening. It's been a while since we've had one.'

'That's what Nav said when I picked it up.'

Aidan put the empty rice carton to one side and turned his attention to the meals. The change in his dietary habits wasn't the only thing that Navkinder had commented on, but he didn't feel the need to mention her teasing him about his black eye. After careful ice packing and liberal applications of arnica and comfrey, he had thought the bruising was fading nicely. Not according to Navkinder, it wasn't. Then she had laughed and said, 'Good for her,' when he had told her who had hit him.

'She said she had to double-check the name on the order, it's been so long since I've been in.'

'We've been spoiled with Eldritch and his culinary expertise. I knew I should have chained him to the stove while I had the chance.' Jane cast a mournful glance at the solid bulk of Gwyn's Rayburn as if picturing a captive wizard, saucepan at the ready. She sighed theatrically. 'Have you heard anything from him, Gwyn?'

Had Aidan not glanced round at that point he would have missed it – the momentary flicker of *what?* on Gwyn's face in response to Jane's question. But then the older woman shifted, an odd movement that was half dismissive shrug, half squaring of her shoulders and it was gone, leaving him wondering exactly what it was he thought he had seen.

'No.' Currents of annoyance and frustration rippled through Gwyn's voice, very much at odds with her laughter of a few moments before. She scowled as she took an assortment of cutlery from the drawer by the sink. 'Not that there's any reason why he should feel obliged to phone me.'

The mismatched spoons and forks rattled as she turned and banged them down on the table.

Aidan winced, not so much at Gwyn's outburst – it was her silences that were most worrying, not her shouting – but at what it might be covering. He knew from experience just how well his ex-guardian could mask her true feelings, especially if something – or someone – had hurt her. He had been guilty of misreading her badly in the past but these days he felt he was better than most at deciphering her moods. Given the exaggerated sharpness of her tone, he wondered if it had been a trace of sadness he had glimpsed. That made more sense than his initial thought, that it had been fear that he had seen in those peridot eyes. Either way, it was clear that something to do with the wizard had got under her skin.

Nothing new there, then.

Jane shot Gwyn a sympathetic look. 'No reason, apart from the fact that you're his friend and he should realise you'd like to know that everything's okay,' she suggested.

Gwyn gave a little snort, although it was hard to judge whether she was dismissing any such obligation on the Englishman's part or her own foolishness in expecting such a courtesy. She was silent for a minute while she arranged the place settings and Aidan thought she wasn't going to respond. He was about to change the subject and tell her about the latest team-building exercise he and Matt had devised for their students at Red Kite Adventure Training when she said, 'I've tried phoning him myself, but I didn't get an answer – not from his mobile and not from his home number either. All I got was voicemail and the answerphone. I left a couple of messages, but he's not phoned back.'

Her tone was suitably dismissive, but watching her adjust the layout of the cutlery as though the relative positioning of each spoon and fork was of vital importance, Aidan decided his reading of her had been correct. Whether or not Eldritch should have been in touch was a moot point, but he didn't like the idea of Gwyn making herself unhappy worrying about him.

'I guess he's had other things on his mind,' he said and then, partly because he thought it might lighten the mood but also because he couldn't help teasing her, he added, 'Come on, Gwyn, it's not like he's forgotten you. Cut him some slack. The man's been reunited with his wife after two years.' He leered at her suggestively. 'He's going to be a little busy.'

He had expected the comment to generate a sarcastic response. Instead, Aidan was surprised – and thoroughly amused – to see a faint flush spread up the back of Gwyn's neck, clearly visible on the pale skin between her shirt collar and the dark mass of her hair, which was currently piled up into something reminiscent of a Sumo wrestler's topknot.

On the other side of the table, Jane chuckled. 'Even so, he's got to come up for air some time.'

Gwyn stopped fussing with the cutlery and drew herself up. Even then, she was several inches shorter than Jane and a good eight inches shorter than Aidan himself. It shouldn't have been possible for her to appear threatening, but what Gwyn lacked in physical stature she made up for in attitude. The look she gave her guests would have had Satan commuting to work on ice skates for the rest of the week. Aidan hastily dismissed the idea of calling her out about the blush still staining her cheeks.

'I appreciate that, right now, Eldritch is going to be thinking about no one but Helen,' Gwyn said caustically. 'Given what they've both been through, I can understand that. But, when he does indeed surface,' the icy gaze focused briefly on Jane who winced visibly, 'it would be nice if he'd have the decency to return a call.' Her attention came back to Aidan and he found himself fighting the urge to hang his head and fidget. 'I bumped into Rowan this morning and apparently she's been trying to get hold of him about the book signing. Lady forbid that he'd feel the need to phone me, but he's not bothered to get back to her either. She was worried and asked me if there was any news.'

For a moment more Gwyn kept her guests skewered, wordlessly accusing them of being in league with Eldritch and his conspiracy of silence. Then, as abruptly as she had turned on them, she seemed to reconsider. She sighed and shook her head as though physically dismissing her bad mood.

'None of which is the fault of either of you two,' she conceded. She still looked faintly annoyed, but Aidan was reasonably certain that that residue of emotion was aimed solely at the errant wizard. 'So, on that note, I suggest we forget about Marcus Eldritch for now and enjoy our meal.' Gwyn gave a rueful smile and gestured towards the table. 'Let's sit down and eat.'

'Are you working on any interesting articles at the moment, Gwyn?'

'As a matter of fact, I am. I'm writing a summary of research on the decomposition rates of bodies under different environmental conditions.'

'Nice.' Aidan's expression made it clear he thought it was anything but. 'You should know better than to ask a question like that over dinner, Jay.'

Jane shot him a look of dazzling innocence, even though they both knew her choice of topic had been deliberate and intended to distract Gwyn. Given the enthusiasm evident in Gwyn's response, Aidan had to admit it was a good one, but his objection still stood. Inwardly, he resigned himself to several minutes of hearing about things he might prefer to remain blissfully unaware of – particularly at the dinner table. By way of protest he skewered one of Jane's prawns and popped it into his mouth.

'Hey!' She retaliated by helping herself to a forkful of his rogan josh but carried on talking to Gwyn. 'That's not your usual field, is it?'

'No, it's a new commission – *Forensic Science Today.* Mal Dickinson put them in touch with me, Lady bless him. I wasn't certain at first, but forensics is a growing field so it's a good one to get into and to be honest with you it's proving fascinating. I've been talking to the world expert in the decomposition of hanging bodies.'

'I'll bet he's a bundle of laughs.'

'Actually, Aidan, he is a she and we got on very well, thank you. We found we have a surprising amount in common.'

Aidan snorted. 'Why am I not surprised?'

Gwyn looked down her nose at him. 'I'll have you know I happen to get on well with a lot of people. Her husband was charming too, although I have to say the man's completely obsessed with parrots.' Gwyn's brows drew together as she frowned a little at the recollection.

'What? Hanging them?'

'Sweet Lady, no! Conserving them.'

'So, he's a taxidermist?'

'Conserving, Aidan, not preserving.' At that point Gwyn realised she was being teased and she rolled her eyes heavenwards. Aidan smirked, satisfied with her reaction. His grin widened further as Gwyn said pointedly, 'Anyway, I've been learning all sorts of things about disposing of dead bodies. You never know when it might come in handy.' Her dark brows winged together as she eyed him in what she presumably thought was a threatening manner.

Unintimidated, Aidan chuckled. 'So, when Rowan bumps off Eldritch for standing her up over the book signing, we know who'll be helping her—' The look on Gwyn's face stopped him in his tracks.

Nice one, Aidan! Open mouth and change feet, son.

'That was meant to be a joke, Gwyn.'

But clearly it was no laughing matter. When Gwyn didn't respond but merely looked down at her dinner, Jane leaned over and touched her arm. 'You really are worried about him, aren't you?'

The way Gwyn's face had drained of colour was answer enough for Aidan, although he couldn't understand it. 'But why? He's been out of touch for a few days. What's so terrible about that?'

'Nothing.'

Gwyn shook her head, but she wouldn't meet his eyes. She pushed a forkful of rice across her plate and Aidan realised she had barely touched her food. That in itself was unlike Gwyn. The woman had a bird-like appetite, always assuming the bird in question was a vulture.

'Come on, Gwyn, something's bothering you. There's more to this than the fact that Eldritch hasn't phoned. What's got you so worried about him?'

Almost reluctantly Gwyn raised her eyes from her plate. She looked first at Aidan and then at Jane as though silently weighing up how they would respond to her next words.

Her lips thinned. 'I know this is going to sound stupid, but I had a dream.'

'A dream?' Jane kept most of the scepticism out of her voice, but her eyebrows gave her away.

Aidan was as surprised as she was by Gwyn's admission, but he had experienced the power of dreams.

The bathroom mirror reflecting the razor against his throat ... watching as the water in the basin turned crimson ... then waking to find his hand on the bathroom door and Sula barking at him like a mad thing.

The hellishly vivid nightmares he had experienced the previous autumn had been caused by a demon manifesting in the local hills, the occurrence that had first brought Eldritch to Llancathan. A twist of fear knotted itself around Aidan's gut and he put his fork down.

All of a sudden, his own appetite had deserted him. 'What sort of dream, Gwyn?'

For a moment she didn't answer. She met his eyes briefly but then her gaze flicked away, coming to rest on a point beyond his shoulder, as though she was watching an image being replayed on the whitewashed kitchen wall.

'I saw Eldritch.'

Her fingers played with the rope of rose quartz spheres around her wrist, turning them against her skin as if praying over the beads of a rosary. Aidan recognised the bracelet as one of the ones Gwyn had lent Eldritch last year to ward him against demonic influence. Was that significant?

'He was surrounded by darkness.' Gwyn stared at the wall. Her voice went flat, as if waiting for her audience to make something of her next words. 'And he was naked.'

Jane's eyebrows hiked skywards again as she glanced across at Aidan, but he shook his head, not wanting to interrupt Gwyn's account.

After a moment's silence, Gwyn continued. 'He couldn't speak but I could tell he was afraid. Mortally afraid.'

Aidan sensed the echo of that fear in Gwyn now.

Her fingers stilled on her bracelet and she seemed to draw into herself as she went on. 'The darkness was rippling, crawling.' She shuddered, screwing her eyes shut as though that could stop her seeing what was there in her mind. 'It was like a curtain of black ink, slithering up behind him and yet somehow it was alive, sentient.'

Her hands slid over her forearms, mimicking the movement of those shadowy tendrils. The hairs on the back of Aidan's neck stood on end. He had no difficulty picturing what Gwyn was describing; he had seen it for himself deep within the tunnels of the abandoned Greenfields lead mine.

'The boundary of the Unseen Realm.' Bile rose in his throat at the memory of long, slithering pseudopodia of darkness, reaching between the worlds. He swallowed it down, his stomach curdling. 'You don't think it's another demon, do you?'

Gwyn's eyes opened and she looked at him. She shook her head helplessly. 'Honestly? I don't know. But there was something there, in the darkness, something that took shape from it. A woman. I couldn't see her properly because she was standing behind him, but she was holding him.' She mimed an embrace. 'He wanted to scream – I know he did – but he couldn't.'

Gwyn bit her lip and Aidan felt a cold sense of dread at whatever she was about to reveal. She took a steadying breath and visibly pulled herself back from the nightmare. In a cold, controlled voice she concluded, 'She pulled his head round and then she kissed him, and I knew once she'd done that he wasn't going to be Eldritch any more.'

CHAPTER 15

There was silence in the wake of Gwyn's words. Not sure what else to do, Aidan put his hand over hers where it had fisted on the tabletop. It felt awkward and somehow wrong to be offering Gwyn comfort. Until recently any reassurance in their relationship had flowed strictly in the opposite direction.

'I'm not surprised you were freaked out, dreaming something like that.'

And surely it was just a dream. There was no real reason to think it was anything else, no matter how unnerved Gwyn had been nor how uneasy the image she described made him feel. He turned to Jane, curious to hear her perspective. She raised her shoulders in a shrug but said nothing.

'Well?' he prompted.

Jane might sometimes choose to keep her own counsel rather than say something she knew would be upsetting but, when invited to give her opinion, she was never one to mince her words. 'It's all a bit Freudian.' She turned to Gwyn. 'If I was into dream analysis, I'd say you've got a mystery woman who holds power over Eldritch – well, that's got to be Helen. She's lurking in the shadows because you've never met her. You know your friendship with him is bound to change now that they've been reunited and that upsets you, but your mind doesn't like to admit that. Instead it twists things around and that upset becomes fear for his safety in your dream. Then finally Helen kisses him and all of a sudden Eldritch is no longer the man you knew. His relationship with her has changed him.' She sat back in her chair and folded her arms, treating Aidan to an expression that clearly said, *you did ask*. 'Sorry,' she added. The word was addressed to Gwyn but without there being any genuine sense of apology attached to it.

Gwyn looked at Jane with something akin to loathing. 'Do you think I've not thought of that? Do you really believe I'm so shallow that I hadn't considered that as a possibility?'

'Okay, hold on, Gwyn.' Aidan didn't care for the coldly vicious tone Gwyn was using, but nor did he like what Jane was suggesting. He turned to her next. 'Dreams can be more than just your subconscious. Trust me, I know.'

Jane took the reprimand calmly. Of the three of them, she seemed the least upset by what Gwyn had shared. 'I appreciate that. I'm just saying that that's how someone who doesn't have any knowledge of the supernatural would interpret it. The dreaming mind throws up some pretty weird stuff, none of which we can be held responsible for. You know that, Gwyn. Just because you dream something it doesn't mean that's what you think when you're awake. As for the supernatural? Well, I'm the wrong person to be asking. I wouldn't know a premonition in a dream if it came up and hit me over the head. I've never had one so I'm not the person to judge, but if you say there are such things and that this was some sort of warning then who am I to disbelieve you?'

Gwyn was silent for a moment, staring at her plate again, and Aidan had the sense, as he often did with her, that she was sifting through her thoughts like a gambler sorting a hand of cards deciding what she would and wouldn't reveal. Eventually she sighed as if, with that exhalation, she was letting go of the sudden squall of defensive anger.

'I don't know if it was, Jane.' She pushed her fork through her curry, doodling patterns in it, but the edgy nervousness of earlier had passed. 'My first reaction was much the same as yours – that my subconscious was having a field day. But after speaking to Rowan, I began to wonder, so I thought I'd phone and, of course, I couldn't get through. Since then, I've been unable to shake the feeling that something's wrong. Every time the phone's rung I've rushed to answer it, hoping it would be him.'

Gwyn scowled and this time it was clear it was her own behaviour she was irritated with. 'You wouldn't believe how many cold callers I've had today. I think word's got around that there's some crazy woman desperate to talk to people, and they've all been ringing here, trying their luck.'

'Then why not phone him again?' Jane suggested. 'Or, tell you what, I'll phone him. If he doesn't answer I'll leave a message telling him to phone back or we'll assume something terrible has happened and we'll be forced to send the police round to his house to check on him.'

Aidan had to laugh at the enthusiasm in her voice. 'You wouldn't.'

'I might.' Her expression shifted, her eyes narrowing fractionally, the corner of her lips turning up in the faintest of smiles in a way he knew meant *just watch me*. Even the dojo seniors trod carefully when Jane gave them that look. The juniors learned to ignore it at their peril. Then she gave a little shrug. 'Well, okay,' she relented, putting aside the pleasure of such devilment for another time. 'I wouldn't set the police on him, but he's not to know that. And anyway, it might get the message across that he's being rude. It's not as though we want to monopolise his life, but we do want to know that everything's okay. A two-minute phone call isn't so much to ask, surely?'

Gwyn looked from Jane to Aidan. 'You're humouring me, aren't you?'

But there was no bitterness in her voice. She sounded almost amused by the idea.

'No,' said Jane.

'Yes,' said Aidan.

'But only because we care,' Jane added.

Gwyn laughed and this time the humour was genuine. 'Thank you both. If that idiot would just answer the phone, I wouldn't have any reason to worry.'

'And where would be the fun in that?'

'You're right, Aidan. I'll try him again when we've finished dinner.'

'It's the answerphone again.' Gwyn rolled her eyes heavenwards but she kept hold of the phone when Jane gestured for her to pass it over. 'Here we go.' She took a deep breath. 'Listen, Eldritch, if you don't answer the phone, or at the very least return your messages, Jane's promising to send the police round to check on you. And you know she's more than capable of doing that. Seriously, though, we'd all like to know that everything's okay—'

Abruptly Gwyn stopped talking.

'Oh … hello. I didn't think anyone was going to answer. Is … is that Helen?'

Aidan shared a surprised look with Jane. Unconsciously they both leaned in, trying to catch the voice on the other end of the phone.

'We've not spoken before. My name's Gwyn. I've called a couple of times. I hope I'm not disturbing you, but I do need to speak to Eldritch if that's possible. It's about the signing he's agreed to do for his new book. Is he there, please?'

There was a pause. Aidan held up crossed fingers which Jane returned with an optimistic thumbs up. Together they watched Gwyn in anticipation.

'Oh, I see.' Gwyn didn't try to keep the disappointment from her voice. 'Okay. Well, could you ask him to call me when he gets in, please? It's just to sort out a few details. It won't take long but I really would appreciate— yes. Yes, he has the number. Okay. Thank you. Goodbye.'

Gwyn stood and put the phone back in its cradle. She didn't speak and Aidan thought it was that sense of being let down once again that was keeping her silent, but when he looked at her face he read more puzzlement there than frustration.

'Well?' he prompted, his own curiosity piqued. He wanted to know what Eldritch's wife had had to say for herself. Gwyn's side of the conversation hadn't suggested anything untoward. 'Is everything okay?'

Gwyn didn't answer immediately. She ran her hands through her hair, heedlessly dislodging the topknot so that half of it came loose and sagged to one side, pulling her white streak over the crown of her head like a sideways skunk. Then she looked at him, acknowledging his question, but when she did speak it wasn't to answer him, or at least not in a way that made any sense.

'That was odd.'

She came back to the table, absently clearing space among the detritus of curry-streaked plates and fragments of poppadom so she could sit with her elbows propped on the worn pine. She rested her chin on her interlaced fingers, her expression pensive and her eyes distant. Whatever insights she had gained from her brief conversation with Helen, Aidan thought they hadn't reassured her. But nor did she seem overly inclined to share them. Her body might be sitting there with them, but her mind was clearly elsewhere.

He gave her a minute, waiting for the explanation that would decipher her cryptic remark. When none was forthcoming, he gave a mental shrug and asked the obvious question, rather as he suspected he was meant to. 'What was odd?'

'That was Helen.'

'I think we guessed that much,' Jane said with a smile and more patience than Aidan thought Gwyn deserved. 'So now we know she's alright – that's good. Where's Eldritch?'

'She didn't say, just that he was out.'

'But she'll get him to call you back?'

Sometimes getting information out of Gwyn was like pulling teeth. For a moment Aidan entertained the idea of picking his ex-guardian up and shaking her like a piggy bank, as if doing so would release the details trapped in her head like a child's horde of salted-away pennies. It was a satisfying image. He held on to it as he waited for her response. This time she graced him with a slightly longer answer.

'When he gets in, although she wasn't sure when that would be, so she said not to expect a call tonight.'

Well, that was something. 'So, at least we know they're both alright now.'

'Do we?' Gwyn's voice was unexpectedly sharp.

Aidan blinked in surprise. 'Well, yes.' Wasn't it obvious? 'You've spoken to Helen, and you've just said she's going to get Eldritch to call you.'

'That's not the same as speaking to him myself.'

'No.' Aidan could see that. 'But if he's not there …'

There were times when having a conversation with Gwyn felt like reasoning with a four-year-old.

'We only have her word for that.'

Aidan looked at her curiously, not sure he understood what she was implying. He ran the words through his head a second time but still came to the same conclusion, unlikely though it seemed.

'Are you really suggesting Eldritch has been done in by his wife and she's covering it up by telling anyone who phones that he's gone shopping?'

When she didn't answer he raised his eyebrows incredulously.

'Oh, come on, Gwyn. Maybe it's a bit weird that he's out – if I was him, I don't suppose I'd leave her side – but it's a long way from there to having her down as suspect number one for bumping him off.'

'Whereas if she has done something to him she's going to admit it straight off,' Gwyn countered. She shook her head, dismissing either him or his logic, Aidan wasn't sure which. 'It wasn't just that, Aidan.'

'Okay, what then?'

For a moment he thought her scowl would be the only

answer she gave him, but then she said, 'She called him Marcus.'

Aidan waited for the rest of the revelation but, when Gwyn said nothing more, he realised that that was it. He studied his knuckles for a moment, trying to think of something appropriate to say. He didn't think, *Are you completely nuts?* would be helpful, but that didn't mean he wasn't tempted to try it.

But this was Gwyn, he reminded himself. She wasn't generally given to overreacting to anything. He swallowed the sarcastic comment and counted to ten. When he thought he could do so without sounding too scathing, he ventured, 'Well, that is his name, isn't it?'

Gwyn looked at him as though he was being particularly dense. After a second, she took a deep breath, her nostrils flaring. 'I know that, Aidan,' she said, speaking slowly as if he might otherwise have trouble understanding her. 'But when we first met, he introduced himself to me as Eldritch. He said that the only people who ever called him Marcus were his parents. He was quite adamant about it.' She paused for a moment and a hint of wickedness flashed in her eyes. It warmed her voice as she added, 'Why else do you think I sometimes call him that, if not to annoy him?'

The wickedness morphed into a mischievous smile that brought a welcome lightening of the mood. 'He told me that all his friends call him Eldritch.' Gwyn shrugged. 'Somehow I can't see his wife being an exception to that.'

Aidan sat back and considered this for a moment. He tried to think of all the times he had heard Eldritch introduce himself to anyone. With the exception of their own first meeting, when the wizard had deliberately tried to obscure his identity, it had always been, 'Hi, I'm Eldritch.' Beyond that one stage-managed encounter on the sailing club jetty, he couldn't think of a single time Eldritch had so much as mentioned his first name. But there were different reasons for changing your use name.

'Maybe Helen always called him Marcus and he decided to change after she was possessed.'

He could understand why someone might do such a thing. He had stopped answering to David the day his mother died, opting to use his middle name instead, ever since.

He read the recognition of that in the widening of Gwyn's eyes. She reached over and rubbed a finger across his knuckles, her touch light as a cat's paw and equally unsentimental, but comforting nonetheless.

Yet still she shook her head. 'I got the impression he had always preferred to be known as Eldritch.'

'Well, it's not as though we can ask him.'

Aware that it had been him and Gwyn doing all the talking, Aidan cast a glance at Jane. Like Gwyn, she sat with her elbows on the table, but her right hand was held in a loose fist, her left hand cupped lightly over the top; *I'm able to fight but I choose not to.* She looked very much as she did in the dojo when watching two fighters sparing: analysing their fighting styles and mentally cataloguing their weaknesses.

'What do you reckon, Jay? You're the expert on picking up nuances. How would a security ninja read the situation? Any alarm bells?'

Jane leaned back in her chair and crossed her arms. She chewed her lip for a moment as she ordered her thoughts. 'It's hard to say without actually having heard her. She was speaking to someone she doesn't know so maybe she called him Marcus because she was being formal. If I was talking to someone I didn't know I'd refer to you as Aidan, not Aide, or Tarzan, or—'

'Okay,' Aidan interrupted quickly, sensing the quickening of Gwyn's interest in the sharp lift of her head.

'But you called him Eldritch, didn't you, Gwyn?' Jane's eyes briefly lost focus as she ran the overheard conversation back through her head, mentally confirming what had been said. 'In a situation when you're building rapport with someone new to you, the tendency is to shift to using the same vocabulary. Of course, she might have made a point of using a pet name for him, in which case I'd say she was staking her territory.'

'Because she doesn't like the idea of some strange woman wanting to speak to her husband.'

'Yeah, but it was you she was speaking to, Gwyn, not Rowan.'

Aidan smirked, enjoying the idea that someone would think of Gwyn as a sexual predator, especially where Eldritch was concerned.

Jane laughed too, but she wasn't going to be distracted from the point she was making. 'But, if she wasn't being territorial, I'd expect her to use the same name that you'd used.'

Aidan's smile slipped as he realised what she meant. 'Wait a minute. You're saying you agree there's something wrong?' He hadn't expected that.

'Based on the evidence we have – which admittedly isn't much to go on – yes. If you accept the possibility of Gwyn's dream being some kind of warning, Eldritch is MIA and his wife is acting out of character, then something's going on.'

Aidan looked at the two women. One of them he could dismiss, but if they were both in agreement … Just because he didn't like what they were suggesting didn't mean it might not be true.

'Okay,' he said carefully. 'What do we do?'

'We could go and visit him. You've got his address haven't you, Gwyn? London's not that far away.'

'Yes. But what if there's nothing wrong?'

Aidan gave a short laugh. Having spent the best part of the evening trying to convince them that Eldritch was in trouble, it was typical that Gwyn would now be thinking of the downside of them taking action to try to help him.

'And what if there is? Look, he's either going to answer the door, in which case you can explain to him about your dream and he can have a good laugh about it, or he isn't and we'll know that something odd's happened.'

'And potentially we'll have walked straight into whatever trap he's fallen foul of.'

Aidan gave a tight smile, admitting Gwyn had a point. Let's beam the first officer down to exactly the same spot the captain has just disappeared from. Not such a great plan.

'It's not so much whatever as whoever, isn't it?' Jane put in. 'If something has happened to Eldritch, it has to be Helen who's behind it.'

'Do you really think so?'

Aidan realised he was the one back-pedalling now, but it felt like a betrayal of Eldritch to be casting his wife as the villain of the piece without any real proof of her wrongdoing, or indeed of there being an actual crime.

'You've never heard of Ockham's Razor?'

Aidan looked at Jane blankly. They had known each other since childhood and had been lovers for two years now.

If pressed he would have said that they were mentally and physically in tune, but occasionally there were times when her logic defeated him.

'Ockham's what? Is that one of those techno bands you come back raving about when you've been clubbing with Joan and Ruth and the rest of the yoga gang?'

He shuddered. The yoga class's monthly night out was something he made sure he stayed well clear of. As he had explained once to Eldritch, a dozen strong-minded and very bendy women, loud music and too much over-coloured and overpriced alcohol was a mix that any sane man should avoid.

Jane gave him a pained look. 'Ockham's Razor is a principle. It states that when there are multiple explanations for why something's happened, it's usually the simplest one that's correct. Eldritch gets a phone call to say his wife has miraculously woken up in hospital. He goes home to be with her and then he goes missing. It's got to be Helen who's to blame.'

'But why would Helen hurt Eldritch?'

'She wouldn't.'

Aidan digested this, following the chain of what Jane had said and the one thing she hadn't put into words.

'You're thinking she's still possessed. Or that she's been possessed again.' He frowned as Jane answered him with a one-shouldered shrug. 'Are you serious? You're the one who was so sure that she could have recovered when everyone said it was impossible.'

Jane squared her shoulders, hearing the unvoiced accusation in his tone and meeting it head on. 'At the time, that was a reasonable conclusion, based on what we knew.' Only the thinning of her lips suggested she might be harbouring her own regrets about what she had said that night. 'But things have changed and if something weird has happened to Eldritch that throws up a whole new set of data to factor in. You work with the evidence you've got – whether or not you like what it's telling you. So yes, there are reasons why Helen might have been the first person ever to have survived demonic possession – there still are. But it would be one screwy coincidence if that was the case and at the same time that she wakes up some other supernatural thing turns up and threatens Eldritch.' She met Aidan's eyes with a fierce, blue stare. 'I don't believe in coincidences.'

Aidan rubbed his hands over his face. This was turning into a bad dream – one from which there seemed no likelihood of waking any time soon. He looked at Gwyn for support. This was more her area of expertise than his.

'But Eldritch would have sensed that, surely? If there was another demon involved and Helen had been possessed again he'd realise, wouldn't he? I mean, come on – he is a wizard, after all.'

But instead of agreeing with him Gwyn shook her head, a small negating movement that stabbed at his heart like a stiletto of ice.

'It's not that simple. When a demon takes a physical body, the energies that mark it as having crossed from the Unseen Realm are masked by the life force of the host – it becomes almost impossible to trace. On top of that, once it's assimilated, a demon can mimic a host so well that even those people closest to them can't tell what's wrong.

'When he first told us about Helen, Eldritch said that it was a long time before he realised what had happened, that it was only after Paul's death that he truly believed it. And he knew she'd been exposed to a demon then. If Helen has been possessed by some new entity then it's hardly going to be the first thing he thinks of if she behaves a little oddly, given that she's been in a coma for two years.'

'Which she shouldn't have woken up from. Christ!' Aidan rounded on Jane, but Gwyn spoke before he could.

'We all wanted to believe it was possible, Aidan.' There was no anger in her voice, just the weary clarity of hindsight. 'What Jane suggested was plausible and, when he was presented with the one thing that meant more to him than anything else in the world, Eldritch chose to believe that a miracle could happen. We wanted it to be true for his sake.'

Jane sighed. 'Yeah,' she agreed softly. 'We did. We really did.'

For several moments they sat in silence, each of them recalling that last evening together and the stunned joy on Eldritch's face as he had begun to accept the possibility of Helen's recovery.

'Oh crap,' Aidan muttered, but the venom had gone from his voice. He pushed his hands through his hair. 'Like I said before, what do we do? What can we do?'

'Well, what we can't do is go and talk to Helen. Jane's right: if something has happened to Eldritch, and she's behind it, then I'd rather we knew a little more about what we're dealing with before we show our hand.'

'Even if Eldritch's life is at stake?'

'We're not going to help him by wading in unprepared. As you once said to me, Aidan – who's going to come to the rescue if we both get into trouble? From what little I know of her, Helen is – or was – a powerful sorceress. If she's been possessed, she will still have access to that power. The days are long gone when I could hope to win an arcane duel against her and, I'm sorry to have to say this, Aidan, you don't have the necessary skills to do so. Not yet.'

Gwyn's words recalled another council of war in this kitchen, an October evening, the night outside the windows chilly and damp, a world away from the warmth of this evening's velvety dusk. They had eaten takeaway curry that night too, Aidan remembered – him, Gwyn and Eldritch – the night he had first learned how much chaos a demon might cause in the Mortal World. He remembered too the fray of tempers between Gwyn and Eldritch as Gwyn had tried to convince Eldritch not to take what she felt was an unnecessary risk, and how right her fears had ultimately been proven to be.

Yet there were times when risks had to be taken. 'We've got to start somewhere, though. If Eldritch is in trouble we can't just ignore it, even if it is dangerous.'

'I'd say we start with the obvious, the clinic.' Jane's tone was decisive. 'That has to be the best place to find out if there was anything odd about Helen waking up – apart from the fact that she actually woke up, I mean. Let's see if they noticed anything.'

'Such as?'

Jane rolled her eyes. 'How should I know? I keep telling you, I'm not the expert on the supernatural. But, if a woman in a coma recovers consciousness against all odds, something had to trigger it, and that something had to happen at the clinic. Besides, I'll bet I can get us in to see Helen's doctor.'

'You can?' Then the full implication of what Jane had said struck him. Aidan studied his girlfriend. 'Us?'

'Yes, us. You'll need to come along so you can sense anything weird.'

'Or I could come,' suggested Gwyn.

Jane shook her head. 'You wouldn't look right. Aidan would. And trust me, this is all about looking the part.'

Aidan and Gwyn exchanged puzzled glances.

'Okay, cyber ninja, what are you thinking?'

'The Greenman Clinic's privately funded.' Jane stopped at Aidan's bemused look. 'What? You mean it never occurred to you to Google it, after Eldritch told us Helen was being treated there?'

Aidan shook his head. 'Er, no.'

'Seriously?' Jane's eyebrows quirked down as she considered this possibility. She eyed Aidan doubtfully for a moment as if she couldn't quite believe his lack of curiosity but then shrugged, visibly putting the matter to one side. 'Well, never mind, it is. Anyway, it's not every day that one of their patients recovers. I reckon our good doctor would welcome the chance to boast about it in the scientific press. You get to come along as my photographer. Obviously, I'd want a picture of Doctor Ashwood for the article, maybe one of Helen's room, too. I don't know if you'd be able to sense if anything weird was going on, but you've got more chance than I have.'

Aidan stared at Jane, his expression an equal mix of amazement and incredulity. 'And you just thought this up now, on the fly?'

Jane gave him a small smile, trying for nonchalance and not quite pulling it off. Even cyber ninjas enjoyed a little flattery. 'This is what I do for a living.'

'Ashwood's going to want Helen's consent before he speaks to you,' Gwyn chipped in, but Aidan could tell from the thoughtful way she said it that she too was impressed.

'Ah, but if I go to see him at the clinic, posing as a friend of Helen's – who also happens to be a journalist – and I give him a letter signed by her giving her approval, he'll probably jump at the chance. She was unconscious when she was admitted, remember. They won't have her signature on record to be able to check it.'

For several seconds no one spoke, and Aidan and Gwyn weighed up Jane's plan. They exchanged another look. It sounded feasible.

'What if he phones Helen to check your credentials?' Gwyn wanted to know.

This time Jane grinned. 'Chances are he won't. But, if he does, I play my ace. I tell him I'm not a journalist; I'm a security expert. I've been sent by the relevant health authority to check if he'd fall for a phishing scam and reveal confidential patient information. Congratulations! He's passed the test. Then I have to be a bit more creative to find out if anything odd happened.'

'So, you check his security and while you're doing it you keep telling him how fascinating his work is. By the time you've finished he'll be dying to tell you all about it. You'll have him eating out of your hand.'

Jane regarded her lover like a cat finishing a plate of canary à la crème. 'Something like that,' she conceded, her voice edging towards smug.

Gwyn laughed and shook her head admiringly. 'You watch yourself with this one, Aidan. Lady help you if you ever cross her.' Looking back at Jane, she offered, 'I have a National

Union of Journalists card, if you need to copy one. Or I could probably get Mal Dickinson to vouch for you. I could tell him it was a security test you were running.'

Jane nodded. 'Both could come in handy.' Her face split into a satisfied smile. 'I think we can make this work.'

CHAPTER 16

Watching Jane at work was a revelation. Aidan had been surprised at just how easily she had secured an interview with Doctor Ashwood. He had expected the head of the Greenman Clinic to be more reticent about talking to a journalist, but apparently he had welcomed the idea as enthusiastically as Jane had said he would, to the extent that he had found time in his schedule to meet with them the following day.

Now, sitting in the doctor's first-floor office and trying his best to behave like the press photographer Jane had introduced him as, Aidan wondered if he would dare to believe anything she told him ever again. Even knowing she was lying through her teeth, it was hard not to accept what she said at face value. Somehow, she exuded an air of credibility.

Part of it was the clothes she was wearing – her props, as she called them, like his borrowed camera. For her role as a journalist, Jane had opted for a pair of draped wide-legged trousers and a silky blouse the colour of egg yolks, topped with a cropped linen jacket in a deep indigo blue, a far cry from her usual uniform of jeans and a T-shirt. 'Dress the part,' she had explained as he sat on the bed in their hotel room watching the final stages of her metamorphosis, 'and ninety per cent of people won't question you.' At the time, Aidan had wondered why dressing the part involved subjecting her hair to a device that looked like it might have seen use in the

Spanish Inquisition. He liked her hair's soft waves, although he had to admit that the resulting poker-straight strands looked sleekly sophisticated – and surprisingly sexy, in a rather prim and proper sort of way – when she caught them back in a clip at the nape of her neck.

At that point he had been sorely tempted to wander over and undo that clip, curious to find out what those polished strands would feel like as he shook them out around her shoulders, but he had resisted the urge. Jane would not have been amused to have her preparations disrupted and there wasn't time for him to convince her otherwise, much though he would have liked to. Instead, he had filed the image away for future enjoyment, trying not to whimper out loud as she applied a slick of the palest pink gloss to her lips and then blew him a knowing kiss in the mirror. His control might have fractured, but the next second she turned to face him. Her chin lifted, her posture shifted, and in that instant the transformation was complete. His Jane had been replaced with … well, Aidan couldn't quite have said, but watching her now he could see how carefully she had captured the balance between smart and casual; she was relaxed enough not to stress a potentially nervous interviewee but sleek enough to convince anyone of her credentials.

She certainly looked more professional than Gwyn ever did, thought Aidan, although he had to concede he had never seen Gwyn interviewing anyone. He wondered briefly what she had worn for her discussions with the world expert on hanging bodies. A lab coat and an expression of ghoulish delight, knowing Gwyn. An image popped into his mind of her sitting at a table with another woman and a man who had a parrot on each shoulder and – for no reason Aidan could think of – a huge, bushy beard. A rack of flaccid bodies hung in the doorway behind them, like shirts waiting to be put away after having been ironed. Aidan shook himself mentally and brought his focus back to the office, tuning in as Jane assured the doctor that, while she would take notes throughout the interview, she would respect his wishes about any details he wanted to keep off the record.

Doctor Ashwood nodded at this. 'Good. Yes, yes, that's good.' He straightened his tie and then loosened it again. Aidan did his best not to smirk. It was clear who was in charge of the interview.

'Now, Doctor Ashwood.' Jane smiled warmly as she said the physician's name. 'Talk me through what happened that day.'

'It's quite amazing, really.' Ashwood's eyes lit with enthusiasm; this was a story he wanted to share. Such was his eagerness, Aidan could almost feel sorry that he and Jane wouldn't be helping to publicise it. Then again, Helen's amazing recovery wasn't necessarily the medical marvel the doctor believed it to be. Thankfully unaware of Aidan's thoughts, Ashwood leaned forward in his seat and stared earnestly at Jane. 'Helen simply woke up!'

When that revelation elicited no more than a raised eyebrow and a one-shouldered shrug he frowned but then regrouped and continued. 'Ah, of course. Well, you should realise that, while we work on the principle that all our patients have the potential for recovery, in reality, the number of people who do recover from Unresponsive Wakefulness Syndrome is small. When it does happen, however, it's usually a gradual process. There are signs that the level of consciousness is changing. But with Helen, well, I've never seen anything like it. When I did my rounds that afternoon there was no change in her condition. She was completely unresponsive, just as she had been since she was admitted. Then, a few hours later, she was fully awake and talking, almost as though nothing had happened to her.'

Jane cocked her head, projecting polite scepticism coupled with journalistic curiosity. 'Really? She woke up, just like that?'

'Absolutely.' The doctor nodded vigorously, but when Jane made no response he sat back in his seat, looking thoughtful. Almost as if speaking to himself he said, 'Well, I suppose it's possible that Bob and Terry really did hear her making a sound that afternoon.'

'Bob and Terry? Are they members of the nursing staff?'

'What? Oh, no. They're … er, well, they're workmen, or handymen if you like, here at the clinic. They were in Helen's room that afternoon.'

'That sounds a little unusual.' Jane treated the doctor to a smile that was both amused and slightly quizzical.

He laughed. 'Well, yes, quite. That's what I thought. I was rather surprised when I found them in there but when I asked what they were doing, Bob said that they'd been in the corridor and had heard a noise as though someone in the room had cried out. There wasn't anyone else around – as I said, I was doing my rounds and was in with another patient at the time – so they did the correct thing and very sensibly went in to check if everything was alright. If I hadn't come in at that point one of them would have come to find me. As it was, Bob told me what they'd heard. Of course, when I checked her, Helen was still unresponsive, so I thanked them for their vigilance but dismissed it. Maybe I did them a disservice and they really did hear something.'

'Fascinating.' Jane made some notes. 'Going back to Helen, did you find her awake when you did your next rounds? What actually happened?'

'Well, as I told you, Bob and Terry had looked in on Helen that afternoon. When I spoke to them, they commented on the fact that she didn't have any visitors and Terry in particular thought it was very sad that a young woman like her didn't have any family with her. In fact, he was so moved by her situation that he took it upon himself to visit her that evening. Consequently, he was actually there when she woke up. It was Terry who fetched me.

'I must say, he was quite unsettled by it all. He's normally a very quiet young man, the type that wouldn't say boo to a goose, especially with members of the clinic's medical staff, but he was quite forceful when he came to fetch me. He came into my office, just after eight o'clock, and demanded that I come straight away.'

The doctor chuckled at the memory and Jane laughed too. 'I can imagine it must have come as quite a shock to him, but what a wonderful thing to happen. I'd very much like to speak to him about it and to Bob, too. Could you arrange that?'

Doctor Ashwood's whole demeanour changed. 'I can certainly ask Terry if he'd talk to you – when he's back in work, that is – but I'm afraid you won't be able to speak to Bob.'

'Oh? Why not?'

'Ah, well, this might seem a little strange. In fact, it's really rather sad, especially when you think of the happy circumstances with Helen. Bob would have been delighted with what happened, absolutely delighted. He was a lovely chap—'

'You're using the past tense,' Jane interjected, cutting off the rambling explanation. She pinned the consultant with a sharp stare that even Gwyn would have been proud of.

Doctor Ashwood looked back at her like a ten-year-old schoolboy asked to explain to his headmistress exactly what he had been doing behind the bike sheds.

'Um, yes, yes, I am. You see, the morning cleaning staff found Bob in the toilets, just down the corridor, actually, from Helen's room. There'll be an autopsy of course – sudden death and all that – but from looking at him I'd say he'd had a heart attack. Terry did say he'd complained of feeling unwell when he'd last seen him.'

Aidan started, mental alarm bells ringing at the doctor's words. He wanted to jump in and question him himself but to do so would mean breaking character. Reluctantly he sat back and let Jane continue.

'Let me get this right. You mean Bob died at some point between reporting Helen making a noise and her actually regaining consciousness?'

'Well, we don't know exactly when he died. It might have been later in the night, although why he'd have been at the clinic outside his normal working hours I don't know. But yes, he was found the next morning. I'll admit it's a bizarre set of circumstances, isn't it? Totally unconnected, of course, but bizarre nonetheless.'

'Very bizarre,' agreed Jane. Her gaze flicked sideways to meet Aidan's. 'Very bizarre indeed.' She focused back on the doctor. 'When we came through from reception, I noticed that you have CCTV cameras in the corridors. Do you have them in the patients' rooms?'

'Ah, yes, but—'

'And has anyone reviewed the footage from Helen's room for that day?'

For the first time during the interview Doctor Ashwood stiffened, as though Jane had suggested something inappropriate.

'No. Why would they? While we do have coverage in the patients' rooms, those videos are on a separate system. The recordings aren't monitored and would only be reviewed in the event of a serious incident; some sort of security issue or – heaven forbid – if a question were raised about staff conduct or the treatment a patient received.'

'And of course, no one's going to complain about the circumstances around a patient waking up.'

For a second Doctor Ashwood looked blank, but then he chuckled as he realised Jane had been teasing him. He relaxed again, sending her a smile as he settled back in his chair. 'I doubt it.'

'Then the recordings from the rooms are kept?'

'Yes.'

'In which case, would it be possible for me to view the tape from Helen's room?'

The suggestion seemed to take Ashwood by surprise. For several moments he seemed unable to think of what to say. 'Well, I don't see why you would want to,' he protested eventually.

Jane put down her pen and notebook and folded her hands in her lap. 'It's all about accurate reporting, Doctor Ashwood.' She angled her body slightly towards the physician as though confiding in him. 'I can imagine what a patient with UWS is like, but to be able to convey that accurately to the readers of this article I would like to see someone. Now, personally, I don't feel it would be right to observe some of your patients, even if we can be fairly certain that doing so wouldn't affect them. I think you would agree with me on that. It would be an invasion of their privacy, just as you've quite rightly said would be the case if you actively monitored the video feeds from their rooms. However, Helen has given her permission for me to review her records and anything pertaining to her stay here in the clinic, as you saw in her letter. I feel, therefore, that it would be less intrusive for me to view the recordings – with you present, of course, if you felt that was the correct thing to do – than to ask you to let me see another of your patients. I simply want to understand the sequence of events and to convey it accurately.'

She leaned further forward, subtly mirroring the doctor's posture at the start of their interview. 'I'm sure you agree that UWS is an under-reported condition, one that's poorly understood outside the small community of clinicians who specialise in dealing with it. An accurate portrayal of Helen's waking moments would be highly beneficial to anyone who has relatives in this state, or to fellow medics and scientists who encounter it.' Jane looked gravely at the doctor and nodded her head. 'I'm sure you'd agree with me.'

It was like watching a snake hypnotising its prey. Aidan tried not to gawp at his girlfriend. The good doctor had no chance.

'Oh … er … yes, I see what you're getting at.' Unconsciously following Jane's lead, Ashwood nodded. His voice grew more positive. 'Well, as you say, Helen has given her permission so I don't see that there would be any issue.'

'Excellent.' Jane beamed at the doctor. 'Can we view the footage here or do we need to go to another office? I don't want to monopolise your time when you've already been so generous with it.'

Doctor Ashwood blinked as though a little surprised by what he had agreed to. 'Er, well, the system is housed in reception. There's an office there you can use.'

CHAPTER 17

The security office that housed the clinic's CCTV systems was little more than a glorified cupboard, its door tucked into an alcove behind the clinic's reception desk and half hidden by a sleek floor-to-ceiling shelving unit and an enormous flat-screen television displaying images of happy-looking patients being tended to by a variety of nurses, consultants and physiotherapists, all of whom were tanned, smiling and had, in Aidan's opinion, improbably white teeth. Small and windowless, it was already stuffy, and with the door closed – 'So we don't disturb you,' Jane had informed the receptionist who had pulled up the recordings of room 18 and shown her how to fast forward, rewind and pause the images – it was only going to get worse. Aidan undid the second button on the neck of his polo shirt and ran a finger under the collar resignedly, easing the fabric away from his neck. Hot summer days were for spending outdoors on the hills or in the forest or building rafts on the Clywedog, not for sitting in offices. That dislike of being hemmed in was precisely why he had founded Red Kite Adventure Training. He pitied anyone who had to watch their summers go past through an office window. Aidan cast a sour glance at the featureless walls enclosing him and Jane.

At least most office workers get a window. Eldritch definitely owes me a pint for this.

It was easier to think in terms of Eldritch being able to settle his obligations in the Unicorn than to worry about what might have happened to the Englishman. But he and Jane would find out, even if it meant spending the rest of the day locked away in a broom cupboard. He pushed a hand through his hair, feeling the sweat already prickling on his scalp, and sighed. He could only be grateful that he wasn't claustrophobic.

Jane had slipped out of her jacket but otherwise seemed unbothered by the heat or the cramped conditions. Maybe this was the sort of environment cybersecurity consultants regularly worked in. Aidan grimaced and made a mental note to add cyber ninja to his list of careers to avoid. Still, Jane seemed comfortable enough in front of the keyboard. A few tendrils of hair had come loose from the clip at the nape of her neck and were starting to kink in the heat. She pushed them back absently, tucking them behind her ears, then looked round at him as if aware of his scrutiny.

'Do you think Bob's death and Helen's waking up are related?'

'I don't see how they can be.' Aidan scowled as he leaned on the back of her chair and shook his head. 'But I'll bet every one of our new climbing harnesses that they are.' He huffed out his breath in frustration. 'There's just so much of this stuff I don't know anything about. Gwyn's the expert, not me.'

And she had been teaching him, it was true. But, at his own request, those lessons had been focused on refining his ability to harness and use power, that psychic energy that all humans had, to a greater or lesser extent, and which those who could wield it sometimes referred to as magic. It was an approach that Gwyn had agreed with. Power could be deadly enough in the hands of a trained practitioner. She made no bones about the danger an untrained wizard could pose. Now Aidan wished he had also asked her to teach him more about the denizens of the Unseen Realm. But he hadn't expected to be facing another supernatural threat after he and Eldritch had destroyed the demon manifesting in the old Greenfields mine. And, he realised, neither had she.

'Do you still want to check these videos out?' Jane's voice cut into his musings.

'Yeah. There may be something there, there may not. But this is going to be our only chance to find out. Anything extra we can tell Gwyn has got to be worth it.'

Jane nodded her agreement. 'That's what I thought. So,' she turned back to the keyboard, 'where do you want to start?'

'Let's find the point when the workmen go into Helen's room. I know Doctor Ashwood didn't seem to think that they could have heard anything, but they must have had some reason for going in there.'

'Hmm. You're thinking that it wasn't her that they heard.' Jane's words weren't phrased as a question.

'Maybe. Maybe they heard whatever it was that woke her up.'

'Do you have any idea what you're looking for?'

For the first time since they had entered the clinic Jane sounded uneasy. A little line formed between her brows as she eyed the video monitor as if worried about what images they might encounter.

'Not really.' Aidan gave a small shrug, trying for nonchalance but suspecting he only managed to convey uncertainty. 'I've only seen one demon manifest.' And that had been the second most horrific thing he had ever witnessed. The most horrific had been what had happened when that newly manifested demon had taken Griff Howell as its host. The thought of seeing that happen again made him queasy, although he tried telling himself that watching a recording had to be easier than having it happen live in front of him. At least if it was on a screen he could pretend they were watching an overly graphic horror film. The thought didn't help.

But maybe that wasn't what they would see.

'I've no idea if they all manifest the same. I never thought to ask Gwyn.'

The admission made him feel stupid and ill-prepared. *Some demon hunter you are, son.* He glanced sheepishly at Jane, but she seemed unfazed by his omission.

'To be fair, we weren't expecting to see video footage,' she reminded him.

'I guess not, but I did think that if a demon had manifested anywhere near here I'd be able to sense the hole it made in the boundary.' Despite the stuffy warmth of the enclosed office he shivered, thinking once again of that aching void he had seen on the twenty-five-fathom level of the Greenfields mine. 'I know we didn't get to see Helen's room, but I haven't picked up anything from the general atmosphere. And I did try.'

Following Doctor Ashwood to his office, he had lowered his shields and tried to sense that prickly static that would have signalled the nearness of the boundary to the Unseen Realm. But there had been nothing – or at least nothing he had been able to pick up.

'I wondered why you were keeping so quiet. But absence of proof isn't proof of absence. Even if demons don't all manifest the same way, we know the workmen reported hearing Helen cry out and that's what prompted them to go in to investigate. Why would they make that up? And, even if they did – even if there was no sound – there had to be something that made them go into her room.'

Once again, Aidan was grateful for Jane's habit of breaking any puzzle into a logical sequence of facts to be reviewed and questions to be answered. It made him feel they had a chance of working this out.

Even so. 'I still wish I knew more about this,' he said ruefully.

To his surprise Jane twisted round and kissed him on the cheek. 'You know what, Tarzan? I'm rather glad you don't.' She gave him an awkward smile as though she felt guilty admitting to even that small an uneasiness about the task in hand. 'Come on, let's find out what there is on the recording and then we'll start worrying about what we can and can't see.'

'Thanks, Jay.' Aidan shot her a grin as he took his seat next to her. 'Okay, let's see what we've got.'

The CCTV footage was shot from above and to one side of Helen's bed. It showed her lying on her back, unmoving. Only the time stamp in the bottom corner of the screen gave any indication that the recording was advancing at all. After a couple of minutes of watching Jane increased the speed of the playback.

'It's not very exciting, is it?' she said, drily. 'I can understand why Eldritch didn't visit.'

Aidan could too, but not just because of the boredom. 'What's the point when you know the other person's not going to wake up?'

They continued watching the screen.

'Hang on. There are the two workmen.'

Aidan pointed at the screen where two men had appeared in Helen's room. Jane paused the replay.

'Back it up so we can see if anything happens before they come in.'

Jane complied and they sat and watched the image of the unconscious woman.

'It's a shame there's no sound on this.'

'Yeah, it would help if we could hear whatever it was that they heard.'

They studied the image.

'There's no sign of anything in the room with her.'

'Or at least nothing that's showing up on the camera. Okay, here they come,' Jane commented as the two men were picked up on the camera. 'Bob and Terry. I wonder which one's which.'

Aidan had been about to surmise that Bob was probably the older of the two, given he had reportedly died of a heart attack, but the look on their faces as they walked towards the bed stopped him.

'They don't look as though they're investigating a noise.'

'No.'

Beside him Jane had gone dangerously still, her body as tense as her one-word answer.

'This is wrong. This is …' Her voice trailed off as, on the screen, the younger of the two workmen stepped up to the bed.

Aidan tensed, his gut telling him what was going to happen, even as his mind tried to reject the possibility.

No!

Unconsciously he shifted his weight, half rising from his chair as if he could lunge forward and stop the man. He was aware of Jane's half-formed gasp of protest but then they both froze as the mood on the screen abruptly changed from lust to anger.

'What the—'

They watched transfixed, torn between disgust and puzzlement at the images playing out in front of them. Even when the video showed the arrival of Doctor Ashwood interrupting the two men neither of them relaxed. Silently they watched the doctor examining Helen and then shepherding the two workmen from the room. As the recorded image returned to the unchanging shot of Helen lying unaware and unmoving in her bed Jane pressed pause. She and Aidan eyed each other.

'What the hell was all that about?'

From the time stamp on the screen the whole incident had taken less than five minutes.

'One thing's for sure; that wasn't anything to do with a demon.' Aidan felt slightly queasy that, given a choice between a demon and what they had just seen, he would have preferred to have witnessed a manifestation. At least he felt he understood demonic evil. 'There's no way they went in there to investigate a noise.'

'I think that's a fairly safe bet.' Disgust dripped like venom from Jane's every word.

'I'm not sure what the one in the black T-shirt was going to do—'

'I thought that was obvious.' Jane turned and gave Aidan a withering look.

'Yeah,' Aidan admitted. He shifted uncomfortably, embarrassed and understanding that, in some primitive way, he was implicated in the crime by virtue of his gender. He knew that was unreasonable, but he felt disgusted enough by what he had seen to accept that guilt. 'But then it looked like he was going to hit her and the older guy stopped him.'

Jane snorted derisively. 'He didn't seem to mind his friend mauling her after that, though.' She made a low, angry sound in the back of her throat, reminding Aidan of Sula when she was defending her territory. 'Who knows what they would have done if Ashwood hadn't come in when he did.'

'Thank God he did.'

'Once we've found out what happened to Helen he needs to see this. He should know what his staff get up to.'

'One of them's dead,' Aidan pointed out, not that that changed or excused what had been done, just that the universe had taken one of the men beyond any justice they could mete out. Jane looked at him, her jaw set, her eyes glowering. As clearly as if she had spoken, Aidan could hear her saying, *And your point is?*

When he made no response, she said coldly, 'And the other one's going to wish he was if he has the misfortune to meet me.'

Aidan chose not to argue that point, but there were other questions still to be answered. 'Okay,' he said, deliberately refocusing on the one thing they had come to the clinic to learn. 'We still don't know what caused Helen to wake up but, whatever it was, it must have happened between … 17:03 …' he read the timestamp from the bottom of the screen '… and whenever Terry reported Helen being awake.'

'He alerted Doctor Ashwood just after eight. That's three hours elapsed time – give or take.' A wealth of anger formed an undercurrent to Jane's voice but they had come to the clinic for a reason and her next words made it clear she was still focused on that. 'We don't have the time to view all that. What do you reckon – take it to seven o'clock, see if anything's happened and go from there?'

'Yeah, that sounds good.'

CHAPTER 18

'Sweet Lady!' Gwyn looked from Aidan to Jane and back again, her green eyes wide and shocked. 'You're absolutely sure about that? About the kiss?'

'Oh yeah.' Aidan nodded emphatically. 'It wasn't something you could mistake.'

Recalling those video images made him cringe inwardly. Thinking about what they might mean for Eldritch made him sick with dread. It was only the knowledge that he had no real understanding of what he would be dealing with, or how to combat it, that had stopped him going straight to Eldritch's house from the clinic. His head knew it was the right decision, but his heart was still telling him that he had signed his friend's death warrant, always assuming that Eldritch wasn't already dead at the time he and Jane were watching the recordings.

'He walked up to the bed and put his hands on either side of her face as if he was expecting her to struggle.'

Aidan made a vague movement with his hands as though mimicking what he had seen. When he realised what he had done he balled them into fists. The look on Jane's face mirrored his own disgust.

'Then, bang! He kissed her,' he continued. 'Three seconds later he's on the floor, dog food.'

'Bringing a whole new meaning to the phrase "kiss of death",' Jane said sharply.

It was the first time she had spoken since they had rendezvoused with Gwyn back at the town house hotel where they had stayed the previous night. She sat on the squashy two-seater settee beside Aidan, her arms folded around her, hugging herself as though she was feeling cold, despite the early afternoon sunshine filtering in through the diaphanous curtains. Aidan could sympathise. He remembered how he had felt the first time he had seen a demon kill, but he also knew his girlfriend well enough to know that meaningless reassurances would not be welcome. And right now, those were the only type he could give.

He had hoped that Gwyn would shed some light on what they had seen but, after her initial, startled reaction, she made no comment. In fact, she barely seemed to have registered what had been said, staring at the floor as though deep in thought. Aidan might have believed she had developed a sudden fascination with the cobalt and ochre zigzags of the faded kilim running alongside the bed, but for the way she had one hand fisted in her hair, twisting the dark strands round her fingers until it surely had to hurt. Yet still she said nothing, her mind focused elsewhere on lord alone knew what.

Aidan found himself talking to relieve the silence. 'Bob couldn't have been something like a Dementor, could he, Gwyn? You know, those ghost things in Harry Potter that kill with a kiss, only in reverse, obviously …' He knew he was babbling.

Gwyn's head came up and she glared at him as though she herself might choose to kill with a look. 'No.' Her voice was as sharp as her one-word answer. 'This isn't Harry bloody—' She stopped abruptly and shook her head as if dismissing something from her mind. 'Dementors don't exist, Aidan,' she said in a softer voice. Almost as an afterthought, and quieter still, she added, 'I could almost wish they did.'

Beside him Jane stiffened as she registered the significance of that comment and Aidan felt his stomach knot with genuine fear. What could be worse than those creations of darkness and despair?

He swallowed uneasily and asked the questions he wasn't sure he wanted an answer to. 'What is it, Gwyn? What are we facing?'

Gwyn let out her breath in a long sigh, perhaps as unhappy to answer his questions as he was to ask them. She pinched the bridge of her nose between her fingers and closed her eyes as if marshalling her thoughts. When she looked at them again her face was calm but her eyes held a bleakness that Aidan hadn't seen since she had first told him of the existence of demons.

'They're called grieves.' Gwyn raised a hand to forestall any comment. 'You won't have heard of them.' She looked at Aidan and attempted a smile. 'Nor would JK Rowling, not unless she had access to some very arcane sources. Accounts of them in folklore are sparse, to say the least.' One corner of her lips twisted upwards, but no warmth reached her eyes. 'There will be two of them.' She let out a small huff of breath, too bleak to be mistaken for a laugh, and shook her head. 'Lady bless us, there are always two of them.'

She sounded tired. Not just that, thought Aidan, she sounded old and – the thought made him deeply uneasy – vulnerable. But that was absurd. Gwyn had been dealing with the Unseen Realm all her life. She had been raised to it. He pushed the uncomfortable issue aside before he could examine it too closely and decided he would concentrate on establishing the facts instead. Unsettling though that might be, it was less so than analysing Gwyn's response. 'Does that mean that Terry is one as well?'

Jane snorted derisively. 'I think we know that much from what happened afterwards.'

Aidan would have agreed with her but for the fact that he knew from bitter experience that there could be another explanation. 'Humans and demons can sometimes team up.'

And all hell could, very literally, break loose as a result. He tried not to think of the chaos they had faced when that had happened before. Gwyn's skunk stripe of white hair was the most visible, but the three of them – him, Gwyn and Eldritch – carried scars from that time. Absently he rubbed his thumb along his forearm. They had all come very close to dying. The tightening of Gwyn's lips suggested she was thinking along similar lines, but she shook her head when he invited her opinion with a shrug.

'From what you described I think it's more likely that Terry is host to the second grieve, rather than a human partner.'

It said a lot for their current situation that a statement like that could be deemed to be good news, thought Aidan. Beside him Jane digested the information silently.

'So at least we know who we're looking out for.' That was something. 'But what do these … grieves,' he looked quizzically at Gwyn, checking he had this new name right, 'do? I mean, it's not like Bob was forced to kiss Helen. He obviously wanted to, but it's not much of a life if you kiss someone and then you drop dead, is it?'

Gwyn's response was an exaggerated raising of her eyebrows as if inviting him to think more carefully about what he had just said. 'You know better than that, Aidan. Bob was already dead when he walked into Helen's room.'

Her tone was matter of fact, but Aidan wasn't fooled into thinking that meant she didn't care, even for a man she had never met before. He knew of old just how well Gwyn could hide her emotions.

'First Dementors and now zombies?' Jane tried to make a joke of it, but her voice was tentative and held no more humour than Gwyn's had. Still, she unwrapped her arms and made a visible effort to relax. Aidan thought she was handling her first encounter with the Unseen Realm with more composure than he had. He risked a smile of encouragement – in reality more grimace than grin – and received a rather shaky one in return.

'What you saw was the grieve switching hosts. Once it had moved from Bob's body into Helen's, Bob's body ceased to function.'

'So, they're like demons? When they possess you, you die.'

'They're similar to demons, yes. They both come from the Unseen Realm. Grieves aren't as common though.' Gwyn thought about that for a moment. 'Or perhaps it's more a case that they're not as noticeable,' she qualified. 'They're not driven to create misery and suffering, as demons are. They don't feed off negative emotions so you couldn't track their existence through a trail of suicides and despair.'

She glanced at him as she spoke and Aidan knew from the little twitch of those elfin brows that she was thinking of Eldritch's method of locating manifesting demons. He swallowed down the lump that rose in his throat and the sudden fear that the English wizard and his demon-tracking abilities might now be a thing of the past. Not trusting his voice not to betray him, he kept quiet as Gwyn continued.

'Grieves are creatures of the senses. They seem to be driven by a desire to experience the sensual side of human existence.'

'They were certainly doing that alright.' There was a wealth of commentary contained in Jane's voice, but for all that she sounded calmer, more herself. Her expression veered from wryly amused to horrified as she added, 'Although I'd describe it as more carnal than sensual.'

Aidan gave her a supportive smile. They were both going to have to come to terms with those images. Still, when he thought of his experiences with the behaviour of demons, grieves seemed almost benign by comparison. Apart from the not so small matter of them killing their hosts, of course. The fear he had been feeling for Eldritch eased fractionally.

'But where did they come from? Bob and Terry can't always have been hosts, surely.'

'Doctor Ashwood didn't mention any other sudden deaths at the clinic,' Jane pointed out.

She tapped her lip with her finger as she thought over what the doctor had revealed in his interview. Aidan could almost see her breaking what they knew down into logical segments and laying them out in her head. As a way of coping it was certainly more useful than floods of hysterical tears or head in the sand denial, reactions that many people in her position would have felt entitled to. Then again, Jane would probably flatten anyone foolish enough to suggest she would crack under pressure. The thought made Aidan grin inwardly. He held on to it as a grain of comfort against the nightmare they were facing.

'On the other hand, that's probably not something he'd want to draw attention to,' Jane concluded, unaware of Aidan's internal delight in her logical nature.

'Well, they must have come from somewhere, unless they'd only just broken through from the Unseen Realm, and I couldn't sense any weakening in the boundary.'

'The other alternative is that Bob and Terry inadvertently released them.'

Aidan looked at Gwyn curiously. 'Is that likely?'

'Likely? No. Possible? Yes. Not that it makes any difference to what we're dealing with.' She pulled a face as if admitting that that wasn't very helpful.

'Then that's not something we need to worry about for now.' Jane wasn't one to get sidetracked by peripheral information. Her focus was on the hard facts, such as they had. 'We know Helen's not Helen and Terry's not Terry, either.' The way she said it made it sound almost mundane. 'But the thing that I don't get is that if both of these grieves already have hosts, then what would they want with Eldritch? Besides the obvious, I mean, and even Rowan's had her eyes on him for that.'

The ghost of a smile flickered at the corners of her mouth and, for the briefest moment, it seemed that this situation could be something they would eventually tease Eldritch about, rather than a life-threatening crisis he needed saving from. Then Jane sobered. She looked first at Aidan and then Gwyn for enlightenment. 'What am I missing?'

CHAPTER 19

'Ah.' Rather than answer immediately, Gwyn drew her feet up, folded her arms across her knees and dropped her chin onto her forearms. With her crazy mane of hair spilling over her shoulders and her bare feet she looked like a displaced pixie, thought Aidan, or some sort of wood sprite that had inexplicably wandered into the city and taken up residence in this odd little remnant of bohemia with its wooden floors and faded rugs and packs of Tarot cards alongside the Gideon Bibles in the bedside drawers. Then he saw her eyes. No, not a pixie. Gwyn looked more like an oracle, cursed to see images of a future she feared but could do nothing to prevent.

Pity Cassandra. The snatch of verse echoed in his mind. He realised then that she had never considered the grieves to be a lesser threat than a demon. Even before he heard what she had to say he knew it would be bad.

'I'm guessing Terry wants a host with power to match that of his mate.' Gwyn's voice was flat, as if she spoke of some stranger whose fate was of no great consequence, rather than a friend.

Jane's head jerked up as though she had been slapped. She stared at Gwyn in disbelief, her eyes wide, her body rigid with a sudden startled tension, as though poised to react but uncertain what to do. 'You mean it's not Helen that's the threat after all?'

A thought struck Aidan. Despite the afternoon's heat he felt his hands and face go cold as the blood drained from them in shock.

'Doctor Ashwood told us that Terry was off work,' he said thickly. Jane's eyes darted to his and he saw from her expression that she had made the same connection he had.

Dear God, no!

'We know Helen was still—' Jane hesitated, visibly weighing up the appropriateness of using the word 'alive' to describe a woman they had just learned was effectively an animated corpse. She was silent for a moment, frowning as she searched for an alternative term, then she shook her head as if dismissing the matter as irrelevant. 'Well, the thing in Helen was still in her two days ago when you spoke to her. But Terry ...'

Like Aidan, she shied away from saying what they both feared, as if giving voice to the possibility might make it more real. Instead, she looked questioningly at Gwyn.

'And this isn't reversible?'

Her voice sounded very small in the stillness of the room. Wordlessly, Aidan reached for her hand, uncertain if he was comforter or comforted, simply needing the reassurance of that physical contact. For a moment he and Jane hung on to each other, a single entity, joined by a common dread.

'No.' Gwyn's answer was both fierce and raw. 'When a grieve takes someone as a host, they die. That's definite.' Her voice softened fractionally. 'But even if we assume that's what Terry's planning to do to Eldritch – and I think it must be – he may not have been able to do so yet. A wizard's shields are stronger than an average person's,' she added by way of an explanation. 'They're going to have to break them before they can take him.'

She took a deep breath and uncurled from her chair, stalking to the window to push aside the fine cotton swags and stare out at the street below them. Her hands pleated the thin sherbet-coloured fabric – a small, fidgety movement from a woman who could sit still enough that wild birds would perch next to her. 'That would explain why he's not been in contact. If Terry had already taken Eldritch there'd be no reason for him not to have spoken to me when I called.'

'You really think there's a chance he's still alive?' Aidan wasn't sure he dared hope.

'I think we have to believe that.'

Gwyn let the curtain fall and turned back to him. Unlike those in her cottage, the windowsills here weren't deep enough to sit on so she propped one hip on the wide cast-iron radiator instead. Her fingers strayed to the rose quartz beads encircling her wrist, turning them absently as she spoke. 'Helen and Terry would have to hold him prisoner while they worked on breaking his shields.'

'How are they going to do that?'

Gwyn stopped twisting her bracelet. She lifted her head and returned Aidan's gaze without flinching. 'Prolonged and extreme pain can do it.' Her voice and her face were schooled into neutrality as though she was delivering some footnote of magical theory in one of their lessons. 'Although I would hope the neighbours would notice if someone set up a torture chamber next door. Even in London.'

It might have been meant as a joke, but neither Jane

nor Aidan laughed, too horrified to react, even to the inappropriateness of that throwaway comment.

Gwyn spoke into the silence left by her own words. 'The alternative is to use drugs.' She pushed herself upright and walked back to her chair. 'There are certain herbs that can be used to weaken a wizard's shields, just as there are others that can be used to strengthen them. Helen was a healer. It's likely she'd know about them.'

She let them digest that information in silence before she added, 'We just have to hope she was as good as Eldritch said she was.'

Her scowl suggested she wanted to berate both the absent wizard and his wife about Helen's healing capabilities.

'What do you mean?'

'Interfering with someone's psychic energy is inherently dangerous. The herbs used are very powerful and getting the dosages right is critical. You've seen yourself what happens when someone's energy crashes. If Helen doesn't know what she's doing and she gets it wrong, there's a good chance that she'll end up killing him anyway.'

'Dear God.' There was more prayer than blasphemy in Aidan's shocked whisper.

'How long does it take?' By contrast Jane's voice was cold, as though she were deliberately cutting herself off from the fact that this was Eldritch's life – and quite possibly his death – that they were discussing.

Objectively, Aidan could appreciate her detachment. It was the same as her fighting style in the dojo, clinical and clean and very much like Sensei's. Sensei always said there should be no emotion in a fight, just an absolute focus on doing whatever it took to overcome your opponent, regardless of what that entailed or, indeed, who you were fighting. It sounded simple when Sensei said it in the dojo, but the knife scar that sliced across his forearm was a reminder of how difficult it had been in practice. Aidan found himself thinking that, given the same set of circumstances, Jane wouldn't have held back. His eyes slid to where she sat beside him. He could understand the logic behind her attitude but a small part of him hated her for it.

Gwyn, however, reacted to the question as though it was perfectly reasonable, no more than a discussion of an aspect of magical theory. Her head cocked to one side and her eyes grew distant as she weighed up the different factors involved. 'I'd say it would take a minimum of three days. That's the fastest you could do it with any degree of safety. First, you have to block the body's energy channels. That locks down the core, the innate power that a wizard draws on to do anything magical. That way Eldritch wouldn't be able to fight them. Not only that, but his ability to shield would start to decay as a result.'

She toyed with a strand of hair, twisting it round her finger and pulling it tight. 'It's tricky though. Doing that is going to result in psychic shock. They'd have to give it twenty-four hours for him to stabilise, maybe more.' Her teeth worried at her lower lip as she thought this through. 'But, once he has, they can start adding other things to the mix. His shields will weaken anyway because he won't be able to replenish them, and there are other herbs they can use to speed up the process. Three days and his shields would probably be weak enough for them to break.' Gwyn's mouth thinned to a narrow line at the thought of what that breaking might entail. 'Then they'd be able to take him.'

'Three days.' Aidan's face tightened as he mentally checked off the elapsed time. 'That means they could have taken him last night.'

'No, I don't think so. We're talking about some very specialised ingredients. They're not something that Helen will have simply lying around the house, not least of all because some of them need to be fresh. She'll have to get them from somewhere before she can make the first potion.'

'She's not going to hang around though, is she? How long do you think it would take for her to get her hands on what she needs to make this witch's brew?'

'Twenty-four hours, maybe, if she still has the right contacts. Even if she doesn't, in somewhere like London it's not going to take her much longer than that. And the potion itself takes less than half a day to make.'

'So they could be getting ready to take him today.' Even as he spoke Aidan was on his feet. 'What are we waiting for? We need to get him out of there.'

'No.'

'For God's sake, why not?'

Gwyn looked up at Aidan. 'Because if I'm wrong and he's already been taken, we'll be facing Lady knows what kind of trouble as a result.' Gwyn shook her head. 'Grieves may not be driven by the need to cause death and misery, but that's not to say that they won't. They'll fight for their lives if they need to. If Eldritch has been taken, and we charge in there like the Seventh Cavalry, we'll be facing two fully trained sorcerers fighting for survival.' She stood up and a small part of Aidan's brain registered the fact that she had positioned herself between him and the door. Looking him in the eye she said, 'I'm not taking Jane into that.'

'At least, not without a plan,' Jane suggested, her voice silky and ever so slightly dangerous. She looked pointedly at her two companions, facing each other as though about to go head to head in some arcane duel. The challenge in her own words was evident.

Aidan swore under his breath, his thoughts mutinous for all that he knew Gwyn was right. And so was Jane. It was the first rule of search and rescue – assess the situation before you run in and become a casualty yourself. But knowing that didn't make him feel any happier about the delay.

'Then what are we going to do?' he snarled, angry and frustrated and scared that time was running out for Eldritch. Surely Gwyn could recognise that? Maybe she could, for her lips quirked in a tight and utterly humourless smile as she regarded him.

'We are not going to do anything. You, however, are going to have to go in there on your own and scout things out.'

CHAPTER 20

'Why Aidan?' The sharpness of Jane's tone made it clear what she thought of Gwyn's proposal. She eyed the older woman incredulously, but Gwyn met the inherent criticism without flinching.

'Because no matter how good you are at bluffing your way through any situation, Jane,' a slight inclination of Gwyn's head acknowledged that this was a valuable part of Jane's peculiar skill set, 'if anything went wrong, you'd have no defence against a grieve.'

'Except a solid mawashi geri to the jaw.' Jane smiled with exaggerated sweetness at Gwyn. 'I'd like to see one of them try the kiss of death on me with a mouthful of broken teeth.'

'Not good enough, Jay.' Aidan spoke before Gwyn could. 'Helen's a wizard, a sorceress. She'd hit you with a Levin bolt.'

Jane turned on her lover, her expression venomous. 'Oh, just like you tried to in the dojo? It didn't work, remember?' she said caustically.

'And we don't know why,' he retorted, annoyed that his earlier failure could make her feel she was invulnerable now. Though he wouldn't say so, his irritation was seated in a very real fear. He would back Jane against any mortal opponent, but the Unseen Realm was different. He intended to keep her safe from it even if she hated him for doing so.

'Enough.' Gwyn's voice was sharp enough to cut across a battlefield, let alone a hotel room. She glared at her two companions as though they were children caught fighting over whose turn it was to play with a favourite toy. The pair of them subsided under that fierce peridot gaze.

Gwyn waited a moment longer perhaps judging whether they were ready to listen to her. Then she continued. 'It has to be Aidan for several reasons. You both saw how easy it was for the grieve to take Helen. You'd be equally vulnerable, Jane, and as Aidan rightly says, Helen wouldn't have to tackle you physically to overpower you. She'd use a Levin bolt and it wouldn't be a half-hearted attempt like the one he threw at you in the dojo.'

Both Aidan and Jane bristled, albeit for very different reasons.

Gwyn ignored them. 'Your shields aren't as strong as mine or Eldritch's, Aidan, but they're better than an ordinary person's. A grieve wouldn't be able to break them easily.'

'Then why Aidan and not you, Gwyn?' Jane asked with barely concealed ill grace. 'If your shields are better than his, why aren't you the one to go scouting things out?'

The older woman huffed out an irritated breath, her nostrils flaring, but when she spoke it was clear that it wasn't the question that had annoyed her. Instead, it seemed she was unhappy with what she was about to say.

'I'd far rather it was me who went.' Gwyn's mouth thinned in annoyance, underlining the sentiment. 'But I've already spoken to Helen, remember. It's going to look suspicious if I show up in London two days later, wanting to see Eldritch. Aidan, on the other hand … well, she doesn't know him, so he should be alright.'

'Should be?' Jane wasn't happy.

'Yes. He should be.' Gwyn looked at her ex-ward and sighed. 'There are no guarantees, but if you're not comfortable with this then I'll go, Aidan.'

Aidan looked at her, his raised eyebrows like a question mark.

Really?

He shook his head, dismissing the suggestion. 'No, it's okay. It makes more sense if I do it.' He turned and offered Jane a lopsided smile, part apology and part peace offering. 'It will be okay, Jay.'

'Huh! It had better be.'

She sounded disgusted but he recognised it was because she was worried for him; that and the fact that she would have preferred to be the one going into a potentially dangerous situation. He could understand that; he would have felt the same way if their positions had been reversed. He leaned over and quickly kissed her on the nose, then leaned back out of range of easy retaliation. Jane folded her arms and glared at him.

Knowing not to push his luck, but hoping he had been partly forgiven, Aidan turned back to Gwyn. 'Okay, I go round. I'll find out if anyone's home, or at least if anyone's answering the door.' He gave a wry smile, acknowledging that the two scenarios might not be the same. 'And if Helen's there, I ask to see Eldritch.'

'If she stalls you then we can assume he's not been taken yet. You say, "Oh well, let him know I called," and leave.'

'Alright.'

So far so good. But there was one scenario Aidan didn't want to contemplate, and yet he knew he had to face it. He looked at Gwyn, his expression painfully serious. 'And if it's Eldritch who opens the door?'

He had hoped for reassurance. What he got instead was a look of raw grief that told him that, for all Gwyn's earlier assertions that the grieves wouldn't have had time to break the wizard's shields, this was the one thing she was dreading. He opened his mouth to offer some response, something comforting but ultimately meaningless, but his mentor cut him off with a shake of her head.

'If it is, and he's clearly not under any duress, then I think you have to assume he's already been taken.'

Dear God . . .

Aidan swallowed the words along with the sense of desolation that threatened to overwhelm him. Hearing Gwyn say what he feared was somehow far worse than merely thinking it.

Yet Gwyn hadn't finished. Looking him in the eye, she went on inexorably, 'In which case, you're going to have to treat him as normally as you can.'

What?

Aidan knew his expression was screaming, *How do I do that?* But how could he be expected to act normally if he came face to face with his friend's animated corpse?

Jane took one look at him and rounded on Gwyn. 'And that,' she said, jabbing an angry finger towards his face, 'is exactly why I should be the one to go. He'll give the game away.'

'No!'

Aidan and Gwyn spoke together. For a moment they looked at each other in surprise, an acknowledgement of how rare it was for them to be in absolute agreement over anything. Gwyn raised her eyebrows. Aidan managed a lopsided smile in return. If nothing else, it diffused some of the raw emotions flying between them.

'I still think it's unlikely, Aidan. Honestly, I do. Sweet Lady, you know how pig-headed that man can be.' Gwyn gave a little tight-lipped smile, as if Eldritch's stubbornness could be any help against the threat he faced. 'But, if it comes to it, you shouldn't be in any danger so long as you don't give them any reason to think that you know there's anything wrong.' That much at least, Gwyn sounded sure of. 'You can tell him that Rowan's been driving you crazy asking for news, so you thought that while you were here in London you'd take the opportunity to call round. Or blame it on me – that should seem reasonable enough.'

She hesitated as if she would say something else, then shook her head, dismissing whatever it was she had thought to add. Instead, she said, 'You're going to need a good reason for being in London, though.'

'Beyond wanting to save a crazy Englishman's neck, you mean?' Aidan tried unsuccessfully for humour.

Beside him, Jane swore under her breath. 'That's not the reason I'd choose,' she muttered sarcastically.

Gwyn just looked miserable.

'Jay?' Aidan turned to his girlfriend. 'I could do with a little security ninja expertise here.'

Jane looked down her nose at him. 'Oh, so now you want my help.'

Well, at least she was talking to him.

Aidan shot her a reproachful look. 'You don't want to see a grown man beg.'

At least he hoped she didn't. For good measure he turned his best pleading puppy-dog eyes on her, what Matt referred to as his 'kicked beagle' expression.

'Don't count on it, Tarzan.' Jane's tone was venomous but her expression was already softening. She pursed her lips, rolled her eyes heavenwards as if appealing to a higher power, then gave an exasperated huff of breath as she relented. 'The trick is to pick a reason that rings true for you.' Her voice shifted to the bright tone he recognised from the dojo, the one she used with the juniors that meant, *Do what I tell you and this will work.* 'Don't worry so much what Eldritch is going to think of it – it's how you feel about it that matters. If you believe it then he will too.'

Aidan digested this silently. 'Thanks. I think.'

Presumably it was sound advice, but he had been hoping for a more concrete suggestion as to why he was here. What on earth would have brought him to London? From the moment his feet hit the platform at Euston and the rank, trapped diesel smell caught in the back of his throat, his main preoccupation was with getting out of the city again as soon as possible. He couldn't think of one reason why he would choose to come here in preference to being out on the hills, and he wholeheartedly wished he was back at the station now, headed for a train rather than having recently got off one. But as he thought that, his mind brought back the one sight that had cheered him up as he and Jane had arrived the previous evening.

'Got it. The Rock and Snow Show is on at Earl's Court this week.'

He grinned at Jane triumphantly, recalling how she had responded with a martyred sigh and a muttered comment about there being no escape when he had pointed out the advert he had seen on the side of a bus.

'Matt and I did think about having a stand there once, back in the early days when we were setting up Red Kite. We never did get round to it – it's too expensive for starters – but I could say I've come to check it out again, weigh up the competition, that sort of thing.'

'Hmm, not bad.' There was enough approval in Jane's tone that Aidan felt a momentary glow of satisfaction. She might even have forgiven him for his agreement that she should be kept out of the conflict. Then she poked him none too gently in the ribs and added, 'For an amateur,' and he revised his opinion. He was still in the doghouse but if it kept her safe he would gladly stay there.

Under normal circumstances their verbal sparring would have elicited either a raised eyebrow or an indulgent smile from Gwyn, depending on her mood. More often than not she would then wade in with her own waspish comment. But now she let it slide past her, responding only to the merit of Aidan's suggested cover story.

'Okay. That's good. So, you go in and talk to him. You tell him that you're delighted for him that he has Helen back, that you're hoping he'll come back to Wales at some point, but that you already suspect he may not want to.'

Gwyn paused and a bittersweet smile lifted the corners of her mouth, briefly lighting her face like a shaft of winter sunshine breaking between the clouds. The sight of it cut Aidan to the core. He knew without asking she had just put into words all her own tangled feelings about Eldritch's absence.

'Gwyn …'

Aidan fought down the unfamiliar urge to get up and give her a hug, unreasonably scared that if he did so she might cry and certain that neither of them would cope very well if she did. Gwyn started a little at her name. She blinked and rubbed her hands over her face as if the thoughts she had just vocalised were something she could wipe away, like clinging spider webs.

When she continued her voice was level and brisk. 'Make your excuses and get out of there as soon as you can without it seeming suspicious. Neither of the grieves is going to want you there. They'll probably be only too glad to get rid of you.' She paused and then added, 'But I meant it. If you're not comfortable doing this, Aidan, I will go.'

She met his gaze, her own expression carefully neutral, and Aidan realised she was weighing his confidence in pulling this off against the risks inherent in going herself. He wondered what she would do if confronted by a grieve wearing Eldritch's body and realised he couldn't let her face that. In that instant he knew his decision was made.

'No way, Gwyn. We've agreed. It makes more sense if I go.' He conjured up a smile to cover his real feelings and forced confidence he didn't quite feel into his voice. 'Besides, just like you said, he's not been taken yet. It's going to be Helen who answers the door if anybody does.'

'Of course.' Gwyn nodded, her own smile just a fraction too bright to be genuine.

Aidan noticed but carried on with the charade. 'So, what are you and Jay going to be doing while I'm playing James Bond?'

'We're going to be drinking tea and eating cake.' Gwyn almost managed to sound cheerful at the prospect. 'I did some research of my own while the two of you were at the clinic. There's an arcade of shops about five minutes' walk from Eldritch's house and there's a rather pleasant looking café in the middle. Jane and I will wait for you there.'

CHAPTER 21

Jane glanced down at her smart trousers and blouse.

'Give me two minutes to get changed.' At Aidan's quizzical look she added, 'I'd rather not be wearing my best clothes if we end up having to ride to your rescue.'

Aidan didn't even try to keep the sourness from his voice. 'You're not going to be riding to anyone's rescue. You're going to be stuffing yourselves with tea and cake.'

'I hope so, but that's if everything goes to plan. If it doesn't, we're your backup.' Jane smiled with false sweetness and Aidan's scowl deepened. 'If we don't hear from you after half an hour then we're coming in to get you.'

Some arguments simply weren't worth having and Aidan recognised instinctively that this was one of them. He noticed that Jane hadn't bothered to confirm this addition to the plan with Gwyn and he knew that if he didn't check in within the allotted time she would come after him, regardless of what Gwyn thought about it.

'Okay, but you'd better make it an hour. If I do find Eldritch then it's going to seem weird if I cut and run too soon.' He laughed humourlessly as a thought struck him. 'It's crazy – we came here wanting to find him. Now I'm hoping that I don't get to see him. Well, not straight away.' He gave her a lopsided smile. 'You know what I mean.'

Jane nodded her understanding. 'We're going to be in time

to save him,' she said. 'We have to believe that.' She gave him a tight-lipped smile of her own in return. 'I'll be two minutes.' Then she was gone.

Aidan looked round at Gwyn, wondering if she had anything to add. While he and Jane had been speaking she had swept her hair back and was busy fastening it into an untidy plait. The effect emphasised her white skunk stripe, serving as an unpleasant reminder of their previous run-in with the Unseen Realm. Griff Howell had been human enough, but under the influence of the demon he had come very close to killing Gwyn. That streak of white hair was the only visible memento of where he had fractured her skull, but Aidan knew she still suffered from headaches if she got overtired or when the weather turned stormy.

He was suddenly conscious that the danger they faced might be physical as well as supernatural. 'Are you preparing for battle too?'

He could understand Jane's reticence but having Gwyn preparing for the worst as well was like a slap in the face. Given that she'd been the one to propose he do the reconnoitring, the least she could do was to show faith in his abilities.

Perhaps she heard the tetchiness he had tried to keep from his voice, because she cocked her head to one side, considering him like a thrush weighing up a snail it was about to crack against a stone. 'No, Aidan. It's simply cooler to wear my hair up in this heat.'

There was a trace of exasperation in the cant of those elfin brows, as though she felt that much should have been obvious. She wound the finished plait into a knot at the nape of her neck. Holding it in place with one hand she looked distractedly around the room. Finally, she spotted what she wanted on the bedside table, tucked between a large brass Buddha and the bedside lamp. 'Pass me that pencil, will you.'

Bemused, Aidan did as he was asked, and watched her stab it through the knot of her hair. She shook her head experimentally; a few tendrils fell round her face but the bulk of the plait stayed put. Satisfied, she smiled and then, in that unerring way she had of picking up on what he hadn't said out loud, she said, 'Jane's right. It's only sensible that we have a contingency plan.' She raised her eyebrows, inviting his comment. When he said nothing she continued. 'But if I thought you were going to get into trouble, I wouldn't have suggested you go.'

'Yeah.'

Somehow her words, the reassurance he had been hoping for, didn't make Aidan feel any happier. Restlessly he prowled over to the window and stood staring out at the London skyline, the glittering glass and concrete towers of office blocks and apartments intermingled with the curious delicacy of the church spires scattered amongst them. Above that mix of buildings the sky was a sweep of hot summer blue hazed with the smog of city fumes and crosshatched with the slow dispersing contrails of a dozen planes. God, he hated cities. More than anything he wanted to be able to go home, but first … His fist clenched where it rested against the glass. They would be in time to save Eldritch, he told himself, pushing down against the roil of emotions building in his gut. They had to be. But if they weren't …

'What if it's too late, Gwyn?' Aidan kept his eyes on the skyline, hating the way his voice cracked as he spoke.

'We're not going to be too late, Aidan.'

'But what if we are?' He turned to face her, feeling the fear and anger he had been holding in come spewing up, congealing in his throat so that his voice thickened, and he had to fight to get the words out. 'What are we going to do if he has been taken? I go there, I find out, I get out again. I understand that, but what happens then?'

It wasn't just that Eldritch would be dead. Appalling though that thought was, it wasn't the only thing they had to face. In a voice as bleak as midwinter, Aidan asked, 'What do we do?'

'I don't know.'

The simple honesty of Gwyn's answer caught Aidan by surprise. For a moment he stared at her blankly, certain he must have misheard. The blunt, unequivocal nature of that statement left no room for doubt and yet it made no sense.

'But we have to do something. We can't just leave them running loose,' he protested as though Gwyn had suggested doing just that. 'Surely we've got to stop them, send them back to the Unseen Realm?'

'We can't.'

It was back in her voice, that edge of weariness he had caught earlier, accompanied by a sense of something that if he'd heard it in anyone else, Aidan might have described as helplessness.

He stared at her, the woman who had once been his guardian and who was now his guide to the world of the arcane. 'But …' He still couldn't believe what he had heard, couldn't make sense of what she seemed to be telling him.

Gwyn's chin lifted. 'You can't just rip a hole in the boundary and shove something like a grieve back into the Unseen Realm,

Aidan. Once an entity is here in the Mortal World, once it's taken a host, it can only be bound – as I think these two probably were – or destroyed.'

Aidan shrugged off her lecturing tone. This was nothing more than semantics as far as he was concerned. 'Okay, so we can't send them back. But binding them or destroying them – you can do that, can't you?'

He might have phrased it as a question, but Aidan didn't really expect anything other than a positive response from Gwyn. As a child he had believed she could fix anything he asked her to. Though it was many years since he had regarded her with a child's innocent expectations, he still felt certain that this was something she could remedy. When she turned away from him without answering he felt obscurely let down. The pain he had glimpsed in her eyes only confused him.

'Gwyn?'

Maybe Gwyn heard the echo of that long-ago child in his voice for she turned back. She tried to smile as she said, 'Honestly? I don't know. Once upon a time, yes, I could have done it. Now ...'

The brittle smile disappeared without coming close to reaching her eyes. In its place Gwyn made a small gesture, a turning up of her palms like a magician demonstrating she had nothing in her hands or up her sleeves, and she shook her head.

No, this wasn't right. Aidan fought down the urge to throw that accusation at her. Gwyn had to be able to deal with this. Who else was there, if Eldritch was lost to them? He took a deep breath, as much to force down his own fear as to give himself time to marshal the right words.

'Last year, after John's death, you realised there was a demon about to manifest. What were you going to do about it?'

The question startled an incredulous laugh out of her. 'That seems like a lifetime ago.' For a moment her smile returned, genuine this time, as though she was looking back through the months at another woman sourcing crystals and books on demon lore from Rowan's shop. Then her expression turned rueful. 'Truthfully? I don't know,' she admitted. 'I didn't know then and I don't know now.'

She must have read the disbelief in his eyes because she shrugged and made that same dismissive gesture with her hands. 'I mean it, Aidan. I had no idea. Then a crazy English wizard came along, and it all became academic. You know I don't have that kind of power any more.'

Aidan shook his head, dismissing her words. There had to be something they could do. Gwyn might lack the flashy power that Eldritch seemed to call so easily – though he had learned that it wasn't as easy as the wizard made it seem, nor as limitless – he understood that. But even though Gwyn's power wasn't conspicuous, it was there. He had felt it. It was something he would never forget.

'The first lesson you ever gave me on shielding, you called on something … a watcher … the watcher?'

He groped for the words, the hackles standing up on the back of his neck as he brought the memory back. He shivered, feeling the gooseflesh rising on his arms. He remembered how they had sat in the small lounge at the front of her cottage, and he had felt the energies in the room shift and change as she had made her invocation.

Gatherer of Souls, Watcher on the far horizon, you who stand against the darkness—

'I always do, Aidan.' Gwyn's voice brought him back to the present. 'I say a prayer every time I set a circle. Or hadn't you noticed?' Just for a second her voice was that of a teacher whose student has failed a simple test.

'But that night … that first night, you called on something and it came!'

Gwyn dropped her gaze. She looked down at her folded hands.

Aidan recognised what she was doing – organising her thoughts like a gambler sorting a hand of cards, weighing what she would and would not lay out before him – and he felt his anger flare again. 'Gwyn …' He growled her name, angry, frustrated. He wanted an argument, something – anything! – to release the tension building inside him.

Her head came up and the look on her face dried the words on his tongue. 'I called on something, Aidan. Yes. I called on it and it came. That once. I also told you that it doesn't always happen. There's a difference between a prayer being heard and one being answered.'

'But—'

She cut him off with a look. 'I place my soul under the protection of the light. My soul, Aidan, my spirit, not my physical body. I make a declaration that whatever I'm doing, I'm doing with the intention that it is for the higher good.' She let out a small huff of breath, like a dragon venting steam. 'Whatever that may be,' she added, and her tone was as wry as the unexpected smile that caught at the corners of her mouth. She shook her head, dismissing both smile and the lecture she had been giving. 'I'm not asking for that power to be given to me for my use and, even if I were, I couldn't guarantee that it would happen. It's not something I can force.'

She turned her palms up again in that gesture of emptiness.

A maelstrom of conflicting emotions boiled through Aidan, momentarily rendering him speechless. He opened his mouth but couldn't get the words out.

Finally, he muttered, 'So that's it? You're saying that we've got two supernatural creatures on the loose that have already killed God knows how many people, and if Eldritch is dead too, there's nothing we can do? Oh, but we could ask for our souls to be protected because, obviously, that's what counts!'

He stared at her, his sense of disbelief turning rapidly to anger. 'That's not good enough! What the hell is this "higher good" that you're talking about,' he held his hands out, mimicking her gesture, then flung them up, tossing her arguments away, 'if it's not about saving people's lives?'

He spat the words at her, bitter and vicious, wanting to hurt, as if spreading the pain he was feeling could somehow make it more bearable. He drew a shuddering breath, choking on the words that felt like they were ripping him apart. 'We're just going to let them get away with killing him?' Aidan stopped, feeling grief clenching round his throat. He forced it back down with anger, clamping his mouth shut, refusing to let the feelings out, though part of him wanted to howl at the sky. The muscles of his clenched jaw ached and he welcomed the pain.

'That's not what I'm saying at all.' Gwyn's voice was like a whip crack flaying across his skin.

He looked at her, ready to fight, adamant that there could be no compromise. She seemed to draw herself up and for a moment he thought he felt the air crackle with power, like a storm before a lightning strike. He had his shields up and a Levin bolt of his own forming in his hand before he was consciously aware of what he was doing. Then she subsided and, after a moment, so did he. A detached portion of his brain registered that Jane was standing poised in the doorway, watching the pair of them intently as though weighing up whether she should step between them. Her smart journalist persona was gone, and in its place she was wearing what Aidan thought of as her 'world-traveller look' – faded jeans, battered trainers, and a nondescript indigo T-shirt that looked as though it had been washed too many times in saltwater and dried in the sun. With a tan and sun streaks in her hair – both of which she had told him authoritatively could be obtained from a bottle should she want that extra authenticity – she would look like any one of the carefree student adventurers he had met on his gap-year travels. But no student traveller he had encountered had ever looked at him with such sharp-eyed assessment. Though Jane said nothing, Aidan felt he and Gwyn were being judged and had been found wanting.

'Sorry,' he muttered, not sure whether he was addressing his teacher or his lover.

Jane responded by flicking a disgusted look at him and Gwyn. She stalked over to the settee and sat down, her silence more pointed than any verbal reprimand.

Gwyn, however, seemed to accept that his contrition had been directed at her. 'So am I,' she said. 'I would hope you'd think better of me than that.'

'Gwyn …' Aidan wasn't sure he was up to any more of an apology. His emotions were too raw.

Gwyn shook her head. 'It's alright, Aidan.' She swallowed and Aidan realised belatedly that she was as unsettled as he was. 'I don't want to lose him any more than you do, and I still do believe that we have a chance to save him. But if we don't, we will find a way to stop them and avenge his death. I promise you.' She put her hand out and touched his arm. 'I just have no idea, at the moment, how I'm going to do that.'

CHAPTER 22

Aidan walked down the street from the café where he had left Jane and Gwyn. The traffic was heavy and the afternoon air smelled of car exhaust and hot tarmac, reinforcing his prejudice against the metropolis. The heat was bearable, he admitted, but he'd rather take fresh air on rainswept hills than this grimy city stink. Back home, the roadside verges were hip deep in grasses and bracken or awash with a foaming mass of cow parsley, studded here and there with the first bright pink bells of the early foxgloves. He and Sula would come back from their morning walk liberally covered in tiny white petals where they'd brushed against the dew-soaked foliage. Here, not even dandelions had managed to gain a foothold between the grey concrete paving slabs. Even the occasional plane tree, fenced in by protective iron railings – although for the life of him Aidan couldn't imagine what they were being protected from; he hadn't noticed herds of deer or sheep rampaging down the London streets – looked dusty and tired.

Still, the physical act of walking – even along a city street – helped to settle the churn of his thoughts. One step at a time, Jane had counselled on their way to the café, when he'd tried to revisit the subject of how they could handle the grieves without Eldritch's help, niggling at it like a man with toothache poking at a sore molar. He understood her logic, but it was only now he was doing something tangible that it felt bearable.

A gap opened up between the tall town houses with their elegant marble facades and a white and black sign announced that he had found Victoria Mews. Though the entrance was little wider than a car, once he had passed between those end houses the mews widened out. A row of trim brick houses lined either side. Not as grand as those on the main street, they were still three storeys high and with large windows, the ground-floor ones bordered by painted shutters and well-maintained window boxes.

In its way the mews reminded Aidan of some of the backstreets of Llancathan; the front doors opened directly onto a doorstep on the street with only a change in the pattern of the cobbles to denote what was footpath and what was road. Of course, here the cobbles were tightly laid granite sets, light grey for the three feet immediately in front of the houses and then a darker grey down the centre of the road, and the ornate planters outside each front door were genuine terracotta that could have been shipped back from the Cyclades, rather than plastic from the local hardware store. All the front doors were painted in deep reds, blues or greens – good, traditional colours for the front door of an Englishman's castle, with heavy brass knockers and letter boxes. But the window boxes and the planters were cheerful, and Aidan found himself admiring the neat yellow brick frontages as he walked down between them. The traffic noise didn't fully penetrate the mews and, while he was aware of it as a distant drone, Aidan felt able to tune it out. He could imagine children playing in the street and neighbours chatting. It was the sort of area he could picture holding a street party for the Queen's Diamond Jubilee, rather as they had in Llancathan, although he supposed there would be Pimm's and champagne here rather than cider and beer.

The houses had built-in garages but there was still a scattering of cars parked out on the street. Aidan couldn't see Eldritch's anywhere – he imagined the wizard would be a stickler for putting it in the garage – but, as he edged past a sleek two-seater sports car, he realised he had found the correct house. He looked up at the windows but there was no immediate sign of life. As he stood there a young woman came out of the adjacent house. She saw him and stopped in the doorway.

'Hello.' Aidan thought it best to be friendly.

Eldritch's neighbour made a vague noise that might have been a response. She closed her door and checked it was locked before she turned back to him. 'I hope you're going to paint those shutters,' she said by way of an introduction.

Aidan looked at her bemused. 'I'm sorry?'

'The shutters. I hope Helen and Eldritch are getting you to paint them. I wanted to tell them we've decided to enter for the borough's best-kept-street award. I know Eldritch has been away and Helen's only just come out of hospital and all, but it's things like that that will lose us points.'

Aidan looked at the offending shutters. It was true the paint on them was a little more faded than those on the neighbouring houses but there were no major signs of wear.

He turned back to Eldritch's neighbour. 'Um, I'm not here to do the decorating. I'm a friend of Eldritch's.'

'Really?' She looked him up and down and raised her eyebrows.

Aidan glanced down at his clothes. He was dressed casually but not that casually, surely.

'Oh.' The neighbour visibly adjusted her social scale. 'Sorry. My mistake.' She seemed inclined to be a little friendlier now she had established that he wasn't hired help. 'You look the type though, you know; young and fit.' She looked at him appraisingly again and smirked. Aidan hoped he wasn't blushing. 'Helen must have been spoiled for choice these past couple of days. Mind you, the bloke who's been working for them, he's nice looking but he's a bit intense. Fancies himself too. I've seen him giving me the eye when I've walked past.'

Aidan opened his mouth to respond, thought better of it, and shut it again without saying anything. He wasn't sure quite what to make of this deluge of information. Had Eldritch not returned Gwyn's calls because the phone was lost under a dust sheet? Or perhaps fear of predatory neighbours had made Helen wary of any female interest in her husband. Surely not.

'I'm Carol, by the way. You're not from round here, are you?'

'Not really. I'm from Wales.'

'Oh, lovely. I went to Cardiff once.'

Aidan decided against telling Carol-by-the-way that there was more to Wales than Cardiff and bit his tongue.

She went on regardless. 'I went to watch the rugby. I do love the Welsh accent.'

'Thanks.'

Whoever had said that Londoners kept themselves to themselves could never have encountered Carol.

'Are they in?' Aidan nodded towards Eldritch's front door.

Carol shrugged noncommittally. 'I haven't seen them today, but the decorator's been in and out a few times so one of them must be around.' She looked at the road and sniffed. 'At least he's moved that wretched van. I didn't like the way he kept parking it right up against my car. He was bound to scratch the paint, sooner or later. Anyway, I must be off, but remind them about the barbecue we're having for the nursery next weekend.'

'The nursery?' Aidan couldn't imagine a garden centre in the middle of London, let alone one that would host a barbecue.

'Kiddies' Corner. Down at St Martin's Churchyard.' Carol nodded her head to indicate the direction. 'We're raising funds for the refurbishment after the fire. We're still waiting on the building inspector to give the final damage report but it's going to cost thousands at the very least. Those bastards,' she muttered, glaring over Aidan's shoulder as though the vandals responsible for setting the fire were lined up behind him. Then she shrugged and gave him a tight-lipped smile. 'Never mind, we'll get the money raised to get it open again. The barbecue's going to be at the Methodist hall just round the corner from St Martin's. Here.' She slid her bag from her shoulder, unzipped it and produced a brightly coloured flyer which she thrust into his hand. 'There's a map on the back. I popped one of these through the letter box earlier in the week, but you can give them another one as a reminder. I know they don't have children but as a community we should be taking care of the next generation, so we need everyone to come along and help fundraise. It's important.'

She walked over to the driver's door of the sports car and opened it, leaning in to drop her bag onto the passenger seat, apparently dismissing him. Aidan stood where he was, rather bemused by such an abrupt end to a conversation, but then Carol straightened up and turned back to him.

'I'll call round over the weekend and invite them properly, make sure they're coming.' She gave him another blatantly appraising look and then raised a suggestive eyebrow. 'You could always come back for it. It will be fun.'

Before Aidan could decide on a suitable response she was in her car and pulling away. Feeling the need to catch his breath he watched as she navigated the tight entrance to the mews and then turned out into the traffic and was gone. With a small sigh Aidan stepped up to Eldritch's front door and rang the bell.

CHAPTER 23

Aidan's first impression was of casual, understated elegance. The blonde woman who opened the door was tall – close to Jane's height – and slender. She wore loose trousers the colour of duck eggs and a creamy-white sleeveless tunic that fell to mid-thigh. Heavy embroidery in a fractionally richer cream edged the low-cut keyhole neckline, emphasising the slender column of her throat and then drawing the eye down to the hint of softly shaded skin between her breasts. She looked cool and comfortable in the afternoon heat. With her bare feet showing off toenails painted in a pale blush and her fine blonde hair casually tousled, she might have stepped off the pages of a magazine, one of the articles on bohemian city chic that Jane enjoyed reading.

Helen tilted her head to one side and eyed him curiously. 'I'm sorry,' she said, her tone polite but subtly dismissive. 'Whatever it is you're canvassing for or selling, I'm not interested.' Her smile took the sting out of her words but didn't warm her eyes.

'What?' Aidan was nonplussed by her greeting. Then he understood. 'Oh, this? No, your neighbour gave it to me. Here.' He passed Carol's flyer to her. 'It's for a barbecue in support of the local kids' charity or something.'

'Really?' Helen glanced at the brightly coloured paper and then looked back at Aidan. 'Has Carol started to dragoon passers-by into handing out her flyers?' There was a subtle emphasis on the word passers-by and she looked pointedly at the walled-off end of the street. Aidan guessed that very few people came into the mews without a purpose. 'Or did you have another reason for calling?' Her dark blonde eyebrows raised like two well-groomed question marks. She looked at him expectantly, still maintaining that polite smile.

'Oh. Of course. Yes.' Aidan took a deep breath and started again. 'I've come to see Eldritch. Is he in?'

Helen's smile became apologetic. 'I'm sorry. He's out at the moment.'

'Oh.' Aidan tried to keep the relief from his face. Hopefully that meant that Eldritch was still a captive, and not a host. He mustered what he hoped was realistic disappointment. 'That's a shame.' He wondered if he should say more but reminded himself to stick with the plan. 'Can you tell him I called?'

'Of course I can.' There was a fraction of a pause and then Helen added, 'If you tell me who you are.' Somehow, she managed to combine charming and teasing in the one polite smile.

Despite himself, Aidan couldn't help but grin in response. 'I'm Aidan.'

A little furrow appeared between Helen's brows and then her polite expression was replaced by a broad smile. 'Aidan,' she exclaimed. 'How lovely. Marcus has mentioned you. What on earth are you doing here in London?'

Aidan offered up a silent prayer of thanks that he had prepared for this. He thought of the Welsh mountains and smiled. 'I'm down for the Rock and Snow Show at Earl's Court. I go most years.'

Don't babble, he told himself and refrained from giving her the rest of his story about checking out the competition in the adventure training market.

'We're quite a way from Earl's Court,' Helen noted.

'I know.' Aidan gave her a sheepish look, as though worried she would think him foolish. 'But everyone's been worried about Eldritch because he's not been in touch. Rowan's been on at Gwyn. Gwyn's been on at me.' He pulled a face as if to say, *What else could I do?* 'So, while I was going to be in London anyway, I thought I'd take a chance and call round.' He waited an instant and then dropped his gaze. 'You must be Helen,' he said, as shy as if he had just met a famous star in the supermarket.

'I am.' Helen's smile grew arch. 'Did he tell you about me?'

'A little.' Aidan nodded. 'But he only ever referred to you in the past tense. To be honest, we all thought you must have died before he came to Wales, that maybe you'd had cancer or something. It was pretty clear he didn't like talking about it, so no one pushed. We didn't realise you were in hospital.' He paused and smiled diffidently. 'I'm glad you're better.'

Helen laughed, a delightfully relaxed sound. 'So am I. Look, Aidan, he probably won't be long. Why don't you come in and wait for him?'

'Oh.' *Crap! Does that mean Terry's already taken him?* 'Well, I wouldn't like to impose,' Aidan said to cover his hesitation.

'Don't be silly. He'll be delighted to see you, especially after you've come all this way. Then you can put everyone's minds at rest when you go home.'

Aidan's own mind was racing. This sounded more and more as though Eldritch was already a host. He thought of

Gwyn's warning about not doing anything risky, but she had also said the grieves would have no reason to harm him if he did nothing to arouse their suspicions. He had to know about Eldritch. He couldn't walk away now, without finding out for sure.

Try to act normally, he told himself. But what was normal in a situation like this? Steeling himself, he conjured up a delighted smile. 'Well, if you're sure you don't mind.'

'Not at all, in fact I positively insist on it. Come inside.'

The hallway was high ceilinged and pleasantly cool after the sticky afternoon heat. Aidan looked around him, taking in the soft muted colours of the walls and the richly patterned rug decorating the wide oak floorboards. Framed black and white photos hung on the walls and a carved Asian goddess, one hand resting on the hood of a rearing cobra, gazed serenely at visitors from the top of a delicate table. At the far end of the hall an open wooden staircase ascended to the first floor.

He caught Helen watching him as he looked around.

'It's a beautiful house,' Aidan said truthfully.

'Thank you.' Helen gave a pleased smile. 'We like it.'

She trailed one elegantly manicured finger over the goddess's head as she glanced around as if seeing it afresh in the light of his reaction. 'I'll make us some coffee. Come through into the kitchen and you can tell me how you like it. Marcus always tells me I make it too strong. He says I'm trying to poison him.'

Without waiting for an answer, she turned and carried on down the hallway. Not sure what else to do, Aidan swallowed his sense of trepidation and followed her.

Helen led him to the back of the house where a large kitchen faced out over a terrace and a small walled garden. Oak floorboards gave way to limestone tiles and an expanse of pale wood cabinets and marble work surfaces. A central island was positioned to take advantage of the garden view and the light coming through a glazed panel in the roof. Aidan was impressed. No wonder Eldritch enjoyed cooking.

Helen flicked the switch on the kettle and then turned back towards him, spreading her arms out along one of the marble worktops. 'He does like to tease me.'

She leaned back and the swell of her breasts pressed obviously against the slubbed linen of her tunic.

Aidan felt his mouth go dry. Was she flirting with him? Everything Gwyn had said about grieves' appetites came flooding back into his mind. Maybe Eldritch hadn't been taken as a host. Maybe Helen was simply enjoying her husband and he was enjoying her. He felt a sudden apprehension that Eldritch – perfectly normal, untaken Eldritch – would come home to find his wife draping herself all over his friend. Dear God, he should have let Jane come to investigate. At least she wouldn't be subject to Helen's flirtatious advances. Then again, maybe she would; who knew what a grieve's appetites extended to? The image that flashed into his mind made his cheeks burn.

'Are you alright?' There was a huskiness to Helen's voice that he hadn't noticed before.

Aidan swallowed and wiped a hand over his face. 'Yes. Yes, of course. It's just the heat. We're not used to it in Wales.'

Helen nipped her lower lip between her teeth and studied him from under her lashes.

Aidan tried not to stare at her. Though she stood several feet away his skin tingled as though she was pressing herself against him.

'Hmm.' Slowly she lifted her head until she was looking at him directly. He was aware that her eyes were very blue.

'What are you used to?' She ran the tip of her tongue over her lips. The skin was flushed and pink where she had bitten it. 'In Wales.'

She straightened up from where she had been leaning against the counter. Aidan took an involuntary step backward. The sound of the front door opening made him jump.

'That will be him.' Helen smiled at him so innocently that, for a moment, Aidan could almost believe he had imagined her seductive posturing. 'We're in the kitchen, my love,' she called. 'Aidan's here.'

Thank God!

Aidan heard the urgent slap of footsteps on the oak boards of the hallway. His heart was pounding but, even if Eldritch proved to have been taken as a host, finding out had to be better than being seduced by his friend's wife. He turned towards the door, ready to greet the man who came through it, and a blast of energy hit him squarely between the shoulder blades.

The bolt drove the breath from his lungs and knocked him forwards, almost into the arms of the man who came through the door. It wasn't Eldritch. Aidan had just enough time to register that much before something solid connected with his temple. He fell sideways into one of the banks of cupboards, fumbled vaguely with the marble worktop as if trying to find his balance, then slid soundlessly to the floor. The world went dark around him.

CHAPTER 24

Terry stood just inside the kitchen doorway, the wooden statue of the snake goddess still held in his fist like an elaborately carved club. 'Who is he?'

His gaze flicked briefly over the unconscious man sprawled at his feet before returning to focus on Helen, who was leaning casually against the cupboards on the far side of the kitchen. For all that he had asked the question, Terry's tone suggested indifference towards both the man's identity and his fate.

'No one of any importance.' Languid and unhurried, Helen straightened, smoothing an invisible wrinkle from the hem of her tunic. She came over to join him, propping one elbow on the counter and resting her chin on her palm as she leaned over to contemplate the crumpled figure.

'His name is Aidan,' she said dismissively, straightening again. 'He's one of the wizard's friends.' One elegant shoulder rose in a half shrug to underline her lack of concern, but her voice hardened slightly as she added, 'But not one of mine.'

Terry's lip curled into a sneer at the distinction and Helen smiled indulgently at her mate. Unlike her, he had little interest in the shifting layers of human relationships, the subtle nuances that brought such pleasure and pain. He preferred to concentrate on those things that brought more immediate gratification. Such inclinations made him a passionate and inventive lover, Helen admitted with an inward smile. Still, violence suited him too, she thought. His previous host had been foppish and physically rather weak, relying on his status as a nobleman's son and the fear and deference that inspired to get whatever he wanted.

The young man he inhabited now, though, was very different. His was a body used to manual labour with lean, hard muscles to prove it. Helen looked him over approvingly. He had moved like a warrior to defend her, striking down their enemy before he had had a chance to react. Not that she had needed defending, of course. She felt a glow of pleasure in the capabilities of her own body. The magic came easily to her and she would have taken her visitor down without difficulty had she needed to. Still, the feeling of being protected, of being cherished by her mate, made her preen. She moved closer to him and ran a proprietary hand down his arm, enjoying the feel of corded muscle under her fingers. She liked it too when her mate was happy, and underneath the carefully cultivated disdain, she sensed the visceral pleasure he had felt when he had clubbed the other man to the floor.

As if feeling her approval, Terry drew himself up. He hefted the statue in his hand as if it were truly a weapon. 'Do you want me to kill him?'

He made the offer as casually as another man might have asked if she wished to go out for dinner.

Helen's smile broadened at the enthusiasm in his voice. 'No. At least, not yet.' She didn't dismiss the idea entirely. 'There are some things I want him to tell me.' She looked again at Aidan's still form and her smile grew sly and calculating. 'Besides, I think he might be useful to us.'

Terry's disgusted huff of breath said everything he needed to on that topic.

Helen blinked lazily at her mate, unfazed by his lack of belief. 'Watch and learn.'

She crouched down beside Aidan, studying him carefully for a few moments. There was a lump just above his temple and a little thread of blood ran from the split skin, but his breathing seemed regular and unlaboured. For all his enthusiasm, her mate hadn't inflicted too much damage when he had hit him.

Good.

Satisfied, she settled into a kneeling position at the crown of the unconscious man's head. 'Well now, little wizardling. Let me see what I can do with you.'

Slowly, almost tenderly, she slid her fingers through Aidan's hair, spreading her hands so that her fingers cradled the rounded bulb of the skull, while her thumbs rested over his temples. A little frown line dinted the skin between her brows as she concentrated, feeling for the energy points she required. This was something her host had been skilled at, although she had never used the technique for the purposes Helen was about to. More fool her; she and the wizard might have enjoyed all sorts of games if she had done so. Helen licked her lips. Well, she and her mate would enjoy them instead, maybe even with this youngster. Ah, now that would be interesting, but first she wanted to understand the real reason for his visit. Then there would be time for play. Subtly she adjusted the position of her fingers, extending little tendrils of power to brush the surface of the young man's aura as she did so.

'Ah, yes.'

She felt what she sought, there, beneath her fingertips. Satisfied, she glanced up at her mate. He was watching her closely, his expression a blend of impatience and suspicion. He was jealous, she thought, not just of her abilities, but also – and this was foolishness itself – of the young man whose head she was cradling, as if the careful way she held him was the result of a lover's tenderness, rather than the finesse required for a subtle power working. Helen's lips tightened briefly into a little pout of disappointment. His lack of awareness was regrettable, even if it was not entirely unexpected. From what she knew of the man who had become her mate's latest host, he had lacked the imagination to believe in magic. That, combined with her mate's cynicism when it came to a woman's ability to wield power of any sort – despite the fact that it had been the crone Melindra who had been responsible for their previous captivity – made him scornful. Still, she told herself, his attitude would change when he had power of his own. All this flashed through Helen's mind as she met Terry's belligerent scowl.

'Wait until you have taken the wizard,' she promised. 'Then you'll understand.'

Without waiting for a response, she turned her focus back to Aidan, pushing away all extraneous thoughts as she reached into her host's body for her power. She gave a little sigh of pleasure as it flowed through her, filling her like the warmth from a draught of mead. Her eyes slid closed and she sank her consciousness down into the fine webs of energy that made up the young man's shields.

Aidan surfaced slowly from the blackness. His head hurt. At first that was all he was aware of. Pain radiated out from his temple, washing through his skull like a dirty tide that surged and retreated in time with the beat of his pulse. It was hard to think through it, to think of anything beyond the nauseous certainty that any attempt at movement would make him vomit. The fear of how much that in turn would hurt was more than enough to keep him still while he tried to work out what had happened to him.

He was lying on his back on a hard, flat surface, that much he could tell, but he couldn't quite recall what he was doing there. Or where exactly 'there' was, for that matter. The lack of memory bothered him, but not sufficiently to make him want to risk moving. Instead, he made a concerted effort and opened his eyes.

The blonde wood cupboards and polished granite worktops towering above him blurred a little so that he had to concentrate to focus, but at least he could recognise them. He was still in Eldritch's kitchen … except he couldn't be. The units in Eldritch's kitchen were painted a soft sage green. He knew that; he had helped repaint them the weekend after the wizard had moved into the little house in Caeglas. But then, he wasn't in Caeglas, was he?

Oh God!

The full memory came back to him, settling into his consciousness once more like a stone sinking to the bottom of a muddy pond. Helen must have hit him with a Levin bolt. The soft sigh of his exhaled breath was like an admission of stupidity. He had been completely blindsided by her pretence of seduction.

You should have known better than to turn your back on her.

What an idiot. And then, just to make sure of him, whoever had come through the door – he presumed it must have been

Terry, he couldn't quite recall, although he knew it hadn't been Eldritch – had cracked him round the head with something solid, and everything had gone black.

Aidan felt the first prickle of unease as his brain worked its way through the obvious corollary to that sequence of events. He had been unconscious and completely at the mercy of the two grieves. He didn't know why they had chosen to attack him but the only reason he was alive now was because they wanted him that way. Somehow that wasn't a very comforting thought. Aidan knew he needed to get up and get away before they came back for him. Given how he was feeling, fighting his way out wasn't going to be an option, but neither was lying there waiting for the grieves to return. He would need to move quietly but he reckoned that once he was on his feet he would be able to—

A low, throaty laugh from somewhere just behind his head stopped his thoughts in their tracks.

Helen. Training took over then and, almost without conscious decision, Aidan went to roll towards her, betting his freedom on the fact that she wouldn't be expecting an attack. He might not be able to stand but he didn't need to to run a full-knuckle strike down the length of her shin. It wouldn't do much physical damage, but the pain alone would incapacitate her before she could think of using a Levin bolt on him.

As plans went, it was a good one. It might even have worked, but for one thing; his body didn't respond. For a split second he refused to believe it. He tried again, but it was as though his nerves had been cut. For all his effort, his limbs wouldn't move. Worse still, he realised he couldn't even turn his head to see where Helen stood.

No!

Cold shock lanced through him, the beginnings of panic curdling his gut as he realised he was paralysed. He wasn't numb – some hyper-rational part of him reminded him that he could still feel his body – but he was unable to make even the smallest movement of his limbs or head. Desperation drove him to keep trying but, though he strained until the blood pounded in his ears and sweat stood out on his skin, whatever spell Helen had laid on him was too strong to break. His flesh might have been fused to the floor for all the good it did him. Defeated, he stopped and lay there, panting.

'Good. There's no point trying to fight it.'

Helen's face appeared in Aidan's field of view, radiant and beautiful as before as she bent over him. 'You can't move.' Her eyes sparkled with amusement, as though every one of his failed attempts to do so had been visible to her, a sideshow laid on for her personal delight. She leaned closer, fixing him with her cornflower gaze, and added in a conspiratorial whisper, 'Not unless I tell you to.'

Her smile as she straightened up was vulpine and utterly devoid of pity. She tapped her bottom lip with one manicured finger as though considering something, the shaped oval of her nail resting like a pale shell against the deeper rose of her mouth, effortlessly seductive. 'I think it's time you got up now.'

And somehow Aidan found himself on his feet. His headache blossomed anew and his vision blurred so that Helen seemed to sway backwards and forwards towards him, like a mermaid caught in some unseen current, but despite the roiling vertigo that threatened to overtake him Aidan was aware that he was standing perfectly still.

Helen moved closer until she was only inches away from him. He could smell the light scent of her perfume and beneath it, the warmer musk of her skin. It seemed like a lifetime ago that he had been scared she was trying to seduce him. Now he felt genuine fear for whatever she was going to do. He felt the panicky skitter of his pulse and he wondered if she could sense it or if she was aware of the cold sweat prickling out on his body. He hoped she couldn't see his fear in his eyes.

'Now, little wizardling.' Helen's voice was as light and pleasant as it had been when they had stood and talked on her doorstep, but Aidan's stomach twisted at her casual use of that epithet. If she knew that about him, how much else did she know? 'Why are you here?'

Go to hell. I'm not telling you anything.

But, to his horror, he heard himself say, 'To see Eldritch.'

Helen's lips pursed as she considered this answer. 'Really.'

One finely shaped brow lifted and she studied his face dispassionately. Then she walked around him, her head tilted to one side as though she was judging something about him. Aidan didn't know what it was and that lack of knowledge unnerved him. Unable to turn his head to watch her, all he could do was follow her with his eyes to the edge of his field of vision, then turn his eyes quickly in the hope of catching her coming up on his other side.

Finishing her circuit, Helen stopped in front of him. The fact that she hadn't so much as laid a finger on him did nothing to ease Aidan's fear, nor did the way she eyed him for a few seconds, the slightest of smiles lifting the corners of her lips.

He felt like a mouse being toyed with by a beautiful pedigree cat. Helen dipped her head and looked at him teasingly from under her eyelashes.

'And why would that be?'

No! Stop it! Don't say anything else.

Aidan fought to clench his lips shut, to lock the words in his throat, but to no avail. 'To find out if you'd taken him as a host.'

Helen's elegant eyebrows lifted again, but this time in genuine surprise. 'You know about us?'

'Yes.'

'How?'

That was a man's voice. Aidan assumed it was Terry, although he couldn't turn his head to find out. Strangely, he didn't feel the same compulsion to answer him, so he stayed silent. It was a small victory, but he would take what he could.

'I said, how?'

It was Terry. Aidan recognised the handyman from the video as he stepped in front of him. He saw the flash of anger on the other man's face at the realisation that he wasn't going to respond and wondered just how much his defiance was going to cost him. Inwardly he steeled himself, but Helen put her hand out as Terry moved towards him, the promise of violence clear in his eyes.

'It doesn't matter.'

Her tone was soothing but Aidan thought he saw amusement at her partner's discomfiture in the brief curl of her lips. Amusement and a certain amount of condescension. He filed that knowledge away, hoping he might find some way to use it, as she turned back to him.

'Who knows you are here?'

It would have been better if she had let Terry beat him. Desperately Aidan tried to wipe his mind clean, to fill it with thoughts of an empty hotel room rather than answer that particular question.

No one, no one, no one.

He shouted the words in his head to the hammer beat of his pulse. He pictured himself as he had been earlier, walking down the street on his own, the afternoon heat bouncing back from the pavement and the tall, slab-sided buildings, the sunlight bright and crystal sharp on the paintwork of the passing cars. The litany echoed with the remembered slap of his feet on the paving slabs.

No one.

He could all but feel his mouth shaping the words, but as he did he sensed the grip of Helen's power tightening around him in spite of everything he tried to do to the contrary. He thought his heart would burst with the desperate struggle not to speak the words he knew were coming.

'Gwyn.' And as he choked out her name he wished that it would. 'And … Jane.'

Helen studied him, her cornflower blue eyes thoughtful. 'Gwyn.' She rolled the name on her tongue, weighing it, considering it. Then she turned to Terry. 'The Welsh witch. She is the one who has been phoning. Jane is this one's girlfriend,' she added with a slight nod towards Aidan. 'She is of no concern to us, but the witch …' Her lips tightened briefly, but then she gave a negligent shrug, dismissing the problem. 'Well, I have a way to deal with her.'

Once more she turned back to Aidan and he felt his heart clench with fear at what she would ask him next, but the grieve merely studied him for a moment.

'So, you've come to see my husband, to find out what has happened to him.' Helen seemed to think this through. She nodded thoughtfully as if passing some unknown judgement, and then smiled her radiant, predatory smile. 'Would you like to see him?'

She sounded like a witch offering gingerbread to a child she had found in the woods.

To Aidan's surprise, this time he felt no compulsion to answer. The question was all but rhetorical but he answered anyway. 'Yes.'

'What are you doing?' Terry's voice was an angry snarl. He caught Helen's arm and pulled her towards him. Her hand came up, her fingers splayed, and Aidan saw the faintest nimbus of Levin fire shimmer round them. But she did not strike out. Nor did she deign to struggle out of Terry's grip.

'Letting this youngling see his friend,' she said, as though explaining the situation to a backward child. 'There is no harm in it. Besides, it will do my husband good to learn that no one is going to rescue him. When he truly understands that he may break more easily.'

Whether or not this was true, Terry was unswayed by the argument.

'And what of this one?' He gestured angrily at Aidan who stood frozen, wondering what might happen to him if the two grieves fought. 'What if he breaks your control, eh? What then?'

'He can't.' Helen sounded supremely self-confident, as well she might, Aidan reflected bitterly, given that he had been able to do nothing against her compulsion so far. 'His powers aren't strong enough and, even if they were, he doesn't have the knowledge.' Her tone was icily regal. She shook her head dismissively, but Terry scowled, unconvinced. In a sudden, quicksilver shift Helen smiled coquettishly. 'But if he does, you can kill him.'

The promise did little to appease Terry but Helen's chin lifted. 'Enough. He is under my control. I will show you.'

She turned, twisting her arm free from Terry's grip with a practised shrug. She went to one of the drawers and when she turned back she held the slender curve of a boning knife in her hand. Aidan watched the silver glint of the blade warily, wondering just what proof she was about to offer. He had an awful fear that she could make him stand still while she carved the flesh in dripping slices from his bones. For a moment, he wondered if she would let him scream while she did so. But Helen didn't so much as look at him as she walked past.

'Come.' She gestured imperiously. 'Both of you.'

Drop dead, thought Aidan, his mind torn between shaky relief and panicky fear for whatever else she intended. But his body followed her into the hall and up the stairs.

CHAPTER 25

The first-floor bedroom was stiflingly hot after the cool of the downstairs rooms, the air thick with the smell of sweat and a rank muskiness that raised the hackles on the back of Aidan's neck. The curtains were three-quarters drawn so that only a thin bar of sunlight fell over the queen-sized bed that took up most of the floor space. Fitted wardrobes lined the farthest wall, the elegance of their sleek, minimalist lines casually negated by the discarded clothes piled in one corner. A long cherry wood dressing table filled the space beneath the window, its lacquered top empty save for a teacup sitting in splendid isolation at one end. As in the hallway the flooring was bare oak, softened beside the bed by an intricately patterned rug in shades of ruby and midnight, emerald, ochre and sand. The pattern was called Tree of Life; Aidan knew because Eldritch had told him. He had seen the rug's twin in the lounge of the wizard's rented cottage. It covered a worn patch on the otherwise serviceable, if dull, oatmeal carpet, filling the space between the settee and armchair and the small wood burner that nestled in the hearth. Usually Gwyn claimed it, sitting cross-legged by the fire like a displaced Arabian sorceress poised to utter the magic spell that would heave the carpet into life and allow her to fly away across the desert, her midnight hair billowing out behind her in the wind. He and Jane generally opted for the settee, leaving Eldritch – for all that it was his home – to settle for the armchair.

All this Aidan noted with a kind of detached awareness, for the focus of his attention was the bed and the man stretched out upon it, still alive despite all fears to the contrary. Or at least, he told himself, Eldritch must be alive because – surely – no one would have bothered to tie the wrists and ankles of a corpse to the fancy scrollwork of the bed frame. Nor would they gag one. The possible implications of that twisted strip of blue silk made Aidan go cold.

Dear God, what have they been doing to you?

As if she heard his thought, Helen turned and put a hand on Aidan's cheek.

'Feel free to take a look, my pet.'

Her soft murmur held the tones of a mother revealing a longed-for toy to a child. She smiled knowingly at him as she stepped aside, but it was her will that moved his body closer to the bed and then forced him to stand there, motionless, staring at his captive friend.

On the plus side, Eldritch was definitely alive. Aidan could see the steady rise and fall of his chest; a little slow – he counted the respirations, judging them against his own – but reassuringly unlaboured. Set against that reassurance was Eldritch's overall appearance. He looked, if not quite like the corpse that Aidan had feared he was about to see, like a man who had been ill for some time. His skin, while normally pale, was an ashy grey, a fact only emphasised by the darkness of several days' stubble shadowing his cheeks and jaw. The flesh under his closed eyes was bruised and sunken, making the high cheekbones and beaky nose seem more prominent than ever, while pointy with sweat, his dark hair clung in tendrils around his face and spread in damp rat tails across the pillow wedged underneath his head.

Had he been able to, Aidan would have turned away. What relief he had felt was turning rapidly to embarrassment, knowing Eldritch would be mortified to be seen like this, stretched as if crucified across the stained and crumpled sheet, his body exposed and vulnerable. Aidan's own sense of failure at being unable to help only made his embarrassment worse. But he couldn't move. Held in place, subject to Helen's whim, he made himself take it all in.

You need to know if he's hurt for when you get him out of here, he told himself, refusing to contemplate the fact that he couldn't see a way out of this for either of them.

Yet, beyond the raw and swollen abrasions that marked his wrists and ankles, mute testament to the wizard's stubborn – and futile – attempts to free himself, Eldritch's body bore no obvious signs of injury. The wizard kept himself in good shape. He swam regularly, first thing in the mornings, as soon as the Llancathan swimming pool opened. He said it was because he preferred to swim when the pool was quiet, but Aidan knew it was also because there would be fewer people around at that time to see the scars that patterned Eldritch's chest and shoulders. Not that anyone was likely to comment, although the senior partner at Llancathan's veterinary practice had once asked Aidan if he knew what sort of animal had caused those semicircular marks. She had claimed it was professional curiosity that had driven her enquiry. Aidan had responded with a story about Eldritch's boyhood encounter with a giant squid, which had caused raised eyebrows and a lot of laughter, after which Jules McFaddon had looked thoughtful and asked if he knew if Eldritch was dating. 'It would be a shame for a body like that to go to waste.'

But, in his own quiet way, Eldritch had politely sidestepped all offers of romantic – or purely physical – involvement. It hadn't stopped people trying; Rowan, in particular, had taken Eldritch's chastity as a personal challenge, but Eldritch had stayed faithful to a woman he had thought was as good as dead. And this was where it had got him.

Damn you! Hot anger surged through Aidan as Helen brushed past him to lean over the bed, bending close to her husband's body.

'Now, now, don't be shy, my love.' Her voice was husky and sweet as though the man she addressed was still her lover rather than her captive. 'I know you're not asleep.'

As if to prove the point she dug him sharply in the ribs with her knuckles. Eldritch flinched involuntarily, but he didn't open his eyes.

'One of your friends has come to see you,' Helen murmured enticingly. 'Don't you want to see who it is?'

Almost grudgingly, Eldritch's eyes opened. His pupils were huge and dilated leaving only a thin band of iris visible, like two silver-grey moons in eclipse. He moved his head slightly on the pillow, blinking up at Helen as he tried to focus. Then his eyes widened and Aidan saw recognition and then shock flit across his face as he realised who was standing behind her. The sinews of his neck stood out as Eldritch strained to raise his head from the pillow, twisting so he could get a better look. There was fear in his eyes, but Aidan didn't think the wizard was frightened for himself. He was frightened for him.

'Don't you have anything to say to your friend, my love?'

Eldritch was trying to speak around the gag, but all he

managed was to bare his teeth, his eyes going wide and furious. Frustration showed in every line of his body.

Watching all this, Helen laughed delightedly. 'Oh, of course. Let me help you.'

She knelt on the bed beside Eldritch, pushing his head none too gently back onto the pillow. Deftly her long fingers dealt with the knot securing the gag. She pulled the crusted fabric from between his lips and dropped it on the sheet beside his head.

'Aid …' The wizard struggled to speak. His lips were dry and cracked and the corners of his mouth were bruised and swollen from the gag. He stopped and swallowed convulsively, his jaw working as he tried to bring saliva to his mouth.

Don't, Aidan wanted to tell him. *There's no need to. Don't hurt yourself,* but he couldn't say a word.

'Aidan?' The name came out as a barely audible rasp. Eldritch swallowed again, his head shifting restlessly on the thin pillow. His voice was a little clearer as he asked, 'Are you okay?'

You idiot. You're the one we're all worried about.

Aidan felt a surge of affection for his friend followed by a wash of bitterness that he had no way of communicating with him.

'Aidan?'

The confusion in the wizard's voice was coupled with a wariness that had come into his expression. The grey eyes stared at him for a moment but when it became clear that Aidan would not – or could not – respond, Eldritch turned his head to look at Helen.

'What have you done to him?' he demanded.

Helen lowered her eyes demurely, the action at odds with the secretive smile teasing the corners of her mouth. The bed frame rattled as Eldritch jerked against the ties that held him as though he had tried to lunge at her, forgetting for a moment that he was restrained.

'What?' he repeated. He didn't struggle again but nor did he relax.

Helen laughed. 'Nothing permanent.' She sat back on her heels and regarded her husband for a moment with her dark cornflower eyes. Her lips parted seductively and she nipped the tip of her tongue between her teeth. 'Not yet anyway. Why, what are you frightened I might do to him?'

'You're not a blood mage, Helen.'

Eldritch's answer made no sense to Aidan, but it seemed to strike a nerve with the grieve.

Helen looked at him, the seductive teasing replaced by something colder and more clinical. 'But I'm not Helen, am I?' There was defiance and arrogance in the tilt of her head and the way her chin lifted. 'I am far more than she was.'

'Aidan!' Eldritch's head whipped round towards him, the grey eyes focused and determined. 'Think of the sigils Roc and Sho and—'

Fast as a striking snake Helen backhanded Eldritch across the jaw and Aidan felt the slap of power backing up the blow. Eldritch's head snapped sideways.

'That's not polite.'

Before Eldritch could gather himself, Terry was on him from the other side, stuffing the gag back between his teeth. Dazed and bound, Eldritch had no chance of resisting him. He tried but his struggle was short-lived. Watching helplessly

Aidan saw fresh blood staining the edges of the gag as Terry tightened it cruelly.

His mind was in turmoil, trying to make sense of what Eldritch had tried to tell him. He knew the two sigils Eldritch had named, the glyphs for safety and protection, remembered the hours Gwyn had had him tracing the sweeping curves of the former, the strange spiky angles of the latter, learning their shapes by heart, but he couldn't imagine how that knowledge would help him now.

Raised voices brought him back to the present.

'I told you this was a bad—'

'Enough!'

Helen was off the bed and facing down the handyman and, though he topped her by several inches, it was Terry who backed down from the confrontation.

'He was going to tell him how to break your spell.' Terry's voice was sulky but he didn't meet Helen's eyes. He shot Eldritch a look of pure hatred.

'But he wasn't able to, was he? The boy doesn't know enough to protect himself.' Helen turned from Terry to address Eldritch, her voice becoming mocking. 'You and your Welsh witch haven't taught him that, have you?' She seized Eldritch by the jaw, forcing him to look at her. 'This isn't blood magic, not yet. I will use that on him, yes, but for now I think you need to learn just how well I can control him without it.'

She dropped her hand, releasing Eldritch's jaw as though he was no longer of interest to her. 'All of you need to learn,' she said, giving Terry a coldly contemptuous look.

Aidan tried to watch where she went but she passed out of his field of vision. He felt his heart hammering as he waited for her to reappear. He wondered if Terry had the imagination to feel apprehensive too. Then Helen was standing beside him and he saw with a flash of terror that she held the boning knife in her hand again.

'I think it's time for that demonstration now.'

CHAPTER 26

'Hold out your right hand.'

Helen's voice was calm again but all pretence of softness had gone from her eyes. Unable to do anything else, Aidan obeyed. He felt sweat sliding down his body as he tried not to imagine what she was about to do to him. A hand was a complex marvel of nerves and muscles and sinews – and a source of unspeakable pain if you slowly picked one apart with a knife. Had he been able to, he would have shut his eyes; instead, he wondered again if Helen would let him scream. He tried to prepare himself, tried to will himself to be brave. His certainty of what the grieve was about to do was so strong that it took him a moment to realise what was happening when Helen put the handle of the knife against his palm and wrapped his fingers round it. Confused, he could only look at her, wondering what she intended.

Helen gazed at him coldly and then moved once more to stand at the head of the bed.

'You see my husband?' She gestured at Eldritch.

'Yes.' Aidan heard his response, flat and devoid of emotion, with a sense of disbelief. How could the racing of his heart, the sudden flare of panicky realisation not spill over into his voice? This was worse – far worse – than enduring torture himself, for he had a horrible inkling of what Helen was about to do.

'Cut out his left eye.'

An inarticulate whimper tried to force its way from Aidan's throat. He felt the grip of Helen's control tighten around him.

From the far side of the bed he heard Terry's shocked exclamation. 'No! What do you think you're doing?'

'You don't trust me that this child is under my control? Well, now we'll see, won't we? Go on.' This latter comment was addressed to Aidan. With every ounce of strength he could muster Aidan tried to open his fingers and drop the knife. But his hand continued to hold it securely. In utter horror he felt his body turn and take a step forward, and then another, bringing him level with Eldritch's head. He turned once more towards the bed, leaning forward to look down at Eldritch. Though tension tightened the wizard's muscles like wire he wasn't struggling against his restraints. He stared back at Aidan, his eyes fiercely determined, as though willpower could help him get his message past the gag that rendered his words unintelligible. Sweat beaded Eldritch's forehead. Aidan saw the oily gleam of it as he leaned forward, the knife in his hand moving inexorably towards the wizard's cheek. He felt sweat sliding down his own face, stinging his eyes.

'Slowly, my pet.'

Vaguely, Aidan was aware that Terry was shouting at Helen. The blood thundered in his ears. He tried to stop himself reaching out with his left hand, catching hold of Eldritch's head, holding the wizard still. Now his friend's body bucked as he fought, twisting helplessly against the restraints and against Aidan's relentless grip. Aidan felt sweat-slicked skin slide under his hand and his fingers tightened, digging into those high cheekbones, compressing the nose as he gripped harder. He heard the frantic gasp of Eldritch's breath, felt the damp warmth of it against his palm as he leaned his weight down. Now he could see the fear in Eldritch's eyes.

OhGod!OhGod!OhGod!

He laid the curved steel against Eldritch's cheek, the point under his eye, feeling for the edge of the socket. In utter desperation, he tried to close his eyes but found he was unable to do even that. Under the point of the blade, the first drop of blood welled up like a cabochon ruby.

'No!' Terry howled and threw himself at Helen.

She gestured and he slammed back against the dressing table. Aidan felt the knife dig in a little deeper as he leaned more pressure onto the wizard to hold him still, heard the sharp hitch in Eldritch's breath and felt the choking scream of horror building silently in his own throat. Eldritch's body was locked rigid now, his chest and torso arching off the bed as Aidan pressed his head down into the pillow. His own breath was coming in short, panting sobs as he fought as desperately as the wizard not to do this and felt Helen's will bind tighter and tighter around him.

'Stop!'

Aidan's muscles locked solid. Then, without his conscious volition, the hand holding the knife pulled back and he let go of the wizard's face. He was vaguely aware that Eldritch's body had gone limp and he wondered if the wizard had fainted. God knew, he thought he might do so himself. The world greyed out around the edges but still he stood there, the knife frozen only inches from Eldritch's face. He watched the blood bead up and spread in a little trickle along the edge of Eldritch's eye socket, shockingly bright against the charcoal-tinged flesh.

'Never, ever doubt me again.'

CHAPTER 27

'We must change our plans.'

His mind still reeling from what Helen had forced him to do, Aidan tried to collect his wits and concentrate on what he was hearing. The voice seemed to come from a long way away although he knew the two grieves were standing just behind him.

'Why?' Terry sounded subdued, not challenging Helen this time, but seeking information. 'The boy is under your control. You have proved that.' There was grudging admiration in his voice.

'He is not the one I am concerned about. It is the woman, Gwyn. I do not know how she has found out about us, but she has. When her little wizardling fails to return, she will come herself.'

'What of it?' Aidan could not see the two grieves but he could picture the dismissive shrug that accompanied the handyman's words. 'She is just a woman.'

'I am just a woman, my mate. You have seen it does not do to underestimate me.'

There was just a hint of reprimand in Helen's tone but, having made her point, she did not press it. She continued more thoughtfully, 'My husband said she was strong.'

'You overcame the boy.'

'He was just a scout.'

Perhaps Terry pulled a face because Helen added, 'Would you send your best soldier in first? He was here to reconnoitre. When he does not return, she will know something is wrong. Then she will come to find him.'

'And you will kill her.' Certainty and relish informed Terry's voice.

Helen laughed, a cold sound without any humour. 'Perhaps I could, but why should I? I have a better idea. We will take the wizard to another place, somewhere we will not be interrupted while we finish breaking him. If this Welsh witch does come here to seek him, she will get an unpleasant surprise.'

Aidan's stomach twisted with apprehension. He supposed he should feel relieved that Helen didn't feel the need to try to kill Gwyn but instead he was terrified that whatever the grieve considered to be an unpleasant surprise might prove an even greater threat. Uneasily he recalled Jane's parting comment as he had left the two women at the café, reminding him that she and Gwyn would come and get him if they hadn't heard from him after an hour. She had said it lightly, her tone half-joking, as Gwyn had turned to look at the selection of home-made cakes displayed in the glass-fronted case, but he knew she had been deadly serious.

Dear God, how long was I out for?

He had felt the phone in his pocket vibrate as Helen had led him up the stairs to the bedroom. It wasn't too great a leap to think that that had been a text from Jane asking if all was well. Did that mean his hour was up? If it was, would she give him any leeway and wait to see if he responded or were she and Gwyn already on their way here? Surely, if they were, they would consider the possibility that they could be walking into a trap. Wouldn't they?

Please, Jay, stay out of this. Don't put yourself in danger trying to help me and Eldritch.

If Aidan had had any means of sending that message, he would have done. Though he suspected there was no way that he and the wizard could get out of this on their own, he didn't see what Jane and Gwyn could possibly do to help. Gwyn had been blunt about the limits of her ability to tackle the grieves. Now he had first-hand experience of what Helen was capable of, Aidan could only hope that his mentor didn't try. She might withstand an initial exchange of Levin bolts, but he couldn't imagine her beating the grieve. As for Jane, she would be just so much dog food. With only a non-magical level of shielding she wouldn't stand a chance. No, it would be better if they stayed away. Fear clutched at him at the thought of what was likely to happen to him and Eldritch, but if they were as good as dead anyway he didn't want to take Jane or Gwyn with him. Looking down at the unmoving form of the wizard on the bed he was certain Eldritch would prefer it that way too.

'Come here, little wizardling.'

Unable to do anything else, Aidan turned away from the bed and went to where Helen stood by the dressing table. He was conscious of the knife still in his hand but didn't fool himself that he was capable of doing anything with it, other than what she would tell him to. The thought of what that might be made his breathing go shallow and his pulse surge as the involuntary spike of adrenalin flooded his system. Had he been capable, he would have flinched when she reached out towards him, but all she did was take the knife from his unresisting fingers and place it on the polished wood top of the dressing table. For several moments she studied him, her head on one side in a way that reminded him painfully of Gwyn. Then she reached up and, to his intense surprise, gently placed her hand over his temple where Terry had hit him, cupping his cheek as tenderly as a lover. He felt a surge of warmth that seemed to melt into the bones of his skull and the pain he had felt since waking slid away as though it had never been.

Maybe his confused gratitude at this small act of kindness showed somewhere in the depths of his eyes, or perhaps the sorceress simply understood how he must be feeling, for Helen said evenly, 'Don't thank me, little wizardling. One doesn't set a half-crippled dog to guard one's house.'

She lowered her hand.

'My husband spoke of blood mages.' Helen shot a glance at the still figure on the bed and her lips lifted in a brief half smile. It was the expression of someone amused by the antics of a child. She turned back to Aidan, studying his face. 'Yet you have no idea what one is, do you?'

Her tone was gentle, almost reassuring. She studied him for a moment longer and then shook her head in wonderment as if answering her own question. Her eyes locked with his. 'Oh, but you are going to learn.'

The eruption of sound from the bed was as shocking as it was unexpected. Aidan would have sworn that Eldritch was unconscious, yet Helen's words provoked a startling reaction from the captive wizard. Eldritch jerked against the ropes tying him to the bed, frantically pulling against them as he sought to free himself. Muffled behind the gag, his words were reduced to an incomprehensible agony of sound, but still he continued, the painful, guttural noises a hoarse counterpoint to the metallic squeal and creak of the bed frame as it rocked with the violence of his struggle.

Locked in his unresponsive body, Aidan could only listen in horror, shaken by the ferocity of his friend's response and the realisation of what it must mean. Whatever Helen was about to do was anathema to the wizard. The knowledge terrified him and yet he was as helpless as Eldritch to prevent it.

'Silence him.' Helen's command was a sharp slap across the noise of Eldritch's protest.

From the corner of his eye, Aidan saw Terry swagger towards the bed. Aidan flinched inwardly as he heard the smack of a fist impacting against flesh and the resulting silence as Eldritch stopped struggling. A moment later the unmistakeable sound of a second blow landing left him feeling almost physically sick.

You bastard!

Aidan swallowed down the sourness of bile and promised himself he would make Terry regret his casual brutality. He was aware that his chances of doing so were remote, but the alternative was to meekly accept what had just happened and he couldn't do that.

Helen flicked the briefest of glances towards the bed. 'I hope you've not damaged him too much.'

'You told me to shut him up.' Aidan couldn't see Terry's face but he could picture the sullen sneer. 'What do you think? Anyway, you're the one who claims to be a healer.'

Helen's nostrils flared and she gave a dismissive snort. She eyed Aidan as though she could read his disgust, even in his expressionless face.

After a moment she leaned her head close to his. 'Don't fret, little wizardling. You can be sure I'll take care of him.'

From her tone, Aidan couldn't tell whether she meant Terry or Eldritch.

Putting her hand to his cheek like a lover about to share a secret, she murmured, 'You don't have to worry your pretty head about it.' She leaned closer still and he felt the warmth of her lips brush his cheek. She dipped her head and whispered in his ear, 'Very soon you won't be able to worry about anything at all.'

She straightened then, pulling back from him. Almost casually she reached for the knife on the dressing table.

Oh God!

Aidan felt his heart lurch wildly as adrenalin scalded his blood.

'Look at the blade.' Helen's voice was soft and seductive. 'Concentrate on my voice.'

He fought to do neither, but he found he couldn't tear his eyes away from the wicked curve of steel. Helen's words wormed into his brain past the wall of silent curses he threw up to stop her.

She smiled at him then, her eyes heavy lidded, her lips softly parted as though she were about to partake in some exquisite pleasure. Slowly she raised the hand holding the knife. Her eyes locked on his over the blade.

This is it.

Aidan tried to steel himself for whatever Helen was about to do to him. Cold sweat prickled between his shoulder blades and slid down his back. He thought his heart might burst as she leaned closer to him. He felt his heart might stop when she drew the blade over her own flesh.

With no discernible change of expression Helen dropped the knife back onto the dressing table while Aidan stared in appalled fascination at the blood spreading across her left palm. He didn't know what to make of this unexpected development. Partly he was relieved that Helen had put the knife down without using it on him or – worse still – compelling him to use it, but he was equally certain that nothing good was going to come from what she had just done. Held motionless by her will, he could do nothing but wait for her to reveal what that might be.

He didn't have to wait long.

Still smiling, Helen ran the tip of her index finger along the cut, picking up a smear of blood. 'Hold out your hand.'

Unable to do anything else, Aidan did as he was told. Helen took his hand in hers, tilting it towards her like a fortune teller examining the lines of his life. She studied it for a moment and then pressed her bloodied finger to his skin, leaving a neat carmine fingerprint in the centre of his palm.

Aidan looked at the mark in confusion. He had expected pain or searing heat; something that would reflect the violence of Eldritch's reaction to the prospect of Helen using blood magic. But what he felt was nothing. He risked a glance at Helen's face, almost daring to hope that things weren't working as she had planned but, if that was true, there was no indication in her expression. A faint line of concentration marked the skin between her brows and her eyes had grown distant, as though she was focusing internally, but she showed no sign of frustration at her plans being thwarted. With a frisson of fear, Aidan recognised that faraway look as the same one that Gwyn or Eldritch had at the start of a power working. Helen was merely drawing on her power. Whatever she intended for him wasn't finished; it had barely begun.

Even as he realised it, Helen took his hand again, brushing her fingers over his skin as though she was tracing some strange design of barbed spikes and angles upon his flesh. The lines radiated out from that bloody fingerprint, stretching in a web to the base of each finger and back towards his wrist. Where her fingers touched his skin, Aidan fancied he could feel a slight scratching as though she traced the design with her fingernails and not the pads of her fingers. Following that odd, chitinous sensation was a sense of chill that sank into his flesh, lingering after her fingers had passed.

The design was complex but finally Helen's fingers stilled. She held her hand outstretched over his palm and closed her eyes, exhaling a slow, even breath as she did so, and for a heartbeat Aidan thought he could see the sigil she had drawn, showing clear and solid on his skin as though Helen had laid it out in lines of silver and rust. It lay there on his upturned palm and then, even as he watched it, the glyph disappeared.

Yet it wasn't as though it had simply vanished. Rather it was as though his flesh had turned liquid beneath it and it had sunk down through skin and tendon and bone until it lodged in the centre of his hand, tangible and weighty, his flesh reforming and solidifying around it. Aidan would have dismissed the idea as fanciful but, with a growing sense of horror, he realised he could feel the shape of the sigil within his flesh. It lay there like some queer, alien spider, its body wrought of frost and lead, its outstretched legs a mass of barbs and hooks and spikes, tangling amongst his bones. The idea turned him queasy with shock. He stared at his hand, searching for some evidence of what Helen had done, but there was nothing to be seen except for that bloody fingerprint. But there was no denying the presence of that foreign body lying within his flesh.

'Give me your other hand.'

A silent whimper of fear clogged Aidan's throat at Helen's command. He tried desperately to resist, fighting as hard as he had when she had ordered him to cut out Eldritch's eye, but to no avail. Though he struggled to lock his muscles rigid, feeling as though the tension in his body would tear tendon from bone, he could not stop his arm lifting, his hand turning palm up in front of Helen as though offering itself up for her touch.

His breath ragged, his heart pounding, Aidan watched as Helen dabbed a little more blood up from her own palm. Then, regal as a queen bestowing a gift, she pressed her bloodied finger into his skin. Had he been able to he would have cried out, for this time he felt the glyph building under her fingers, the icy chill starting even before she held her hand over the completed symbol to imbue it with her energy and life force. It was terrifying, knowing what was coming and yet being utterly helpless to prevent it. A small, hyper-rational part of his mind told him to focus on the shape of the sigil – it was like none of the glyphs Gwyn had had him memorise – as if by doing so he could work out its name or deduce what properties it drew to it, but mostly Aidan was too terrified to care. He only knew that whatever attributes Helen was weaving into those savage spiky angles and inward-hooking curves they were deadly to him. Then Helen's hand shifted and he felt her release that second shape into his flesh and all such thoughts vanished in a wave of heart-stopping fear.

No!No!No!No!No!

Never before had Aidan experienced anything so hideous as this studied violation. His universe shrank down to the feel of Helen's fingers gliding over his skin and a hyperawareness of those foreign shapes lurking where she had placed them in his flesh. He thought he might pass out when he felt her draw a third sigil on his forehead. He wished he could die when she lifted his polo shirt and drew another over his heart. And each time the sensation of the slow, inexorable invasion of his flesh that followed was beyond torture.

'You belong to me now, little wizardling.'

Helen's voice seemed to come to Aidan from the far shores of nightmare, at once impossibly distant and yet somehow there within the very bones of his skull.

'Head, heart and hands.'

No … he tried to shape the response in his mind but even thinking of resistance was incredibly hard. His body felt drained, his spirit dazed and drifting. *Never.*

He wasn't sure if he was still conscious or had passed into delirium.

Dimly he was aware of someone leaning close, of hands clasping his temples. He breathed in and his nostrils filled with the complex notes of Helen's perfume. He breathed out and felt the slippery slick of sweat on his skin as she pressed her forehead against his. As his vision cleared there was nothing to be seen beyond the deep forget-me-not blue of her eyes.

For a seemingly endless moment he gazed into them, feeling as though he lay in the eye of a storm, his mind and body wrung out and exhausted, no strength left to fight, no capacity left to resist. If he chose not to think, just allowed himself to surrender to that sense of the inevitable, it was almost peaceful.

Helen's voice, when she spoke again, was the singsong melody of a lullaby, a mother crooning to a restless child, a woman singing to a sleeping, sated lover. Aidan didn't know the words she used but some ancient part of him understood that visceral sense of ownership, the passion and protectiveness of the creator having brought something into being. For a second he knew those things and his spirit lifted with hers … and then he felt it, the sickening moment when those awful, alien shapes she had planted within his body began to move.

Like the probing tentacles of some unholy parasite, he felt each whirl and barb uncoil and start to spread, twining themselves around his nerves, delving into his synapses, infiltrating themselves into the microscopic spaces between his cells. Inexorable as an encroaching tide they spread through his body and Aidan shrank back before them.

He was aware on some level that he was drawing back behind his shields, retreating into some central point in his being, pulling out of his flesh and leaving it behind. No conscious decision made him do it. It was pure instinct that drove him to flee. He understood that in doing so he was giving himself utterly over to Helen's control, ceding even the small amount of awareness that was left to him, but he could think of nothing else to do. He had no way to fight this, knew of no way to resist this invasion and so he fled before it. He pulled his shields closer around him, as tightly as he knew how, scrunching himself into an ever-smaller space, somewhere in the heart of his being. Yet still those searching tendrils followed him, seeking, probing, trying to find a way to reach him. They circled around his shields, nudging blindly at them, indefatigable and relentless. Aidan felt them as they moulded themselves around his refuge, insinuating themselves into the top layers of those great protective wings that were how he envisaged his body's psychic defences, delving and testing and pushing through. And Aidan knew that if they touched him he would be completely lost. He shrank back into himself, pulling in until he could retreat no further. There was nowhere else for him to go. He felt Helen's will pressing against him, felt as though she was pulling the threads of her control closer and closer around him. Unable to do anything else, Aidan curled his essence into the tiniest seed of consciousness and cowered while the hooks of Helen's binding tangled along his nerves and through his brain, overwhelming and engulfing every neuron and synapse, and he became hers completely.

With a shuddering breath, Helen released the grip on her power and looked at the young man she had just enslaved. It had almost been too easy. Child that he was, he had had no idea of how to resist her. She shook her head, dismissing any notion of guilt. He was a tool now, nothing more – one that would serve her well.

She glanced at her mate, signalling that she had finished.

Terry approached the mute and motionless form of the young man. 'What have you done to him?'

'I have bound him through the power of my blood. He has no will, no awareness of his own. Whatever I tell him to do now, he will do, whether or not I am here to watch over him. He is my servant, absolutely and forever.'

She ran a proprietary hand along Aidan's outstretched arm, feeling the muscles rigid under her fingers. He would stand there until he died if she so wished. She smiled, running the tip of her tongue over her teeth. The thought of such power was deliciously intoxicating.

'So.' Reluctantly she released it. There were things that must be done before any such indulgences. 'He will remain in this house and if anyone enters he will kill them. I will not have our existence jeopardised by the snooping of some mortal witch nor the mewling interference of this one's girlfriend. If he kills them, it will not be our responsibility.'

Terry's eyes narrowed as he considered the implications of this. 'And then?'

'And then, when you have successfully taken the wizard, I will have him kill himself. It pays to leave no loose ends, mate of mine.'

She walked over to the bed and looked down at Eldritch's unconscious form. The mottled red and purple discolouration of fresh bruising stood out across the side of his face and blood had spilled and clotted in the stubble along his jaw. For the first time Helen noticed the scattering of silver hairs running through the dark. She reached out and brushed them with her fingertips, touching the red stickiness and tracing it back to the swollen and split lips that had pleasured her so enjoyably. The faintest needle of regret pricked at her. Angry with herself, Helen pushed it away. There was no denying that the wizard was a skilful lover. Had he taken other partners, she wondered, while her host had lain insensible, incarcerated in that clinic?

'Did you lie to me, my husband? Were you unfaithful to me with your Welsh witch?'

Something within her went hot and tight at the thought, surprising her. Was she really jealous of some mortal? She huffed out an irritated breath, dismissing such foolishness, but the sensation of anger remained. 'It matters not.'

She touched her fingers once more to Eldritch's lips, trailed them slowly down over his chin and throat, lingering where she could feel the pulse beating just beneath the skin.

Fragile, she thought. *Vulnerable.*

And hers to do with as she pleased.

Her fingers spread out, her hand gripped and then, on a sigh, she released him.

She glanced up as Terry came to stand by her.

'Where should we take him? It needs to be somewhere we will be unobserved.'

Helen chuckled. 'Ah, but our little wizardling has provided a solution to that as well. There is a place not far from here that should suit us very well. We will be undisturbed there for as long as we need.'

CHAPTER 28

'You're sure this is the right house?' Jane stopped outside number seven and eyed the deep burgundy front door curiously.

'Yes.'

Gwyn's voice was flat and expressionless and as utterly devoid of emotion as her face. She was as certain of the address as she was of her own name. The only thing she questioned was whether she and Jane should be risking what they were about to do or whether, by doing so, she was condemning the younger woman to the Lady knew what sort of fate. Just – an unforgiving voice inside her head informed her – as she had condemned Aidan. Gwyn pushed down the uncomfortable roil of emotions that accompanied that thought. She and Jane had talked through what they would do if Aidan didn't return and, when it became apparent that he wasn't going to, had discussed their options carefully. Now was not the time for second thoughts.

'Very nice.'

Jane's response held no indication that she had guessed Gwyn's reticence from her tone. It might have been a genuine assessment of the merits of Eldritch's London residence but, if this trip had given Gwyn anything, it was the understanding that her ex-ward's girlfriend was nowhere near as easy to read as she had thought, and Gwyn prided herself on not being one to make snap assessments of people. Jane had enough hidden depths to put Llyn Clywedog – along with every one of its doomed and drowned farms and houses – to shame. Dropping into character and simply acting as though everything was the way she wanted it to seem, so that onlookers saw what they expected and not what was actually happening, was one of her skills. She was doing it now, making a play of checking something on her phone as she glanced casually over the front of the house.

'No obvious signs of alarms. Not that that means anything and not that I can do anything about them, anyway.' Jane delivered her verdict. 'I didn't think I'd be doing my cat burglar routine on this trip.' That was offered as a wry addition almost under her breath.

Despite the seriousness of their situation, Gwyn was tempted to ask just how often Jane did employ her housebreaking skills, but reluctantly put the thought to one side. That was a conversation that deserved to be kept and savoured at some unspecified future time when all of this would be looked back upon with humour and relief. Despite the stories Jane told about her work escapades, Gwyn found the confidence with which the younger woman had said she could pick a lock both surprising and a little disconcerting. But, as Jane had pointed out, there was a lot to her job that she didn't talk about openly, preferring to compartmentalise work and personal life, rather as Gwyn herself kept all trace of anything mystical away from the editors who commissioned her technical writing.

Jane put her phone away, smiling and nodding as though she had just confirmed this was the house they were looking for. With no visible change in expression she murmured softly, 'No neighbours in evidence either, but just stand by the step here as if you're waiting for your good friend Eldritch to open the door, and let me know if anyone comes up the street. It's a decent lock but it shouldn't take me long.'

Without waiting for a response Jane mounted the doorstep, putting one hand over the doorbell as though ringing it. Blocked by her body, her other hand was already probing the lock with a slender pick. Gwyn tried not to stare, pretending to herself – and to any casual observers – that she was indeed expecting a happy, healthy Eldritch to open the door at any moment. She rested one hand against the door frame, pushing her own senses into the fabric of the house, trying to gauge what might be waiting for them. Conventional alarms might not be the only thing to confront a would-be burglar; certainly not now. Gwyn sank her awareness around the door, specifically seeking out any wardings they would need to deal with, but the only ones she could sense were years old, simple suggestions that anyone seeking to get rich on the stolen contents of this house would find easier and better pickings elsewhere. She sifted through those faded ribbons of magic, sensing the faintest echo of Eldritch's power in the weave of those glyphs and sigils. It came to her as a hint of sandalwood and cedar, the feel of sun-warmed stone and the half-heard murmur of a voice like silver threaded through granite. There was a familiarity to those traces, like touching the collar of an old flannel shirt, worn into softness. The thought made her smile even as the realisation that those sensations were only ghosts stung her like a razor slicing across her skin. Absently she wondered if Eldritch's neighbours had suffered a greater rate of predation as a result of the wizard's defences, or if that sense of *go somewhere else* had worked as a protection for their houses as well.

You can ask him about that when you find him, she told herself and steadfastly refused to listen to the traitorous voice that added, *if he's still alive to be found.*

However well it had worked in its heyday, the warding was worn almost to nothingness by the passage of time. Certainly, it didn't seem to be putting Jane off her stride.

With a small hum of satisfaction, Llancathan's answer to Raffles straightened from her nonchalant leaning against the door. 'We're in. Come on.'

Without waiting for a response, she pushed the door open just enough to scan the hallway and stepped inside. For a second Gwyn held her breath. Limited though it was, her own power burned in her hands ready to throw at whatever danger might materialise, conjured by Jane's intrusion. But nothing happened; no alarms went off, no bolts of energy fizzed across the hallway, nor did anyone appear, protesting against their entry.

Without turning, Jane hissed softly, 'Don't stand there like a lemon, Gwyn. Come in and close the door.'

So she did.

It hadn't been her intention to let Jane go first but the younger woman was already edging silently along the hallway. Gwyn thought about calling her back – *What? And let everyone know we're here? Not that there's much chance they don't know already* – but dismissed the thought almost immediately and went after her, trying to keep her shields tight while simultaneously probing for any danger. She was horribly conscious that first Eldritch and now Aidan had gone missing here. While she and Jane weren't wandering in blindly, heedless of the danger they might face, Gwyn was uncomfortably clear of her own limits when it came to defending the pair of them against anything arcane that lay in wait. She could only trust that Jane knew what she was doing when she said she could handle any physical threat posed by the two grieves.

It felt strange to think of these high-ceilinged rooms as Eldritch's home, but the place undoubtedly bore his signature. Gwyn could see echoes of the way he had furnished his rented house in Wales in everything from the colours of the walls to the minimalist frames that held a gallery of black and white photos. She slipped past a slender table – no doubt a convenient dumping ground for house keys and other random ephemera, though she herself would have put a statue of Tara or some other welcoming goddess on it – and followed Jane through into the lounge. A swift glance round showed that the room was empty, but Jane padded silently to the far end, moving the curtains aside just to be certain, even though Gwyn doubted anyone could have hidden behind the thin voile. Still, it was best to be thorough.

Gwyn scanned the room too, trying not to wonder where Eldritch and Helen had bought the thick Persian rug that softened the polished wood floor or be distracted by the titles of the books in the tall shelving unit. She brushed her fingers over the arm of the settee, feeling the cool smoothness of the leather and the soft weight of the wool throw draped over its back. There was no trace of Aidan but again she had that sense of Eldritch, that feeling that came like a reminder of a scent and the whisper of a half-heard word. Unlike the wards, this was warm and recent; she barely had to extend herself to feel it. Her throat tightened with an emotion that felt uncomfortably like grief. It was as painful as catching a glimpse of him in the distance and knowing that was the last time she would see him.

Irritating and infuriating man!

She swallowed hard, pushing away her fear for the wizard, trying to get a sense of when he had last been here but, whether it was because the trace was too slight or her own powers were insufficient for the task, she could not pin it down. Yet there was something else there. Mingled with that sense of the wizard was another impression, sparkling like sunlight on water and full of life. It came with the scent of lilies and jasmine, heady as a garden at twilight. For a moment Gwyn found herself distracted, both entranced and delighted. She wanted to sink into that sensation, to fold it around her and have it envelop her. But underneath that initial fragrance was an unpleasant, cloying sweetness. Heavy and almost overpowering, it was the scent of a funeral wreath starting to rot. Gwyn pulled her senses back sharply, feeling as though she had reached to touch a lover's face only for her fingers to encounter the slime of decomposition. She swallowed down her sense of disgust. The grieve had been here too.

Jane returned to her side, her expression questioning. Gwyn shook her head, unwilling to explain. There was nothing here that could help them.

Where would they put him?

If the grieves had been working on breaking Eldritch's shields, surely they would have held him in the house. Maybe Aidan's visit had scared them and they had taken the wizard elsewhere, but if they had overpowered Aidan, would they have taken him with them or had they left him lying unconscious – or worse – somewhere out of sight?

Gwyn felt a queasy sense of fear clutching at her gut. Anything could have happened here. But with that sense of fear came anger; a slow-burning rage that told her she would do everything in her power to save her two friends and if – *Lady forbid!* – it turned out that they were beyond saving she would call down the very legions of hell to avenge them.

Grim-faced and silent she gestured to Jane – out and carry on down the hallway.

Jane nodded once and turned, stealthy as a cat, moving towards the door. She took two steps and abruptly froze, and Gwyn could almost imagine the young woman's ears pricking like Kali's as she turned her head, listening intently. Gwyn stretched out her own senses, both normal and preternatural. Something brushed against them, the faintest touch of an aura at once both familiar and yet subtly changed. She was reaching her hand out to touch Jane's sleeve in warning, even as the younger woman glanced sharply back towards her.

'Someone's there,' she mouthed, and Jane nodded in silent agreement.

By unspoken accord they separated, moving apart so as to present two targets. Jane inched forward as the door was pushed open and a familiar figure stepped into the room.

'Aidan!' Gwyn couldn't help but smile at the relief that lit up Jane's voice. 'Hell's teeth! We thought the zombie wife had got you.'

But even as Jane spoke Gwyn realised something was wrong. Her silent prayer of thanks turned to a shouted warning as Aidan flung up his hand. It was the only thing she could do in the second she had, but she knew it wasn't enough. The air crackled with the static discharge of power as Aidan hurled a full-force Levin bolt straight into his girlfriend's face.

Gwyn expected Jane to go down as if she had been pole-axed, yet incredibly the young woman didn't so much as flinch.

What the—

The sheer impossibility of what she had just seen made her hesitate a fateful fraction of a second. It wasn't so much that Jane had shrugged off Aidan's attack; it was more that she didn't even seem to notice it. The power was there in Gwyn's hand, ready to be flung, but for the space between one heartbeat and the next she thought she had to be mistaken. Jane couldn't have withstood such an attack; therefore, Aidan couldn't have made it. Momentarily bemused Gwyn froze, and Aidan's second Levin bolt slammed into her chest. Though she was fully shielded, the force of it was enough to drive her backwards, knocking her off balance as though she had been rugby tackled. She staggered, caught her foot as she backed into the coffee table and half fell, arms flailing as she tried to turn, to catch herself on thin air. Then gravity took over and she went down, the back of her head cracking into the side of the bookcase in an explosion of starburst lights.

CHAPTER 29

Jane heard Gwyn's shouted 'No!' even as she saw Aidan fling up his hand. Almost in the same instant she registered the unnaturally fixed expression on his face and realised he hadn't responded to her. She braced instinctively but the hand he had raised didn't lash out in any sort of attack. Instead, he made a strange gesture as if flinging something into her face. A small part of her brain registered it as the same movement she and Sensei had noticed him making in the dojo – *Was it really less than a week ago?* – only this time it wasn't a subtly camouflaged flicking of the fingers but an extravagant full arm movement as if whatever it was he was throwing was tangible, at least to him.

Before she could decide how to react to this odd non-attack, Aidan stepped sideways, making the same gesture again, but this time he was looking straight past her. Though she had felt nothing herself, Jane heard the forced exhalation behind her, followed by the sound of a body falling heavily against something solid.

Gwyn!

But she didn't so much as glance round, keeping all her attention focused on Aidan – if indeed it was still Aidan who stood in front of her. Jane felt an unfamiliar knot of fear tighten in her stomach. Everything she had seen on the CCTV footage from the clinic and everything Gwyn had said that morning came home to her as real in a way that it hadn't before. She swallowed against the sudden tightness in her throat. Yes, she had seen what had happened to Helen and Bob. It had been shocking, but in the same way that viewing news footage from a distant war zone was shocking; even though Helen was Eldritch's wife she hadn't known her personally, and she hadn't known Bob at all. Possession by some supernatural entity was a very different matter when the person affected was someone you knew and loved.

'Come on, Tarzan.'

Jane wasn't sure if Aidan was still reachable, but she wasn't going to give up on him without trying. The cold stare and lack of response were unnerving, but she kept her tone deliberately light as though this was all part of some ridiculous joke. She held her hands loosely by her sides and concentrated on keeping her body language relaxed and unthreatening, even while she was poised and ready to react to whatever he might do next. 'Stop playing around and talk to me.'

Aidan's head tilted fractionally to one side, in that quizzical way he and Gwyn shared as if he was weighing something up, and Jane felt a glimmer of hope that she had managed to get through to him. Then he lunged forward, and, in that instant, she realised how wrong she was. She had already lost him.

She and Aidan sparred frequently, both in and out of the dojo. Like all the seniors, they were competitive, each pushing the other, testing limits and working to gain the upper hand, but there were boundaries you did not cross; you didn't use techniques that would hurt or maim or strike with killing force, even though you could. Now, Aidan went for her eyes, fingers speared and rigid, and as she blocked his arm he drove a hard kick in towards her solar plexus which, were she not already turning, would have ruptured her diaphragm. As it was Jane felt the bruising force of it skid across her tensed abdominal muscles. She retaliated with an instinctive back-knuckle strike towards his cheekbone, snapping her hand away as he blocked and tried to pull her into an armlock. Adrenalin surged through her system, sending her pulse hammering as she kicked hard into the muscle just above his knee and pivoted away from the punch he threw after her. She knew what he had just tried to do, and a cold and fierce anger settled over her.

Screw it, Aidan! I don't want to hurt you.

But she would if necessary.

His next attack was a mawashi geri straight at her head. He was quick on his feet and he had several inches more reach than she did. In the dojo Jane might have danced backwards out of range or moved inside the arc of his kick to score a point of her own against him. Here, with limited space to move and the certain knowledge that if she closed with Aidan she would be putting herself in range of any number of far more deadly techniques, she opted for a double-armed block instead. It was a defensive move, but she drove it in as an attack, one forearm smashing into his shin just above the ankle, the other connecting just below his knee. Sensei would have had strong words to say to any student using such a technique in the dojo and for good reason; it could easily result in broken bones for either fighter. Jane felt the force of the impact jar through her body and knew her forearms would be black with bruising by the morning. Aidan's leg would be too.

And if that's the worst of it we'll have got away lightly.

Yet it worked to take the edge off Aidan's attack. Whatever was driving him, he still had the sense to fight tactically. Instead of coming up with the second roundhouse kick he would normally have followed up with, he backed off, keeping his weight on his back foot, nursing that right leg and giving the bruised muscles a moment or two to recover. Jane felt a fierce satisfaction as she weighed the thought of going in against him while he was still off balance. She had no qualms about fighting as hard and dirty as the situation required, regardless of who her opponent was. Rules were for the dojo; that was another thing that Sensei drilled into her students. But Sensei also taught that it was always better to walk away from a fight if there was any option of doing so. Hoping that might yet be possible, Jane took the moment's respite to try that other path.

'Gwyn?' She didn't look behind her; she could only pray that the other woman was able to hear her and respond to the urgent demand in her voice. 'Can't you do something to unhex him?'

But there was no answer. Jane swallowed down the horrible certainty of what that silence meant. She looked at the man who was her lover and her friend and her heart twisted. Their first meeting had been in the dojo when his mother had brought him along to the club, hoping that taking up karate would help his recovery after a fall on the school stairs had almost crippled him. Later, Aidan would joke that the physiotherapist had recommended tai chi but that his mother hadn't known the difference between that and karate. Whether or not that was true, Sensei had agreed to let him train and Jane, a year older and already a junior black belt, had been the student she most often paired with him. Over the years they had grown close as friends and fellow students, warriors in training in the curious camaraderie of the dojo, nursing bruises and broken bones, celebrating competitions won and gradings passed. They had gone their separate ways when university beckoned, but when eventually they both returned to Llancathan their friendship had resumed and then deepened into something new. The childhood friends had become lovers. And now it had come to this.

Jane looked into Aidan's icily blank eyes one last time, acknowledging all that they had had between them before putting it to one side.

I'm sorry, Aidan. I guess we do this the hard way after all.

What she was about to do might break her heart, but that wouldn't stop her doing it.

CHAPTER 30

There had been a lot of joking amongst the seniors of the karate club when she and Aidan had first started dating. The post-training pint in the Unicorn became the forum for many half-teasing questions about who would win if it came to a fight between them. Mostly Jane had preferred to stay out of the debate, laughing at the suggestions but offering little comment. If pushed, she would shrug and point out that Aidan was stronger than she was and that his extra height gave him more reach for techniques, and invite whoever was asking to draw their own conclusions. The more experienced fighters – those she sparred with regularly: Keith and Martin, Deb, Erika and Tigger – would sometimes counter that she was faster and more flexible than Aidan, not to mention a grade higher. All of that was true, but Jane knew that most of the men would still bet on Aidan. She had never asked him outright, but she suspected, deep down, that so would he. It didn't offend her. She would have been disappointed if Sensei had expressed that opinion, but she was quite happy to let the rest of the club think what they wanted. What she had never said to any of them was that she had thought through in detail how she would approach such a fight.

Not that she had believed it would ever take place but, just because her planning had been theoretical, that didn't make it any less thorough. Of course, the fact that she had thought through her tactics didn't mean that it would be easy, either.

All that flashed through her mind as she watched Aidan watching her intently. He had his weight spread between both feet again so she knew he would come at her at any moment. Apart from the utter stillness of his expression he held himself very much as he would if they were facing off for a normal fight. Jane smiled grimly to herself. That was good because she was about to bet her life on his using the techniques he favoured in the dojo.

She gave him the slightest inclination of her head, acknowledging him as her opponent, and bounced a little on the balls of her feet, her hands fisted in front of her, guarding head and chest. She made a couple of feints, like a fighter weighing up her opponent, not quite ready to commit to an attack. It was the sort of thing she pulled the juniors up on. A good fighter would read the pattern and use that fraction of a second of dead time between bounces to attack. And Aidan was a very good fighter.

Knowing that, Jane bounced. Feint left. No reaction. Feint right. No reaction. Feint left. There! Aidan spun and drove in a reverse kick towards her. It was a favourite attack of his and for good reason; he had a kick like a mule. The speed with which he could turn often caught people moving in on him and it would have gone straight through her overly high guard if she hadn't been expecting just that. In the dojo, she would have slid a block along his leg and countered with a controlled strike to the head as he moved past her. Now she stepped wide and powered a kick of her own into his hip. Like her earlier block, it was another technique that wouldn't have been tolerated by Sensei. Aidan's leg dropped heavily as the ball of her foot connected with his hip joint, crushing muscle into bone with devastating force. Even so, he tried to spin for the reverse mawashi geri that would have been his natural follow up, single-minded in his determination to catch her, but his leg would barely support him, the muscles deadened by her blow, and he staggered, off balance.

Jane didn't give him time to try anything else. Her foot wasn't fully on the floor before she came up with her left leg, catching Aidan across the temple with the side of her foot in a roundhouse kick. As his head snapped sideways she flicked her leg round in a reverse mawashi geri, just as she would on one of the heavy punchbags she regularly practised on, catching him on the left side of his jaw. She stepped in to finish the attack with a tetsui strike to the bridge of his nose, but he was already crumpling, his eyes rolling back in his head even as he went down to the floor.

Relentless as death, Jane followed him down, fist poised and ready to deliver the strike if he showed the smallest sign of trying to regain his feet, but she saw from the way he landed with no attempt to break his fall that he was unconscious. Even so, she dropped her knee onto his neck, ready to apply pressure if he moved, while she twisted his arms behind his back. But Aidan never stirred as she pulled out the cable tie she kept in her back pocket and used it to fasten his thumbs tightly together in a simple but brutally effective handcuff.

Ordinarily, Jane would have considered that sufficient to incapacitate any opponent but, knowing Aidan and considering the single-minded determination with which he had just tried to kill her, she wasn't taking any chances. There were a number of things she could do, some of them more permanently disabling than others. She smiled nastily as she weighed up her options. For a moment, the unconscious man on the floor in front of her was no longer her lover and friend but an anonymous assailant fate had thrown on her mercy. Given the circumstances, she wasn't feeling particularly merciful. Her smile turned wicked as she made her decision.

Sorry, Tarzan. Her fingers found the buckle of his belt. *But you asked for this.*

CHAPTER 31

The sheer dead weight of him made her task harder than she had expected – *Come on, Aide, you usually cooperate when I do this!* – but, with some determined tugging and twisting, Jane pulled Aidan's jeans down around his knees.

There. Possessed or not, he wouldn't be getting up in a hurry. Satisfied with her handiwork she sat back on her heels, huffing out a quiet sigh of relief at the fact that she had neutralised the current danger and she could relax.

The sound of movement behind her had her spinning round, body coming up in a half crouch, right hand fisted, left hand open and ready to grab or defend before she had consciously thought what she was doing. Then her brain caught up with her body and she swore venomously as she realised what this new threat was.

'Gwyn!' Jane's glance went from the older woman's face to her own hands. With a disgusted groan she relaxed, lowering her guard and sinking back to the floor. 'Hell's teeth,' she muttered, shaking her head. 'Don't do that to me. I could have killed you.'

Her anger was directed more at herself than it was at Gwyn, but that did nothing to soften her words. The frantic spike of her pulse served only to reinforce the realisation of how badly she had been taken off guard. If it had been anyone but Gwyn behind her … Jane scrubbed her hand over her face and resolved not to waste energy by thinking too much about what might have been. Absently she ran her fingers through her hair, then combed the strands straight again while she let her heartbeat settle.

Belatedly she thought to ask, 'Are you okay?'

Gwyn was sitting up now, but looking at her more critically, Jane could see the hand she was casually resting on the coffee table was there to steady herself. Her other hand was gingerly probing the back of her head. Never one to worry unduly about her appearance, Gwyn's current look could only be described as dishevelled. Her plait had come loose, its sloppy remains drooping over her shoulder, while stray tendrils of hair tangled crazily around her face. Framed in that haphazard curtain her naturally pale skin seemed almost translucent – as white as bone china and similarly delicate – and, from the pinched tightness around her mouth, Jane guessed Gwyn was nursing a killer headache.

Still, the older woman nodded in response to the question. 'More or less, yes.' As if to prove the point she sat up straighter and took that telltale hand off the coffee table. 'The question is, how in the Lady's name are you okay?'

Gwyn's tone held confusion and an odd trace of wariness that Jane hadn't heard from her before. She sighed inwardly. She supposed she shouldn't feel disappointed that the other woman would have bet on Aidan winning their fight, but somehow it still rankled.

Oh well.

She gave a one-shouldered shrug and tried for nonchalance rather than peevishness as she answered. 'I don't make an issue of it, but I am a higher grade than he is. Whether he likes to admit it or not, I ought to be able to take him.' She was aware that her voice had gone fierce but didn't much care. She might not like what she had had to do but, given the circumstances, surely Gwyn should be grateful it was Aidan who was stretched out on the floor and not her. She almost said as much but instead she added truthfully, 'It also helps that Sensei told me I should be ready for something like this.'

Gwyn had been about to say something, but this revelation stopped her in her tracks. Her mouth snapped shut on whatever comment she had been about to make while her eyes went wide with disbelief.

'What?' Jane couldn't help but laugh at the incredulous look on Gwyn's face. 'Oh, not for Aidan being possessed. I don't mean that. She's good, but she's not *that* good.' A fleeting grin lifted the corners of her mouth as her words conjured other memories, ones she wasn't about to share with Gwyn. 'She always says she knows every one of her students by our different fighting styles and that she also knows exactly how she'd take each of us out if it ever came to it. When I passed my second Dan, she took me to one side and told me I should do the same.

'It was the first grade I'd taken as a senior – as an adult, I mean. Sensei said you never know who you might have to fight and when you might have to do it for real, but that it could be anyone. Anyone.' Jane's gaze flicked briefly to the still form beside her and her lips tightened. She huffed out a breath, dismissing whatever else she had been going to add. 'At the time, I thought it was a bit overkill. She didn't mention it to the guys who graded – just to me. I did wonder if it was because I was, well, another woman, that she was trying to give me an edge.' Jane frowned for a moment but then continued. 'Anyway, I thought about it for a while and then I started to do it, just as an exercise really. How do I counter someone who does this? What would I do against this combination? If I really did have to fight so-and-so, how would I do it? Trust in God but change your passwords regularly. It's the same sort of thing. Over time I guess it became a habit. A lot of things do when it's Sensei who's suggested them.'

Gwyn's expression hadn't changed as she listened to Jane's explanation, but now she nodded slightly as if she approved of this sentiment.

'I really should get to know that woman,' she mused. Then she shook her head and her focus returned to more immediate concerns. 'That wasn't what I meant, Jane. When Aidan came through that door, he threw a Levin bolt straight at you. I saw him do it. Sweet Lady, it should have flattened you as though you'd been tasered! I had full shields up and the one he hit me with had enough power to knock me flying. How did you stop it?'

Jane looked at Gwyn, nonplussed. 'There wasn't anything for me to stop. He nearly caught me with that first mae geri.'

Now *that* would have taken her out if it had connected properly. In fact, all the techniques Aidan had thrown at her had had the potential to maim or kill. She rubbed her hand over her bruised abdominal muscles and scowled. Handling those and taking Aidan out without doing him permanent damage – hopefully – *that* was what Gwyn should have been getting excited about.

'I don't know why you're getting so worked up about these Levin bolt things. I told you, Gwyn, they don't work on me. I mean, sure, I saw him do that twitchy thing with his fingers, just like he did in training, except that this time he wasn't bothering to hide what he was doing. But that was it. It didn't do anything. It was just like in the dojo – I didn't feel a thing.' She shook her head, at a loss as to what Gwyn was making so much fuss about. They needed to move past that, get Aidan back on his feet and find out what the hell had happened to Eldritch. She shrugged and turned her empty palms up to the ceiling. 'What can I say? They don't work on me.'

'That's impossible. You simply can't not be affected by a psychic bolt, it's not—' Gwyn stopped in mid-sentence. For several seconds she said nothing, but Jane could almost see the thoughts darting through her mind; argument and frantic counterargument chasing back and forth behind those wide green eyes until finally they emerged as a single word. 'Oh.'

Jane would have liked something more enlightening. She waited but, when nothing was forthcoming, she gave up. 'Oh? For crying out loud, what the hell does that mean, Gwyn? Screw all this hocus pocus mumbo jumbo. Tell me in words I'm going to understand.'

'Sweet Lady.' Gwyn was staring at her as though she had just grown two heads. Jane could brazen out most things but now she felt the hairs lift on the back of her neck. Gwyn's scrutiny was unnerving her.

'Gwyn …'

Gwyn didn't seem to notice the warning tone or, if she did, she took no notice. In a voice somewhere between wonder and incredulity she said, 'It actually is possible, after all. You really are a null, aren't you?'

She frowned and once again Jane had the sense of thoughts racing behind those forest-green eyes. She would have questioned Gwyn but at that moment the other woman broke into a smile that lit her face, making her seem much younger.

'The wards on the house.' There was a childlike delight in Gwyn's voice that made Jane wish, however briefly, that she too could be party to whatever crazy delusion the older woman was experiencing. 'It wasn't their age that stopped them working on you, was it?' Gwyn shook her head, her eyes wide and sparkling as though she had just solved a puzzle.

'What are you on about?'

'This house has protective wards on it – just as mine does. They should have stopped you from breaking in. I thought they weren't working because they were old.' Gwyn smiled at her own foolishness.

Jane knew nothing about protective wards but the name gave her a starting point and she could take an educated guess. That led her to a very different explanation. 'Why would they? I was breaking in to save Eldritch's life, not to steal his savings. Besides,' she challenged, her logical brain bringing back all she had heard Gwyn and Eldritch saying about nulls, 'you and Eldritch said that nulls don't exist.'

'They don't,' Gwyn confirmed with a shake of her head. She was still smiling. 'Except they must do, because that's the only explanation I can think of for what's just happened. Oh, we are going to have to test this.'

'Hang on.' Jane didn't back away from Gwyn but for a split second she felt like doing so. She reacted to her own discomfort by putting on her fiercest expression. 'I'm not going to be anyone's lab rat.' She was adamant about that. 'Besides,' she countered, and her scowl morphed into a pointed smile, 'Aidan's already tested it. It didn't work when he tried it on me in the dojo and you saw for yourself what happened here while the bolt he threw at you knocked you out—'

'It didn't knock me out, it knocked me backwards. Which is why I tripped over the coffee table.' Gwyn treated the offending item of furniture to a glare that should have reduced it to a slag of fused metal and glass. 'Then I hit my head on the bookcase, a concussive blow that had me seeing stars for a minute or two.'

Jane raised her eyebrows but managed to keep the scepticism from her voice. 'Right.' But it wasn't amusement at Gwyn's bruised ego that brought the edge of satisfaction to her voice. 'But what you're really saying is that Helen can't pull any magic tricks on me. If I go up against her – or even against Eldritch,' her voice cracked a little at that, but she rallied, 'it's hand to hand. They can't touch me.'

'We can't be sure, Jane.' Caution drew Gwyn's brows down, carving a line between them. 'We can't take that risk.'

'Gwyn, we're going to have to take a risk. This whole escapade has been one huge risk. Now it looks like we might have a genuine edge—' With a conscious effort Jane stopped herself. This wasn't the time for an argument. 'Anyway, we're getting ahead of ourselves.' Jane looked down at Aidan and grimaced as the unfamiliar prickle of concern stirred her conscience. 'The first question is, is he going to be okay when he wakes up?'

'I think that depends on how hard you hit him.'

'As hard as I had to,' Jane murmured, a touch of venom creeping back into her voice. Doing anything else would have been a risk she hadn't been willing to take. 'Seriously, Gwyn, will he be okay? I was hoping that knocking him out might cancel out whatever's been done to him.'

'Like rebooting a PC?' Gwyn's dark brows raised like a visible question mark.

Jane shrugged. 'It works,' she muttered, but she felt more sheepish than confident.

Gwyn snorted unhelpfully. 'Not that well for people, I'm afraid, or at least not where magic's concerned. It rather depends what we're dealing with.' She scooted herself over to Jane's side. 'Let's take a look at him,' she said, and her tone was more sympathetic than her words.

Jane moved out of the way, watching as Gwyn felt Aidan's pulse and then lifted each eyelid in turn to look into his eyes. Given the circumstances, she had been expecting something more esoteric from Gwyn. Seeing her give Aidan the sort of examination that any competent first aider might carry out was somehow reassuring. She allowed herself to relax a little.

'What did you do to him?'

'A mawashi geri – that's a roundhouse kick, side of the foot – to the right temple then a reverse mawashi, side of the foot again, to the left side of the jaw. He was already out when he hit the floor so he may have banged the back of his head too.'

'Hmm. So, we're probably looking at concussion, but let's hope nothing more serious. Anything else?'

Jane bit her lip. 'You might want to look at his right hip and maybe his shin too. I don't think he's going to be running anywhere for a while.'

'Right.' The simplicity of Gwyn's response held a wealth of commentary.

Jane winced. 'He was trying to kill me, Gwyn. To kill us,' she amended.

'I know.' Gwyn's lips pursed into a little moue of disapproval, though who exactly it was aimed at was hard to tell. 'Well, we'll worry about getting him back on his feet when he's conscious and we'll worry about bringing him round when I know a little more about what's been done to him.'

But instead of looking at Aidan she cocked her head to one side and studied Jane. 'I think Aidan will be very glad you took Sensei's advice.' She paused and then added curiously, 'I'm also wondering where you found the cable tie.'

'In my back pocket.' Jane took in Gwyn's astonishment. 'You mean you don't carry one?'

Judging from the scowl she received Jane decided that maybe it wasn't quite the right time for humour. 'Yeah, okay. It's something I picked up at that conference I went to last October. I'm not that much into the personal security side of things. I've no plans to go into close protection and be a bodyguard, although there are people – the rich Arabs, especially – who pay a lot of money to have female security details for their wives and daughters.' She wrinkled her nose dismissively. 'Not my idea of fun. I'd rather hack systems – at least code does what you tell it to. Still, you never know when something will come in handy. I spoke to a guy who worked out in Africa. He demoed how well they work as a handcuff. They're easy to carry, don't get picked up on security scans – he said he's never without one. It was another one of those things that seemed like a good idea, so I've carried a couple ever since.'

She produced a second strip of black plastic and waved it

at Gwyn with the flourish of a conjurer pulling a rabbit out of a top hat. 'See?' Still smirking she slipped it back into her jeans pocket.

'Huh! Remind me never to get on the wrong side of you.' Gwyn looked from Aidan's bound thumbs to his neatly displayed underwear and raised a questioning eyebrow. 'And the jeans?' she asked pointedly.

'Ah, they're a personal touch. I didn't want him able to get up in a hurry.'

Jane's fingers strayed to touch Aidan's cheek, just above the darkening mark her foot had left on his jawline.

'Tell me he's going to be okay, Gwyn.' She heard the plaintive note that crept into her voice and pulled her hand back. 'It's not good for the male ego to be beaten quite this solidly by a woman.'

It was a brave attempt at nonchalance, but Jane knew Gwyn wasn't fooled.

She reached out in a rare gesture of comfort and squeezed Jane's hand. 'We'll get him sorted.' She settled herself cross-legged beside Aidan, placing her left hand over his forehead and her right over his solar plexus. She caught and held Jane's gaze. 'I promise.'

'That bitch!'

Watching Gwyn working was a little like watching paint dry. Nothing visible had happened for several minutes and, though she had tried to stay focused, Jane's attention had drifted. Gwyn's exclamation brought her back to the present like a slap.

'What?'

Gwyn didn't answer. Instead, she brushed Aidan's hair back and stared angrily at his forehead. When Jane looked for herself she saw what appeared to be a smear of dried blood on his skin.

'I didn't do that.' There was no obvious wound that the blood – if that was what it was – had come from. Nor was there enough of it to seem significant, but Gwyn's reaction suggested otherwise. Curious and concerned in equal measures Jane asked, 'What is it?'

'Pull his shirt up.'

Gwyn's words made as little sense to Jane as an instruction as they did as an answer to her question. 'What? Why?'

'His shirt. Lift it up. I need to see his chest.'

Jane might have baulked at anyone using that tone of voice on her, but she dealt in emergencies on a daily basis and knew the difference between someone who was being rude and someone who was utterly focused. She did what she was asked.

Another smear of blood was scrawled across the skin on the left side of Aidan's chest, along the bottom edge of his pectoral muscle.

Gwyn looked at it and her expression hardened. 'Damn her!'

Gwyn rarely swore, other than when she invoked the Lady, and Jane had never heard such cold fury in her voice before. She felt her own icy control snap into place in response. 'What is it?' she asked, her voice calm though her pulse was starting to race.

'Blood magic.' Gwyn spat as if the very words had a foul taste associated with them. 'That bitch has used blood magic on him.'

Jane had no idea what that meant but she wasn't one to waste time on unimportant details. There was only one thing she needed to know.

'How bad?' she asked bluntly.

'If she'd used it on someone without power it would be lethal.' Gwyn's small frame was almost vibrating with anger. She took a sharp breath, visibly reaching for control. 'Blood magic wipes out the subject's will. It puts them utterly under your control and, to all intents and purposes, it's impossible for a third party to break.

'Oh, theoretically, you can do it. If you're stronger than the practitioner who set the spell, you can smash through it with brute force. That's academic in this case. I don't have anything like that sort of power.' There was a curious mix of emotion in Gwyn's voice. Another time Jane would have liked to ask her why that admission was so painful, but she held her tongue. Such information wasn't relevant now.

'The other way you can do it is by killing the person setting the spell.'

Now that held more promise, but as Jane went to make the obvious comment Gwyn held her hand up, silencing her.

'But no sane practitioner is going to do either of those things, not if they care about the person the magic has been worked on. In either case you would cause such a backlash of power that you'd kill the subject. You just can't do it. That's one of the reasons blood magic is forbidden.'

A mix of shock and anger washed over Jane as she listened to Gwyn, followed by a deep and terrifying sense of grief. Her throat knotted tight on the words of denial she wanted to shout in Gwyn's face and for a moment she couldn't speak. She swiped impatiently at her eyes as they blurred and reached for anger instead. That, at least, she knew how to use.

'But people still teach this stuff, don't they?' She slapped at Gwyn with her words, wanting to hurt as if doing so might relieve the pain she was feeling. 'Sure, you might say, "Oh, I'd never do something like that," but you still teach it, so when people go over to the dark side, they know how to use it.'

To her credit, Gwyn did not react to Jane's needling.

'The fundamentals are taught, yes, by those who know them. Blood magic is an obscure discipline, even by the standards of the arcane world. The information is shared so that those of us with power can protect against it.'

'Oh, well that makes it alright then.' Jane snarled, rounding on Gwyn. 'That's the sort of pathetic argument American gun owners spout every time there's a mass shooting. Magic doesn't kill people. People kill people.' Her words dripped contempt.

Gwyn sat a little more upright. While her voice remained calm there was a degree of precision in the way she spoke that suggested her words were carefully chosen.

'Think of it like your karate, Jane. Aidan just used his training to attack you but normally he'd only use it in self-defence. It's not the karate that's changed.' She studied the younger woman as if over a pair of imaginary glasses. 'It's the same as you being an ethical hacker. You have the same skills as the cybercriminals, but you use them within the law. How did you describe it to me once – think bad, act good? Well, this is the same.' Gwyn stared at Jane as if daring the younger woman to contradict her. Then she let out a shuddering breath. From her fierce stance she seemed to shrink in on herself as she added, 'As it happens, I didn't teach Aidan about blood magic because I didn't want to expose him to it. There really aren't so many of us that I thought it was a risk. I never dreamt he'd have to deal with it, let alone fall victim to it himself.'

The naked pain in Gwyn's voice brought Jane up short. She met Gwyn's eyes and her angry retort died unspoken as she saw her own grief and anger mirrored within them, magnified by a torment of self-blame. Gwyn wasn't responsible for what had been done to Aidan, but that didn't mean she considered herself innocent. Ashamed of her own reaction, Jane swallowed down the words she had been about to use. Instead, she asked, 'Would it have made any difference if you had?'

She wasn't expecting Gwyn to nod.

'Oh yes. Blood magic is relatively straightforward to block if you have power and you know what you're doing.'

The return of hope was so strong it was almost a physical pain.

'But Aidan has power,' Jane pointed out tentatively. 'Are you saying that he could break this himself?'

She scarcely dared listen to Gwyn's answer.

'He could, yes.'

This was better than Jane had expected. 'Then—'

'The problem is that he doesn't know how. I'm going to have to teach him.'

Jane shrugged. One thing she knew for sure was that Aidan was a quick learner. She didn't see why Gwyn should be so despondent.

'And? I mean, how hard will that be?'

Gwyn's eyebrows raised. 'Given that he's likely to try and kill us both as soon as he wakes up, what do you think?'

'Oh.' Jane looked from Gwyn to her unconscious lover and back again. 'I guess we'd best not untie him, then.'

CHAPTER 32

There were voices. Drifting somewhere between consciousness and oblivion, Aidan could hear them, echoing weirdly as though they were both inside and outside his head. One moment they seemed to be far away and then they were so close as to be part of him, worming their way through his brain like the whispered commands of the grieve. The possibility that that was what they were terrified him, and even in his semiconscious state he did his best not to listen. He dared not take the chance that if he did he would be compelled to do even more horrific things to the people he loved.

'Aidan, listen to me.'

The worst thing was that it sounded like Gwyn's voice. And her voice had been used to try to trick him once before. The memory twisted around him, sending him back to the night he had learned first hand about demons. Waking in the frigid darkness of the forest hut he had refused to believe it could be Gwyn outside, pleading with him to open the door. That refusal had saved his life – his and Eldritch's, he remembered – and the thought of what he had so nearly done to the wizard today brought fresh pain.

'I know Helen's been controlling you.'

The voice came again, resolute and unyielding, demanding that he listen.

'But you can beat her. I need you to remember the sigils I've been teaching you and weave them into your shields. If you can do that, Aidan, I promise you, you can block her influence.'

Eldritch. Even if the wizard forgave him for what he had done, Aidan was certain that Gwyn never would. And if she wouldn't forgive him, why would she be talking to him now? It had to be another trick. Miserable and despairing, he turned his awareness away.

'Sweet Lady! He's not listening to me.' The familiar voice cracked with frustration. 'Aidan, come on. It's me, Gwyn.'

No, it's not, he countered silently. It couldn't be. He wouldn't let it be her.

'Okay, let's try this.'

A different voice, no less beloved. Before he could place it, a palm cracked across the side of his face, sudden and stinging.

'For the love of God! Open your eyes, you moron!'

Hands gripped his shoulders and shook him, sending a wave of pain and nausea through his head. He couldn't prevent the groan that slipped from him, but it gained him no sympathy. If anything, it seemed to infuriate whoever was talking.

'Don't play the wounded hero with me. If you give up on me now I'll do more than give you press-ups. You want to keep that black belt? Then you show me you've got the balls to wear it. You open your eyes right now or I'm going to kick your sorry carcass right out of this dojo and you won't be coming back again.'

Jane?

It hurt to try to speak. The bones of his jaw, and even his teeth, ached ferociously. His lips and tongue felt swollen and thick so that he could barely shape her name, but he did his best.

'Ja … y?'

'That's *Sensei Jane* to you, Aidan Morgan. Now open your eyes! You can do this.'

The fierceness slipped and, just for a moment, there was something close to desperation in that insistent voice. The idea shocked him. He had never known Jane to sound desperate before. Aidan opened his eyes and she was there, leaning over him, beautiful and fierce. Gwyn was there too. From the angle at which he lay he couldn't see her face, but who else would be wearing that chunky silver and turquoise cuff and the crazy assortment of crystal bead bracelets? He felt an instant of pure love for the pair of them … and then magic slapped at him, the grieve's spell dragging fire along every nerve. He felt his eyes rolling back and the world spun as blackness poured over him, poisoned silver barbs tearing at his nerves and the awful alien presence of the blood magic tightening its grip around his consciousness.

'Oh no you don't!'

Jane released his shoulders and caught his jaw. Her fingers dug into bruised and tender flesh, sending pain screaming down his nerves. For a moment the shriek of it almost blocked out the voice of the grieve in his mind.

'You open your eyes again and you listen to me!'

But he couldn't. The power of the grieve was overwhelming him. He had only one purpose and that was to kill whoever had entered the house. Now his eyes did open so he could see his target, beautifully close, perfectly vulnerable. Immediately he struck out at her but something was restraining his hands. He pulled against the bonds, thrashing and twisting as he tried to get free, barely registering the sting of tearing skin.

The woman must die! He would choke the life from her. He would pound her head against the floor until it burst open like a melon.

The pain in his jaw intensified. It was nothing compared with the strength of the blood magic. He existed only to kill. It was what he had to do.

'Gwyn, I'm losing him.'

He heard fear, almost panic. It meant nothing to him other than that his prey knew she was done for. He would get free and then he would kill. He wrenched again at the restraints pinning his hands behind his back but to no avail. Changing tactics he sagged back against the floor, letting his body go limp, neither struggling to free himself nor fighting to strike his captor. He almost laughed when the grip on his jaw eased fractionally. Instead, he jerked savagely using his head as a weapon. Bone crunched into flesh and the woman cried out, her grip loosening further. He rolled, trying to lash out with his legs but they were tangled somehow. Then his head was caught again. Strong limbs locked around him, but they wouldn't be able to hold him forever and once he was free … He bellowed his rage, thrashing and bucking his body to get rid of the woman who clung to him.

'Do something!'

He felt her hands slip as she tried to hold him then lightning blasted through every nerve and his world went black.

Breathing heavily, Jane rolled to her knees, putting a hand out to steady herself when the world seemed to shift sideways. The side of her head throbbed where Aidan had driven his skull into hers. Tentatively she pushed her hand through her hair, exploring the tender area with her fingertips. It was bruised, she concluded, but that was nothing compared with the damage he'd have done if he'd managed to hit her on the nose or the cheekbone.

Damn it, Tarzan!

But the anger she felt didn't make it any easier to look at the body stretched on the floor beside her. Unconsciousness had erased the bestial snarl from Aidan's face, but it would be a long time before the image of it faded from her memory.

Feeling sick, Jane turned to Gwyn. 'What did you do?' Even to her own ears, her voice sounded flat and heavy with defeat.

'I hit him with a Levin bolt. At that close a range it's pretty much guaranteed to knock someone out. It's not entirely without risk, but it was safer than you having to hit him again.' Gwyn eyed her unconscious ex-ward sadly. 'And it was certainly better than leaving him as he was.'

Jane nodded mutely, understanding but not feeling ready to comment. Instead, she busied herself teasing out one of the strands of hair that clung to Aidan's forehead. This year's sun had already started to bleach it and the threads of copper were more noticeable than ever among the lighter brown.

'I thought we were getting through to him.' She wound the hair around her finger, creating a kiss curl. 'I'm sure we were. He … he tried to say my name, he recognised me, just before he …' She broke off, looking at the older woman with desperation in her eyes. 'Screw it, Gwyn! What are we going to do?'

The silence stretched between them, as mutely accusing as Aidan's unconscious form.

Gwyn broke it. 'There is something I can try.' The words might have been hopeful but the tone was reluctant, as though whatever solution she was about to offer might be worse than doing nothing. 'It's not going to be nice though,' she added, confirming Jane's fears. 'It all depends on how well he can concentrate when he's in pain.'

Jane's hand closed protectively on Aidan's shoulder. 'What do you mean?'

'You said it yourself – there were a few seconds after he regained consciousness when he was thinking for himself, before the blood magic overpowered him.'

'And?'

'And that means we have an opportunity – however brief – to get through to him. I can bring him round and then, before the blood magic takes hold, I can throw pain at him. It won't cause him any physical harm, not really, but it's going to feel like it is.' She looked from Jane to Aidan and then back again, her expression uneasy. 'Lady help me, he's going to be in agony.'

'And how's that going to help?'

Gwyn offered a grimace that might have been meant as a reassuring smile. 'I'm hoping that the pain will hold the blood magic at bay long enough for him to shield himself. But it's going to depend on whether he can concentrate enough to understand what we're asking him to do. What you're asking him to do,' she amended. 'He responded better to you than he did to me, so you're going to have to be the one to talk him through it.'

Jane stared at Gwyn, appalled. 'But I don't know anything about what he needs to do!'

'I know. But I think I've got a way round that. You just need to do what I'll tell you.'

Gwyn sighed and her shoulders sagged as though all her energy had left her along with that little huff of breath. There was concern written across her face as she met Jane's gaze. 'This isn't going to be nice, and I can't even guarantee it will work. I'll understand if you don't want to try this, Jane.'

Jane bit her lip, worrying it between her teeth as she considered this. 'What other options do we have?'

'Frankly? None. If we don't get this to work then we've lost him. Forever.'

CHAPTER 33

Awareness came with the agonising suddenness of someone sliding a hot knife under his fingernails. One moment there was nothing and then, a heartbeat later, pain as though every cell in his body had been dipped in acid. He wanted to scream but he couldn't find the breath. He longed to retreat back into unconsciousness, but something was holding him present, forcing him to endure pain like nothing he had experienced before. If this was torture he would willingly give up any secret, but no one was asking him questions. And yet there was a voice. Over the laboured pounding of his heart he could hear someone speaking. In desperation he tuned into the sound, frantically seeking anything that might distract him from the pain.

It sounded like Jane but she was talking about sigils. What did Jane know about sigils?

'Come on, Tarzan, Gwyn's drawn them on the floor. You don't even have to remember them yourself. All you have to do is open your eyes and look at them and then draw them on your shields.'

How could he look at something when it was taking all his focus to keep breathing? It was impossible. And then, in the back of his mind, he felt the malevolence of blood magic awakening.

No!

Without conscious thought his eyes flew open, seeking his target, and fresh agony speared through him. He thought he had known what torment was but this was worse still. His body arched, spasming, and from a long way off he heard the animal sound of pain torn from his throat as his muscles went rigid, driving the air from his lungs.

'Screw this, Gwyn! He's fitting. You're killing him.'

'I'm saving his life! Sweet Lady, keep talking to him – I can't do this for long. Get him to look at those sigils.'

Black spots danced on the edge of his vision. He couldn't breathe. It didn't matter, he was going to kill everyone there.

'Aidan!'

Hands were turning his unyielding body.

'Look at the fucking sigils!'

Desperation and a woman's sobbing breath. Pain slicing through his body with every heartbeat. A hand fisted in his hair, holding his head above the floor.

'Look at them!'

A pattern of random lines adorned the floorboards, scant inches from his face. They held no meaning, no interest, but his body was locked in a spastic rictus and he couldn't look away. The shapes glittered and swam as he stared at them, unblinking, his brain slowing with the onset of hypoxia.

And then something happened.

He was still aware of the pain racking his body, still conscious of the absolute need to break free and to kill these fools who dared trespass against his mistress's command, but it was as if all those sensations and desires had shifted somehow, as though his consciousness had slipped free of his body and in doing so had left them behind. In that moment he was simply floating above those strange patterns.

But they weren't strange. He knew them.

The world seemed to shiver as something altered within him.

He knew them.

Their names seemed to sing in his mind, beautiful and impossibly ancient, the sounds of them echoing with melancholy and filling him with a longing for something he had no words to describe. Roc and Sho and Bel – even as they came to him, he remembered Gwyn drawing them for him on her kitchen table, covering its surface in flour and making him trace the lines over and over again with his finger as he memorised their names.

No, that line goes right to left. You're lining it up east–west, remember … start at the centre and work clockwise … it's always clockwise – a sudden huff of laughter – *unless maybe you move to Australia …*

His eyes moved along the lines and he felt power following, sticky and resistant, but it was his power still. As he stared at the sigils, tracing each shape in his mind, he felt them lift from the floorboards to swirl around him, their shapes glittering as though they were drawn in starlight rather than lines of white chalk. There were the sweeping curves of Roc enfolding him like the high walls of a safe harbour; the prickly spikiness of Sho, barbed like an ancient throwing star to be wielded for protection; the spreading lines of Bel radiating outward like the light of a guiding star or the fingers of an outstretched hand reaching towards him with the offer of sanctuary. Their names rang through his consciousness, blending together like a peel of crystal bells.

Aidan felt as much as heard the sound of them and, in that moment, he was no longer pinned on his side staring at chalk marks on a polished wooden floor. Instead, he stood in a vast and cavernous darkness. Gritty dust whispered under his feet as he shifted his weight and there, in front and all around him, his shields glowed like angel wings, the repeated sigils of safety and protection and sanctuary woven into them in threads of phosphor and quicksilver. Of the grieve's control he felt nothing. Those sentient hooks and barbs that had crawled through his flesh, burning like ice and vitriol across every synapse and coercing and controlling his every thought and action were gone. The realisation left him feeling sick with relief.

Dear God, it's over!

His vision blurred and he sank to the ground, wrapping his arms around his chest to still the tremors that shook him, heedless of the tears that ran down his cheeks.

It's over.

He closed his eyes and let the knowledge fall with him into darkness.

'Come on, Aidan. You need to wake up.'

Aidan wasn't so sure about that. If it was up to him, he would be happy to continue lying where he was, letting a vague awareness of the world wash over him. Not that he was particularly comfortable – his muscles felt as if they had been racked and his head ached as though the bones of his skull had been prised apart with a crowbar – but still, it was his pain, in his body, and its presence told him that he was no longer a numb and mindless automaton under Helen's control. Seen in that context the pain was almost welcome, which was more than could be said for the voice. But perhaps its owner would get bored and go away if he refused to respond.

'Open those baby blues. We know you're in there.'

Or perhaps they wouldn't. He let out a sigh that was almost a groan as his befuddled brain finally placed the owner of that voice. On the bright side, she might be able to do something about the pain.

Gingerly he cracked his eyes open and waited while the resulting blur of nightshade hair and pale skin resolved itself into a rough approximation of Gwyn's face. Focusing took more effort than it should have done, but then he hadn't expected her to be quite so close. It came to him then that the lumpy pillow his head was cradled on must be her lap. He thought about that for a moment as he studied her, trying to get his eyes to work properly. Even blurred she looked tired. There were shadows under her eyes and her face had the pinched, slightly strained look she got when she had been writing into the early hours of the morning.

'You look as bad as I feel.' He felt she should know that, even if he had to struggle to force the words out. Then, 'Who hit me with the truck?'

He caught the toss of her head and could imagine the eye roll that accompanied the movement, even if his vision chose that moment to blur so he didn't actually see those green eyes turning heavenward. Gwyn didn't answer with words but looked pointedly to one side.

'That would have been me. Mostly.'

Aidan turned his head fractionally in the direction of the new voice. The joints between his vertebrae seemed to have been filled with ground glass while he had been unconscious, but he did his best to ignore the discomfort and tried for a smile as pleasure welled up inside him. 'Hey.'

'Hey, yourself.' Jane reached out and laced her fingers around his. 'It's nice to have you back, Tarzan.'

'It's nice to be back.' He would have said more but his vision flipped again and this time his stomach went with it. Concentrating on his breathing helped a little. Around small sips of air he added, 'Be even better if I could see straight.'

He tried squinting but that only made his head pound and did nothing to help his vision. Swallowing against the sudden rush of saliva that flooded his mouth, he closed his eyes but he kept hold of Jane's hand. 'I think you've given me a concussion.'

He managed a small laugh at the creative, though physically improbable, suggestion she made in response.

'Maybe later.' He gave her hand a weak squeeze but chose not to open his eyes. 'I don't think I'm up to that right now.'

'Gwyn?' There was hesitation in Jane's voice, cut with an edge of urgent, desperate hope.

Aidan processed that along with the fact that she had spoken to Gwyn and not to him. *I must be looking bad, then.*

He couldn't quite bring himself to care. From a long way away, he thought he heard Gwyn sigh, but she only said, 'I'll do what I can.'

Aidan felt the brush of fingertips along his jaw and up over his cheekbones to his temples. Light as moth wings they stroked his skin, leaving a tingling warmth behind them. He sighed as his muscles softened and relaxed. He was no longer aware of the sensation of his head being cradled in Gwyn's lap, just a feeling of floating, weightless, as if in some thick, warm syrup that trickled through his flesh and seeped into his bones. The pain was still present, but that creeping warmth had swaddled it, muffling the shape of it, soothing its jagged edges, so it no longer had the power to slice him open.

For a timeless moment he lay there, feeling muscle and bone melting together, dissolving and sinking into that soothing warmth. He drifted somewhere on the borders of consciousness, but gradually the dreamy fuzziness receded and he began to feel more like himself. He spoke without thinking. 'Remind me to come to you next time Jane and I—'

Horror closed his throat, choking off the words.

Dear God!

His eyes flew open as memory flooded back. He jerked upright, barely registering the fact that the pain that would have floored him only minutes before was gone.

'I tried to kill you. Both of you.'

He twisted to look first at Jane and then at Gwyn. Now he was able to focus properly the signs of fatigue on Gwyn's face were obvious but, although there was an ashy grey tinge to her lips that worried him, he saw no indication of any injuries. Jane looked – well, like Jane really – as unfazed by life as ever, until he saw the bruises spreading like ink stains along the outer edges of her forearms. He knew exactly what had caused them.

'Jay—'

Jane rolled her eyes. 'Defensive wounds only, Tarzan,' she said, shrugging off his reaction. She cast a dismissive look at her arms. 'You've got a matching set on your shin, so don't feel too bad about them. You took some putting down,' she admitted. 'I had to play rough.'

Ordinarily, Aidan would have met a statement like that with a suggestive leer, but his natural comeback of *I love it when you do that* dried in his throat. He swallowed round the tangle of words and emotions. 'I'm glad.'

For the briefest of moments Jane's eyes met his and he saw, behind her nonchalance, his own despair at having to hurt someone he loved reflected back at him. Then she shook her head and her mask was firmly back in place.

'You may not be quite so pleased when you try to stand up. Gwyn might have fixed that thick skull of yours, but I've probably screwed your hip up. And you're really going to have to work on your blocks. You fall for that double mawashi geri every time.' Her hand closed around his, squeezing his fingers.

'Yes, Sensei Jane.'

Another thought occurred to him, one that stopped him in his tracks like a slap across the face. A slap, or a psychic bolt.

'I tried to hit you with a Levin bolt. *I did* hit you with a Levin bolt. Full force.' He knew he had thrown them effectively because he saw, in his mind's eye, the image of Gwyn falling backward under the impact of his second bolt. 'What the hell happened?'

To his intense surprise, Jane smirked. 'Yeah, well, we're going to have to talk about that. Apparently, the whole magic thing doesn't work on me.'

Aidan blinked in surprise. That was not what he had been expecting to hear. 'Really?'

'Seems that way.' A typical Jane shrug accompanied the words, dismissing conjecture – however entertaining that might be – in the face of facts. 'What can I say? I'm a cyber ninja, after all.'

She was trying for nonchalance, but Aidan thought his girlfriend sounded rather smug. He wanted to ask more but Gwyn coughed, pointedly.

'I hate to interrupt, but Aidan, we need to know – did you see Eldritch?'

'Yes. Yes, I saw him.'

His voice sounded hollow in his ears and some of the warmth that had flowed back into his world with the realisation that Jane and Gwyn were safe drained away.

Put the guilt away, son. It's not helping anyone right now.

Aidan forced himself to take a slow, steadying breath, grounding himself as he twisted to face his mentor. 'And I saw Terry. They've not taken him yet.'

'Thank the Lady.'

The sense of relief embodied in Gwyn's words was almost palpable.

Aidan hated having to bring her down again. 'But they're going to, Gwyn. They plan to do it today.'

Gwyn's mouth tightened but she didn't seem surprised. She gave a small nod as though he was telling her something she already knew. 'Do you have any idea where they've taken him?'

Her voice was businesslike, and it was only the long years of knowing her that allowed Aidan to hear the emotions underlying that cool tone. He felt that fear too, but he did his best to put it to one side as he groped in his memory for any details he could offer, sifting through everything he had overheard Helen and Terry discussing. He hadn't cared about any of it while he had been wrapped in the influence of the blood magic – it had been nothing more than noise, irrelevant to the task that had been set for him – but concentrating now he realised he could recall it, like the soundtrack to a film that had been running in another room. And there it was. Terry had asked about where they should take Eldritch and Helen had said that he, Aidan, had provided them with a solution. Surely, there was only one place that could mean.

'I think so. There's a kid's nursery at one of the local churches that's been damaged in a fire. They're having some sort of fundraiser for it next weekend. The woman next door gave me a flyer, wanted me to remind Helen and Eldritch, to make sure they were going.' Aidan's eyebrows drew down as he recalled the force of nature that was Carol. 'I gave it to Helen.'

He hadn't thought she had paid any attention to it, but she must have done.

'She told Terry about it, about the church, just before they left. I guess she didn't think it mattered if I overheard.'

He frowned, torn between anger at Helen's dismissal of him and relief that the grieve's oversight had given them the information they needed.

Jane snorted. 'Little mistakes. It never pays to get cocky.' There was an element of superiority in her own voice.

Gwyn was more objective. 'We were lucky though. It wouldn't have done us any good if we hadn't been able to get Aidan to break through the blood magic. Do you know where this church is, Aidan?'

Aidan nodded. 'St Martin's – no, St Martin's Churchyard – deconsecrated, I guess. There was a map on the flyer. I got the impression that it wasn't very far.'

'Then what are we waiting for?' Jane was halfway to her feet as she spoke. 'We need to find the flyer and go gatecrash the party.'

'Just a minute, Jane. Before we go anywhere there are some details we have to work out.' Gwyn held up her hands to forestall any protest. 'I know we may not have much time so don't waste it by arguing with me. Aidan, when you saw Eldritch, how was he? Had they hurt him?'

'I don't think they'd tortured him, if that's what you mean. They had him tied to the bed upstairs.'

Jane had sat back down. Now, she widened her eyes at him in exaggerated interest.

'Really?'

Aidan couldn't help but grin, reassured by her response that, despite all that had happened, things were alright between them. 'Don't start.'

Reluctantly he put her teasing to one side and concentrated on the image of the wizard as he had seen him on entering the bedroom, forcing himself to think of him not as a friend but as a stranger, assessing his condition just as he would a stray hiker on Plynlimon.

'He looked dehydrated and I don't suppose they've fed him. He's got some nasty looking abrasions around his wrists and ankles, painful but not deep enough to have done any lasting damage. He also has a cut under his left eye that might need a couple of stitches.'

His composure slipped and he swallowed bile as he remembered the feel of the knife in his hand. *Please don't ask me about that.*

Thankfully, Gwyn didn't. 'Was he conscious?'

'Yes, and he still had a fair bit of fight left in him, even though he was tied up. When Helen took the gag off him he tried to tell me the sigils I needed to free myself.'

The briefest of smiles lifted the corners of Gwyn's mouth, rueful appreciation for the wizard's efforts. 'I don't suppose she liked that,' she said drily.

'No.' Aidan shook his head, remembering Helen's fury. 'She gagged him again straight away. He still tried to fight though. Then, when she told him she was going to use blood magic on me, he went crazy trying to get free, to get her to stop. She … she told Terry to shut him up, to stop him.'

He bit his lip, reliving the sense of helplessness at being so totally under Helen's control he couldn't even turn his head to look at his friend. 'I heard him hit him.'

He closed his eyes briefly, trying to bring back any other details that Gwyn might deem useful, and for a moment the hot, stuffy air of the bedroom closed round him again. He could hear the ugly note in Terry's voice and the sound of flesh striking flesh, but all he could picture was the cool silver of the blade in Helen's hand. He opened his eyes again, not wanting to remember any more. Gwyn might want to know the how of what had happened, but he could only report back on the result. He gave a small shrug, uncomfortable and apologetic and a tiny bit defiant.

'He knocked him out – I know that much – but I couldn't actually see what he did.'

And when Helen had stepped towards him, knife in hand, a large part of him had stopped caring. He wasn't proud of that, but he thought that Eldritch, at least, might have understood. Whether or not Gwyn did he wasn't sure. Certainly, if she noticed his discomfort, she made no comment on it.

Instead, she said, 'He wasn't able to use his magic?'

She spoke softly, her voice flat and distracted, as though her thoughts had already raced far away, beyond that simple statement. Aidan considered what she had said. He hadn't given the possibility any thought, but he realised it must be true. How else could four short lengths of rope keep a wizard captive?

'No, I guess not.'

Gwyn let out her breath in a long sigh. 'That's what I was afraid of.'

She bowed her head, pinching the bridge of her nose between her thumb and forefinger as though she was trying to stop a headache.

'Why, Gwyn? What difference does that make?'

But Gwyn didn't answer Jane's question. Her eyes were closed, shutting her two companions out. Jane looked at Aidan but he shook his head, as baffled as she was by the raw, haunted look he had seen on Gwyn's face. For a moment his ex-guardian had looked not so much afraid but terrified, as though she had seen some critical balance shift in favour of the grieves, yet he couldn't understand what had changed. Then it hit him.

'Oh.'

He couldn't think of anything else to say.

CHAPTER 34

'For crying out loud, what is it with you two? Why are you both so reluctant to say what it is that you're afraid of? I don't do this hocus pocus stuff so how can I help if neither of you is willing to come straight out and tell me what's wrong?'

Aidan winced. He could understand Jane's frustration and the fact that her usually ice-cool temper was fraying was a sign of just how unsettled she was. But if he was right, it wasn't his place to explain.

'It's kind of complicated, Jay.'

The glare he got in return would have sent the dojo juniors running for cover – and a fair few of the senior ranks too. Aidan was desperately trying to think of something he could say that wouldn't make the situation worse when, against his expectation, Gwyn spoke.

'No, Aidan, actually it's very simple.' She straightened up and looked at her two companions. 'And I'm sorry, Jane, I wasn't meaning to be secretive. Of all of us, you may be the one best placed to survive this particular hocus pocus stuff.'

Gwyn's lips twitched briefly, a fleeting attempt at a smile that came nowhere near warming her eyes. She pushed one hand restlessly through her hair, loosening the final remnants of her plait so that it fell in disarray around her shoulders. But for all the storm-wrack chaos of her hair, she herself seemed to have taken on a grim focus, channelling her fear into something sharp and deadly that made Aidan wonder if her choice of verb had been deliberate. Gwyn had the air of someone who wasn't sure she would survive her chosen path coupled with an absolute determination to see it through regardless. He prayed he was reading the situation wrongly but a prickly feeling in the pit of his stomach told him he wasn't, and the thought petrified him.

Gwyn continued relentlessly. 'The problem is that even if we rescue Eldritch and – let it please the Lady! – we *will* get there before Terry tries to take him, but when we do, he's not going to have any power. He won't be able to help to destroy the grieves, which means I'm going to have to do it on my own.' She exhaled a small huff of breath that, under other circumstances, might have been a self-deprecating laugh. 'And the problem with that,' she added, forestalling the obvious question, 'is that I simply don't have the power to do it any more.'

For several seconds nobody spoke, Gwyn's words hanging between them.

'Okay, we go in and we rescue Eldritch and we leave the grieves.' In the light of his recent experience, what had seemed an unacceptable compromise earlier now made sense to Aidan. 'At least we can save him. That's something, isn't it? The pair of you can come back and finish the job when he's got his power back.'

Gwyn looked at him and the smile that spread over her face was as sweet as a half-remembered love song. For an instant the weariness lifted from her eyes and she looked almost young. 'Bless you, Aidan.'

It was as though he had offered her something unknowably precious. But she shook her head regretfully, unable – or unwilling – to take it.

'You were right when we spoke earlier. We both know I can't leave them on the loose.'

'But you said—'

'I did. But what happened here has upped the stakes. You have no idea how close we were to being unable to save you. If Helen was willing to use blood magic once there's nothing to say she won't do so again, this time on someone who has no hope of freeing themselves.'

'And you'll put your life on the line because of that?' Aidan fought down the sudden urge to grab those narrow shoulders and shake them until he rattled some sense into her. He balled his hands into fists to keep himself from doing just that as the unease that had been building in him erupted. 'Christ! You've been hanging out with Eldritch for too long.'

It was his fear talking, he knew that – his own fear of facing Helen again and his fear for Gwyn and for what she might be prepared to do if he couldn't persuade her otherwise.

If his voice was cracking with temper, Jane's was coldly clinical. 'Couldn't we just kill them? Helen and Terry, I mean.'

Aidan turned and stared at his girlfriend, aghast. 'Have you gone crazy too?'

'No.' Jane sounded almost offended that he would say such a thing. 'If they died when they were taken as hosts, we wouldn't be killing them as such, we'd just be stopping their bodies.'

'I don't think the police would see it quite like that.'

'And it wouldn't solve the problem,' Gwyn added, though her tone suggested she might have considered Jane's solution if that weren't the case. 'Killing the hosts will set the grieves free. If anything, it makes things worse because they'd then be able to take new hosts and we wouldn't be any the wiser as to where they had gone.'

'But we wouldn't have a rogue wizard terrorising London.'

'No, just two dead bodies and a probable life sentence for murder.' Aidan rolled his eyes. 'I thought I was the one who'd had my brain scrambled.'

'We'd also have two more people killed when the grieves take new hosts,' Gwyn said as if she hadn't heard Aidan's final comment. 'I appreciate the thought, Jane, but no.'

'Then we're screwed?'

Against all odds, Jane's summing up of the situation drew a small smile from Gwyn.

'Not yet. Lady willing, there is one way that I might still be able to access some of Eldritch's power.' She swallowed and despite the lightness of her tone Aidan saw the desperate intensity in her eyes when she turned towards him. 'When you saw Eldritch, did you notice whether he had his grandmother's ring, the one he wears on a chain round his neck?'

It took him a moment to process the question. His mind was still dealing with the notion that Jane had been serious about killing the grieves and Gwyn seemed to be serious about getting herself killed. But he knew the ring Gwyn was describing and why Eldritch wore it. It was a power sink.

Sometimes, just sometimes, they can save your life.

That was what the wizard had once told him, just before Eldritch had used the power stored in the ring to save both their lives. The way Aidan thought of it, a power sink was the wizardly equivalent of having a bar of Kendal mint cake stashed in the pocket of your rucksack. No one in their right mind wanted to eat the stuff unless it was an emergency, but when you were stuck on a hillside in a blizzard with nothing else, it was very welcome. A spark of hope flickered into life, deep in Aidan's belly, not quite enough to replace the queasy fear, nor the anger he had been using to mask it, but it was a start.

In a calmer voice than he would have used mere moments ago he said, 'No. No, he didn't.'

'You're absolutely sure about that?'

His hand forcing the wizard's head down against the crumpled pillow. Sweat beading Eldritch's face above the blood-flecked gag as he fought to twist away from the knifepoint inching towards his eye, the sinews of his neck straining … and no chain.

Aidan nodded, momentarily unable to speak. He swallowed, choking down the memory along with a mouthful of bile. 'Yes, absolutely.'

'Then Helen must have taken it from him. There's not much point drugging someone to deprive them of their power and then leaving them with access to a power sink.' Gwyn's lips thinned into a tight line as she thought this through. 'I don't think she would have taken it for her own use though. Eldritch and I talked about power sinks once and he was surprised I used them. I got the impression he didn't know anyone else who did. And she wouldn't have taken it with them – it would be too great a risk that he might get hold of it. So it's got to be here in the house. We need to find it.'

'It could be anywhere.' From anyone else the comment would have been defeatist; from Jane it was merely a summing up of the reality of the situation. Still, Aidan could have done without having that pointed out quite so bluntly. And yet …

'No. He was in the bedroom.'

There had been that scatter of discarded clothes – jeans, a

man's shirt – Eldritch's presumably. That would be the place to look first. Aidan started to push himself upright and pain knifed through his hip. He clenched his teeth as he shifted position, getting his left leg under him to lever himself up, but Jane beat him to it.

'I'll go. It will be quicker. You won't be running anywhere for a while.'

Aidan sagged back, gripping his thigh with one hand. He was simultaneously angry with himself for giving in to his body's weakness and grateful that Jane wasn't going to make a fuss about it. Through gritted teeth he managed, 'Bedroom's on the first floor, across the landing from the bathroom.'

'Thanks, Tarzan.' She stopped in the doorway. 'Is there anything else you need, Gwyn?'

'Several things, including a cup of the strongest coffee available, but first, find me that ring.'

CHAPTER 35

Eldritch was aware that he had been drifting in and out of the grey no-man's-land bordering unconsciousness for some time. At first it was difficult to be sure what was real and what was only the fractured dreamscape of nightmare, but each time he surfaced there was a little more certainty; a little more of the world made itself known to him. Each time he slipped back under the world retreated slightly less. He hadn't quite worked up the resolve to open his eyes, but he promised himself he would soon. Even if he didn't, he knew already that he had been moved. The smell alone told him that much. The stale, sickroom fug of the bedroom that had surrounded him like a miasma for the last three days had been replaced with the ashy reek of charred wood overlain with an acrid taint that could only be burnt plastic. Wherever he was – and Eldritch struggled to think of anywhere that might spawn that particular olfactory cocktail – it smelled like the tail end of Bonfire Night or perhaps one of the lesser waiting rooms of hell. In the phantom safety behind his closed eyes he considered that for a moment. It had a certain grim appeal. It said a lot for what he had been through that a sojourn in hell could be viewed as an improvement in circumstances.

So, they had moved him. He really would open his eyes in a minute but, as consciousness flowed back, he found there were other aspects of his situation that clamoured more insistently for his attention. And they weren't pleasant.

His head hurt enough to make him wonder queasily whether opening his eyes was such a good idea after all.

His body hurt too, a mass of individual discomforts that coalesced to form one aching, miserable whole.

His arms … *dear God!*

Full awareness collided with him like a truck, overwhelming, inescapable and unstoppable. With it came the realisation that, with his knees buckled, he was all but hanging from his wrists, his body's weight dragging through his arms and shoulders and turning them into a single, screaming mass of pain. Now he was aware of it, it really was astonishing just how much it hurt.

Clenching his teeth on a groan, Eldritch fought to get his feet underneath him and stand up, ungainly as a newborn foal and hampered by the fact that his ankles were also bound. Had it not been for the rope around his wrists he would have fallen – there was no strength in his legs and his head spun with vertigo – but somehow he managed to lock his knees and hang on, swallowing bile as a wave of nausea rolled over him, forcing it down. Not that there would be anything left in his stomach to throw up, not after days without food, but he doubted that would make the experience any more pleasant.

Briefly he cursed Terry and his fist-happy attitude. He had known Helen wouldn't tolerate his attempt at distraction and it had needed no great leap of Holmesian logic to deduce how she would respond. He winced at the recollection, tasting blood as the small movement made his split lip crack open again. Yes, it had been stupid, but he couldn't have lain there and done nothing, no matter how futile his efforts. Pig-headed stubbornness, Gwyn would have called it. The thought brought a momentary smile, so brief it barely troubled his bruised and swollen mouth before a heart-wrenching sense of grief wiped it away. She would never forgive him for what had happened. Then again, he would never forgive himself. *Aidan!*

When he had first surfaced from the drugs Helen had given him to find himself tied naked and helpless to his own bed, he had felt too sick and disorientated to care much what was happening. If anything, he had thought himself caught in some delirium-born nightmare. Then came the awful, tearing grief as he had realised the truth – that whatever was animating his wife's body it wasn't Helen. The knowledge had come close to finishing him. He couldn't go through that again. Had he been able to access his power, he would have released it in a final strike, willingly sacrificing himself if it had meant destroying the entity inside her. But he quickly found that his power had been sealed away from him, making such an action impossible. So instead, he had tried to free himself physically.

Of course I did, he told the spectre of Gwyn lurking silent and reproachful within his head. *Don't tell me you wouldn't have done the same.*

He had struggled, fighting against the ropes holding him until the skin of his wrists and ankles tore and the blue nylon strands were spattered with blood. But still they had held. And still he had kept up that desperate struggle. In the end it had been exhaustion that had stopped him, finally forcing him to admit the sheer impossibility of the task. And as he lay there, beaten and vulnerable, Helen had come to him. The creature pretending to be his wife had sat cross-legged on the bed beside him, as the real Helen had done so often in the past, and laughed, taunting him with his utter helplessness and with the details of what she and her mate intended to do. Then, almost as if proving a point, she had clamped her hand over his nose until lack of breath had forced him to open his mouth and when he did so, she had poured the second dose of poisons down his throat.

At that point he had shut down. Eldritch swallowed thickly at the memory, turning away from Gwyn in his mind, not wanting to see the contempt he imagined stamped across her features. Part of that had been a physical reaction to the toxins flooding his system, the drugs designed to sap his strength and shred his resistance, ravaging his body like a hundred hungry mouths, gnawing and sucking at the marrow of his bones, leaving him weak and retching, his body trembling with shock. But it had been a mental response too. Eldritch could see that now. His grief had turned inwards and he had reacted to the unbearable by withdrawing from it. Helpless to prevent whatever was being done to him, he had done his best to stop caring. It had been the only option left to him.

But then he had seen Aidan.

The sight of his friend's panicked eyes in his otherwise frozen face, his body moving like an automaton under another's control, had filled him with a mix of anger and fear beyond anything he had felt for himself. In all likelihood, it was too late to save Aidan – Eldritch knew the reality of blood magic too well to dare to hope otherwise – but if Helen had stooped to such evil once she could do so again. And that meant he had no alternative but to fight. Somehow, he had to find a way to stop her. But first he had to escape.

Gingerly, hoping the movement wouldn't make him sick, Eldritch lifted his head and looked around him. His new prison was a large room some thirty feet wide and easily twice as long.

Community hall, he thought, taking in the high ceiling and the tall windows that dominated the walls along either side.

Derelict, he added. He had been right about there having been a fire here. The walls were dark with soot, the windows too so that only a thin, grubby twilight filtered through them for all their size. At the far end of the hall, where perhaps the fire had burned fiercest, a heap of twisted metal frames suggested the remains of a stack of chairs, the floorboards beneath them charred and blackened. At this end the floor looked relatively unscathed, for all that there were scorch marks licking up the walls. Maybe that was why the scaffold he was tied to was at this end of the hall. He looked at the couple of stacked crates, the metal toolbox and the bundled shape of what looked like a decorator's dust sheet that lay to one side of the scaffold and wondered briefly about the people who were – presumably – working here. But Helen had ways to ensure they wouldn't be disturbed; he couldn't rely on help from that quarter. Eldritch looked around him one final time but there was little else to be seen amid the gloom and shadows and nothing that gave any indication of where the hall might be.

He considered that fact for a moment. It was late afternoon; he knew that from his own innate sense of time. He had been unconscious for no more than a couple of hours, not overly long, but sufficient for Helen and Terry to have taken him almost anywhere.

Okay, a derelict hall … somewhere.

He decided that was all he needed for now. It didn't matter where here was; he didn't intend staying for a moment longer than he had to. It was time to act.

Peering sideways at the ties around his wrists, Eldritch had to admit that his captors had done a good job. The rope was the same type they had used on him at the house, a quarter of an inch thick and with the knots tied on the opposite side of the scaffold pole from his hands so there was no way he would be able to reach them – not even if he suddenly developed Houdini-esque levels of flexibility. Nor was he going to be able to twist free. The raw flesh on his wrists and ankles bore ample testament to which wore out first – nylon rope or human skin – and it wasn't a contest he was in any hurry to repeat, not when it would be so pointless. Eldritch gave a grudging huff of breath at Terry and Helen's thoroughness. In other circumstances he might have been flattered that, even now, they still considered him an escape risk.

Worried you're going to lose your precious new host?

But maybe that level of diligence also meant that they were going to leave him alone for a while. He could only hope so. What he was about to attempt wasn't something he could rush.

There had been one unforeseen consequence of his anger at Helen's enslavement of Aidan, one outcome he was confident that Helen herself couldn't have anticipated. Sinking his focus inward, Eldritch felt it within him still – the tiniest thread of power born of adrenalin and fury. Ordinarily he wouldn't have noticed such a minuscule amount. It was like a single spark compared to the fury of a wildfire, a prickle of static against the surging glory of a lightning bolt. It was only because his power was reduced to almost nothing that he was able to sense it. Even so, had his circumstances been less dire, he wouldn't have thought it worth bothering with. But Gwyn had taught him that a lot could be done with a tiny amount of power, if you went about it in the right way, and Aidan – bitter rage filled

Eldritch at the realisation that Aidan and his love of climbing were now things of the past – had taught him a lot about ropes.

He held the memory of those conversations in his mind like a handful of precious jewels – Sunday evenings around the kitchen table or tucked into his small lounge, Jane and Aidan sprawled across the settee and Gwyn cross-legged on the rug, luxuriating in the heat of the wood burner like one of her cats, trading stories backwards and forwards between them. Aidan invariably had some tall tale involving the latest challenge he and Matt – his partner at Red Kite Adventure Training – had inflicted on their trainees, or sometimes, more harrowingly, about the stray hikers and climbers the mountain rescue team were called out to help. It seemed there were a lot of things that could go wrong in the great outdoors and Eldritch – city born and raised – had found the stories fascinating. Ropes didn't only break because they got frayed. They could be damaged by friction too or, more accurately, by the heat it caused. Studying the rope around his right wrist, Eldritch reckoned he could use that tiny spark of power to burn through it, not all at once, but one strand at a time. If he could do that then he could untie himself and escape. Admittedly, the thought of wandering the streets naked wasn't one that thrilled him, but if he got picked up by the police he would be quite happy. He would gladly take a charge of public indecency over what Helen and Terry had planned for him.

So … His eyes slipped closed as he exhaled slowly, centring himself. Awareness of the hall, of the scaffold, of his own aching body slid away as he turned his focus inward and reached for that tiny wisp of power. Such things had been a part of his life for so long he could no longer remember a time when he had been unable to wield the power that lay like molten fire in the core of his bones. Yet reaching for that fragment now was like trying to grasp a silk thread while wearing welding gauntlets. Though he knew exactly what he needed to do, and how it would feel to hold it, he couldn't quite close his senses around that elusive spark. He tried again and once more it slipped away from him. He made another attempt, bringing all his concentration to bear until the muscles of his jaw bunched and jumped and the tendons stood out on his neck with the effort. Yet still that precious ember remained just out of reach. The blood pounding in his temples, Eldritch opened his eyes.

Breathe, he counselled himself.

He let his head drop forward for a moment, feeling the movement pull at the stiff muscles of his neck. He was aware of sweat breaking out all over his skin, how it plastered the matted spikes of his hair to his head and prickled in the heavy stubble along his jaw. It stung in his eyes and burned in the raw flesh of his wrists and ankles. He would have given a lot to be able to wipe it away. He would have given even more for a drink.

Dear God, he was thirsty. Helen had given him a little water – along with the potions she had forced down his throat – but not much. He ran a dry tongue over his lips, feeling the cracked and flaking skin, and tried not to think about it. At least he wasn't gagged any more; that was a small mercy. Probably they hadn't wanted to risk him throwing up when he came round.

Wouldn't want your precious host to choke on his own vomit now, would you?

He raised his head and eyed the hall once more. There

was a door down there, he thought. He could just make out the shape of it in the shadows at the far end. Maybe it led to a kitchen or even just a toilet, anywhere with a sink and taps where he might be able to get a drink. Not much, just a mouthful or two, enough to help clear his head a little and give him the strength to get away.

Damn it, you're not helping yourself.

Annoyed that he had allowed himself to be distracted Eldritch forced himself to straighten up, not quite sure how his knees had come to sag or why he had barely noticed the renewed agony in his wrists. A distant part of him registered the hair-fine tremor in the deep muscles of his legs and he guessed that even standing would be beyond him soon. At this rate he was going to be making his escape on hands and knees. For a moment the thought made him sick and then he pushed it to one side.

Hands and knees will be just fine.

The alternative was infinitely worse.

Resolutely Eldritch turned his focus inwards once more.

Take it. Use it.

Take the thirst and the nausea. Take the dull, wearying ache that seemed woven into bone and sinew and the raw, soul-shredding grief that overlaid everything, as grey and as bitter as ashes. These were things he could use, resources he could beat together into a weapon, even though the one he would use it against was himself. Inwardly Eldritch quailed, knowing what it would cost him.

It won't be the first time.

He had done something similar last autumn after defeating the demon that had broken through in the depths of the Greenfields mine. Injured and exhausted from the battle to overcome it, the only way he could raise the power needed to seal the boundary between the Mortal World and the Unseen Realm had been by tapping into his own pain. He had had nothing else.

In the smoke-scented gloom of the abandoned hall, Eldritch smiled, bittersweet and weary to the bone. He would do this. There was power to be had just from making such a decision. Closing his eyes once more, he sank his consciousness down into his battered flesh, actively seeking and acknowledging each of those separate agonies he had been trying so desperately to hold at arm's length. Every torment he uncovered he embraced, allowing himself not only to feel it but to surrender himself to it. He teased out the jagged red energies of physical pain and waded through the muddy ashes of mental and physical exhaustion. He stood alongside the hole where Helen had ripped the heart from him and let the cold, burning rawness of reawakened grief flood through him. Each sensation was a strap with which to flay his soul and a strop against which he could sharpen his will.

And there, finally, was the little spark of power, glowing softly in the darkness. Gently, lovingly, Eldritch closed his mind around it. He cradled it close and brought it to bear against the rope.

One fibre at a time. It took precision, not strength, to separate each strand in his mind, teasing them apart and then letting that little flare of power sear them. Muscles cramped and twisted, bones ached and flesh burned with sweat until it felt as though his body had truly been flayed, but still Eldritch held firm. It was an agonisingly slow process and the knowledge that Helen and Terry could return at any moment was like vitriol, eating away at his concentration. He pushed the thought away and focused on that tiny flare of power, burning through the rope like a white-hot needle, one strand, one fibre at a time. Dear God, it was taking so long!

Keep going, you're doing fine.

Patience: that was all he needed. It had been the first discipline he had been taught when, as a gangly child of ten, his power had begun to manifest. That power had burned through him, as hot and as bright as phosphorus, but even though its use had come naturally to him, still his teacher had insisted on his repeating the simplest of exercises again and again, instilling in him that all-important discipline, that ability to focus. He sank into it now, giving himself over to it with a whispered prayer of thanks to the wisdom of the tiny grey-haired matriarch who had raised him.

You can do it, El.

Through closed lids he could see Helen – the real Helen, his Helen – standing part way down the hall. Paul was beside her, a comforting hand resting on his sister's shoulder. Steve was there too, a sturdy figure, solid and competent looking in the dusty khaki of his desert fatigues, feet braced, arms folded. Eldritch felt them willing him on, willing him to concentrate, to hold steady.

Keep going, wizard.

He couldn't see her but the voice he heard was Gwyn's and then it morphed into another's.

You're doing okay. He could almost see the speaker's grin as the disembodied voice added, *for an Englishman.*

Aidan, he thought. *I'm going to get out of here. I'm going to avenge you.*

A heartbeat. Stillness. Another heartbeat. A moment

to push back against the exhaustion, to hold off the shivery tremor building in his limbs.

Close your eyes and refine your focus until everything you are is concentrated in that one bead of power.

The voices blended in his head, mingling with his own thoughts. Time seemed to slow and still as, with the delicacy and precision of a surgeon teasing apart nerves and blood vessels, Eldritch separated the rope into its constituent strands and, one by one, severed them. He felt the bindings around his wrist start to loosen.

Yes!

And from behind him came the sound of a door opening.

CHAPTER 36

'There are ways to overcome your shields, my love.' Helen stood in front of the scaffold and eyed Eldritch flirtatiously. She wound a long tendril of hair around one finger as she spoke. 'Pain is one of them.'

She leaned towards him, angling her body so that the linen of her tunic pulled slightly over her breasts. There was little doubt she wore nothing underneath it.

'But what of pleasure?'

Deliberately she brushed against him, sinuous and graceful, and then drew back, watching him closely, weighing his reaction. Working to keep his expression neutral, Eldritch forced himself to meet her eyes.

Keep her talking. 'Why would I care?'

His mouth was so dry it was hard to speak. It was harder still to maintain his focus as he did so, keeping that tiny needle of power searing through the rope one fibre at a time. 'I'm still going to be dead at the end of it.'

That seemed to amuse Helen. She laughed prettily then looked down her nose at him as though he had said something incredibly naïve.

'Of course you will be. But why wouldn't you want to enjoy your last moments?'

She unwound the strand of hair and ran her fingers along his cheek instead. Eldritch turned his head away from her caress. As well as her physical touch he felt her energy prickling him through his too-thin shields. It grated against him like sandpaper, rasping at his own aura until his nerves howled at her nearness. He was aware of Terry too, standing a few feet away. Though he leaned indolently against the stacked crates, the second grieve followed his every movement with almost predatory interest.

'Isn't your friend going to mind if you hurt his new host?' Eldritch tried to keep his voice level, as though it wasn't his pain they were talking about.

Helen's lips curled appreciatively but the flicker of amusement in her eyes told him he hadn't quite succeeded. 'You forget, my love, there are ways of causing you pain that won't significantly damage your body.'

She ran a proprietary hand along his arm as though judging the quality of his muscle. When she reached his biceps her fingers tightened, the nails digging into his skin for the briefest of moments before she released him. An echo of pain scratched along Eldritch's nerves.

'Besides, I'm a healer. It would only be a minor inconvenience.' She gave a little shrug as her gaze returned to his face. Eldritch swallowed, fighting not to think of what her words meant. For a moment his mind went blank as he searched for a response, something – anything – to keep the conversation going.

'You should watch yourself. You know how it ended last time.' The gravelly rasp of his voice sounded false in his ears. Could she tell that he was playing for time? If she did, would she care?

'How sweet.'

Helen stepped closer, the soft weight of her breasts pushing against his chest, the thin linen a barely noticeable barrier between them. The scent of her perfume rose up, threatening to overwhelm him, but beneath it Eldritch thought he could smell the hot scorch of burned rope. Silently he prayed that she wouldn't notice, that that treacherous wisp of scent would be lost in the overall bonfire reek of the hall.

Just a few seconds more.

'No demon would try to possess a human already taken as a host. Why would it?' Helen sniffed disdainfully. 'But even so, in this body I can handle any demon.' She smiled with delight at that power, the pleasure radiating from her even as she reached up, slow and languid as a siren, and put her hands on either side of his face. Eldritch felt the warmth of her breath as she bent her head close to whisper into his ear. 'But I would rather handle you.'

Concentrate.

The fibres of the rope were parting, one by one, beneath his magic. All he had to do was to focus on them. He could ignore the woman trying to seduce him. It wasn't as though she meant anything to him now. But he was forgetting what she was and who she had been.

'Mmm ... yes,' Helen murmured.

Her hands skimmed over the muscles of his chest, light and teasing. They stopped and her nails nipped his skin sending little shivers of anticipation of almost-pain almost-pleasure through his system, moving on, passing down over the sensitive skin of his belly, then down further still. She knew his body intimately, just as he had known hers, and she knew how and where to touch him to get the reaction she wanted. The grieve's fingers trailed fire over his skin and Eldritch groaned in mixed despair and desire as he felt himself responding to her.

Helen laughed again, the sound throaty and suggestive. 'You remember, don't you?'

He tried to turn away as she went to kiss him, her lips hot and urgent on his, demanding that he acknowledge her. His body seemed to burn where she pressed against him and all the while her fingers teased and stroked. Desire was building within him, igniting his flesh, burning away all other sensations, overriding even the pain and the physical sickness so that all he wanted was to bury himself inside her. As if from a long way away Eldritch heard Helen laugh again as he moaned.

'Why try to resist me?' she purred. 'You were more than willing before.'

Her teeth nipped provocatively at his lip. Eldritch fought to hold back the part of him that wanted to respond in kind.

Yes, he had loved her, frantically, passionately, losing himself in her body. But that had been when he had believed she was still Helen. His mind squirmed at the thought of what he had done, of what she had done to him. Were those times any less a rape than this would be? His stomach curdled at the thought and in that moment the sourness of shame and revulsion flooded through his system, sweeping before it the cloying miasma of arousal and lust that had saturated his flesh.

Use it!

Eldritch caught the wave of bitterness and flung it towards his wrist and the final strands of rope parted as though they had been drenched in acid. His arm dropped, suddenly free, and Eldritch lashed out, driving his fist into the side of Helen's face before she had time to realise what he had done. Pain burst through his knuckles, shocking him, even as Helen went sprawling. How did Aidan and Jane manage to do this? But in that same instant he was sweeping up the flare of energy it generated and hurling it at the bindings around his left wrist. He caught the almost sweet smell of burning flesh, felt his skin pucker and sear and the rope start to give, but the next second Terry was on top of him.

Eldritch managed to get in another wild punch, sending Terry staggering backwards, his nose streaming blood. He twisted, pulling against the restraining rope as Terry snatched something from the top of the crates. The handyman lunged, blood-rimmed teeth bared in a snarl of berserker rage, arm swinging, and Eldritch caught the glint of metal arcing down towards his head, deadly as a battle mace. In that instant he froze, knowing he should dodge but unable to do anything but watch the descending blow. In some still, small corner of his mind he realised that Terry was too angry to care what damage he inflicted, and part of him welcomed that fact. He would die – yes – but he wouldn't be taken as a host. His power, at least, would never be turned against an innocent.

'No!'

Eldritch's flayed senses felt the slap of power that knocked Terry backwards like a wall of heat from the blast door of a furnace. He heard the clatter of the younger man's improvised weapon as it fell from his hand and onto the floor, but the next second any further thought was beyond him. He was aware only of the shockwave of pain that slammed into him. It went through him like acid, turning his bones to chalk and his muscles to water. His knees buckled and he would have screamed but the pain was so overwhelming he couldn't draw breath. Dimly he was aware that he was still hanging from his left wrist. Cold sweat sheeted down his body, a wave of blackness swamped his vision and he had no strength to push it back. He was going to pass out. His shields would finally give way and Terry would take him as a host.

When you wake up, you'll be dead, he thought, stupid with pain and shock, and could only hope that the agony would end when that happened.

A hand fisted in his hair, dragging his head up, and power slapped him, buffeting his failing senses and jerking him back from the edge of oblivion. He was dimly aware that the scourge of pain had been lifted. What he felt now – bad though it was – was simply the aftermath. But he wasn't so foolish as to think Helen's anger had run its course. He knew the pain would return in a heartbeat when she willed it. Blearily he opened his eyes to face the inevitable.

Helen leaned in close towards him. 'You're going to pay for that.'

All trace of seduction had gone from her voice. She didn't shout, but an undercurrent of fury ran beneath the carefully controlled words. Her grip tightened painfully in his hair as if for emphasis and then she thrust him away from her. 'Secure him!'

Contempt dripped from every syllable.

Before Eldritch could even think of resisting, Terry had jerked him upright, wrenching his newly freed arm backwards and slamming it against the scaffold pole then lashing it in place. For several moments the handyman stood studying his captive, his eyes hard, his lips set in a thin, calculating line. He seemed to reach some conclusion for his expression changed, twisting into an ugly sneer as he half-turned away only to swing back sharply, dipping his shoulder and driving his fist up into Eldritch's solar plexus in a short, hard jab that Eldritch was helpless to avoid. Tied though he was, Eldritch folded around the punch, the breath driven from his lungs. His legs buckled and he couldn't help gasping in pain as his weight dropped onto his wrists, sending fresh agony shearing through his arms. He heard Terry's grunt of satisfaction as the younger man cinched the ropes tighter around his wrists. Then Terry had him by the chin, work-hardened fingers digging into the soft flesh over his jaw as he forced his head up. Terry leaned in close, close enough for Eldritch to smell the other man's sweat, even above the reek of his own body. Close enough to see the hungry gleam that lit his eyes.

'Not long now.'

A smile slid across Terry's lips. Keeping his eyes fixed on Eldritch's he mimed a slow, lingering kiss then released his grip with a shove. He was still laughing as he stepped away from the scaffold.

Eldritch straightened up slowly, moving carefully around the wrecking ball of pain that Terry's fist had left in his gut. He supposed he should be thankful that the grieve hadn't carried through with his charade and tried to take him – not that he was under any illusion that the reprieve was anything other than temporary – but gratitude wasn't easy when even the simple act of breathing hurt. At least the handyman had returned to his post by the crates, ceding centre stage to Helen once more, so he wasn't in imminent danger of another fist in the gut. Eldritch pulled himself up a little straighter, bracing himself on legs that felt like chewed string. Of course, Helen could do things to him that would make a beating from Terry seem almost pleasant.

Ah well . . .

He moved his jaw, trying to work up enough saliva to swallow and overcome the dryness in his throat. Somehow, he found his voice. 'I suppose it's too late to say that I'm sorry?'

Helen huffed a short breath in response, her nostrils flaring, though Eldritch couldn't have said whether she was annoyed or amused by his attempt at bravado. She made no other response but continued to stand silently watching him and his next quip died unspoken.

'I thought so,' he conceded. He half shrugged, the smallest of movements, and let the silence fall between them in the hot, heavy gloom. Taking the opportunity, he studied her face, the full lips and high, arched brows, her hair like a fall of sunshine over those slender shoulders. Beautiful, yes, but there was nothing of his Helen left in the pansy-blue eyes that fixed on him like a hawk's on its prey. He shoved down the grief that threatened to overwhelm him even now and willed himself to stay calm. The mark left by his fist stood out on her jaw like a visible rebuke.

Wait for me, he thought, conjuring a picture of the woman he had loved – his Helen – in his mind. *I won't be long.*

Still, the creature wearing his wife's body made no comment. Instead she waited, patient as a serpent. The message behind her inaction was clear: *There's no need to hurry. You are mine, to do with as I please.*

She knew he had no way to resist her just as they both knew that no one was coming to save him. Every line of her body shouted those two truths in eloquent silence.

Eventually, she spoke. 'That wasn't wise, my love.' Her voice had settled back into its former husky sweetness. She sounded resigned, like a mother forced to reprimand a child for its own good. Only her eyes, cold and unforgiving as a winter sky, hinted that she would enjoy what was to come. 'I offered you pleasure.'

She reached out and brushed her fingertips across his cheek in a parody of her earlier caress. Eldritch held himself rigid, forcing himself not to flinch from her touch. Helen pouted prettily as she lifted her hand away, as though his lack of response had disappointed her. She sighed but her eyes remained hard.

'But, since you refused me, I will use pain instead.' She leaned closer and whispered conspiratorially, 'You think you know what that means.' Her lips were almost brushing his hair as she added, 'But you have no idea.'

Eldritch felt the energy emanating from her, the waves of anticipation that were like a prelude to ecstasy. Though he tried to keep his face expressionless he felt the first coils of fear twist in his belly. His shields were paper thin. It would take almost nothing to break through them, but he understood that was no longer Helen's sole interest. Before they reached that point, she planned to enjoy every moment of agony she could wring out of him. She would make him suffer until Terry's taking him would feel like an act of mercy.

Helen drew back fractionally and Eldritch wondered if she was feeling his emotions as he could feel hers, drinking them in like a fine wine, savouring them. He was aware as never before of his utter helplessness, of the unyielding metal of the scaffold pole against his wrists and the rough tightness of the ropes holding him. He felt the smoothness of the worn wooden floorboards beneath his bare feet and the sweat prickling out across his body and sliding down his skin. The very air seemed hot, clogging his lungs with the smell of ashes. He was aware that his heart was hammering and that his breathing had gone shallow and high in his chest as adrenalin kicked through his blood.

Those of us about to die—

Helen leaned in again and this time Eldritch couldn't stop himself flinching as she brushed the matted hair back from his face.

She looked up at him, her eyes dark and velvety. 'I've made you scream with passion, my love. Now, will you scream for me again?'

CHAPTER 37

'What do you want to do, Gwyn?'

Jane turned a quizzical eye on her companions as they stood at the entrance to St Martin's Churchyard. High walls of rough, age-blackened sandstone flanked what would normally be a wide gateway, but the gap between the two massive pillars had been sealed off with panels of chipboard shuttering. The temporary barricade wasn't as high as the walls, but it made it clear that the churchyard was currently off limits to the general public. To reinforce the point, prominent black and yellow notices proclaimed the building within to be unsafe and warned against unauthorised access, should anyone still feel inclined to try.

'Do we risk the easy way?' Jane jerked her head at the small access door set in the centre of the grey-painted boards like a postern gate in a stage scenery castle wall. 'Or do we go over the top? I can get up there.'

She frowned and bit her lip as though holding back the words 'I'm not sure about you two', but Aidan heard them anyway. At any other time, he would have responded to the implied slight with a few choice words of his own, but now he kept quiet. Though he wasn't about to admit it, the thought of trying to scale the shuttering made him feel faintly sick.

It was ridiculous.

He swiped a hand through his hair, pushing the damp strands back from his forehead, feeling the sweat slick against his fingers. The weather was changing, becoming sticky and humid. Behind them the eastern sky still showed an intense blue but to the west, beyond the churchyard, it had darkened to the colour of a bone-deep bruise. There was a storm building and from the towers of cumulonimbus crowding the sky it looked like it would be a monster.

Nothing good comes from the west …

Aidan grimaced at the old saying and pulled his attention back to the shuttering blocking off the churchyard.

It's not as though it's that high, he told himself, shamed by the sudden dryness in his mouth and the queasy knot of fear clenching in his stomach. A running jump, hit it halfway up, grab for the top and swing over. Yes, he'd have to be careful, make the jump so he pushed off on his left leg rather than his right. It might not be pretty, but it should be possible. Yet, even as he imagined himself making that leap, catching hold of the rough board, the hair prickled on the back of his neck and his palms went clammy. Every instinct screamed at him that it wasn't his hip he needed to worry about; something awful was going to happen the moment he tried to climb that barrier. Despite the heat of the afternoon, he shivered and tried not to think what might have walked across his grave.

'We'll use the door.' Gwyn's pronouncement cut across his thoughts. 'They must have taken Eldritch in that way – they certainly didn't take him over the top. We'll do the same.'

Aidan swallowed thickly. Somehow the prospect of going through the door was no more appealing than going over the top.

He licked his lips. 'Won't Helen have thought of that?'

'Of course she will.' The look that accompanied Gwyn's response could have reduced both the door and the shuttering around it to charred kindling and made Aidan wish he hadn't said anything. 'And, as I don't want any more nasty surprises today or to tip Helen off that we're coming, neither of you are to do anything until I tell you it's safe to do so.'

Though Jane topped Gwyn by several inches and Aidan topped her by several more, Gwyn managed to look down her nose at both of them. 'Is that clear?'

'Crystal.' Jane didn't salute in response to the snap in Gwyn's voice but the sideways look she shot Aidan suggested she hadn't decided whether to be amused, impressed or irritated by Gwyn's newly authoritarian manner.

Aidan wasn't sure either. Gwyn's attitude had changed dramatically since they had found Eldritch's ring – power store intact – and she had accessed the energy held within it. At first, he had thought her increased confidence – a less charitable person might have termed it arrogance – was reassuring, but now he wondered if he didn't prefer her previous, more cautious style. He confined himself to an unhappy nod.

'Good. This may take a few minutes. Don't interrupt me.'

And with that she dismissed them, turning to study the shuttering blocking their way. Aidan held his breath as she raised her hands, stretching them out so that her splayed fingers were almost touching its surface. He knew Gwyn was sinking her arcane senses into the fabric of the churchyard boundary. Like an explosives expert feeling for a wire or a trip plate, or perhaps more like a bloodhound questing for the elusive scent of danger, she would search for the unfathomable traces of any trap or trigger that Helen might have laid. Having experienced Helen's power first hand, the idea made Aidan's stomach churn. All he could do was to keep telling himself that Gwyn knew what she was doing and hope that his growing sense of unease didn't mean that this whole venture was about to blow up in her face.

'How do we know when she's finished the HPS?'

Jane's terminology was new to Aidan but the question was a welcome distraction from the sick dread of watching Gwyn and waiting for something to go wrong. He turned away from the churchyard entrance and the small, still figure standing in front of it and looked quizzically at his girlfriend. 'HPS?'

'Come on, Tarzan, keep up.' Jane offered rolled eyes and an unapologetic smirk at Aidan's confusion. 'Hocus pocus stuff. How do we know when she's finished?'

'Oh.' Aidan considered Gwyn's approach to the arcane in the lessons she had given him. 'It depends what she finds. Probably she'll just stop, put her hands down, maybe swear a bit.' He almost managed a smile.

Unless it all goes wrong. Dear God …

He turned back to watch Gwyn, but he wasn't sure whether he should pray that she found nothing or hope that she would find some evidence of Helen's defences that would stop them entering the churchyard. He rubbed a hand over his sweating face, wishing he could wipe away his apprehension as easily. The gluey heat of the afternoon seemed to settle closer around him, clogging his lungs.

'Are you okay, Tarzan?'

'Huh?'

He jerked back and this time he read concern in the way Jane's brows kinked down over her direct blue gaze.

'Of course. I'm fine.' He tried for a grin and suspected

he succeeded only in baring his teeth. 'I was just wishing that we'd thought about the place being boarded up. We could have brought a ladder instead of a bag of salt and a year's supply of candles.' He thought of the satchel of magical paraphernalia Gwyn had assembled at Eldritch's. 'Unless Gwyn's thinking of burning a way through.'

It was a poor joke and even to his own ears his voice sounded flat and strained. He could see from the way Jane's frown deepened that she had heard it too, but he couldn't bring himself to tell her of his fear.

'My hip's giving me some gip,' he said instead, which was true, although it stung his pride to admit it. He shifted his weight in an unsuccessful attempt to ease the nagging ache of bruised muscle and bone. 'Gwyn's driving didn't help.'

They had taken Eldritch's car and Gwyn had driven it like a woman possessed, cutting through the rat run of criss-crossing side streets that lay between Victoria Mews and St Martin's Lane at a speed that showed little concern for safety or for her passengers' comfort. The narrow residential streets had been riddled with speed bumps and it seemed to Aidan that they had found all of them – and slowed for none.

'It wasn't the most comfortable of rides.'

He saw renewed guilt flare in Jane's eyes and felt bad for putting it there. Still, guilty or not, she didn't apologise. Instead, she let out an irritated grunt.

'You should have tried sitting in the back,' she said with some feeling. The dark look that accompanied her words conjured a genuine smile from Aidan.

'I would have done, but I'd have thrown up over you.'

'Charming.'

The dry tone was so reminiscent of the sort of response Eldritch might have made that, for a moment, Aidan saw the wizard in his mind, leaning nonchalantly against the churchyard wall, his arms folded across his chest and a sardonic smile gracing those saturnine features.

Damn it!

A different fear and guilt of his own smote Aidan. He closed his eyes and tried to reach for calm.

Eldritch is in there, he told himself. *How can you possibly be too scared to go in and save him?*

But the thought of doing so made his chest tighten and his breathing become fast and panicky. The world seemed to swim behind his closed eyes.

'Tarzan?'

He realised Jane was speaking to him again.

Her voice sharpened, demanding his attention. 'You're not okay, are you?'

This time Aidan couldn't find the energy to lie. He opened his eyes and looked at her. 'No.'

Jane swore at him, furious as a she-cat defending her kittens. 'Why didn't you say something sooner?'

She moved to take his arm, but Aidan batted her hand away. 'It's nothing you did. In fact, it's nothing anyone's done to me that's the problem. It's this.' His gesture encompassed Gwyn, the boarded-up entrance and the churchyard walls. 'Everything about this is wrong.'

Jane stopped fussing at him and her eyes went sharp but she said nothing.

Unsure how he could explain the strength of his feelings, Aidan waded on through her silence. 'I'm not scared of facing

Helen again, honestly I'm not.' He had to believe that. 'And the only reason Terry took me down was that I was stupid enough to turn my back on Helen and she hit me first. That's not going to happen again.' A little flare of anger kicked through his system, momentarily displacing the fear. It gave him the impetus to continue. 'But every time I look at those boards, every time I think of climbing over them, or the wall, or going through that door, I just know that something bad – really bad – is going to happen – to you, to me, to Gwyn.'

Conscious that he was clenching and unclenching his fists he hooked his thumbs in the front pockets of his jeans. He had never had premonitions before, but he had never had anyone like Helen mess with his brain before, either.

'This isn't pre-fight nerves or imagination. Something bad is going to happen. I just know it is.'

He stopped, reading scepticism in Jane's continuing silence.

'You've got good instincts,' he said. 'Tell me you're not getting a bad feeling about any of this.'

To Aidan's relief Jane didn't immediately dismiss his fears. She folded her arms and stood there, her lower lip caught between her teeth, as she considered what he had said.

'You mean like evil zombie wife deliberately mentioned where they were taking Eldritch so you'd overhear and now you're leading us into a trap?'

Aidan nodded unhappily. Put like that, it was exactly what he was afraid of. 'So, you can feel it too?' At least he wasn't imagining it.

'Nope, not a thing.'

Aidan blinked in surprise. 'But—'

'Screw it, Tarzan. I don't know what's got you so freaked

about this, but I don't think Helen had any expectation of you coming out of that blood magic stunt with your brain intact.'

Jane moved closer again but, instead of trying to take his arm, she landed a none-too-gentle punch on his biceps. It said more about her relief at his recovery than she would put into words. 'That being the case, why would she waste effort with some sort of double-cross?'

She looked at him expectantly for a moment, eyebrows raised, and then shrugged, dismissing her own argument. 'But hey, what do I know? It's HPS. I can tell you one thing though.' Her voice took on a note of challenge of its own. 'That's a heavy-duty hasp and staple fitted to that door but there's no sign of a padlock. No one goes to all the trouble of boarding up an entrance like that and then leaves the door unlocked.' Her stare turned hard, daring him to contradict her. 'Someone's gone in there and I'm guessing it's zombie wife and her tame handyman.'

'They're in there alright.'

Aidan and Jane turned sharply, neither having noticed Gwyn finish her assessment of the churchyard boundary. She could move as stealthily as one of her cats when she chose to. Sometimes Aidan thought she did it on purpose.

He eyed his teacher unhappily. 'Are you sure, Gwyn?'

Jane might have dismissed the possibility of them walking into a trap but, in her own words, it was HPS; she didn't truly understand what Helen was capable of.

Gwyn didn't answer immediately. Instead, she studied him, her head canted to one side like an inquisitive bird, and Aidan wondered what she was seeing. Was she reading his fear and judging him?

He swallowed the words *Don't make me go in there* and

went for the painful admission. 'I've got a really bad feeling about this.'

It was like waiting for a storm to break. Aidan braced himself for Gwyn's put-down, knowing it would be far blunter than Jane's. Yet, when she finally spoke, what she said was, 'I'd be surprised if you hadn't, Aidan.'

For a moment Aidan felt something akin to relief – vindication perhaps that his fears were justified. 'You mean you've found a trap?'

And perhaps that meant they would need to find another way in.

But Gwyn's next words dashed that hope. 'Not a trap, no. Helen was certain that you'd be able to deal with us, Aidan and – though it galls me to say it – if it hadn't been for Jane turning out to be a null, you would have done.'

The null in question grinned, all guilt forgotten.

'Why would she bother to set a trap here? No, her concern was to make sure she and Terry wouldn't be disturbed by anyone coming into the churchyard. It's too big an area to cast a veil around to ensure no one can get in, so instead she's set wards all along the boundary. These walls are written with sigils of distraction and fear – Shibelth, Trenth, Na'ar—' The very names were harsh and discordant and Gwyn's expression tightened as she spoke them as though they left a bitter taste on her tongue. 'There are others too – you don't need to know them – but they all have one aim: to stop anyone thinking about what's in the churchyard and to make sure that no one tries to go inside. Even if someone passing by heard something—' Gwyn's gaze dropped, her eyes flicking away as though she couldn't quite bear to look at him and Aidan flinched; it didn't take a mind reader to guess what sounds she was imagining. His own expression was grim as she continued. 'They wouldn't investigate. But chances are, they wouldn't even notice with the strength of these wards. Helen has bought herself all the time she needs to do whatever she has to to break Eldritch.'

This time Gwyn's gaze remained steady and her voice was unemotional, as though the man she spoke of was a stranger, his suffering a matter of no concern. 'She wouldn't expect anyone walking past today to have the power to cross the wards she's set.'

'But you can.' It wasn't a question.

'Of course.'

'But what about me and Jane? How do we get in there?'

Jane answered before Gwyn could. 'I don't know about you, Tarzan, but I'm planning on using the door. Cyber ninja, remember? I'm immune. You're the only one who's got a problem with this.'

She turned to Gwyn with a smile like a Valkyrie ready to ride into battle. 'You wanted proof that your HPS doesn't work on me? I think you've got it.'

A slight quirk of Gwyn's lips acknowledged Jane's point. The older woman started to say something but Aidan broke in over the top of her. Jane's newfound abilities weren't the issue here and he could do without any congratulatory speeches.

'Great – but what do I do? I can't …'

He broke off, gesturing angrily towards the shuttering as shame and fear congealed in his throat, blocking the other things he might have said. It hurt more than he cared to admit that he was the one to baulk at entering the churchyard. 'Damn it!'

Disgusted with himself as much as with his two companions

Aidan balled his hands into fists, aware that his palms were slippery with sweat. Even now he knew that his fear was a result of Helen's wards he could no more bring himself to touch that door than he could have thrust his bare hand into the heart of a fire.

He took a deep breath. 'Help me with this, Gwyn.'

'You'd find it easier if you'd strengthen your shields.' Gwyn's voice was surprisingly calm given the way he had spoken to her.

It only served to irritate Aidan further. 'My shields are—'

Oh!

It was surprising how much Gwyn could convey with a raised eyebrow. Aidan felt his anger drain away along with much of the energy that had been sustaining him.

'They were strong,' he muttered. He should apologise but he was tired and his hip was throbbing and above everything else he was aware of the time running away from them, time in which they should be getting on with saving Eldritch. He stared down at the pavement, scuffing the toe of his trainer along the uneven edge of one of the concrete slabs. 'Maybe you should do this without me.'

'Don't be stupid, Aidan.' Now Gwyn did sound annoyed. 'If this is going to work we need all three of us to play our parts. You know that.' She let out an irritated huff of breath, sounding rather like Kali being removed from the kitchen table, but her next comment made it clear that her ex-ward's behaviour wasn't the sole source of her annoyance. 'It's my fault as well. You're a good student – mostly,' she added with a sharp look that told him not to let the unexpected praise go to his head. 'But it's different when you're doing things for real. The amount of power you've expended today is beyond anything that you've done before. Add to that the fact that you've been hurt – physically and psychically – and it's hardly surprising that your energy levels have gone through the floor. You're compensating for that by letting your shields go thin. The sigils are holding.' He didn't miss the relief in her voice as she made that pronouncement. 'That's something, but the rest really isn't worth spit at the moment.' She offered him a one-sided shrug as if to soften the judgement. 'It's to be expected.'

'Like a white belt dropping their guard when they get tired?'

'Exactly, Jane. Even on your last legs I imagine you or Aidan would keep your guard up in a fight. You've been trained to do it but it's not something we've practised with power.'

'So, you're saying all I need to do is to strengthen my shields?'

Aidan cut across the two women. Another time he would be interested – in fact he made a mental note to revisit the subject with Gwyn; he didn't want to be put in this position ever again – but right now he just wanted a way to deal with this incapacitating fear.

'You could, but I'm not sure you've got the energy to do it. A quicker way would be for you to wear this.' As she spoke, Gwyn slid a bracelet from the collection on her right wrist and handed it to him. 'Put it on. It should give you sufficient protection to get past the wards.'

Aidan did as he was told, ignoring Jane's snigger as he surveyed the result. His wrist was larger than Gwyn's and the bracelet was stretched, leaving gaps where the strand of elastic showed through the amethyst chips. He hoped that wasn't going to reduce its effectiveness. It might look ridiculous, but he'd take an armful of girly bracelets if it helped.

'Now, how do you feel when you think about going into the churchyard?'

Aidan considered the question as he looked at the little access door and imagined himself going through it. The strangest idea came into his head.

'Like someone's tapping me on the shoulder and telling me to look over there.' He jerked his head towards the other side of the street. 'And that I should be afraid.' He thought about that sensation for a moment, probing at it, waiting for the paralysing, gut-clenching fear to return but nothing happened. He grinned. 'But really I'm not.'

It was an odd dichotomy, but he was willing to live with it if it meant he could get into the churchyard.

'Excellent.' Gwyn's response was brisk and stopped Aidan asking the questions he would have liked to have put to her. But he recognised that now wasn't the time for a lesson in magical theory; they needed to get to Eldritch. 'We go in carefully. I don't want them to see or hear us until—'

An agonised scream sounded from within the churchyard. For a heartbeat the three of them froze. Gwyn was the first to recover. She wheeled round, lunging for the access door and Aidan would have sworn he saw a pale phosphor glow building around her fingers as she flung it open.

'Change of plan!'

CHAPTER 38

The three of them pelted across the churchyard. Aidan barely registered the neat lawn bordered with cedarwood benches and a line of clipped topiary bay trees in square pewter planters. He was oblivious to the sandpit and the vivid primary coloured plastic of the children's swings, the see-saw and the climbing frame. His focus was on the concrete and brick building in front of him. Aidan had expected a traditional church – deconsecrated or not – but, with its flat roof and slab sides, St Martin's looked more like a 1950s warehouse, an image that wasn't helped by the anti-vandalism mesh protecting the tall grimy windows or the scaffolding surrounding the front of the building. As he ran, it crossed Aidan's mind to wonder if the would-be arsonists had been bored teenagers or aesthetes intent on ridding the neighbourhood of an eyesore.

Wide double doors were visible behind the scaffolding, their moulded wood panels painted an unpleasant mud brown. Though the path led directly to them, Gwyn veered off, heading for a smaller door set in the side wall. Jane followed on her heels and Aidan – much to his chagrin – brought up the rear. They had almost reached their goal when a second scream sliced through the air. Without breaking stride, Gwyn gestured and even in the dazzle of sunshine Aidan saw the flare of light as the Levin bolt she threw hit the door at lock height. The next second Jane was past her, driving the ball of her foot into the wood as smoothly as though they had rehearsed the move a dozen times, bursting the door open.

After the afternoon brightness, the interior of the hall seemed sunk in shadows, murky and dim, as though the smoke from the fire still hung in the air along with the smell of charred wood. Aidan looked around frantically. At first, he thought the place was empty, but then his eyes adjusted to the poor light and he saw them. The next moments printed themselves on his mind as a roller-coaster rush of emotions and images. There was the adrenalin punch of shock and anger at the sight of Eldritch's body, hanging like a carcass from a scaffold at the end of the hall, the grieves crowding in on either side of him, and then relief as he realised that two grieves meant that Terry hadn't taken the wizard yet. He might have laughed at the almost comical look of outrage on Helen's face as she spun to face the intruders, but the knowledge of what she was capable of killed the sound in his throat.

'You,' she spat, and her expression turned to cold fury.

She got no further. Gwyn was already moving, the foxfire glow outlining her fingers clearly visible in the gloom as she flung a Levin bolt straight at Helen. It hit the grieve squarely, sending her staggering backwards and, for a moment, Aidan thought the fight was over almost before it had begun. But Helen didn't go down. Instead, she caught her balance against the scaffold and straightened unharmed and Aidan remembered that – grieve host or not – this was a woman who had hunted demons with Eldritch. She would not be beaten so easily. In that same moment Terry lunged forward and grabbed hold of Eldritch, his hand fisting in the wizard's hair as he dragged the unconscious man's head up.

Aidan didn't know what the handyman intended – surely, he couldn't mean to possess Eldritch now? – but it was a risk he wasn't prepared to take. With no way to get to Terry in time to stop him, Aidan did the only thing he could. He reached frantically for whatever power he could, pulling it from his core, from his faded shields, even – he wasn't sure how – from the string of semi-precious stones around his wrist. With his mind he shaped the disparate energies into a Levin bolt and hurled it at Terry's back, hoping desperately that it would be enough. But it never reached its target. Somehow Helen got there first. The sorceress didn't react as Aidan's bolt spent itself harmlessly against her shields. Then she did something unexpected; she pulled Terry away from the captive wizard.

'Leave him!' she lashed out verbally at her mate, even as she wheeled around, lithe and graceful as a dancer, to block a bolt from Gwyn that – Aidan was fairly certain – should have taken both her and Terry to the floor. 'We deal with them first.'

Her blonde hair whipped around her shoulders and her hands scythed through the air as she returned Gwyn's fire with a double handful of her own. From the corner of his eye, Aidan saw Gwyn's hands come up in a warding gesture. She deflected the first of Helen's bolts, the air crackling with discharge as the two opposing energies collided, but the second passed through her defences, catching the edge of her shields and spinning her round. There was a smell like ozone and Aidan heard his teacher's short sob of breath as she went down on one knee.

For a moment he froze, torn between his immediate instinct to go to her aid – and to hell with the plan – and the knowledge that there was nothing he could do to help her. Then Jane was there, standing between Gwyn and Helen while

Gwyn, clearly dazed, struggled to her feet. With a silent prayer to whatever deities watched over Welsh witches and cyber ninjas Aidan turned his attention to Terry.

If Aidan had been surprised by Helen's actions, Terry had seemed stunned. For several seconds he had remained frozen, a murderous expression on his face, almost as though he wanted to attack Helen rather than Eldritch's would-be rescuers. But now he bent and grabbed something from the floor, hefting it like a club as he scanned his potential opponents. His gaze flicked briefly over the women and Aidan could almost see his thought processes as he dismissed them. Then he turned and his sneer morphed into a nasty smile as his eyes met Aidan's across the hall.

Oh yeah, time for round two.

Aidan had never been one to pick fights, but he was almost looking forward to this.

Sorry, Sensei, he thought, acknowledging his instructor's often repeated philosophy that only fools start fights and only bigger fools stay to fight them. *This one's got it coming.*

He matched Terry's smile with a leer of his own. 'Have you got the balls for a proper fight this time?'

He put every ounce of arrogance he could summon into the challenge. Hoping Jane wasn't listening he added contemptuously, 'Or are you only up to playing with the girls?'

The air fizzed with another bolt. Someone cried out; Aidan wasn't sure who and didn't dare look to find out. Eyes never leaving Terry's, he swaggered forward, his stance matching his leer, arrogant and overconfident. *Look at me. Don't you just want to wipe that cocky grin right off my face?*

The handyman took a step towards him, mirroring Aidan's swagger. 'I will break your arms.'

The improvised club – Aidan noted it was a heavy-duty adjustable spanner – slapped against Terry's palm for emphasis. Another step. 'Then I will break your legs.'

And another. 'After that I will take your friend while you watch, knowing you have failed to save him. And then, finally, I will wear his body when I put your eyes out. In the end you will beg me to kill you.'

Nice. Aidan shrugged negligently. He spread his arms, offering himself as a target. 'You talk a lot, but I don't see much action. Show me what you've got.'

The enthusiasm in his voice wasn't entirely manufactured. The handyman might top him by a couple of inches, but Aidan knew his own abilities, even with a gammy leg. Terry was in for a nasty surprise if he thought this was going to be easy. He took an unhurried step forward, weighing up how the other man moved, considering his tactics if Terry was going to try to disable him … and then all such thoughts vanished as Helen's mind clamped around his.

It was like being engulfed by an alien consciousness. The terrible force that was the sorceress's blood magic tore at the fragile web of his shields. He felt those icy silver hooks trying to catch hold, searching mindlessly for a way to reach him. He sensed them slipping against the protective shapes of the sigils, like blades sliding off a shield boss, and he knew those shimmering cobweb forms were all that stood between him and possession. At the same time Helen's arcane power wrapped around his physical body, squeezing and compressing it. His muscles seemed to liquify and it felt to Aidan as if his brain must burst under the pressure. The air squeezed from his lungs in a terrible, keening whine and he had no strength to breathe in again. Something gave within his head and he tasted the copper of blood in his throat. A wave of red and black washed across his vision as the terrible encircling power tightened still further. Far away he thought he heard Helen's laughter.

No!

He had no breath, but the scream rang through his head, at once both fierce and defiant. He accepted the terror coursing through him, acknowledged the physical pain, and seized the white-hot burn of the adrenalin rush that scalded his blood. Body, mind and soul, he channelled the visceral energy of everything he was and everything he aspired to be – dojo warrior, mountain rescuer, wizard-in-training – pouring it all into his shields and into the glowing sigils that adorned them, until he felt they must surely flare like burning magnesium.

You will not prevail!

Like a genetic memory, the archaic wording rose within him as if from some older, wiser self, bursting in his brain like a thunderclap. In that same instant he felt Helen's thwarted rage slap at him and the pressure of the blood magic dropped away.

Aidan reeled, dazed and half-blinded by the attack. He gulped in a breath, sucking the stale taste of mingled smoke and city fumes down into his lungs as gratefully as he would the moist breezes that danced round the summit of Plynlimon. For a heartbeat it was all that he could manage, but then the world came back into focus and reminded him that Helen's magic was not the only danger to be faced.

It was his training that saved him. With Terry virtually on top of him, Aidan reacted even before he consciously registered the spanner scything down towards his head. Not thinking of blocking Terry's arm, he threw himself sideways, diving under the swing and twisting clear of a blow that would have smashed his skull like a china teacup. The head of the spanner arced past him, missing him by inches, but his breath caught as pain speared through his hip.

Crap!

Off balance he stumbled, his leg folding underneath him, pitching him towards the floor. Reflex turned the move into an untidy breakfall, effective enough to avoid injury but without the impetus to bring him back onto his feet, leaving him stranded half-kneeling, half-sprawled on his side as Terry's momentum carried him past. The floor was not the place to be in any fight. Aidan started to push to his feet, but even if the real Terry hadn't been used to fighting, the thing within him certainly was, for the lanky handyman turned faster than Aidan would have given him credit for. He spun round, balanced and poised on the balls of his feet, the spanner brandished in front of his body. Instinctively, Aidan changed tactic. He sagged, doing his best to look hurt and defenceless. In truth, it wasn't so much of an act, but he chose to ignore that fact. He dabbed half-heartedly at the blood trickling from his nose, tried to rise and sank back with a stifled groan. Terry smiled nastily.

Aidan raised wavering hands in front of him. 'Try it.' He forced the words out, as though the effort of speaking cost him dearly. 'If you think you're tough enough.'

Terry's smile became a feral grin. The grieve within him was enjoying this. Aidan read the change in his stance, saw the slight relaxation at the other man decided his prey was unable to escape and anticipated the prospect of an easy kill. But not a fast one, thought Aidan, remembering the grieve's taunts. He had no doubt that Terry would take great pleasure in making him suffer now he was sure there was no danger to himself. Aidan had met with bullies before.

He swayed, blinked and shook his head as though he was having difficulty focusing. He let his eyes half close, keeping his gaze down, watching Terry's feet, waiting for the move … and drove his good leg up hard into Terry's groin when the handyman stepped in to strike him.

The kick connected as sweetly as Aidan could have wished for. Terry doubled over, the spanner tumbling unnoticed from his hand, and Aidan met his descending chin with a rising punch that snapped the other man's head back. The grieve went down heavily in a groaning heap – conscious – just – but Aidan didn't think he was going to get up in a hurry. Still, it wasn't a risk he was going to take, given the state of his own battered body. He mustered what energy he had left and hit the other man with a close-range Levin bolt. This time Terry's body went limp.

Remind me to mention that to Sensei.

The thought gave him a certain satisfaction. He started to get to his feet but stopped as a wave of dizziness washed over him. Okay, maybe the bolt hadn't been such a great idea. He swallowed against the bile that rose in his throat and sank back to the floor.

Let's just give it a moment, shall we?

His head was pounding as though his skull was too tight for his brain and, now that the adrenalin was receding, his body was reminding him that this wasn't his first fight of the day. Even with the benefit of Gwyn's earlier healing magic, he ached down to his bones.

A hand clamping around his shoulder made Aidan jerk

upright, shocked to realise that his eyes had slipped closed. His fists clenched instinctively before he realised it was Jane.

'Are you okay?' She eyed his cocked fists; no doubt she also saw the hair-fine tremor that ran through his arms, but tactfully refrained from commenting on either.

'What? Yeah.' Aidan shook his head to clear it – a mistake, as the world went fuzzy around the edges – but he did his best to ignore it. He stared up at Jane, relieved to see she seemed unharmed – in fact both of her did. With a struggle he brought her back into focus. 'I'm great. Why wouldn't I be?'

The blonde brows quirked as if suggesting it should be obvious but Jane – being Jane – told him anyway. 'Because you're grey, Tarzan. And you're shaking.'

She crouched down beside him, the better to look into his eyes. At any other time Aidan would have appreciated the closeness but he knew his girlfriend wasn't being romantic; she was checking for concussion. Irritated, he waved her off.

'You can play nurse later. I'm fine.' It wasn't strictly true, at least not at the moment, but he knew he would be. 'He didn't touch me. I'm just sore where someone else beat the crap out of me earlier.' And if he sounded petulant about that then he felt he had earned the right. 'What about Helen?'

Jane greeted the change of subject with an unladylike snort. 'She fights like a girl.' A contemptuous toss of the head underlined the disdain in her voice.

Not when she's in your head, she doesn't, Aidan thought, but he didn't want to talk about that. 'You fight like a girl,' he pointed out instead.

Jane gave him a withering look. 'I am a girl,' she corrected. 'I fight like a cyber ninja.'

An image of Helen going down under a coldly efficient barrage of kicks and strikes – and quite possibly a nerve block or two – filled Aidan's head even as Jane continued, 'Besides, Gwyn was right – zombie wife wasn't expecting to come up against a null.' Her expression morphed into a superior smile.

'Chalk one up to the cyber ninja,' Aidan conceded. A tightness deep within him – he refused to call it fear – eased and slipped away. 'And Gwyn's okay?' He looked round for his mentor. He hadn't forgotten that choked-off sob of pain. 'And Eldritch?'

'Gwyn's fine, as you can see. She said something about making sure zombie wife couldn't cause any more trouble before she's ready to deal with her.' Jane's lips pursed as she looked to where Gwyn knelt beside Helen's body, her hands held out above the other woman's head and chest. 'Personally, I'd have tied her up, but you know,' the cyber ninja gave an eloquent shrug, 'HPS. As for Eldritch—' For a moment Jane's air of self-assurance slipped. 'I've not got to him yet. I … I wanted to make sure you had things under control first.'

She looked at Aidan as though trying to gauge his reaction to her choice of priorities then her expression morphed into a rare, sweet smile. 'I'm glad you're okay, Tarzan.'

'Back at you, ninja.'

Aidan felt a brief, overwhelming urge to gather his girlfriend into a hug. He resisted; one thing would lead to another – probably to him falling asleep in her arms, if he was honest, although the waking up might be enjoyable – but this wasn't the time for such things. Instead, he pushed himself to his feet trying not to wince as he did so. 'Tell you what. You look after this one and I'll look after Eldritch.'

CHAPTER 39

'Eldritch?'

The wizard hung limply from the scaffold tower, his knees buckled, his body kept upright only by virtue of the rope lashing his wrists tightly against the metal frame. His head was bowed forward, his chin against his chest so that his dark hair fell in a matted curtain over his face, obscuring his features. He didn't move.

Crap!

'Eldritch!'

Not waiting for a response Aidan ducked his head so he could look into his friend's face and his heart sank. Although he had been half expecting what he saw he couldn't help wincing; if Eldritch had looked bad as a spreadeagled captive in the stuffy gloom of his bedroom, now he looked worse. Under an ugly patchwork of dried blood and bruises his skin was fish-belly pale and sheened with sweat. The thick stubble on his cheeks and jaw stood out like smears of ink on the sunken flesh.

'Oh Christ!' Aidan's eyes went to the dribbles of blood patterning Eldritch's forearms – fresh, sticky red tracking across the flaking traceries of older, darker rust. In his mind he heard again the awful, trapped animal sound of Eldritch's screams and the image came to him, unbidden and unwanted, of that bound form jerking convulsively, the sinews of his arms and neck standing out in agony as he pulled uselessly against the unforgiving ropes. The thought brought a rush of anger and a strong desire to inflict similar suffering on the two grieves. 'Those bastards—'

With an effort Aidan pushed back the dark fantasy that wanted to run riot through his mind. The grieves could wait. He took a slow, deliberate breath, focusing on keeping his feelings from leaching into his voice as he turned back to Eldritch. 'But it's okay. It's okay. We've got you now.'

He spoke as much to calm himself as for Eldritch's sake. He thought it unlikely that the tall Englishman could hear him but the act of talking to the other man, of engaging in that soft, steady litany, made him feel better. 'We're going to get you out of here. You're going to be alright.'

Aidan fumbled out his pocketknife, conscious that his hands were shaking. He decided to put that down to anger rather than any lingering after-effects of his own encounters with the grieves. Opening the blade, he bent and sliced through the ropes hobbling Eldritch's ankles and if he harboured a brief fantasy that it wasn't rope he was cutting – well, he didn't think anyone would blame him. Smiling darkly at the thought he straightened, knife in hand.

Okay, let's get you down.

He had been certain that Eldritch was still unconscious but somehow those grey eyes were open and had locked on the blade. From there they jerked up to Aidan's face and Aidan remembered Eldritch had very good reason to be afraid of him wielding a knife.

'Crap!'

The younger man couldn't tell how much Eldritch was able to process but what the wizard could take in clearly terrified him. Eldritch thrashed wildly, straining against the ropes, fear lending his movements a ferocity that shocked Aidan. There was no chance of Eldritch breaking free, but that wasn't going to stop him trying and he was going to hurt himself in the process.

'Eldritch, no! No!'

Aidan dropped the knife and did the only thing he could think of. He grabbed at Eldritch, trying to hold his friend still. 'It's me. It's alright.' He couldn't stop the panic scaling his voice upwards.

Please God, don't think I'm holding you so I can cut you.

'I'm not going to hurt you.' He wasn't sure what he would do if the wizard proved to be beyond his reach. Praying it was the right thing to do, he pulled the matted head close, holding Eldritch to him. 'It's over now, I promise. It's over.'

Maybe it was the desperation in his voice that got through. Certainly, Aidan would have sworn Eldritch wasn't rational enough to take in his words, but one moment the body pressed against his was rigid and straining and the next it went limp as Eldritch stopped fighting. For several seconds Aidan simply hung on to the wizard, unsure if he was restraining him or clinging to him for support. The twin rasp of their mingled breath sounded loud, even over the pounding rush of blood through his ears.

'It's okay.' Slowly Aidan allowed himself to relax. 'Hey, it's okay.'

Maybe if he said it enough times he would start to believe it was true. After everything that had happened today, he desperately wanted to. He wanted Eldritch to believe it as well. Keeping his hands on either side of the Englishman's face he drew back so he could look into his friend's eyes. They were tracking him now, the man emerging from the nightmare.

Eldritch's brows creased fractionally. 'Aidan?'

Had he not been standing so close Aidan wouldn't have caught the breathy whisper of sound. 'Yeah.'

It was all he could manage, sudden relief closing his throat. He swallowed down the roil of emotions that threatened to choke him.

In the silence it was Eldritch who spoke first. 'You … okay?'

Naturally deep, the wizard's voice sounded as rough as the plates of the earth grating together, but the unexpected question wrung a bark of laughter from Aidan.

'Am I okay? Christ!' He shook his head, disbelieving. 'You're the one we've been worried about, you idiot!' He resisted his initial urge to land a companionable punch on Eldritch's biceps and settled for ruffling his hair instead, leaving the matted strands standing up in random spikes. 'I'm fine.'

A brief spasm tightened the muscles along Eldritch's jaw, and his eyes slid shut. When he opened them again Aidan thought they seemed a little clearer.

'How?'

Aidan rolled his own eyes heavenwards, understanding the multitude of questions condensed in that one short word. Trust a wizard to want to know the details of his escape from Helen's spell.

'Jane and Gwyn lured me back from the dark side. They had cookies.'

Eldritch's forehead creased into a frown as he tried to process what Aidan had said and singularly failed to make sense of it. Despite the gravity of the situation, Aidan found himself laughing again. He wondered briefly if it was the onset of hysteria. Given the day he had had it wouldn't surprise him.

'It's an old joke, don't worry about it. Jane beat some sense into me.' He turned his head to display the darkening bruise along his own jaw. 'Then Gwyn pitched in and between them they managed to convince me to draw the wards I needed on my shields.'

He decided to leave out any mention of the excruciating pain that had accompanied those desperate instructions. Eldritch didn't need to hear that and it wasn't something Aidan was in any hurry to revisit.

'I tried …' Eldritch sounded so remorseful that for a second Aidan was tempted to grab those broad shoulders with their patina of crescent moon scars and shake them.

'I know you did. And you earned a fist in the face as a reward.' Aidan grimaced; he knew very well how much such things hurt. If either of them ought to be feeling guilty it should be him, but Eldritch just shook his head, wordlessly dismissing the need for an apology when he said as much.

Aidan blew out his breath in a huff. 'Yeah, well.' They could carry on like this all afternoon and it wouldn't resolve anything. He bent and retrieved his knife. 'Let's say we forget about it for now and get you down.'

He set the blade against the ropes around Eldritch's wrist but didn't start cutting. 'Listen, before we do this I need to know – are you hurt anywhere?' He kicked himself mentally as soon as the words were out of his mouth.

Of course he is, you idiot. Look at him!

'More than cuts and bruises I mean. I know they're not good.' He shot Eldritch an apologetic look to let his friend know he wasn't trivialising the beating he had taken. 'But is there anything I'm going to make worse if you keel over and I have to catch you?' The screams he had heard echoed in his voice as he added softly, 'What did she do to you?'

Because somehow he knew it had been Helen who had been responsible for the wizard's agony and that only made things worse. He locked eyes with Eldritch. *You need to tell me the truth.*

But Eldritch only shook his head again, a small, tired motion, leaving Aidan unsure if it was an answer to his initial question or a denial that anything had been done to him. It wouldn't be the first time the tall wizard had played down an injury.

And remember where that got us.

Maybe the memory showed on his face for the corner of Eldritch's mouth twitched as if he could follow Aidan's thinking. It was a long way from a smile and gone almost before it registered, but for a second it softened the planes of the Englishman's face making him seem less haggard.

'She threw pain,' Eldritch said as though that explained everything. His voice was expressionless, but Aidan had to turn away from him, fixing his eyes on the cold steel of the scaffold pole, while he got his own emotions under control. Gwyn had explained to him how she and Jane had broken the blood magic and he knew first hand the agony hidden in those deceptively simple words. It occurred to him then that however excruciating the pain he had endured, at least Gwyn had been trying to save his life. And she had probably held back. Helen would not have been so restrained.

'No real damage,' Eldritch continued as Aidan turned back to him. Those broad shoulders moved fractionally in the smallest of shrugs, dismissing what had happened, but his eyes slid closed and Aidan thought the tall man looked as though he might be sick. He couldn't blame him; he felt queasy himself. Eldritch's head drooped and his Adam's apple bobbed as he swallowed convulsively. 'I'm alright.'

The weariness in that gravelly voice made a mockery of the claim and Aidan fought down the urge to say something scathing in response even as Eldritch drew a shuddering breath and lifted his head. 'But I've felt better.'

His grey gaze fixed on Aidan and for a moment the younger man saw misery there along with a host of other emotions before Eldritch locked them away.

'Just get me down. Please.'

CHAPTER 40

Contrary to expectations, Eldritch didn't collapse the moment his first wrist was freed. Even so, Aidan didn't think he was going to stay standing for very long. The wizard clung to the scaffold, a fine tremor shaking his limbs like palsy, while Aidan dealt with the ropes around his other wrist. He said nothing but he hissed in pain as his arm came free and he started to sag. Aidan reacted, grabbing him even as Eldritch staggered and tried to straighten. With the pair of them off balance, the resulting tangle of limbs ended with them both on the floor.

For several moments neither of them moved, then cautiously Aidan propped himself up on his elbows, regarding his recumbent friend with a mixture of amusement and exasperation. Eldritch didn't seem to have noticed that he was lying sprawled across Aidan's thighs.

'We really are going to have to stop meeting like this.'

The comment brought a huff of breath that, under other circumstances, might have been a laugh; perhaps the other man wasn't completely unaware of his position after all. Aidan was about to suggest that Eldritch might like to move when the wizard flinched. A small groan escaped him and his muscles bunched as if protesting a sudden cramp. Aidan's pulse spiked. Despite the weight of Eldritch's body pinning his legs he sat fully upright.

'Eldritch?'

'She used drugs—' Another spasm cut off the words. Eldritch rode it out with clenched teeth and small panting breaths. 'Not so good.'

'Is there anything I can do?' Aidan guessed it was unlikely but he had to ask. 'Or Gwyn?' He cast a worried glance towards where his mentor knelt between the bodies of the two grieves, Jane having dragged Terry's unconscious form over to lie beside Helen's. He didn't want to interrupt, yet surely what she was doing could wait if Eldritch needed her? But the clutch of fingers on his arm stopped him before he could call out.

'No.' Eldritch's face twisted even as he spoke. His fingers tightened briefly and then released, his face relaxing into a sort of wary watchfulness, as if anticipating the next attack. 'It will pass.'

To Aidan's ears it sounded as though the tall man was trying to convince himself of this fact, rather than to reassure him, but he didn't push it.

'It feels better … lying down.'

Unconvinced, Aidan waited, but the wizard's eyes drifted closed and some of the strung tension seemed to ebb out of the lanky body. Eldritch's breathing softened and, after a few moments, he added, 'I'll just stay here for a minute.'

'Sure.' Uncertain what else to do, Aidan patted his friend's arm in what he hoped was a reassuring manner. 'Take as long as you need. There's no rush.'

He looked again at the prostrate body pinning his legs and, knowing Eldritch's own habit of hiding behind humour, couldn't resist adding, 'It's not like I'm going anywhere.'

Still, if he was going to spend time as an impromptu cushion, Aidan decided he might as well be comfortable doing so. Moving carefully, so as not to jostle the wizard, he shifted backwards so he could lean against the scaffold. Eldritch seemed oblivious to the manoeuvring but Aidan thought that his friend's colour was a little better, his face less ashen than it had been when he had first cut him down. There was no escaping the fact that the man needed – and would probably want, when he was feeling better – a bath, and it would take some careful work with a razor before Eldritch looked his normal well-groomed self, but at least he no longer resembled a freshly executed corpse strung up by some medieval land baron as an example to the other troublesome serfs.

Clothing wouldn't go amiss either, he thought wryly. It was an indication of just how rough the wizard was feeling that he hadn't protested his current state of undress, but Aidan couldn't imagine that lasting; not that he blamed him. He wondered briefly how Helen and Terry had dealt with that. Had they smuggled Eldritch out of the house rolled up in a decorator's dust sheet, like Cleopatra in her infamous carpet? His lips twitched at the thought; the idea was both amusing and appalling. Fortunately, they wouldn't be resorting to such measures to get Eldritch home. His friend could thank him later for having the foresight to gather up – or rather to get Jane to gather up – a set of clothes for him to wear.

He should ask her if she wouldn't mind fetching them from the car, while he was currently indisposed, but when he looked round for her he saw that she was already ahead of him. He gave her an appreciative grin and a thumbs up as she came through the door, Gwyn's battered canvas satchel in one hand and a white plastic carrier bag in the other. She deposited the satchel on the floor beside its owner and then came to join him.

Many women would have been disconcerted by the sight of six feet of naked wizard lying sprawled across their partner's legs, but not Jane.

'That doesn't look comfortable,' she said, totally deadpan.

Aidan shrugged noncommittally and reached for the bag, but instead of handing it over Jane crouched down and peered more closely at Eldritch. 'Jay, I don't think—'

Maybe it was the sound of their voices, or perhaps the wizard had felt her scrutiny, because Eldritch chose that moment to open his eyes.

'Hey, welcome back.' Relief and affection warmed Jane's voice as she leaned in. 'We missed you, you know.'

But, while Jane might have been delighted, Eldritch's eyes went wide with alarm. He made an odd noise that Jane probably took as 'Hello', but which Aidan guessed was more likely to have been 'help' or even 'hell' and his hands jerked to cover his groin in a hasty, if somewhat belated, attempt at modesty. Even dazed and flat on his back it seemed that the Englishman was going to maintain a sense of decorum if he could. Jane appeared not to notice Eldritch's embarrassment – she continued to smile down at him as though waiting for a more eloquent response – but Aidan decided it would be best if he hurried things along. Though a small part of him was amused that this was the most life Eldritch had shown since being cut down, he pulled the bag from Jane's hand and shoved it at Eldritch. The wizard all but snatched it from him, clamping the white plastic protectively over his groin. Then he lay very still watching Jane rather as a mouse might watch a snake.

'Thanks, Jay, that's great.'

Trying to be subtle, Aidan made a shooing gesture, hoping she would get the point and go away. When she didn't move he glared at her.

'What?' Jane looked genuinely puzzled.

Aidan widened his eyes and jerked his head towards Eldritch. 'Jay, he's naked,' he hissed in a half whisper, as if by keeping his voice down he could avoid adding to the wizard's embarrassment. But, for someone usually so intuitive, Jane seemed oblivious to the problem.

She shot Aidan an odd look. 'Yes, I can see that. That's why I thought I'd bring his clothes in.' Her tone suggested that that much should have been obvious.

'Well, can't you turn your back or close your eyes or …' Jane gave him a pitying look and Aidan had the horrible feeling of the ground slipping out from under his feet. 'Or something,' he concluded, annoyed and now embarrassed himself – which only added to his sense of annoyance.

Jane raised her eyebrows. 'Oh, come on, Aidan. It's not like I haven't seen it all before.'

Eldritch made a strangled, choking noise and his hands clenched more tightly over the carrier bag as though the young woman might prove her point by tearing it from his grasp. Aidan opened his mouth to reply, realised he couldn't think of a single coherent thing to say in response and closed it with a snap. He stared at his girlfriend incredulously.

Jane looked from him to Eldritch and back again. 'Well, not Eldritch naked, obviously.' Her mouth firmed into a thin, disapproving line as if Aidan had dared to suggest such a thing. 'But you know what I mean.'

Aidan did, but it didn't make things any better. Not

sure he could articulate what he was feeling he settled for a glare. Jane tossed her head and looked down at Eldritch, but if she had expected him to agree with her she was going to be disappointed. The wizard was doing his best to avoid eye contact with either of them.

'Oh, for goodness' sake.' Jane folded her arms and stared pointedly at the ceiling. She looked as though she was mentally counting to ten, but Aidan noted she was blushing. So was Eldritch, and the flush didn't stop at his cheeks.

'Jay. Please.'

Aidan tried for conciliatory, but Jane stopped him with a look.

'Maybe you'd prefer it if I got Gwyn to help you?' she asked, her voice sweet as honey dripping from a razor blade. Aidan swallowed his first response. He hoped she was joking but he couldn't be sure.

'I think we can manage.'

'Huh!' Jane didn't look down, but her tone said very clearly what she thought of that. Without altering her eyeline she said carefully, 'I'll leave you boys,' there was just the slightest accent on that last word, 'to it, then.'

And, keeping her gaze pointedly away from the floor, she stalked back to join Gwyn.

Aidan watched her go. 'I think I'm going to pay for that,' he commented to no one in particular. Then he looked down at Eldritch. 'Come on, let's get you sorted before she really does sick Gwyn on us.'

'She wouldn't.' The wizard shook his head, a small movement that barely stirred the long strands of his hair against the faded denim of Aidan's jeans, but there was more disbelief than certainty in his voice.

Aidan looked at him sceptically, even less sure of his girlfriend's benevolence. 'How much do you want to bet on that?'

He grinned at the momentary look of panic that suffused Eldritch's face. The man who could face torture and the threat of imminent possession by grieves with stoicism was far less certain about the prospect of dealing with a stubborn cyber ninja and a temperamental Welsh witch.

'I thought not. Okay, let's see what we've got.'

As tactfully as possible, given the position of the bag, Aidan leaned over and pulled out the clothes Jane had packed, leaving Eldritch's modesty to the dubious protection of the empty plastic.

'We'll do that in a minute.' He dismissed the white shirt, putting it to one side. 'First things first.' He shook out the dark jeans and realised what was missing. 'Hmm, I'm afraid you're going to have to go commando – Jane forgot about boxers.'

Eldritch smile wanly but made no comment. Given the circumstances any clothes would be an improvement, but his hand was shaking as he reached to take the jeans from Aidan. It dropped back across his chest once he had them, as though even that little effort had exhausted him. Aidan waited a few seconds to see what the wizard would do, but when Eldritch didn't move he made his decision.

'Okay, let's see what we can do here.' He squirmed out from beneath Eldritch and before the wizard could grasp what he was doing he took the jeans from him. 'Stay still. I'll help you.'

Aidan kept his voice light and the contact brisk and methodical as he slid the bunched-up denim over Eldritch's feet. Despite the lack of protest, he could all but feel the waves of embarrassment radiating off his friend's lanky body. Still, he thought, it was better that it was him providing the unwanted help rather than Jane or – he winced at the thought – Gwyn. Looked at in that light, the wizard should be grateful for what he was doing.

'You know, I recall it being a whole lot easier the last time we did this.' He lifted Eldritch's knees so he could ease the jeans up over his legs.

'That's because last time … you were taking my clothes off.' The granite and silver voice was a grating whisper, breathy and stilted, but the wizard's tone was as dry as the Sahara. There was a pause as he gathered the energy to add, 'And I was unconscious when you did it.'

'Oh, yeah.' Aidan looked at Eldritch's face, gratified to see the ghost of a smile on those bloodless lips. He grinned in response. 'That was one hell of a first date.'

As he spoke he wrangled the jeans up to Eldritch's hips, then stopped, deciding there was a fine line between assistance and assault. It wasn't one he wanted to cross.

'Tell you what, you can do the rest yourself.'

Aidan waited until Eldritch had finished fastening his jeans and then helped him to sit up, leaning against the scaffold while he put on his shirt.

The wizard pulled the shirt closed but shook his head when Aidan offered to help him button it. 'In a minute.'

He seemed to sink in on himself, swallowing sharply as if fighting down a sudden rush of nausea, and for several moments his focus seemed to be on his breathing, taking small sips of air through clenched teeth. When he spoke again it was with the air of someone looking for a distraction. 'Tell me what happened.'

'We'll save the full story for later.' Aidan didn't feel he could do justice to the telling on his own, but if his friend needed something to take his mind off his current discomfort he thought he had just the thing. 'As for what happened here, well, Jane and Gwyn took out Helen and I took care of Terry.' Aidan kept his tone light, almost as if dismissing what they had achieved, but he could see he had caught Eldritch's attention. The wizard's dark brows quirked into a frown as he tried to make sense of that particular division of labour. Aidan let him puzzle over it for a few seconds and then, with a negligent shrug, he delivered his bombshell. 'Of course, we had one hell of an advantage, given that Jane's a null.'

Eldritch's eyes widened comically. 'What?' His face tightened briefly as another spasm caught him, but his eyes remained fixed on Aidan's. 'That's impossible.'

Aidan tried not to smirk, gratified with the reaction his words had provoked. 'Honestly, she is. Trust me, we put it to the test and magic doesn't touch her.'

Some of the pleasure he felt at Eldritch's response leaked away as he remembered how he had tested Jane's capabilities. His mouth clamped down into a thin, tight line on his final words.

Queasy or not, Eldritch made the connection. 'You fought her with magic.'

It wasn't a question and the hardening of the wizard's expression told Aidan that he also understood how that fight had come about.

Aidan shifted uncomfortably. 'Yeah. Or at least I tried to. Christ!' He exhaled a long sigh, then shook his head as though doing so might loosen the hold those memories had on his brain. 'A Levin bolt that knocked Gwyn flat didn't even ruffle Jay's hair, thank God.' He smiled ruefully as he added, 'Then she took me apart.'

'Friendly fire?'

'Believe me, there was nothing friendly about it.'

'So, there's no use threatening to turn her into a frog next time …' Eldritch gestured vaguely towards his jeans.

Aidan snorted, appreciating the attempt at humour. 'No, probably not.'

'A null …' Eldritch murmured, testing the word on his tongue as though he was weighing up the possibilities. 'I'd always believed there was no such thing.' Perhaps his stomach had settled again for he seemed brighter as he asked, 'What's the plan now?'

This time, Aidan had no choice but to be vague. 'Honestly? I don't know. Gwyn hasn't felt the need to share any details. She's got something planned though. She's borrowed your ring and she's really buzzed.'

A small frown kinked Eldritch's brow as he digested this. Then he shook his head in denial. 'There isn't enough power there for her to deal with two grieves.'

'Well, she's got something in mind. She's—'

'I will kill you, hag!'

CHAPTER 41

That was Terry's voice.

He's got free! Aidan was on his feet in an instant, adrenalin pumping through his system and a hundred horrible visions of Gwyn being bludgeoned to death by the handyman filling his head. He whirled, clenching his teeth against the pain the movement drove through his hip, his only thought to launch himself into the fight at Gwyn's side … only there was no fight. The two grieves were still lying where he had last seen them, in the centre of the hall, while Gwyn herself was arranging the eclectic mixture of tealights and candles she had gathered from Eldritch's house in a sweeping curve around them, her movements as calm and unhurried as though she were working in the lavender-scented silence of her own living room.

For a moment Aidan froze, wondering if he was somehow misreading the situation. Terry had sounded so vehement it was hard to believe that his words were nothing more than empty bluster. But Jane was there, standing a little to one side of where Gwyn was working, her thumbs hooked casually in the front pockets of her jeans, watching proceedings with the cool assessment she showed when someone new to the club demonstrated an unfamiliar kata. She seemed as unconcerned by Terry's outburst as Gwyn appeared to be. Feeling slightly sheepish Aidan lowered his hands and allowed himself to relax.

'Your pathetic spells won't save you.' Terry spat the words, his voice underlaid with the promise of imminent violence as though he were the captor and Gwyn his helpless prisoner. But for all the notice Gwyn took of him he might as well not have spoken. She bent to add another candle to the curve of her circle and Jane shot Aidan an amused look over the top of Gwyn's head.

The cyber ninja might have been exasperated with him and Eldritch but her raised eyebrows now were for the handyman's bravado and the shake of her head made it clear that she wasn't impressed. It would seem that a strait-laced attitude to male nudity was easier to forgive.

'They cannot hold us forever.'

Jane cast another look down at the grieve as though to double-check that he wasn't about to lunge to his feet and attack Gwyn. Apparently satisfied she sauntered over to join Aidan.

'Pathetic or not, her spells seem to be doing a good enough job at the moment,' she noted. 'I'd still vote for cable ties but hey, what do I know? HPS.' The wry twitch of her lips acknowledged that this was something outside her area of expertise. 'At least this explains why she insisted on bringing all those candles.' She dropped her gaze to where Eldritch was still sitting, propped against the scaffold. 'You haven't got so much as a nightlight left in your house.'

Eldritch gave the smallest of nods to acknowledge her words but made no other response. He appeared to be watching Gwyn, but one hand had strayed to cover his mouth and Aidan wondered if his friend was fighting back another bout of nausea. He looked pale and distracted and Aidan was relieved on Eldritch's behalf that Jane didn't press him for a more eloquent reply.

She studied the silent wizard for a moment and then turned back to Aidan. 'Is he alright?' she murmured. Her tone held more concern than the brief question might have suggested.

Aidan made a so-so gesture with his hand. 'He will be.' He would have to take Eldritch's word on that but, since he knew of nothing he could do to help, that trust would have to be sufficient.

Perhaps Jane understood because she didn't challenge him. Instead, she thought for a moment and then said, 'Nice look, by the way. Jeans and an unbuttoned white shirt – so much sexier than stark naked.'

She treated both men to a predatory leer. Aidan scowled but he appreciated the levity, and the impish look on Jane's face told him she knew it. They shared a fleeting grin and then Jane asked, 'So, what is she doing with all the candles?'

'She's casting a circle.'

At least that was what Aidan thought Gwyn was doing. He shifted his stance to take some of the weight off his sore hip as he took a proper look. It was true that his mentor often had clusters of candles scattered around the room when she was working with power and he had seen Eldritch mark the south cardinal point of his own circles with a single red candle, but this was different. Aidan had never seen either of them set out an entire circle boundary with candles before.

Gwyn took another tealight from her satchel and positioned it on the floor, and Aidan was intrigued and impressed by the accuracy with which the circle was taking shape. He understood that in magical terms a circle was simply a way of defining a space that, despite the name, didn't have to be circular. Indeed, the first circle he had encountered – the one Eldritch had created as part of a veil to protect them from the demon – hadn't been circular at all. But this one was. Aidan reckoned it wouldn't have been more regular if Gwyn had been following a compass line chalked on the tired wooden boards.

Despite the disparity in their shapes, Gwyn's nascent circle reminded Aidan of that first protective veil. She didn't appear to be using sigils – or at least her hands weren't visibly moving to trace those complicated, arcane shapes – but as she positioned each addition to the candle ring he sensed the prickly static of magic being worked, of strands of power being pulled together and pinned in place. Curious, he tried to let his eyes shift out of focus as he watched her position the next tealight and thought he could see something there – a lingering quicksilver gleam as though Gwyn's fingers had left smears of starlight across the stale afternoon air. That faint trace of light had none of the intricacy of the glyphs he had seen Eldritch use, nor the ones that Gwyn herself had been starting to teach him. The shape was softer – smudgier – than the ones he was learning. It seemed more primitive, like the crude lines of a painting daubed onto a cave wall compared with the fine brushstrokes of a Renaissance masterpiece. Yet there was something powerful about it too, powerful and unsettling as though it tapped into some genetic memory of a time when the darkness was closer and populated with creatures inimical to human life. He shivered. Part of him wanted to go across and ask her to explain what she was doing. Another part of him wanted to stay well away.

'It's a containment circle.'

Aidan started a little at Eldritch's comment. He had thought the wizard had been feeling too sick to be paying much attention to what Gwyn was doing.

'Well, that makes sense, doesn't it? She's planning to contain the grieves, after all.'

'No.' Eldritch shook his head but whatever explanation he might have added was silenced as a new voice cut in.

'My mate speaks the truth.'

It was Helen.

Eldritch stiffened.

'Do you really think otherwise, witch woman? The power in my husband's ring is almost spent and your own pitiful store is drained. You do not have the strengtth to bind us. Tell me then, what is it that you think you can do? You cannot hold us forever.'

In contrast to Terry's raging, Helen's tone was calm, like a parent reasoning with a stubborn child. But if she expected a response from Gwyn she too was to be disappointed. Having completed her circle of candles the Welsh witch stood for several seconds eyeing her handiwork. Then she took a new item from her satchel. Aidan recognised the Ziplock plastic bag filled with table salt that Gwyn had requisitioned from Eldritch's kitchen. He watched with amusement as, rather than unseal it in the conventional manner, his teacher tore a corner of the plastic open with her teeth. She spent a moment finessing the hole to her satisfaction and then started to walk around her circle for a second time, the salt dribbling from the bag as she did so, forming a fine, even line on the outside of the ring of candles.

'Let us go and we will cause you no trouble. We will even spare the wizard.' Helen's eyes flicked from Gwyn to Eldritch, but her expression did not change. There was nothing in that passing glance to suggest that Eldritch meant anything to her now. 'Come, you have no choice.' The sorceress's voice was filled with hearty reasonableness, enough to suggest that Gwyn would be a fool not to agree with her.

Not so, Terry's. 'You're going to die, hag!' He hurled the words at Gwyn as though they were the weapons that would bring about her downfall. 'I will take your wizard lover and I will burn you alive with his magic. You're going to die screaming and with your last breath you will wish that you had destroyed him instead of trying to destroy us.'

Gwyn kept walking, impervious to threat and inducement alike. Only when she had returned to her starting point and surveyed this new circle did she finally respond to her two captives.

'I'm not going to be the one to destroy you.' She made it sound as though such an assumption was foolishness.

'Do you really think that my husband can help you?' The disdain in the sorceress's voice was as blatant as the dismissal on her face as she looked once more at Eldritch. 'You fool. He has no power now.'

Gwyn smiled indulgently as though she found the grieve's words comical. 'I wasn't thinking of him.'

Now it was Helen's turn to sound amused. 'Really? Your little wizardling isn't strong enough.'

The sniff with which she ended her judgement suggested eloquently that Gwyn was deluding herself. She didn't deign to look at Aidan as she spoke, but Gwyn did. For several seconds her green cat eyes met his and he had the oddest feeling she was trying to convey something to him through that look. It was almost as though she was giving him the mental equivalent of a hug. He scowled a question at her, but she ignored it, saying nothing – or rather nothing that was addressed to him. To Helen she simply said, 'I wouldn't ask that of him.'

'Then who?'

Gwyn turned her head slightly to look down at the grieve. Surrounded by the storm-wrack craziness of her hair, her face was calm and self-assured. She smiled at Helen and it was the smile of a chess master who has sacrificed every other piece on the board to manoeuvre an opponent into checkmate. A thread of unease wormed its way down Aidan's spine.

'It's not so much who, as what. What do you know of the Rite of Morrigan?'

CHAPTER 42

'Gwyn, no!'

The name meant nothing to Aidan, but it seemed to have hit a nerve with Eldritch and with Helen. The wizard jerked as though he had been slapped and he sat properly upright, his grey eyes wide and shocked.

Helen seemed equally taken aback and for the first time her air of superiority slipped. 'You wouldn't dare!' she hissed, but her challenge rang hollow as though she too were unnerved by Gwyn's words.

'Who the hell's Morrigan?' Jane demanded, but Aidan could only shake his head, as mystified as she was.

'I've no idea.' He wasn't so worried by the grieve's reaction; Helen might consider this rite dangerous, but she had no knowledge of what Gwyn was – or wasn't – capable of. But Eldritch did and he seemed genuinely horrified at the prospect. Aidan shifted uncomfortably, unsettled by the wizard's response. He had seen Eldritch face off against a demon as coolly as he himself might go into a training bout in the dojo. If the wizard believed that what Gwyn was suggesting was a bad idea, then it wasn't something he wanted to experience. He looked at Gwyn, hoping she would take notice of Eldritch's protest, but – typical Gwyn – she seemed more amused by the reaction her words had generated than concerned. She certainly didn't look like a woman about to reconsider her chosen course of action.

With a growing sense of uneasiness, Aidan turned back to Jane. 'But I've a nasty feeling we're not going to like it when we find out.' He sent her a rueful smile that was part apology and part warning that she should be on her guard for whatever was coming. 'What's she talking about, Eldritch?'

But Eldritch didn't answer. His attention was fixed on the Welsh witch to the exclusion of everyone else. He looked stricken, his face strained and paler than ever under the sweat-spiked fall of his hair. 'For the love of everything holy, Gwyn, don't do this.'

The gravelly rasp of his voice did nothing to disguise the emotion behind that plea.

Across the hall Gwyn stiffened, all trace of amusement disappearing from her expression. In its place was a prickly irritation as though she heard mistrust in the wizard's words rather than concern. Annoyance tightened her lips into a thin line that suggested she would have expected better from a man she counted as a friend, and the hard glitter in her eyes told Aidan that Eldritch's words had stung her in a way that all the grieves' comments could never do. And yet she and Eldritch were friends and perhaps Gwyn remembered that, for in the next instant she let out a long huff of breath like an exasperated dragon. For the space of several heartbeats she studied the wizard, her expression somewhere between irritation and resignation. Watching her, Aidan could almost see the chain of thoughts running behind her eyes. Finally, she seemed to reach some conclusion.

She shook her head as though already regretting what she was about to do and came over to join her three friends. 'Do you have a better idea?' Gwyn stood by Eldritch's feet, her arms folded, glaring down at the semi-prone man.

'Gwyn—'

Gwyn's elfin brows raised in repetition of her question, effectively silencing the wizard.

Eldritch swallowed down whatever he had been about to say and tried again. 'We could leave here now.' The wizard's voice was low and urgent. In his lap his fist clenched, the knuckles whitening as if he could force his arguments on her physically. 'The four of us … we'd be safe. I don't think they'd come after us.'

The hairs on the back of Aidan's neck stood up. Whatever the Rite of Morrigan was it must be bad if Eldritch was suggesting they run away rather than risk it. Jane's eyes widened and he heard confusion and outrage in her sharp 'What?', but it was Gwyn's reaction that held his attention. A slight inclination of the witch's head acknowledged the truth in Eldritch's words and, for the briefest of moments, Aidan thought he saw something else – a yearning in those forest-green eyes, as though the thing she wanted most in all the world was to go along with his suggestion. Aidan swallowed, waiting for her to say something, but then that hint of vulnerability was gone, replaced by a wall of calm thoughtfulness more unnerving than any emotional storm.

'We might be,' she agreed, but the bittersweet smile that accompanied her words dismissed that truth as irrelevant. 'But they'd swap bodies as soon as they got the chance, you know they would. And that's two deaths I refuse to have on my conscience. I think Helen—' She stopped and the look she cast back at the grieves held a wealth of sadness and regret. 'The real Helen would have agreed with me.' Her eyes sought Eldritch's once more, locking on to his as if she would pass more than words between them. 'I think, deep down, you do too.' The fleeting smile she offered him might have been an apology.

Eldritch bowed his head. 'I don't want to lose you too.'

The words were little more than a breath, but Gwyn had sharp ears. 'That makes two of us,' she said drily. She tossed her head, shaking the dark swags of her hair back from her face. Yet her expression was softer than her tone. Her hand lifted briefly as though she would reach out towards him, but she let it drop without completing the gesture.

'You really have no shields left at all, do you?' She made no apology for the abrupt switch of topic. Instead, she treated the wizard to a scowl as though his current incapacity was somehow his own fault. 'I imagine you're feeling sick as a dog too.'

Eldritch didn't offer a reply but the slight tightening of his lips confirmed Gwyn's assessment.

'I thought as much.' Then she added more gently, 'It will pass, I promise you. I've a fair idea what she used and there are things I can do to help counter it when we get you home. It will take a few days to get it out of your system but then you'll start to bounce back. Until then, this will help.'

As she spoke, Gwyn slid the rose quartz bracelet from her wrist. She held the strand of pale pink spheres in her hand for a moment as though weighing its value. 'I seem to be giving out a lot of these today.' She shot a swift look at Aidan, too fast for him to read her expression, and added, 'Maybe I should go into business.'

But for all her gruffness she was careful as she bent and slid the bracelet over Eldritch's right hand, positioning it to ensure that it didn't rub the raw and abraded skin of his wrist. Eldritch jerked fractionally as the crystal spheres touched his skin and

Gwyn smiled knowingly. 'I've keyed the stones to you. All you have to do is open yourself to them.' Then she added sternly, 'Don't take it off.'

The instruction was reinforced with a basilisk glare as if to say *Remember what happened last time.* Eldritch's shoulders moved in the briefest of shrugs, acknowledging the hit. Gwyn's bracelets had proven their worth last autumn after his encounter with the avatar. At the time he had dismissed the strings of crystal beads as hippy trinkets and had worn them purely to humour her. He hadn't realised how effectively they had been shielding him until he stopped wearing them, a mistake that had nearly cost him and Aidan their lives. Still, that memory didn't stop him commenting, 'It's not me who's dabbling with possession.'

His voice was quiet, as though it wasn't his intention to argue with her, but Gwyn's expression still hardened.

'I'm not dabbling with anything. I know what I'm doing, wizard.' She scowled as if deciding that arguing with him in his current state hardly constituted a fair fight. 'You can give it back to me in a day or two.'

For a moment it seemed she would say more but then she shook her head, dismissing whatever comment she had been about to make as irrelevant, and straightened up. She turned to Aidan and Jane, but Aidan spoke before she could.

'What are you planning, Gwyn?' His tone was sharper than he intended but her exchange with Eldritch had unnerved him. 'What's this Rite of Morrigan?'

Gwyn let out a small huff of breath, although whether in irritation or amusement it was impossible to say. 'I can see I've neglected your training.'

She might have left it there, but Aidan moved and caught hold of her arm. He held it a little tighter than was necessary, not enough to hurt but sufficient to let her know he wasn't going to be fobbed off with half an answer.

'Gwyn.' He almost growled the name. The words 'tell me the truth' hung unspoken between them.

For a long moment Gwyn merely looked at Aidan. She didn't tell him to take his hand off her – in fact she gave no indication that she even noticed she was being held – she simply studied him, her head cocked to one side like a blackbird contemplating a particularly juicy worm. It was a look that had made him squirm as a child but now he steeled himself against it. Perhaps she realised because she nodded almost imperceptibly.

The truth, then.

Her gaze lost focus for a few seconds but for once Aidan had the impression that Gwyn was ordering her thoughts rather than sorting through them to decide what she would – or would not – share. When she spoke, it was in the direct and unemotional tone he was familiar with from her lessons in magical theory.

'I told you that there were sources of power, entities if you will – or perhaps elemental principles might be a better term – that can be summoned as a way of raising power.' She waited for his nod. 'Well, the Rite of Morrigan is a summoning ritual.'

'So, you're going to summon a power source that will give you the energy you need to deal with the grieves?'

'In essence, yes.'

'Okay.'

'Sounds simple enough,' Jane chipped in. 'But I'm getting the sense that—'

'It isn't,' Eldritch spoke across her. His voice was harsh, almost angry.

'Stay out of this, wizard.' Gwyn didn't spare Eldritch a glance but her tone held more than a note of warning. 'None of the elemental principles are straightforward to deal with,' she continued for Aidan's benefit. 'They come if they wish. It's not something you can coerce.'

'Like the Gatherer of Souls?' Aidan recalled again his first lesson in shielding and the prickle of nervous amazement he had felt at the tangible shift of energies in Gwyn's small lounge. Yet there had been nothing truly fearful about that encounter. He remembered it primarily because that evening had been the first step on his journey into what had been a largely unguessed-at world of magic. Gwyn nodded and he saw recognition of that same memory reflected in the briefest lifting of her lips.

'Similar. Morrigan is a female principle, a feminine energy.'

'Feminine as in gentle and easy to deal with?'

The question was half tongue-in-cheek, half hopeful, but surely the cards had to fall in their favour at some point in this venture? Aidan ignored Jane's derisive snort and focused on Gwyn, waiting for her answer. Her black, elfin brows quirked upwards but instead of answering him she looked at Jane.

'You need to keep this one, he's cute.' Turning back, she added more seriously, 'I'd have thought you'd be the last person to make that sort of assumption, Aidan.'

'Hey, it was just a thought.' Aidan felt aggrieved at Gwyn's response. 'I'm sure there must be some females in the world that are easy to deal with.'

'Don't bank on it.' Another time Eldritch's dry response would have been the start of a vigorous – if essentially good natured – exchange with Gwyn, but not now. 'One of Morrigan's other names is the Scatterer of Souls.' Eldritch's voice was grim, his expression as dark as the back road into hell. 'In ancient times the cult of Morrigan worshipped her as a warrior goddess.'

Still irritated with Gwyn, Aidan registered the emotion firming Eldritch's voice as anger. It scarcely occurred to him that it might have been fear.

'You can't do this, Gwyn.'

Gwyn's nostrils flared. She turned, looking down her nose at the semi-recumbent wizard, and for a moment her eyes went cold and hard. Aidan thought she would ask Eldritch who he thought he was to tell her what she could or couldn't do, and he wondered what Eldritch's reaction would be, but instead she said, 'I wasn't much older than Aidan is now when I tapped into wild magic, unshielded and exhausted, and used it to save my best friend from bleeding to death from a uterine haemorrhage.' If her eyes were glacial then her tone was colder still. Now came the warning. 'Don't think to judge what I'm capable of.'

She didn't add 'wizard', her familiar epithet when arguing with Eldritch. There was no endearment in her voice now. Her small form radiated a bitter and righteous fury.

'And you burned out every energy channel in your body doing it.' Eldritch didn't have the strength to raise his voice, but his tone matched Gwyn's icy anger.

'And yet I survived. And if my energy channels are burned out, they can't be reburned, can they?' A curious mix of emotions played across Gwyn's face but none of them settled as she added with an almost studied casualness, 'Who knows, this might even open them up again.'

Aidan thought he could read Gwyn better than most, but that throwaway comment worried him. She had told him the story of how she had saved his mother's life – and his own – and what that intervention had cost her. She had also said that she didn't regret her actions and he had believed her. And yet … he hoped that final remark had been made to bait an English wizard she felt had overstepped himself and not that she was about to gamble her life in the hope of a miracle.

Eldritch's expression suggested he feared she just might. 'Please, Gwyn.'

There was no anger in his tone now, nor arrogance, no hint of that boy scout sense of being so sure he knew what was for the best that could be so irritating, even to those who knew the wizard well, but Gwyn turned her back on him regardless.

'Jane, I need to ask you a favour.'

If Jane was surprised by the request she hid it well. 'Sure, anything.'

'I need you to tie Eldritch's hands, please.'

'What?' At first Aidan thought he must have misheard, but one look at that icily determined face told him otherwise. Outraged, he rounded on her. 'Christ, Gwyn! What are you doing?' He looked at Eldritch, slumped and defenceless. The wizard made no protest but his face was a mask of betrayed hurt. 'He can barely even sit up.'

Eldritch was no threat to Gwyn's plans, though at that moment Aidan might have wished he could be. Anger filled him. He expected anger from Gwyn in return and was ready for it. What he got instead shocked him.

'I know, but it will be better this way. Trust me.'

He didn't know what to make of the gentle reasonableness that had come into Gwyn's voice. While he floundered mentally, Jane looked from Gwyn to Eldritch and then, to Aidan's horror, picked up one of the discarded lengths of rope that had been used to bind Eldritch to the scaffold.

'If the lady wants you tied up …' She winked at Eldritch. 'That's what the lady gets.'

Her attempt at humour did nothing to lighten the atmosphere.

Aidan glowered and held out his own wrists. Though he stepped in front of Jane it was clear that his words were directed at Gwyn. 'No. Absolutely not. He's been tied up for three days. You're not going to tie him up again.'

He brandished his crossed wrists angrily, his fists clenched. 'Come on, I've been under Helen's influence. You never know what she might be able to do with me. Hell, I might cave in and just let her take me over. It's a risk you can't take.'

'Aide—'

'Don't *Aide* me, Jane.'

'Aidan.' There was enough bite in Gwyn's tone to have him swinging towards her. 'I appreciate your loyalty but don't be melodramatic. It doesn't suit you.'

Aidan felt his mouth drop open. He closed it with a snap, but before he could come up with a suitable retort Gwyn smiled at him.

'This is for Eldritch's safety. There's no way he can help me and, given that today seems to be a day for pointless gestures,' her forest-green eyes narrowed slightly but she chose not to press the matter, 'I don't want him getting himself killed trying.'

As if that settled the matter, she turned to the wizard. 'You and I both know that there isn't enough power in your body right now to zap a small rodent. You're holding yourself together by the skin of your teeth.' She raised a hand to cut off his protest. 'There's no shame in that. I don't know of anyone else who could have survived what you've been through without breaking. And that includes me.' She offered that admission to him like a gift, the accompanying smile open and without guile. It lit her face like April sunshine, brief and heart-wrenchingly beautiful in its honesty. 'However, right now there is nothing you can do to help me. Unfortunately, I suspect that rather inconvenient fact wouldn't stop you trying. I know what you're like, wizard.' The affection was back in her voice. 'The last thing I need at this point in the proceedings is to have to worry about you thinking something's going wrong and wading in heroically to try and put it right.'

'Gwyn.' There was no protest in that soft whisper, just a wealth of emotion too complex to give name to. Very deliberately Eldritch held out his wrists to Jane.

'You have your knife, don't you?'

Aidan started at Gwyn's question and then nodded, not yet trusting himself to say anything to her, or at least nothing polite.

Gwyn carried on regardless as if she hadn't considered the reason for his silence. 'Good. Keep it handy.'

But instead of telling him what he was keeping the blade handy for she stopped speaking and simply stared at him. It wasn't a simple glance. Gwyn studied him as though she were seeing him for the very first time, or – it felt to Aidan – as if it were the last time they would meet and she was trying to commit his face to her memory. The thought sat queasily alongside the still smouldering embers of his anger. He tried not to squirm under that curious scrutiny, tried not to turn away from her. Then Gwyn smiled at him and, for the briefest of moments, he understood why Eldritch had given in.

'Your mother would be very proud of you, Aidan.'

Before Aidan could think of how to respond to such an odd statement Gwyn closed the gap between them. Putting her hands on his shoulders she rose on her tiptoes and pressed her lips to his forehead. He felt the warmth of her breath against his skin and a prickly tingle of energy before she released him and stepped back.

'I want you to know that I'm very proud of you too.' Then, as though she realised she was in danger of becoming maudlin, she treated him to a basilisk glare. 'Keep up with your studies. And you,' she added, turning to address Eldritch, her voice still stern, 'you'd better make sure he does.'

'If this goes wrong—' Gwyn stopped, a frown line kinking the skin between her eyebrows as she treated Aidan and Jane to a look that was both quizzical and – to Aidan's surprise – faintly amused. She huffed a breath. 'Actually, if this goes wrong I have no idea what will happen, other than it's unlikely to be my problem any more. Trust your instincts, both of you, but I'd suggest you should probably get out of here. Aidan, don't be too hasty but be ready to cut Eldritch free, just in case. But only if it's absolutely necessary,' she added, giving him a hard stare to underline the point. 'You can judge when that might be.'

She turned to Jane. 'Take care of them, Jane.' Both Aidan and Eldritch bristled at this, but Gwyn ignored their indignation. 'Ask Chris and Kath to keep feeding the cats for me.' The corners of her mouth lifted in a smile, but her eyes had turned sad. 'And give Kali the occasional prawn.'

Jane gave Gwyn a look that was part worried question and part resolute acceptance. Then she stepped in and caught the older woman in a swift, brief hug. 'You know I will. Just make sure you're okay to feed your own cats.'

As fast as she had initiated the contact Jane broke it off. She stepped back, her expression a study in careful neutrality.

Eldritch had been silent since Jane had bound his hands. Now he spoke. 'Be careful, Gwyn.'

'Scared it won't work, wizard?'

Eldritch shook his head, a small negating gesture. In the dim light his face looked ghastly, his eyes full of foreboding. 'No.' He dropped his head but Aidan was close enough to hear the soft whisper as the wizard added, 'I'm scared it will.'

CHAPTER 43

'I am the fever in the blood.'

Gwyn stood within the double circle of salt and fire, the flames from the assorted candles and tealights casting spangles of gold light over her bare feet and across the bodies of the two grieves stretched out in front of her. She tossed her hair back from her shoulders, lifting her face as though she were addressing herself to something that only she could see, hidden in the gloom under the smoke-blackened ceiling. While she barely seemed to raise her voice the sound of it filled the hall, flowing into the shadow-laden corners and lapping at the walls like water rising inexorably from the breached walls of an ancient spring. Aidan shivered, the hairs on the back of his neck rising as something within him responded to that graphic litany.

The fever in the blood.

He winced, his mind conjuring up unsettling images of plague pits and discoloured skin swollen and blistered with pestilence. With an effort he pushed them away, cursing his too vivid imagination.

'I am the unhealing wound.'

The images in Aidan's mind shifted as though Gwyn's words were reaching out to a part of him that had known the bloody aftermath of battle and its consequences in the dark times before antibiotics and the mercy of surgery under anaesthetic. His heart lurched unpleasantly as memories that weren't his own spilled into his brain.

Dear God, he could almost hear the screams. His vision went red as if he were viewing the hall through a haze of blood and he flinched, his shoulders hunching unconsciously as though a surgeon's blade had been touched to his own flesh.

It's not real. Aidan forced himself to take a slow breath, pushing the images back. *It's just Gwyn talking creepy; there's no need to freak out.*

But for an instant he could have sworn he caught the cloying smell of corruption, clinging like a taste to the back of his throat. Eldritch's reservations about the entity Gwyn was invoking suddenly made a great deal of sense.

'I am the trembling of pain.'

Again, Gwyn's voice rang out, clear and yet somehow resonant, the sound suggesting that other voices had joined with hers. Aidan's hands balled themselves into fists as he fought the urge to look behind him to check no phantom shapes were forming along the walls at his back. His skin prickled at the thought, but he forced himself to keep his gaze focused on the circle in front of him. If anything was going to manifest as a result of Gwyn's invocation, surely it would take shape there. He licked his lips, unwilling to admit just how nervous that prospect made him. Gwyn knew what she was doing – dear God, he hoped so! Despite Eldritch's misgivings he had to believe that was the case – but he couldn't shake the feeling that the elemental force his mentor sought to harness was beyond anything she had dealt with before. Beside him Jane muttered something as unlikely as it was inventive. Aidan registered the tension she was trying to hide but he had no reassurance to give and no chance to answer her before Gwyn spoke again.

'I am the crushed and splintered bone.'

No!

The protest rose unspoken in Aidan's throat like bile and he fought against a sudden desire to turn and run, to put as much distance as he could between himself and what was happening. This was Gwyn, he tried to reassure himself, his mother's best friend and the woman she had chosen to be his guardian after her death, irritating, infuriating, reassuring and comforting in equal measures; he had known her all his life. He knew she would never deliberately harm him, knew it in the same way that he knew his own name or the shapes of the hills around his home. It was a tenet of his universe. But that knowledge held no power against the awful certainty rising inside him that for all their shared history, the woman he was watching now was a stranger to him, that he had no idea what she was truly capable of. And, deeper still, some long-forgotten and primitive part of his consciousness was telling him that this small, dark-haired woman held the very powers of life and death in her hands.

'I am the rot and the ruin.'

Aidan felt his breathing grow shallow as each inhalation matched itself involuntarily to the cadence of Gwyn's speech. He was aware that Jane had gone very still. There were no brash comments now, no false bravado. Like him, she was waiting. There was a heartbeat of silence like the pause before the ending of the world.

'I am the absence of breath.'

Gwyn swept her arms upwards in one swift motion, her hands stretching wide as though scooping up the sky to hold it – captive – above her head, her fingers spread rigid like outstretched spears. Aidan's breath became a gasp as he felt the sudden surge of power that boiled through the hall, charging the air like the moment before a lightning strike. He watched, torn between fascination and terror, as the very air around Gwyn seemed to shift and ripple, glimmering like a psychedelic heat haze as if the scarred wooden floorboards under her bare feet were burning with invisible flames.

The slightest smile lifted the corners of Gwyn's mouth, as though what she was doing was nothing out of the ordinary. She had told him once that she had been powerful beyond his comprehension. To his shame Aidan remembered how he had scoffed, choosing only to hear her next words that she had lost most of her abilities. At the time he had doubted that she had ever had any to lose. He swallowed, his mouth gone dry while his palms were clammy with sweat. Watching her now, it would seem she still had every right to claim the title of witch.

'I am the white-faced woman.'

Aidan jerked as Gwyn spoke again. He had thought the invocation was over, that the power he could feel seething within the circle was what Gwyn had sought to conjure. Surely that had to be enough? But as he looked at her across the concentric circles of salt and fire he understood that, whatever had answered her, this was just the beginning. Gwyn's wide eyes shone a luminous green against the pallor of her face. He knew he shouldn't be able to tell that at the distance he stood from her, but he could. They glittered like phosphorescent water at the full moon. Aidan's skin crawled as the chant went on, inexorable and unstoppable as a rising flood.

'I am the blue-limbed man.'

Propped against the scaffold Eldritch made a small noise, a sub-vocal whisper of protest. It was only the fact that his own throat had choked closed in terror that prevented Aidan doing the same. He was conscious of the strands of blue rope wrapped around the wizard's wrists, binding him like an altar sacrifice. Aidan wondered if he would have time to cut his friend free if things went wrong. He slid his hand into the front pocket of his jeans and gripped his pocketknife, feeling its casing slick in his sweating palm. He prayed he wouldn't need it. He wondered if he would know he did before it was too late.

'I am the sound in the dark. I am the stillness in the night.'

Gwyn paused and Aidan found himself holding his breath, waiting for her to speak again as though he had no power to move until she did.

'I am the dawn. I am the light. I am the maiden.'

Her voice was a drumbeat, the gathering throb to which the world had been danced into life. Sweat trickled down Aidan's sides underneath his polo shirt. Surely the temperature in the hall was increasing. He breathed to the rhythm of the words.

Another pause.

When Gwyn spoke again her voice was the sound of a heartbeat, a double pulse, the in and out of breath, the sob and suck of a wave endlessly breaking and retreating on some unknowable shore.

'I am the zenith. I am the heat. I am the mother.'

Aidan felt the blood pounding in his temples, felt his heart pumping hard against his ribs. His body seemed in thrall to Gwyn's words as though by listening to them a connection had been made without his knowing, and now he was inexorably bound as a participant in the ritual.

Another pause, as weighty as the silence after a last heartbeat, and Gwyn's voice became a funeral knell – the tolling of the bell that signals the fall of the final night.

'I am the settling. I am the darkness. I am the crone.'

'Gwyn.' Her name came out as a moan, his voice strangled by a visceral dread. The breath seemed to clot in his lungs as, within the circle, the shimmering air began to move.

Nothing changed within the hall itself, no breeze broke the muggy heat, but on the floor near Gwyn's feet the blonde strands of Helen's hair stirred as if lifted by a sudden wind. The candle flames continued to burn steadily, but now Gwyn's shirt was moving, the loose silk fabric alternately billowing and then flattening against her body. As Aidan watched, Gwyn's long hair swirled around her as though she was caught in a vortex. It lifted out from her head, a boiling midnight cloud with its one streak of white as bright as summer lightning. The sensation of building power was like a physical weight pressing down upon him. Aidan's ears popped as the pressure in the room changed. Jane yelped, her eyes going wide and startled. Aidan looked up, following her gaze, and for a second he had the impression that he was staring at an open sky – black and star-strung and yet pregnant with clouds – instead of the smoke-blackened ceiling. For the space of a heartbeat awe replaced fear. Then there was a crack as loud as gunfire and lightning forked down, the bolt striking into Gwyn's upraised hands. Purple and violet and white fire flashed around her and she flung back her head and laughed.

CHAPTER 44

The silence that followed in the wake of that wild banshee laughter was almost tangible. Typically, it was Jane who broke it. 'Is she …?'

The young woman hesitated as if belatedly realising that even that most muted of whispers might be inappropriate. Aidan glanced from his mentor to his girlfriend, hearing his own concern mirrored in those two words and reading it in the fierce line Jane's scowl marked between her brows.

'Okay?' He kept his own voice equally hushed. 'I don't know.' He ran his tongue nervously over his lips and nodded. 'But I think so.'

Almost guiltily, he looked back at the woman standing motionless within the containment circle, hoping that what he said was the truth and not mere wishful thinking. He was unsure what he could do if that wasn't the case but – incredible though it seemed – Gwyn did appear unscathed by her stint as a human lightning rod. She stood there now, either unaware of his scrutiny or ignoring it – either was possible with Gwyn – just a small barefoot woman in a baggy teal shirt and worn jeans, apparently little different from the woman who had stepped into the circle. Her hair – released from the swirling vortex of power – fell over her shoulders in its usual chaos, the dark swags of it accentuating the elfin fineness of her features. Perhaps her face was a little paler than it had been before the ritual, her eyes standing out a little greener against the porcelain of her skin. Aidan wondered if her silence now was because she was coming to terms with what she had just done, but there were no obvious signs to suggest she had come to any harm.

'I was going to say finished,' Jane murmured. 'But okay is good too.'

The briefest cant of her head acknowledged that Aidan was probably right in considering that to be the more important fact. Aidan felt himself grin in response, but a cold voice sliced across his reply before he had a chance to say anything.

'She isn't. Not on either count.'

The venom with which Eldritch spoke had both Aidan and Jane whipping round to stare at him. The wizard was sitting painfully upright, his posture radiating a tense watchfulness that belied how close he must be to the limits of his endurance.

'She won't be alright until this is over. All of it.' Eldritch closed his eyes briefly as a tremor ran through him. When he opened them again they were as bleak and cold as the Atlantic. 'Even then …' He shook his head, as if dismissing whatever he had been about to say. The harshness of his voice softened into misery as he continued, 'You have no idea what she's doing.'

'But fortunately, *she* does.'

The subject of Eldritch's concern sounded unimpressed by his attitude. In fact, Aidan thought she sounded downright irritated. And perhaps she had every right to be, given what he had just seen her do.

'Don't waste your time worrying about my safety, wizard.'

Aidan winced. He could understand her annoyance but there was a note in Gwyn's voice that he had never heard before, or at least not applied to Eldritch. Coming from someone else he would have taken it as contempt.

'You'd do better to look to your own.' If her words had been meant as a challenge, Gwyn didn't wait for Eldritch to respond. 'Watch and learn.'

And she turned away, her movement as haughtily dismissive as a queen's.

Eldritch made a soft noise like an animal in pain, but didn't speak. He raised his bound hands and wiped his face along his shirtsleeve – perhaps the thin film of sweat that stood out on his skin was stinging his eyes – then he sagged back against the leg of the scaffold as if he no longer had the strength or the desire to support himself. A curious mixture of grief and grim determination emphasised the lines that the privations of the last three days had carved into the wizard's face as he stared across the hall at Gwyn. Aidan's gut twisted as the reality of what Gwyn was about to do hit home.

Unsure what else to do, he dropped a hand onto Eldritch's shoulder. 'Hang in there.'

It wasn't enough, but there were no words he could say that would make what was about to happen more bearable.

When he looked back at the circle Gwyn was standing between the bodies of the two grieves. Although Aidan was sure they were still conscious, neither Helen nor Terry made any attempt to speak nor to move. They lay as they had done throughout the ritual, silent and still, staring up at the woman who controlled their fate. But now Aidan fancied there was an edge to their silence. It was as if they recognised the presence of a predator more deadly than themselves and it was a prey's instinctive wariness that kept them still, not wanting to draw death down upon them. Aidan thought he too would freeze if he were in their place. He remembered all too easily being at the mercy of the demon in the old Greenfields mine and how each heartbeat had seemed infinitely precious as he had waited for it to kill him. It struck him now that just like the demon, Gwyn seemed in no hurry to finish off the grieves. The comparison made him queasy.

What was Gwyn thinking as she studied those two supine forms? Helen Eldritch and Terry – with a kind of shock Aidan realised that he didn't know the man's surname – were already dead. Gwyn would not be killing them when she destroyed the grieves but their bodies would still die as a result. Much though he wanted the grieves dealt with, it was still an uncomfortable thought. But if Gwyn had any such reservations they didn't show in her face. She looked composed, Aidan thought. He might have used the word serene, but there was nothing tranquil about Gwyn's present state. She was as serene as a blade or a hunting cat, poised, purposeful and deadly. He shifted uneasily, feeling the tension building as everyone within the hall waited for Gwyn to make her choice. Aidan thought he heard the catch of Eldritch's breath as Gwyn leaned over Helen but, just as it seemed she had made her decision, she swung to face Terry.

'Do you have anything to say?'

'Bastard witch! A curse on you and all your—'

Gwyn gestured abruptly and the angry tirade was cut off. 'Enough.'

There was the snap of command in her voice and a fierceness wholly untempered by mercy or compassion. She had listened to his ranting earlier, it seemed to say, she was not going to do so again. Terry's eyes bulged. His jaw worked, the muscles in his neck standing out as he strained to speak, but he could not break the control Gwyn had over him. A small smile lifted the corners of Gwyn's mouth, signalling her satisfaction with this state of affairs. It was as cold as her voice and equally unforgiving. Despite himself, Aidan shuddered. He had no sympathy for the grieve but it would be a long time before he forgot the sheer terror of being locked immobile within his own body.

Ignoring all Terry's efforts, Gwyn reached down, her hands fisting in the front of his T-shirt and with no apparent difficulty she hauled the bound man to his feet. Aidan watched aghast at this casual display of strength. There was no way Gwyn was physically capable of what she had just done and he hadn't realised that the power gained by invoking Morrigan would extend beyond the psychic realm. Nor, it seemed, had Terry. The man's eyes grew even wider and now there was real fear apparent on his face. Unable to speak, his expression screamed in silent protest as Gwyn pulled him closer, removing her left hand from his shirt to place it against his cheek. For a moment she held her palm there, the gesture as tender as though she were cupping the face of her beloved. For several moments she stared into his eyes and then she lowered her head and kissed him full on the mouth.

'No!'

'Don't!'

Jane's shocked exclamation mingled with Aidan's own. Whatever rite Gwyn had completed, whatever power she had invoked, still he expected to see her crumple, overwhelmed by the potency of the grieve's dark magic. For what seemed like an eternity, witch and grieve remained locked together. Then Gwyn's hand went slack against Terry's cheek. Her lips still pressed to his, she shuddered. Her eyes closed and her fingers trailed across his skin as her arm dropped to her side. In that second Aidan knew that Gwyn had lost. His heart lurched in a painful contraction of grief and anger but before he could launch himself across the hall to attack her killer she lifted her head, pulling away from the kiss. With the gesture of one discarding a used rag she released her grip on Terry's T-shirt, stepping back as the handyman's knees buckled and he fell face down at her feet.

Anxious fingers clenched around Aidan's hand, demanding his attention.

'Who won?'

For a second he couldn't bring himself to answer Jane's question. 'I don't know.'

The confession clogged in his throat, the words slicing him like broken glass. Had Gwyn's kiss somehow removed the grieve from Terry and taken it captive or had it jumped ship, moving into Gwyn of its own volition and taking her as its new host? The realisation that he had no idea how Gwyn's plan was meant to work made Aidan want to curse his ex-guardian for her stubborn, need-to-know secrecy. The thought that he might have lost her made him want to throw back his head and howl with grief. 'Eldritch?'

Surely the wizard would know what had just happened. But the Englishman didn't respond to Aidan's sharp question. His attention was focused solely on the figures in the circle and if he heard the fear underlying that urgent query he gave no sign.

Within the circle the woman who might no longer be Gwyn was moving. She stepped around Terry's crumpled form as though his corpse was of no more interest to her than a bag of rubbish someone had left in her way and stood over Helen. Aidan scarcely dared breathe, waiting to see who would be revealed by her next action – witch or grieve? Cool green eyes stared down at the bound woman.

'And you? Do you have anything to say?'

Aidan felt he might go limp with relief. He exhaled a shaky sigh. 'Thank God!'

It was Gwyn.

The quick squeeze of Jane's fingers around his own was like a celebratory whoop, telling him that she too had feared the worst. They traded nervous grins, knowing the danger wasn't over yet, but daring to hope that everything would be okay. Aidan looked again at Eldritch, but the wizard seemed more intent than ever on the drama taking place in front of him. Aidan bit back the comment he had been about to make and left the other man alone.

Within the circle Helen lifted her head from the floor, the small movement all she could make within the constraints of Gwyn's binding. Strands of blonde hair clung to her cheeks and a streak of soot showed dark against the crumpled linen of her tunic, but she regarded Gwyn as haughtily as her ancient namesake.

'Who are you to cast judgement upon us?' Her nostrils flared as she openly studied the woman standing over her, as though it was Gwyn who was the captive and not her. 'We are creatures of the senses. When did you last dance because you felt sunshine warm your skin or laugh because you ate when you were hungry and felt sated? We ache – we yearn – for the ability to sense what you take for granted. What right do you have to shut us away, to condemn us to the cold, dark eternity of what you call the Unseen Realm?'

She met Gwyn's unblinking peridot gaze with cold disdain and Gwyn's dark brows raised infinitesimally, as though acknowledging the grieve's point of view.

'And what of the humans that you kill as you swap from host to host?'

Aidan couldn't help but smile at her choice of words. Only Gwyn would risk her life to save those unknown future hosts yet still refer to them offhandedly as humans rather than people.

Helen rolled her eyes in a gesture of dismissal; *Why should we speak of such trifles?* 'Hosts grow old.' The reply was given as casually as though the two women were discussing last season's fashions. 'We are eternal. I am no more Helen Eldritch than I was Robert Finch before her or any of those who came before him.'

'And so you kill them.' There was a trace of ice in Gwyn's voice.

'What of it?' Helen met ice with heated defiance. 'It is not within you to care for any of them.'

Amusement turned to alarm bells in Aidan's brain as Gwyn inclined her head, like a fencer acknowledging an opponent's hit.

'You are right. I care for none of them.'

Er, back up, Gwyn. What do you mean you don't care?

But he could think of one terrible explanation for that casual pronouncement and fear tightened like a cold hand around his gut. Then Gwyn spoke again but if the lightness of her tone suggested her words were an afterthought, her eyes suggested otherwise.

'None except the woman Helen.'

Like obsidian pebbles dropped into the fathomless waters of an underground lake, Gwyn's words sent ripples through the hall. For several seconds there was silence. Neither grieve nor witch spoke, but Aidan felt the energies in the room shift and realign. Jane's fingers were rigid against his and he was aware that, like him, she was holding herself ready. But what they might have to do he couldn't have said.

'What do you have to say about her?'

The sheer reasonableness of Gwyn's tone was unnerving.

Helen ran the tip of her tongue over her lips. Aidan could almost see her shifting mental gears as she eyed her captor.

'It was not I who killed her.' Helen's face was a study in injured innocence as though the very idea was preposterous. 'She was dead before I took her body. I gave her life once more.' She said it as though it had been intended as a charitable act. Twisting round as best she could, the grieve turned her gaze towards Eldritch. 'Surely you will admit that, my love – that it was I who gave you back your wife? You knew the demon had killed her. You knew it when you drove the hell spawn from her flesh.' There was a wealth of sorrow and understanding in her voice, as though she had experienced every moment of his suffering and shared it with him. 'Deep down you knew her resurrection was impossible, that it could not be true.'

Helen's demeanour changed as she spoke. The haughty defiance with which she had addressed Gwyn melted away as though it had been nothing but a shield thrown up in desperation by a gentle and vulnerable soul. The husky contralto of her voice softened, becoming achingly tender as she caressed Eldritch with her words.

'And yet you wanted to believe.' The blue eyes sought his. 'I gave you that chance. You loved me as you loved her.'

The agonised catch of Eldritch's breath was as eloquent as a torture victim's scream. He hadn't moved while Gwyn dealt with Terry, but now he shook his head, a small negating gesture, his face carved into a rictus of pain. Aidan understood that what Helen said was the truth, but that truth was not a comfort but a flail. And yet the grieve continued as if she had no comprehension of the suffering she had inflicted.

'I could be Helen for you again, my love.'

She stared at the wizard, her pansy-dark eyes flooded with emotion. Her lips quivered and she pressed them together briefly to steady herself as though she scarcely dared reveal the secret desire she held within her heart. 'I can give you the child that you and she talked of but never had the chance to conceive.'

Her voice trembling and made throaty by the apparent strength of her emotions, the grieve offered that future vision like a chalice of strychnine-laced honey, yearning for Eldritch's understanding and his acceptance even as her words cut open his heart.

'No.'

That brief exhalation of sound was more a sob of pain than an actual word. Across the hall, Helen continued as though she hadn't heard it. 'That child lies within me now.'

Unable to move Helen could not reach towards her husband yet every line of her body gave the impression that she was stretching towards him as if she could not bear for them to be separated.

'The demon would have tortured you with that child my love, but I will give it to you freely. It is the child of your flesh and hers. Son or daughter, it is her essence that has bound with yours to shape it and now it quickens within me.'

Helen dipped her head, the movement almost coy, as though she would gaze through clothes and flesh to where that spark of life had – allegedly – taken root. Her voice was infinitely sweet, pleading with Eldritch to understand what she offered and to make the right choice.

'I can give you this – give it to you freely. Over time you would forget that there was any difference. You would have what you always wanted, the family you and she dreamed of can be yours.'

Aidan listened to the litany of pleading and promises, the whispered words of love and longing, and his heart ached. Beside him he heard Jane swear softly and venomously under her breath, but he was more conscious of the awful silence emanating from Eldritch. He wanted to clap his hands over the other man's ears – anything to stop him hearing those razor-coated words. S*he doesn't mean any of it. She's not your wife.*

But of course, Eldritch already knew that. And still that knowledge couldn't make the pain of might-have-been any less.

The promise of that alternative future shone in Helen's face as she raised her head once more, her eyes gazing longingly towards Eldritch – *I am your wife. How can you think to reject me?* – and Aidan didn't have to look to know that yearning was reflected in Eldritch's. How could it not be, even though each and every detail of it was a lie?

Helen's lips trembled as she looked across at Eldritch, her eyes huge and brimming with emotion as though they were alone together. 'Could you not love me still?'

How can he bear this? Aidan was aware that his own pulse was hammering. It was hard to look at Helen, to see the tangled blonde hair and the casually elegant clothes, now crumpled and dishevelled, and remember that those things were just a mask for the grieve lurking within her flesh. In his mind he heard her husky laughter as she had stood in her kitchen and teased him.

Before she took you captive, he reminded himself, his fist clenching as if through that pressure he could squeeze those memories from his brain. Eldritch's body was similarly rigid, the knuckles of his own fists showing white, even against the pallor of his flesh. The wizard stared at Helen as though unable to tear his eyes away from her. His face was contorted with pain and Aidan heard the ragged draw of his breath, but he did not answer.

'El?' Artfully projected confusion scaled into desperation as the bound woman seemed to realise the situation was slipping away from her. 'Please!'

She seemed to strain towards him as though if she could only touch his hand, Eldritch would come to his senses and forgive her. Tears brimmed and spilled onto her cheeks and for an instant she was nothing more than she appeared – a frightened and desperate woman, pleading with the man she loved, begging him to see reason and to spare her life. But she wasn't and she never could be. In a moment of heartbreaking clarity Aidan realised that this was the second time Eldritch had lived this nightmare. He wondered if the other man was aware of the tears running down his own face, or how his jaw clenched as he gritted his teeth together. Was he trying to stop himself calling Helen's name or flinging curses at her? Either seemed possible. Aidan wondered if the wizard knew himself.

Please, Gwyn … Morrigan … whoever's running this show now …

'Stop this!' Aidan only realised he had spoken aloud when Gwyn's head snapped round. She eyed him coolly and for the first time as an adult Aidan had to force himself to meet that green gaze. 'Please.' He swallowed to clear his throat, unnerved by the lack of response his words had generated. Only the sense of injustice, of desperation and a growing, amorphous anger at what was happening allowed him to continue. He spoke into the silence, fighting down fear and a dozen conflicting emotions to address the woman he had looked up to for more than half his life. Sweat trickled uncomfortably down his back and it seemed hard to breathe in the dim closeness of the hall. 'There's no need for cruelty.'

Something moved in the back of Gwyn's eyes, an odd shifting of expression that was gone before Aidan could put a name to it.

'Is that what you think this is Aidan; cruelty?' Her mouth tightened into a line of disappointment, and she shook her head. 'Oh no. This is responsibility. Every action has its own consequences, and every decision must be made in the knowledge of what those are. I had as much right as any in this room to deal with him.' Her gaze flicked briefly towards Terry's body before returning to Aidan. 'But for this one,' her dark head inclined slightly towards Helen, 'the decision is not mine to make even if I will be the one to carry out the sentence.'

So saying, Gwyn stepped away from Helen. She came to the edge of the candle ring and looked across at the three of them, but Aidan thought she was only really seeing Eldritch.

'What do you say, Marcus Eldritch? This decision is yours. Do you want what has been offered to you?'

There was nothing of the grieve's poisoned promises in that question. It offered nothing and yet it demanded everything. And it would not be denied. Gwyn's too-green eyes bored into Eldritch, insisting that he answer, and in that moment Aidan hated Gwyn – or whatever power was speaking through her – for compounding the wizard's misery by forcing this awful choice on him. Eldritch's jaw worked and he swallowed convulsively as though choking down a handful of conflicting answers.

He stared back at Gwyn and his face contorted with a mixture of grief and rage and pain. 'No!' He flung the answer at her, ripping it from his throat with the howl of a soul in torment.

For a second Helen stared at him, her eyes wide and an expression of stunned disbelief on her face, as though she could not comprehend what she had heard. 'No!' Her scream echoed her husband's. 'No! El!' Her features twisted as she strained to reach towards him, her voice scaling through shock into outrage and horror. 'Don't do this! El!'

As calm as the eye of a storm Gwyn gestured.

'Enough!'

The grieve's body went limp as though every muscle had been instantaneously severed. With her protests similarly silenced, the shallow pant of Helen's breathing was left as the only sound in the hall, its sharpness suggesting that not all the emotion she had shown had been put on for Eldritch's benefit.

'He has chosen.'

Gwyn's voice was as composed as Helen's had been frantic. For a moment she surveyed the captive host, her head cocked to one side in her characteristic pose, but her expression was as devoid of emotion as her voice had been. If she felt anything about Eldritch's decision or her own role as the soon-to-be executor of that choice she was keeping it well hidden. Aidan wondered at her self-control as she sent a cool nod in Eldritch's direction.

'So be it.'

Aidan had expected Gwyn to deal with Helen the same way that she had done with Terry, hauling the grieve upright with a casual display of physical strength that drove home her dominance, so it came as a surprise when she knelt beside Helen, folding herself down to the floor with a sinuous, almost feline, grace. For several seconds she studied her captive, her face an inscrutable mask. Then, in an act that belied her seeming indifference Gwyn brushed the tangled blonde hair back from the other woman's cheeks, as gentle as a mother soothing a fretful child.

'One might wish things could be different.'

She put her hands on either side of Helen's face, tilting the woman's head towards her own as she bent over her.

'Blessed be.'

The ancient words were offered like a benediction, a whisper of grace before Gwyn pressed her lips to Helen's. For several seconds the two stayed there, frozen in that deadly embrace like lovers, flesh pressed against flesh, and then Helen's eyes rolled back and the life went out of her body. Almost tenderly Gwyn lowered the grieve's head to the floor and pressed her eyelids closed.

So that's it. It's over. Aidan let out a shaky breath, not quite sure he dared to believe it could be true. After the drama of Gwyn's ritual and everything they had been through to get here, this quiet ending felt like an anticlimax. He shook his head ruefully, mentally berating himself for the thought. There was a lot to be said for low-key. And besides, he realised, this final act wasn't without fallout of its own; one look at Eldritch's face told him that much.

He had thought he might see the remnants of anger, slowly cooling, in the wizard's grey eyes. He had hoped there might be the first traces of relief filtering through as it slowly sank in for Eldritch that his ordeal was over. What he hadn't expected was the naked grief that marred the wizard's face. It hit him then that – whatever torment he had suffered at the hands of the grieve – Eldritch had loved Helen very much indeed.

I didn't know what else to do. I couldn't bear the thought of living without her. Eldritch's words of less than a week ago rang in Aidan's head. And Eldritch had just seen his wife die for the second time.

Oh hell!

Guilt at his own sense of relief sliced at Aidan, silencing any comment he might have made, and in that same moment Eldritch turned sharply away. He hugged his knees in towards his chest and dropped his head onto his bound hands, cutting off any sight of the outside world. The eloquence of his turned back made it clear he wanted to be left alone.

'Aide?' Jane's whisper of breath held multiple questions, but Aidan could only shake his head as he turned from Eldritch to face her.

'Leave him,' he mouthed. The only thing they could offer Eldritch right now was the privacy of their silence in which to pull himself together. For a moment Jane looked as though she might argue – she hated being unable to help – but then she nodded, shooting a sad look at the wizard.

Within the circle, Gwyn straightened from beside Helen's body. For a moment Aidan wondered if she would say something, but although she looked over at them there was no change in her expression, no sharing of the satisfaction that she surely must have been feeling at having overcome the grieves. Nor was there even a flicker to suggest she had registered Eldritch's current distress or her own role in it.

She's done this before, he reminded himself. When his mother had died Gwyn had hidden her own anguish in an attempt to shield him from further distress. She had managed it so well it had been years before he had realised that the calm face and level voice she presented to the world were no more than a mask. Still, he couldn't help but wince at her current cool indifference and tell himself he was wrong when he thought that – for the merest second – he had seen dismissal in that brief glance, as if Gwyn had noticed the wizard's grief and considered it beneath her concern. Aidan shook himself mentally. Gwyn was doing what she had to do – putting her emotions to one side while she finished dealing with the situation. She'd have a meltdown later and it would be a wise man who had chocolate and wine on hand to deal with it. *And probably a takeaway too,* he thought. She'd need it to get through the energy crash when she came down from the high she was currently on. Maybe he could talk Jane into going out for one. He was becoming aware of a growing number of aches and pains that suggested that whatever magic Gwyn had worked on him earlier was wearing off. Another hour and he wasn't going to feel like doing anything beyond sprawling on a settee. A hot bath wouldn't go amiss either. He blinked, realising he had been drifting.

Save that for later, son.

He forced his attention back to Gwyn as she lifted Eldritch's ring from where it had hung beneath the collar of her shirt. When Jane had first handed it to her, Gwyn had taken it with a fierce reverence, holding it the way Aidan imagined an ancient warrior might have received a fabled weapon. Now, she lifted the chain over her head almost casually, pulling it over the wild mane of her hair and shaking free the stray tendrils that snagged in its links. Even in the grimy light of the hall the central sapphire and its surround of diamond chips appeared to spark and glitter as she held it up in front of her, the chain tangled around her fingers as though it were a snatched trophy she had looted from an enemy's corpse.

A small smile teased the corners of Gwyn's mouth, but her eyes stayed as cold as the gemstones dangling in front of them. For several moments she seemed to gather herself and then, with great deliberation, she lifted her chin and drew in a long, slow breath. For a second she held it, poised like a diminutive opera singer before the start of a grand aria, but when she opened her mouth it was not song that flowed from it. For all his weariness Aidan became instantly alert at what he saw. A stream of something resembling dark, oily smoke tumbled over Gwyn's lips, pouring forth – not like breath – but like something alive, curling and twisting into sinuous, ophidian coils as it hit the air. Reflexively Aidan shrank back against the scaffold, feeling the metal upright hard between his shoulder blades, pressing his sweat-damp polo shirt into his back. He knew without being told that what he was seeing was the essence of the two grieves and the thought of them being free made the hair rise on the back of his neck and his heart stutter with fear. But that strange miasma did not spread as he feared it would. Instead, it seemed to concentrate around Gwyn's raised hand as though something was drawing it there. It took Aidan a moment to realise that that *something* was the ring. The oily darkness seethed and twisted, spreading around Gwyn's fingers like squid ink in water, but Aidan could see now that the core of that dark stream was centred around the ring as though something inside that cluster of precious stones was greedily sucking it in. The smoke shivered and writhed, and Aidan could imagine the grieves' essences frantically fighting against that pull. But they could not escape. In one tightening spiral the last curls of darkness were drawn together and then they too were sucked down into that central sapphire and were gone.

For the space of several heartbeats Gwyn stood motionless, contemplating the ring dangling at the end of its gold chain, her eyes fixed on it as though it were a stage hypnotist's medallion. Watching her, Aidan wondered if she was seeing something within those sharp-edged facets, some trace of the two entities now imprisoned in the ring's crystalline matrix. He wondered what might be revealed if he looked into the dark heart of that central sapphire and a shudder ran down his spine at the thought. He was relieved when Gwyn let the ring and chain drop onto her outstretched palm. She folded her other hand over it then brought both hands to her chest, palms pressed together, lowering her chin so it brushed the tips of her fingers and closing her eyes. With her pale face framed in the wild cascade of her hair she looked like nothing so much as a Pre-Raphaelite saint, praying over the instrument of her martyrdom.

'Wow.' Jane kept her voice low, but her appreciation was clear. 'Do you think that's it – that she's finished now?'

'Who knows?' The amused lift of Jane's eyebrows told Aidan that his words had come out with more feeling than he had intended. He looked again at his mentor, bemused by what he hoped must be the final stage of the grieves' capture. It galled him to admit that he had no idea if she was finalising the enchantment, offering up a prayer of thanks or simply catching her breath. 'I've never seen anything like this before.'

He cast a glance at Eldritch – he would know – but the wizard was still sitting, hugging his grief to himself, and Aidan wasn't going to bother his friend with trivial questions.

'She'll need to dismiss the circle.' That much he could tell Jane. 'After that, I'm hoping we can go home.'

And with that in mind surely it was time to cut Eldritch free. Leaving Jane watching Gwyn, he lowered himself into a clumsy crouch beside the wizard, trying not to groan as every bruise and aching muscle protested the movement. 'Hey.'

The soft greeting brought no response. Carefully Aidan closed his hand over the other man's shoulder, much as he would have done if he had been dealing with a casualty on the slopes of Plynlimon. He felt a fine tremor racking the muscles under his fingers and his heart went out to his friend. Whether Eldritch's current state was down to emotional shock or the cumulative effects of the physical abuse he had suffered was immaterial. They needed to get him away from here to somewhere where he could rest and hopefully recover. Gwyn would know what to do, Aidan told himself. He increased the pressure of his grip slightly as though by doing so he could pass that reassurance on.

'Let's get these ropes off.' That would be a good start.

Perhaps Eldritch felt so too because he lifted his head. Beneath the matted spikes of his hair the wizard's face seemed paler than before, the charcoal shadows under his eyes more pronounced in the pattern of blood and bruises that spread over cheek and jaw. Even his eyes seemed battered, but Aidan took comfort from the fact that they did at least focus on him. The long fingers clenched momentarily as though Eldritch was physically dragging himself back from whatever refuge he had retreated to.

'Er … guys.'

The odd note in Jane's voice had Aidan's head whipping round. What he saw made his heart lurch.

What the …?

'We've got a problem.'

CHAPTER 45

'What the hell happened?'

'I don't know. She just … changed. One moment she was Gwyn and then …'

The confusion in Jane's voice collided with the shock in Aidan's. Both held an edge of fear. Eldritch noted it even as grief as sharp as pain sliced through him. He looked at the woman standing motionless in the containment circle, her head bowed and hands trailing limply by her sides.

Oh, Gwyn. No.

His chest tightened as though fingers of frost and iron had reached through his ribs and fisted around his heart.

I can't do this! Not now.

A brief and brittle anger flashed through him. Hadn't he lost enough already? He would have thrown back his head and howled the protest aloud, spewing out his bitterness at the uncaring universe, but even as the thought burned across his brain he froze. It made no difference. Quiet despair filled him as that understanding congealed the words in his throat. There were no other options, no one else to pick up the baton if he refused. Either he would deal with this or no one would, and that simply wasn't an option. Stillness settled over him. He fancied he could hear the anguished beating of his heart, monstrously loud against the silence.

'It's a glamour.' A small portion of his mind marvelled

at how normal he sounded, how little of his pain bled into his voice. 'What you're seeing is Morrigan's image of herself incarnated as Gwyn.'

'And?' Aidan crammed a wealth of concern and a dozen questions into that one sharp word. Eldritch dragged his eyes from the object of their discussion. He felt as though part of his soul was torn away as he did so.

'And it means that Gwyn has become Morrigan's avatar.'

'An avatar?' The colour leached from Aidan's face as though Eldritch's words had inflicted a sudden mortal wound. 'You mean …' He stumbled over what he was about to say then tried again. 'But Gwyn's still in there, right? I mean, underneath it all, she is still there.'

The final words came out with fierce defiance as if Aidan could make it so by sheer force of will. With all his heart Eldritch envied the younger man his naïve hope.

'For now.'

It wasn't much but it was all he was prepared to give. A terrible calm filled him as he thrust his bound hands towards Aidan.

'We don't have much time. Cut me loose.'

'What are you going to do?'

Jane crouched down beside the two men but her eyes never left the still form in the containment circle. Gwyn had yet to show any sign of waking from her trance-like state, but the cyber ninja wasn't taking any chances. She continued to watch the transformed woman as she would a known hacker. Concentrating on not flinching away as Aidan's knife scraped against the skin of his wrists, Eldritch almost missed her next words.

'Gwyn said you didn't have any power.'

The comment might not have been meant as a deliberate barb, but it still found its mark.

'Gwyn doesn't always get things right.' This time Eldritch couldn't keep the emotion from spilling into his voice. He winced inwardly as Jane bristled and Aidan's blade stilled momentarily between his wrists, but he didn't apologise. Ruffled feelings weren't the worst thing they were facing here. Still, he made a conscious effort to soften his tone as he added, 'Besides, it's not how much power you have, it's what you do with it that counts.'

'So, what are you going to do?'

Aidan didn't look up as he severed the final strand of rope then folded his knife and slid it back into his pocket.

What indeed?

Briefly Eldritch reviewed what he knew about the cult of Morrigan. It wasn't as much as he would have liked. His grandmother had considered those curious phenomena known as natural or elemental principles too capricious to be treated as power sources and his teenage self had agreed with her. They could be petitioned – certainly – but there was no guarantee that they would answer. Confident in his own burgeoning powers that younger Eldritch had seen little use in a tool that couldn't be relied upon. Two decades later, as he picked the strands of blue nylon from his bloodied wrists, he wondered what that hubris would cost him.

The Scatterer of Souls.

The entity known as Morrigan might choose to grant a fierce and deadly power to acolytes who invoked her successfully. It was said she came most readily to those who could offer her battle and death and the glorious carnage of facing down fearful odds. Eldritch wondered briefly if Horatius had called upon her as he stood upon the Sublician bridge or if there had been believers amongst the Spartans at Thermopylae. Perhaps there were. Certainly, there had been enough deaths in those ancient conflicts to satisfy even the most bloodthirsty of deities. His eyes slid to the preternaturally still figure in her jewel-coloured shirt and faded jeans, the bodies of her vanquished foes lying at her bare feet, and his throat tightened. For that was the other thing his grandmother had warned him about elementals: their help always came at a price. And with Gwyn's transformation, Eldritch was horribly afraid that two deaths would be insufficient to appease Morrigan today.

Not all who summoned the warrior goddess came away from the encounter unscathed. There were tales of petitioners who were destroyed by that which they had sought to harness, literally burning up from within, their bodies consumed by energies the human form was never meant to contain. Having accessed wild magic once himself Eldritch had an inkling of how easily that could happen to those ill-prepared or simply not strong enough to endure an elemental's presence. Yet in some respects, those who died that way – horrific though such immolation was – could be considered the lucky ones. Far worse to Eldritch's mind were the stories of those whose bodies endured, who became vessels of the goddess; the ones who committed such atrocities that they had to be hunted down and killed.

Not again.

In his mind he saw himself as he had been two years ago, kneeling beside Helen's body. Only now the hair he imagined spilling over his fingers was the colour of midnight and a pair of emerald eyes stared sightlessly up at him. Sickened, he pushed the image away, turning back from the dead to face his living friends.

'I'm going to start by talking to her.'

Jane gave an unladylike snort. 'Good luck with that,' she muttered.

Under other circumstances Eldritch might have smiled. 'It may be all it takes, Jane.'

He said it as though he truly believed it, as though an elemental could be persuaded to give up a chosen vessel through words alone. He didn't – but it was better for Jane and Aidan not to know that. Though Eldritch hated to lie to them he wouldn't allow himself the luxury of regret, for he had already decided one thing: it might be too late for Gwyn, but he was going to ensure that Aidan and Jane got out of this nightmare alive.

'And if it isn't?' Jane's question broke through the grimness of his thoughts.

'Then I'll do what's necessary.' This time Eldritch did smile though the warmth of it came nowhere near his eyes. He took a steadying breath and slid the rose quartz bracelet from his wrist, weighing it deliberately in his palm. 'I have enough power for that. Thanks to Gwyn.'

His expression changed, morphing into something more dangerous. It was the smile of Lucifer surveying the heaven he knew he was doomed to lose forever, yet choosing to proceed with his plans nonetheless.

'Sometimes she does get things right.'

And maybe, just maybe, Gwyn had known what she was doing when she had given him the bracelet with its stones already keyed to him.

Dear God, woman!

He wasn't sure if that made things better or worse and he had no time to think it through. His fist closed possessively over the pale pink spheres. 'Now, help me up.'

CHAPTER 46

Standing was harder than it should have been. There seemed to be no strength left in his body. Eldritch drew a ragged breath and did his best to ignore the blackness dancing at the edge of his vision, concentrating instead on what he was about to do. He had no time for weakness. Now he had to be strong for all of them. He locked his knees and willed himself to stand a little straighter, hoping he looked better than he felt.

'Can we do anything to help?' The worry in Aidan's voice suggested he was fooling himself.

Eldritch felt a flash of irritation. *Apart from not being here?*

He knew he was being unfair but that didn't stop him wishing – just for a moment – that Aidan and his girlfriend were anywhere but with him now. Whatever happened in the next few minutes, whatever action he might be forced to take, it would all be so much easier if he didn't have them to worry about. He knew what he was up against; they didn't, and the possibility that they might put themselves in harm's way for his sake made his stomach twist with guilt.

Time fractured and for a moment Eldritch was in another place, booted feet on a different wooden floor as he struggled to gather the shredded remnants of his power together. He knew he had to set a protective veil over the hut in which he and Aidan were sheltering but – dear God! – he was so tired. He could feel the cold weight of his rain-sodden clothes dragging at his body, pulling him down, the agony of nerve-shredding pain radiating out from the torn and mangled flesh of his shoulder. The avatar had come so close to killing him earlier that evening. Now he teetered on the brink of collapse, wanting nothing more than to give in to that overwhelming tiredness and close his eyes. Except he couldn't. It wasn't that he was afraid of dying – if anything, that would be the easy option, to lie down in the unwarded hut and let the avatar kill him as he slept – but he knew that if he died then so would Aidan and he would not allow that to happen. He hadn't asked for help, but that didn't lessen the obligation he had incurred when the young Welshman had turned up on that demon-haunted hillside.

This is what you get when you bring civilians along for the ride.

Eldritch could almost hear his brother-in-law's acerbic judgement echoing around his head.

He opened his eyes, not sure quite when he had allowed them to slip closed, and the bitter cold of the forestry hut faded away to be replaced by the muggy gloom of the community hall. He still felt the queasy sickness of exhaustion, but Eldritch gritted his teeth and dismissed it, denying its hold on him. He hadn't given in to weakness then and he had no intention of doing so now. He glanced at the young couple hovering protectively close while trying to look casual and hide their concern. He read their wariness, the prickly skittishness of fear at a situation neither could control, but also their absolute readiness to help in any way they could. A surge of affection warmed him despite the emotional distance he was trying to retain.

Ah, Paul, he thought, *sometimes you can't stop them.*

And sometimes they were the ones who saved your life, as had happened today. Now it was time to repay that debt.

'There's nothing you can do.' Eldritch shut down his feelings and put the cold snap of authority into his voice. He didn't want either of his friends thinking they had a say in what would come next. 'Just get behind me and – whatever happens – stay out of it. Both of you.'

For a moment Jane looked as though she might refuse, unhappy with the idea of hiding behind anyone, least of all a crazy Englishman who was barely able to stand without help. But as Eldritch steeled himself for an argument he knew he could ill afford, Aidan spoke first.

'Leave it, Jay.' The younger man's expression suggested he was scarcely happier with Eldritch's instruction than his girlfriend but, perhaps because he had seen Eldritch deal with arcane threats in the past, he was prepared to cooperate – at least for now. 'For Gwyn's sake,' Aidan added and then, with a half shrug, 'it's HPS, remember.'

The term meant nothing to Eldritch, but Aidan moved back against the scaffold as though it had clinched the argument and – to Eldritch's surprise – after a moment's hesitation Jane joined him.

'We've got your back.' There was trust in Aidan's voice and the look he shot Eldritch said more clearly than words, *I'm relying on you.* The combination caught Eldritch like a sucker punch. There were so many things about this that he wanted Aidan to understand but no time to tell him.

Eldritch swallowed down a dozen competing statements and went for the most important. 'Just make sure you stay there.'

Then he put aside all thought of his friends and turned to face his opponent.

He had dared to hope that she was still dazed, still adjusting to the constraints of incarnation in a human vessel, but even as he stepped forward the being in front of him inhaled a long and exaggerated breath and looked up.

Gwynyfa Hughes was a small woman. The top of her head barely reached his shoulder, but Eldritch had never been one to equate stature with power. His grandmother had been a small woman too and she would have slapped him down in an instant if he had ever had the temerity to suggest such a thing. Eldritch had little doubt that Gwyn would do the same.

But the woman in front of him now would melt his bones.

She was taller than Gwyn. As her head came up Eldritch judged her to be roughly the same height as Jane, perhaps even a fraction taller. She still had Gwyn's wild, raven-wing hair but hers fell almost to her hips and the pale streak winding down from her crown showed silver not white, like a bolt of lightning in a cascade of darkness. Eldritch saw all this in an instant, but it was the stranger's face that held his attention. While Gwyn's high cheekbones and wide green eyes gave her an appearance that could be described as elfin, this woman's face was unworldly. Her features were subtly different from Gwyn's, stronger and more sensual and yet somehow also pitiless. No one who knew Gwyn could be in any doubt that it wasn't her standing within that double circle of fire and salt.

This was Morrigan.

Even as he thought it, the corners of that generous mouth curved upwards as if the goddess had reached out and plucked the acknowledgement from his brain. Watching her, Eldritch had the oddest feeling that all this time she had been waiting, patient as a lurking cobra, biding her time until he came to her. He ran his tongue over dry and cracked lips and tried not to feel as though he was walking towards a gibbet.

Come into my parlour …

The green, elf-queen eyes swept over him and the wizard was suddenly very conscious of his own dishevelled appearance and of the rank odours of sweat and sickness rising from his unwashed body. In that instant he saw himself as Morrigan must be seeing him and, though her smile didn't alter, the slight hitch of those elegant brows let him understand that she found him wanting.

Is this the sort of man who would face me?

Something shifted within him, rising to the challenge in that haughty, absinthe gaze.

I'm all you're getting, woman. And then, *You should be grateful I'm not doing this stark naked.*

He threw the thoughts back at her along with a wolfish smile dragged out from beneath the morass of weariness and pain and slid into place like familiar camouflage. No one seeing that saturnine flash of amusement and defiance would have realised how tired he felt nor how vulnerable. It was an age-old game and one he had played for so long it was almost second nature. Still smiling, Eldritch crossed his arms in a calculated show of nonchalance, drawing confidence around him like a cloak.

As he did so he consciously altered his focus, letting his vision shift so that it became something other than normal sight. It didn't take power as such, just a change of perception, a mental shift that was primarily an acceptance that there was another way of seeing things. It was something he had been able to do since before he had words to describe what he was seeing, an act as natural as breathing, so it came as a shock that there was a split second of disorientation as though he had stepped sideways within his own body and was now looking out through his eyes as if through two windows. He steadied himself but what he saw brought little comfort. Surrounding Morrigan's projected glamour was a smouldering haze of muddy reds and oranges. The colours pulsed and twisted, bleeding into each other like the pigmented smoke from a distress flare, and Eldritch's heart twisted with them. Gwyn was still alive, but her aura was a soundless scream of pain beyond reasoning and an overwhelming nightmare terror, a desperate, wordless plea for help. It struck him like hot irons through his soul, but even worse was the knowledge that there was so little he could do to help her.

Fight her, Gwyn. He had to believe it would be enough.

Swallowing his fear, Eldritch let his vision return to normal. Doing so felt like a betrayal as though he was deliberately turning his back on the complicated woman who was his friend, but he pushed the idea away. He knew he couldn't afford to think like that if he was going to do what he feared he would have to. Instead, he took a deliberate step closer to the lines of salt and fire. In a voice like granite threaded with silver he said, 'Let her go, Morrigan.'

By way of an answer the woman who was no longer Gwyn threw back her head and laughed. Though he would never have told her so, privately Eldritch thought of Gwyn's laugh as a rare delight, frivolous and playful and surprisingly full of mischief for a woman whose temper – when roused – would match that of a harpy. Morrigan's laughter was different. It might have had the same pitch and tone but there was an edge to it that Eldritch had never heard from Gwyn. Even at her most caustic he had never known her to be wantonly cruel. Eldritch set his jaw against a sudden urge to snarl and waited for the laughter to stop.

'I know she's fighting you and I know you can feel it.' He allowed his features to relax into a wry smile. 'Trust me, she won't stop.' His expression spoke volumes about the stubbornness of witches in general and this one in particular. One hand spread in an expansive gesture as he concluded, 'You might as well let her go.'

'No.'

'But you're killing her.'

Eldritch kept his voice calm and reasonable as though he was talking about a stranger rather than a woman to whom he owed his life and so much more. In response, Morrigan gave a little dip of her head, a gesture that – had it been Gwyn who had made it – would have meant, So?

She studied Eldritch for a long moment and her full lips curved as though she could sense the hurt buried beneath his impassive façade. 'She invited me in.' There was an air of smugness in her voice.

'She asked for your help,' Eldritch corrected her.

The goddess dismissed such pedantry with a flick of her fingers. 'The end result is the same.'

Eldritch pinched the bridge of his nose, rubbing the skin between thumb and forefinger. It did little to ease the headache gnawing at the bones of his skull, but it acted as a displacement giving him a moment to think. He was acutely conscious of the presence of Jane and Aidan behind him – waiting, watching. No rustle of clothing, no scuff of a dragged foot on the wooden floor denoted any restless shifting of position. They were trained to stand silently and so they did, yet Eldritch felt the burn of their eyes on his back, the weight of their expectations nudging at him. Despite the shielding of Gwyn's bracelet their fear and, worse still, their hope pricked at him like a stiletto between his shoulder blades. He hated the probability that he was going to let them down.

What was the tipping point, he wondered? What was it that made the difference, that meant that one supplicant received the goddess's help while the next was destroyed? He wondered if Gwyn had known. If she had, she must have considered her sacrifice worth it. The thought brought no comfort.

Eldritch tried again. 'She's not the right vessel for you, Morrigan. She's not going to bring you death and destruction – she's a healer, not a warrior. It's not in her nature to use her power to hurt.'

'But that's where you're wrong, wizard. She did, didn't she?' Morrigan leaned a little towards Eldritch as though she were inviting him into her confidence, like a gossip about to share a delightful secret. 'She made her choice. She took what little power she had and the paltry dregs in your ring and she chose to invoke me. Me!'

She tossed her head back sending her hair with its lightning streak of silver shimmering around her like a captive storm. 'She made the bargain: her soul for my power.' As she spoke her tone changed, swinging from flirtatious to scathing. 'The power to overcome the entities that you could not.'

The truth of that comment curled across Eldritch's skin like a lash. Regardless of what Gwyn had thought of the risk she was taking, ultimately her predicament was his fault. She had put herself in danger to save him and so had Aidan and Jane.

His breath caught but he kept the hurt from his voice as he answered. 'That doesn't mean that she would want this.'

'And what do you know of it? Do you think you understand how it feels to lose your power, to live crippled, waking each day to the knowledge that what blazed within you is gone, that you have been rendered useless?' She looked down her nose at him. 'You have been without power for less than a handful of days. She has lived that way since before the boy was born.' The hard emerald gaze flicked past Eldritch, the brevity of her glance as dismissive as her words. 'She gave her power to save him, the bastard child, conceived out of wedlock in trickery and deceit.'

Behind him Eldritch heard Aidan's sharp breath and Jane's urgent, 'That's not true, Aidan. You know Gwyn doesn't think that!' He forced himself not to care. In front of him the goddess's beautiful features curled into a sneer. 'And still you would keep her powerless.'

'I would keep her alive!'

Morrigan snorted derisively. 'Alive but crippled.' She drew herself up, haughty as a queen addressing a particularly dense petitioner. 'Yes, she will die. That is the nature of life. But oh, she will pass knowing that she has been glorious one final time.'

The goddess smiled, deadly and radiant, and for an instant Eldritch saw her as though she stood on the field of battle, proud and victorious, the blood of her slaughtered enemies clotting on her skin and gumming the tips of that wild mantle of hair. Nauseated, he shook the vision away. He would not accept that this was how Gwyn was to die.

He drew a slow breath. He was so tired that his flesh ached and the whole conversation was taking on an unreal, fever-dream quality, but his voice was level as he spoke again. 'It's your right to keep her.' The acknowledgement was as sour as wormwood on his tongue, yet he let none of that bitterness leach into his words. 'But let her go, Morrigan. Please.'

The speech was exquisitely balanced between order and plea. There was no servility in that final word, simply a heartfelt request made between equals. Even as Eldritch spoke he wondered if he was making a terrible mistake, but he was running out of time. This close to the goddess he could see the sheen of sweat on her forehead, the blotchiness of colour staining her cheeks like fever spots as Gwyn's body started to fail. He had to get through to her.

And perhaps a warrior goddess didn't want servility for, to his relief, Morrigan didn't react with anger. Instead, she contemplated him, her head cocked to one side in a way that was so quintessentially Gwyn that, for a moment, Eldritch almost forgot his fear.

Then she spoke and her voice remained that of a stranger. 'Then answer me this, wizard. What are you prepared to give to save her?'

Eldritch looked at the woman who wasn't Gwyn. In the silence following her question the ragged draw of his breath sounded loud in his ears, but he smiled and there was no hesitation in his voice as he said, 'Everything.'

He spread his arms as if to demonstrate all that was encompassed by that one brief word. 'You want me to sacrifice?' His voice was light as though what was being asked of him was of no great consequence. 'If that's what it takes then I'm ready.'

'Eldritch!'

'Stay out of this.' Eldritch didn't turn to acknowledge Aidan's shocked protest. Instead, he kept his eyes on his opponent. 'So, what about it, Morrigan? You can have me.' His voice hardened, driving the deal. 'If you let her go.'

Within the containing circles of fire and salt the goddess looked thoughtful. Elfin brows raised as she considered Eldritch's proposition, and the teasing cruelty that had characterised their exchange was absent when she replied.

'What if I asked you for a blood oath?'

Eldritch licked dry lips, waiting for her to continue.

'What if I asked you to kill the boy?'

This time the goddess's eyes didn't so much as flick towards Aidan. It was as if he was neither present nor of any great consequence – a mere trifle with which to test the wizard's fidelity.

Eldritch answered with the same level of detachment. 'If that's what you want.' The accompanying shrug barely moved the crumpled cotton of his shirt.

There was a moment's silence as Morrigan studied him. Then she burst out laughing as though he had made a great joke. 'Oh, but you are sly, Marcus Eldritch. I know as well as you that you don't have the ability to kill him now and if I bound you to perform this task at some future date, still you would evade me. You would confess to your wife's murder and by the time your powers had returned you would be locked away, unable to reach him.

'Enough of this foolishness.' Amusement turned abruptly to cold disdain. 'You say I could have you if I let my vessel go. I could have you anyway, wizard. You are alive only by my grace, as are the children cowering behind you.'

'No one here's doing any cowering, lady.' Jane's voice bristled with anger like the auditory equivalent of a guard dog's raised hackles.

Eldritch sympathised with how she felt but he heartily wished she had stayed silent. It seemed he wasn't the only one.

'Leave it, Jay.'

Eldritch didn't need to turn and see the restraining hand Aidan clamped around Jane's wrist; the warning in his friend's voice painted a clear enough picture. Unfortunately, he could equally imagine the ease with which Jane twisted free. Aidan's girlfriend was not one to hide behind anyone, not even when it might be prudent for her to do so. He groaned inwardly as Morrigan's brows lifted, her interest piqued by the little scene.

Damn you both. Why couldn't you do what you were told and stay quiet?

'But maybe I won't keep this vessel until it fails.' The warrior goddess made a play of leaning to one side to peer past Eldritch. 'Maybe I will take the girl instead.' She straightened up, turning back to Eldritch with a look that was part amusement and part appreciation. 'She has spirit.'

'You can't have her, Morrigan.' Eldritch spoke quickly before Jane had a chance to. Another time he might have been interested in the young woman's response to a supernatural entity's assessment of her character, but not now when it could only make the situation worse. The knowledge that there was so little he could do to protect her was like a sour stone lodged in his belly, but he met Morrigan's acquisitive smile with cold logic. 'She hasn't invited you in and you can't force her to. She's a null.'

He was still struggling to accept that such a thing was possible, but Aidan had been certain of it, and, despite his own reservations, it seemed that Morrigan was prepared to believe it too. Eldritch wondered if she was able to access Gwyn's memories and check the truth of what he was saying, for her nostrils flared as she took a sharp, angry breath. But before he could take any satisfaction from that she spoke, and her words made it clear she was not about to be thwarted.

'I feel sure I could persuade her.'

No trace remained of that momentary flash of temper, but in its place was something colder and more frightening. Those green, elf-queen eyes turned calculating as they met his. 'You would sacrifice yourself to save this woman.' Morrigan looked down at the body she was wearing and her brows kinked together as if she was considering why that should be the case. Then she looked back at Eldritch and the hint of a smile teased the corners of her sensual mouth. Eldritch swallowed thickly. There was nothing pleasant about that smile. It was the look of a torturer deciding where to lay the hot irons on a prisoner's body. 'I think that one would do the same for the boy.'

She raised her steepled fingers, resting her chin on them as she regarded Eldritch with a terrible and icy calm. 'How much pain do you think it would take? How much would I have to hurt him before she was on her knees begging for the chance to give herself to me in order to spare his life?'

CHAPTER 47

There was a moment of appalled silence.

'Stop it!' Eldritch put all the snap and force he could into the command, aware as never before that lives were balanced on the knife-edge of what he did next.

'That means both of you, too!' he added over his shoulder before either Aidan or Jane could respond with some smart retort that would make the situation worse. If indeed that was possible. *Dear God!* He smothered the despairing urge to bury his head in his hands. This was why you didn't let civilians get involved. 'Stay out of this.'

He felt the raw pain of Aidan and Jane's emotions slap at him, sawing at his nerves. Eldritch understood the churning maelstrom of defiance and fear evoked by Morrigan's proposition – he felt that himself – but their shocked outrage at his own words stung. He had hoped for better. For a moment he wondered at the hurt, and then pushed both thought and pain away. It didn't matter; not when he could sense the cold touch of Morrigan's avarice curling around him, brushing his skin like the questing pseudopodia of some creature out of nightmare. That was what he had to remedy, not two cases of bruised feelings.

Something stirred in the dark recesses of Eldritch's soul – intertwined strands of emotion sliding one upon the other like the diamond-patterned coils of a serpent readying itself to strike. Weary as he was, it took him a moment to recognise the sensation as anger.

This had gone far enough. He would not stand by and let Morrigan – nor any other denizen of the Unseen Realm – treat the world as her playground. It wasn't just because it was his friends' lives at stake. There had been too many deaths already. People like Terry, he thought, dead for no better reason than he had stumbled into a situation he had no hope of understanding. Eldritch pictured the young man as he had first seen him at the clinic, standing in the doorway in his faded T-shirt and paint-spattered dungarees, the uniform of his trade. An average man doing an everyday job – until he became a grieve's unwitting host. The poor fool probably hadn't even realised he was in danger. He gave vent to his feelings in a little snort of breath.

And so now it came down to him to stop it. Eldritch shoved the filthy rat tails of hair back from his face, hideously conscious of what that meant he would have to do. Gwyn had had all the time he dared give her. She wasn't going to break free, and he could no longer fool himself that Morrigan could be persuaded to release her voluntarily. It was time he accepted that and acted accordingly. If by some infinitesimal chance Gwyn was still alive, she would understand that what he was about to do was an act of friendship. His hand shook as it tightened around the simple string of rose quartz beads she had given him. He could only wish it didn't feel so much like betrayal. The thought followed him as he turned his consciousness inwards and sank down into the core of his being.

On one level, Eldritch was aware that he still stood in the burned-out community hall, facing down the warrior goddess in her stolen body. Yet at the same time he seemed to have stepped away from that little tableau and into a very different space. Gone were the high, soot-streaked walls and the muggy, smoke-scented heat of the London afternoon. Instead, his senses registered a small room lit by a ghostly luminescence. Its walls pressed close around him, pale and featureless on all sides bar one. It was this fourth wall that held his attention. As black as midnight, it was a sheet of congealed darkness cutting across the room where he knew instinctively no wall should have been. Seeing it, Eldritch smiled to himself, grimly amused. There was no subtlety in the image his mind had conjured. This was the grieve's work, the barrier set between him and his power. Eldritch's smile morphed into something colder and more focused. The grieve's poisons had wrought this. Now he would find out if Gwyn had given him the key to break it down.

He opened his fist and considered the dainty shell-pink beads lying in his palm, remembering how idiotic he had felt the previous year when Gwyn had insisted on his wearing them as a demon ward. That had been in the very first days of their friendship – in truth before either of them would have admitted that there was such a thing as friendship between them. But Gwyn had been proven right about his needing the additional protection as he had found to his cost. His lips quirked a little at the memory. He had learned quickly that the Welsh witch could be both startlingly perceptive and astonishingly blunt when it came to sharing her views. Once more he wondered if she could possibly have foreseen what he would need to do today. He remembered her comment and the accompanying basilisk glare and thought he had his answer.

Oh, Gwyn.

Eldritch swiped his forearm across his eyes, telling himself it was sweat that was making them sting. There was no time for grief. But that didn't stop the string of rose quartz pearls weighing like a traitor's payment of silver in his palm.

Tentatively he stretched his other hand towards the wall's obsidian surface, feeling a little frisson of relief as his fingers touched it. Until that moment he hadn't been certain that such a thing would be possible. And wouldn't that have been one great universal joke if his hand had simply passed through the darkness as though it were smoke or fog, leaving him unable to interact with the barrier in any way. As it was, the grieve's wall felt convincingly solid, its surface slick and chill beneath his skin like the glass in a window that opened onto a winter's night. And, like a night-backed window, now he had touched it the darkness gave back to him a faint reflection of his own image, his face in its frame of matted hair floating ghostly and skull-like above the pale blur of his shirt.

So.

With a nod to his reflection Eldritch brought up Gwyn's bracelet. He paused for a moment eyeing the witch stones hanging from his fingers; so much depended on the delicate traceries of magic held within them. Then he pushed the bracelet against the enigmatic black of the wall, holding it there with the flat of his palm.

He couldn't have said what he expected from that contact. There was no dramatic reaction, no fizzing chaos as with water added to acid. It was almost as though nothing happened at all, and yet the wizard felt something alter beneath his hands. Though the wall remained solid to his touch, for the briefest moment it seemed to shudder as if in the instant that Gwyn's bracelet touched it, it had changed state. Something flickered across the blackness like a shimmer of petrol colours glimpsed in the flash of a raven's wing, and in its wake the wall's appearance changed. It had felt like glass to his touch before but now it looked like glass too, the thinnest transparency separating him from the roiling mass of – what? He had no words to classify that strange condensate of midnight though he knew, in a way that he couldn't explain, that it was organic. Somehow that made it more disturbing. Eldritch felt the hairs on the back of his neck rise as he sensed something moving through the darkness, pushing towards him as though rising through the waters of some ancient and fathomless lake.

Every instinct told him to step away from the barrier, to put as much distance as he could between himself and whatever was in there. He felt cold sweat sluicing down his body, his skin prickling with fear, yet instead of retreating he leaned in closer, pressing Gwyn's bracelet more firmly against that uncanny surface. He kept his eyes fixed on the space framed between his hands and there within the shadows he saw it. Like an image coming clear in a scrying mirror a man's shape formed before him, slowly materialising within the Stygian gloom.

The breath seemed to still in Eldritch's lungs. He had anticipated this from the moment he had found himself in this room, and yet still he was conscious that he was trembling, his hands gone cold as though the blood had drained from his body. Just as Morrigan's glamour appeared as an altered version of Gwyn, so he understood that what he saw looking back at him from the other side of that midnight wall was a reimagining of himself, and yet … he stared at the image in appalled fascination. He had been expecting the similarity. What shocked him was the darkness.

Everything about the man – his jeans, his shirt, the oiled sweep of hair brushed back from his temples – was black. Even the close-cropped beard, neatly shaped to frame that saturnine mouth, was the colour of squid ink unrelieved by even the faintest smattering of the silver that Eldritch knew salted his own cheeks on those rare days that he didn't shave. This man could almost have been mistaken for a younger brother – until one looked into his eyes. Irises the colour of hell-smoke merged into pupils that might have been holes in the veil between worlds. Looking into them was like meeting the gaze of something ancient and inscrutable … and not entirely human. Eldritch had to steel himself to do so and he saw a version of his own wolfish grin spread across the other's face, acknowledging that struggle. Then the grin faded. The grey eyes bored into his own and one eyebrow raised in a silent question as though the other was asking if he understood what he was about to do. Eldritch fought against the sudden tightness in his chest. He knew. He nodded, grateful that that was all the answer he needed to give.

From an impossible distance he heard a voice of granite and silver say, 'You've had your deaths, Morrigan,' and like the ghost of a phantom limb he felt his own gesture towards the bodies lying at the goddess's feet. 'You have new believers.'

Within the white room he pushed Gwyn's bracelet as hard as he could against the barrier's glassy surface even as he stretched his mind towards the crystal matrix at the heart of the stones. The rose quartz spheres felt painfully solid under his hand, their delicate, rounded shapes digging into his palm as he leaned his weight against them. An image formed in his mind of them forcing their way between the bones, splaying the metacarpals apart as they burrowed inwards to nestle, pale and oddly luminescent – like the eggs of some other-worldly parasite – in his red and dripping flesh.

Nauseated, Eldritch thrust the thought from him, resisting the urge to rip his hand away from the barrier. Perhaps he should have expected resistance, although whether it came from the grieve's wall or from his own subconscious he wasn't sure. Either way, it made no difference; he wasn't going to give in. He felt the slipperiness of sweat – or was it blood? – running from beneath his palm and refused to look, keeping his eyes locked on his mirror-self's instead.

'They'll carry the truth of you with them for the rest of their lives.'

He heard his own voice in the distance and wondered vaguely if the goddess was listening. His vision blurred and for a moment it was Morrigan's face staring back at him, the other-worldly darkness of the barrier nothing more than soot-stained walls in the hall's grubby twilight.

No!

With a hideous effort Eldritch willed himself to see the barrier and the shape of his power trapped behind it. Green eyes morphed once more into grey. Holding that ancient gaze like a lifeline Eldritch exhaled, letting all resistance slide from his body along with his breath. Then, as his body emptied, he reached his mind once more towards the string of witch stones, and this time they opened for him.

Helen had never had much faith in power sinks – one of the ways in which her training and Paul's had differed from his own. But Gwyn used them as an integral part of her magic and Eldritch had tuned into these crystals before. His mind remembered their shapes, forming itself to them just as his hands might fit themselves to the chords he had once learned on a childhood guitar, and the stones in their turn seemed to know him too. Connections formed along the pathways that Gwyn had reinforced and the power she had stored there flowed into him.

'Let that be enough.' He heard his voice continue – loud against the otherwise silence of that far-off hall – and knew the goddess's eyebrows raised in amused tolerance at his audacity. 'Because I'm not going to let you do anything else.'

From the epicentre of Gwyn's bracelet a dozen cracks radiated out across the glossy surface of the wall. There was the tiniest of noises, like the brittle fracturing of ice, and Eldritch's hand passed through the barrier to slap against the hand that had risen to mirror it on the other side. Cold flesh pressed for a moment against burning heat, the shock of the contact going through him like a lightning strike. He had the vaguest impression of the rest of the barrier dropping away like a snowfall of splintered glass and then he was pitching forward. Arms caught him with an effortless strength as though he weighed no more than a child. They wrapped around him, pulling him against the other's chest, the heat of them burning like fever against his skin. He felt himself sinking into that embrace while a warmth like alcohol scalded through his blood …

And then he was back in the hall, scarred wooden boards beneath his naked feet and the reality of pain and weakness trembling through his body. Yet somewhere beneath the grinding exhaustion he felt the rush of newly released power searing through the energy channels of his body. Vivid and beautiful, it surged like liquid fire, building within him, ready to burst forth in a conflagration he had no hope of controlling.

In front of him Morrigan frowned, the skin between her elegant brows creasing as she weighed the arrogant certainty in his voice against his obvious state of near collapse. There was no trace of humour in her eyes now. They flashed, mirror-like, seeming to catch and magnify the dirty light in the hall as she studied him. Then she laughed, cruel and dismissive.

'You fool!' She shook her head sending the silver streak dancing in the storm cloud masses of her hair. 'Do you think your words alone can stop me?'

For the briefest of moments Eldritch met and held that terrible emerald stare, beating back against it with his will as if that could possibly be enough. Then his head dropped in defeat. 'No. Not any more.' He made no attempt to keep the weariness from his voice. He thought he should have been afraid, knowing what was to come, but all he felt now was a curious numbness. Maybe he was a fool, just as Morrigan claimed. 'I'm sorry, Aidan.'

He made a gesture which, if he hadn't been so tired, might have been a shrug of regret. It barely moved the skin over his bones. Keeping his hands fisted against the power that keened through his flesh seeking its release, he let his body sag, giving in to the weakness that dragged at his limbs like chains of frost and lead. He heard a sharp intake of breath behind him, a worried voice call his name as he swayed, staggered, his knees starting to buckle. And then he turned that slumping motion into a lunge, hands outstretched, reaching for the goddess. His feet were at the line of salt, his hands spread, the power flaring as he let the fine leash of restraint slip, bursting from his flesh.

But Morrigan was moving too. As Eldritch lunged she brought her own hands together in front of her chest as though scooping something from the air, then thrust them away from her. The air cracked with thunder and a fury of tourmaline fire poured from her splayed fingers even as the leading edge of Eldritch's power reached her. The blaze caught Eldritch in the chest, throwing him backwards.

He went down heavily, hitting the floor with no attempt to break his fall.

He didn't move.

CHAPTER 48

'He's alive.'

Aidan felt the thready pulse beating under his fingers and offered up a silent prayer of thanks, grateful beyond measure that – faint though it might be – it was there at all. The way Eldritch had gone down in that welter of jewel-coloured fire, he had feared the worst. Kneeling on the other side of the wizard's sprawled body, Jane nodded once to show she had heard. The briefest twitch of her lips semaphored her own relief even as it did nothing to lessen the angry hurt in her eyes or the shocked pallor of her face.

'Do you think she is?' She glanced briefly towards the ring of candle flame and then just as quickly looked away. It was as though she didn't want to risk her gaze lingering for too long on the still forms that lay there just in case one of them felt that attention and rose again.

Aidan understood why. His own glance was even briefer than Jane's. 'I don't know. Probably.'

The one thing he was certain of was that he didn't want to go close enough to check.

He looked again at Eldritch. The wizard might be alive, but Aidan didn't think he was going to regain consciousness any time soon. Whatever Morrigan had done – and he had never seen anything like the stream of fire that had burst from her hands – it had been brutally effective. A welted red mark stood out in the centre of Eldritch's chest, clearly visible through the open front of his shirt and vivid as a burn against the pale skin. A burn or a brand. Aidan swallowed queasily at that unwelcome possibility. It didn't take much imagination to form a handprint from that patch of livid red. Did the Scatterer of Souls make a point of marking her victims? He had no way of knowing but on current experience he thought it was the sort of thing she might do. Avoid picking fights with madmen and drunks. He winced and mentally added incarnated elemental principles to Sensei's oft-quoted rule for a long life. 'Either way, we should get out of here.'

Jane licked her lips. Sweat had darkened the tendrils of hair framing her face turning it from blonde to a mink brown and her blue eyes seemed huge in the gloom. She hesitated and then in a small voice she said, 'I don't like leaving Gwyn.'

For a moment all Aidan could do was nod in mute agreement, Jane having given voice to his own thought. He swallowed against the painful constriction in his throat. 'I'm not sure we are,' he managed. 'Not any more.'

Resolutely he pulled Eldritch's arm over his shoulder and tried not to think about what that meant.

'Do you think it will take long?' Jane's question was a whisper of sound that barely carried over the body between them. She glanced again at the three still shapes as she shifted to take a grip on the wizard's other arm. 'I mean, if Eldritch is right and Morrigan … if she is using up Gwyn's body, I can come back and make sure she's … gone.' Jane stumbled fractionally over that last word. 'Later, when you think we've given it enough time. Even if you're not sure how long we need to leave it, if the only way she can get to me is by threatening you then I'm safe enough if I'm on my own.'

Jane's glare managed to be both fierce and frightened. Aidan felt a huge surge of affection for his lover, combined with an urge to grab her by the shoulders and tell her not to be so stupid – there was no way he would let her risk encountering Morrigan on her own – but he wasn't about to waste time and breath arguing over that here.

'We'll talk it through. Later. Let's get out of here first.' He tightened his grip on Eldritch's wrist. 'On three.'

Jane nodded.

'One. Two.' Aidan shifted position so he could push off on his good leg and readied himself to stand. 'Thr—'

'I hope you're not thinking of leaving.'

The voice that wasn't Gwyn's made him freeze.

Dear God, no!

Like a figure risen from nightmare the unnatural gestalt of Gwyn and Morrigan was on her feet once more and – to Aidan's horror – she seemed to have shrugged off the effects of Eldritch's attack. She watched them intently across the barrier of fire and salt.

Still keeping her grip on Eldritch's arm, Jane murmured, 'What do we do now?' She was eyeing the transformed woman rather as a cat might watch an approaching Doberman. 'Appeal to her better nature?'

It was a nice idea but …

'Scatterer of Souls,' Aidan reminded her, 'I don't think she has one.'

He was aware of his own breath going tight and high as that imperious figure took a step towards the circle boundary.

'Okay.' Things were anything but, but he made himself exhale slowly, reaching for calm as he released Eldritch's arm and pushed himself to his feet. Immediately Jane scrambled up to stand beside him, the pair of them forming a living shield between Morrigan and the unconscious wizard. Keeping his eyes on the goddess, Aidan forced a level of confidence that he didn't feel into his voice and said, 'That's a containment circle.'

Somehow that fact wasn't as reassuring as it had been a few minutes ago. Trying not to think of the hand-shaped burn on Eldritch's chest he added firmly, 'You can't cross it.'

But he was horribly aware that he had no idea what Morrigan was capable of.

'Ooh!' Morrigan widened her eyes theatrically like a cynical child too old to be scared by a parent's tale of ghosts and monsters. Deliberately she stepped forward only to shy back again as fire flashed around the circle, surging up in a waist-high ring of peacock-coloured flames. Even at a distance Aidan felt the heat on his face and flung up a hand to shield his eyes, squinting against the phosphor-bright flare from the circle's wards.

But something was wrong.

Relief turned to dismay as he realised that Morrigan was standing mere inches from the conflagration. She had only given the impression of being forced back.

As if she had read his mind the goddess smiled lazily at him. 'Oh, my dear! Do you really think this can hold me?' She reached out and brushed her hand across the fire, her spread fingers trailing so that the edges of the flames caressed their tips, licking at them like fiery lapdogs. 'You don't understand, do you?' she continued, shaking her head reproachfully. 'There's so much that your teachers didn't tell you. You should complain to them but,' she shrugged artlessly, her mouth folding into a little moue of regret, 'it's rather too late for that. Soon it will be too late for you too.'

'Aide?' There was a wealth of questions in that one accented word.

Morrigan turned to address Jane. 'He's quite right; this is a containment circle.' The goddess sniffed derisively. 'Not the best I've seen but adequate for the job. After all, it was only designed to hold back these pathetic creatures.' She nudged Terry's corpse with one slender foot and Aidan noticed for the first time that her toenails appeared a deep and glossy red. When Gwyn painted her nails she tended to favour a rainbow of shades – sometimes quite literally. The goddess's toes looked as though they had been dipped in blood. 'I could break it if I chose but you see I don't have to. My vessel wove it, so of course I can cross it.'

And with a casual toss of her head she stepped calmly and deliberately through the fire, arms outstretched. Once across the circle she stopped. Behind her the flames quivered as if in response to a sudden draft and then all at once snuffed out, leaving behind nothing but puddles of wax and the blackened metal cups of the tealight holders. The smooth line of salt that had formed the outer ward of Gwyn's containment circle was now smudged and broken as though trampled by hundreds of invisible feet.

The gloom of the hall seemed to gather more thickly around Morrigan as she lowered her hands.

'Not feeling so sure of yourself now, are you, little wizardling?' Her eyes flashed with the green fire of a mid-ocean sunset. 'As for you, warrior girl,' that other-worldly gaze turned on Jane, 'you and I have unfinished business.'

Jane swore sharply, anger and fear mingling in her voice.

Aidan wanted to swear too. Instead, he addressed himself to the goddess. 'Leave her alone, Morrigan.'

He had no idea how he was going to enforce that command but nonetheless he moved to step in front of Jane – and almost collided with her as she stepped forward at the same time. 'What the— What are you doing?'

But when she looked at him, he knew.

'I'm sorry, Tarzan.' The words were addressed to him, but Aidan understood they were meant for Morrigan's benefit. The small, sad shake of her head confirmed it. 'I can't stand by and watch her carve you into little pieces. I just can't.' Jane's shoulders drooped momentarily, telegraphing defeat, but then she straightened, drawing dignity around her like a cloak. 'You'll let me have one last kiss.'

It was a statement, not a request. Jane threw the words at the goddess even as she moved closer to Aidan, her hands reaching up to cup his face.

'Are you mad?' He hissed the words at her as she pulled his head down.

'Have you got a better idea?' Her lips found his before he could answer, effectively smothering any possible suggestion with a bruising kiss. There was nothing soft or sentimental about it; it was all heat and defiance, the kiss of a soldier about to go to war.

Aidan's arms came up automatically, pulling Jane hard against him as he returned the kiss with a fervour of his own. There was knotted tension in the muscles under his hands and he felt the adrenalin pound of her heart as she pressed against him. He was aware his own was hammering just as hard; almost absently he wondered which of them was the more scared.

For a moment more they clung together, holding each other with a desperate ferocity, and then slowly, almost reluctantly, Jane pulled back from the kiss. With her body still pressed against his she touched her forehead to Aidan's. Her voice was barely louder than a thought as she murmured, 'Last man standing, Tarzan.'

It was the seniors' catchphrase, taken from Sensei's oft-quoted maxim that anyone with sense walked away from a fight but, if you couldn't, you were to make damned sure that you were the last man – in Sensei's dojo the word meant human rather than denoting gender – left standing afterwards.

Aidan felt himself go cold. He knew what Jane meant to do. He also knew that there was precious little he could do to help her and absolutely nothing he could do to stop her. Fear for her had him struggling to force his words out. 'Stall her.'

It was still the best chance they had but, even as he said it, he wondered if there was another. Acting on instinct he lifted his hands to where hers still cupped his face. Clasping those strong, capable fingers in his own he guided them down between them. Then, with Jane's body shielding what he was doing from Morrigan, he slipped the strand of amethyst chips from around his wrist and slid it onto hers. He felt her frown, her eyebrows pulling down as they stood brow to brow, but there was no time to explain something he wasn't even sure of.

'For luck,' he murmured, and the soft huff of her breath was warm on his skin as she laughed humourlessly in response.

'Enough!' Morrigan's voice cracked like a whip, demanding attention. 'You've had your farewell, little warrior. Now come here.' The goddess's voice turned silky yet somehow only the more menacing as she added, 'You know what will happen if I have to make you.'

'I know.' The slight hesitation in Jane's voice was pitch perfect. Aidan knew that she was acting but still he had to fight the urge to push her behind him, to tell her to run and to hell with what Morrigan would do to him. Then, her face still hidden from Morrigan, she winked at him. 'Bet she fights like a girl.'

Aidan had done many difficult things in his life, but letting Jane walk away from him then surely had to be one of the hardest. It felt wrong. This was HPS, for God's sake; he should be the one to deal with it, not her. The fact that she stood a better chance of defeating Morrigan than he did, both physically and metaphysically – and would probably point that out to him in the bluntest of terms – made no difference to that ingrained sense of propriety. Frustrated and afraid he cast a sharp glance behind him.

You'd better be right about nulls, Eldritch.

But the wizard in question remained crumpled on the floor with only the shallow rise and fall of his chest showing that he was still alive. However this final act played out, he would have no part in it.

If that thing hurts her …

Aidan glared at his unconscious friend, fear for Jane temporarily displacing his concern over the Englishman's condition. But in truth he didn't know what he would do if Jane's strategy failed. He had an inkling that he wouldn't have to live with the problem for very long combined with an unpleasant feeling that it might seem a much longer time indeed.

Halfway across the hall Jane stopped. She looped her thumbs in the front pockets of her jeans and looked at the waiting figure of the goddess, rather as she might weigh up an opponent from another dojo. 'Before we do this you have to promise me something.'

Morrigan stiffened, an expression approaching shock flickered across her features. 'You seek to bargain with me now?'

'You'd better believe it, lady.'

Both impressed and horrified by his girlfriend's bravado, Aidan found himself praying that she wasn't pushing her luck too far.

Jane, however, continued as though such a possibility had never occurred to her. 'I want your word that you won't hurt them. Aidan and Eldritch,' she added with a backward jerk of her head in case there could be any doubt as to who she meant. 'They're nothing to you, but they're the reason I'm doing this. So, when this is done, you leave them alone. You go your way and you let them go theirs. If you want me to do this, then I want you to swear to it.

'I know you wouldn't bargain with Eldritch,' she continued when Morrigan gave no response. 'I understand that – he's a man.' Jane shrugged negligently, dismissing one half of humanity as intrinsically inferior to the other. 'But you and me?' She flashed a quicksilver smile. 'I want your word, woman to woman.'

And with that she crossed her arms and waited.

'And if I choose not to grant your wish?'

Aidan couldn't tell if Morrigan was amused or angered by Jane's demand. Her voice was icy and yet, if she considered the younger woman to be impudent, she made no move to punish her for it.

'Then I guess we all lose.' Jane's mouth creased in an expression of regret. 'But I think you're more pragmatic than that.' Blue eyes met that cold, alien gaze and held it, unblinking. 'And more generous.'

The goddess tilted her head and in that instant Aidan would have sworn it was Gwyn who stood there. Hope clawed at him, but it was Morrigan, not Gwyn, who answered.

'Very well.' Regal as ever, Morrigan inclined her head, a queen condescending to grant a commoner's wish. 'You have my word, little warrior. When this is over your menfolk will go unharmed.'

'Thank you.'

The heartfelt relief in Jane's voice made Aidan's pulse spike as if in that moment she had decided to go through with her sacrifice for real. She was acting, he reminded himself, and she was incredibly good at it. But that knowledge didn't make it any easier to watch.

Dear God.

He wiped sweating palms along the legs of his jeans. How long could Jane keep this up? How long would she need to before the strain of bearing Morrigan's essence became too much for Gwyn's body? He raged silently at the awful dichotomy of wishing Gwyn dead so that Jane would be safe.

Oblivious to his torn feelings Jane continued, 'Right then, how do we do this?

'You will kneel.' Having granted one concession, Morrigan was back to imperious command. 'You too, wizardling.'

Those elf-queen eyes turned sharply on Aidan, pinning him like a mouse in the gaze of a hunting cat.

'Your woman has bartered for your safety. You will not disrupt that bargain.'

Crap!

Jane might not be expecting his help, but Aidan baulked at the idea of being forced into a position from which he couldn't throw himself into the fight. Yet any refusal risked blowing their charade wide open.

'Do it, Aidan. It will be alright.'

Aidan wished he felt as confident about that as Jane, but he knew he had no option. He did as he was told, folding himself stiffly down to the floor. He didn't have to fake the look of sullen compliance on his face. Jane did the same only a great deal more gracefully. She sat back on her heels, her hands folded in her lap and looked questioningly at Morrigan.

'Now what?'

She looked defenceless, Aidan thought, but with her toes curled underneath her she could come off the floor with surprising speed. It was something that caught out many a partner when Sensei had them practising their takedowns and floor work. He forced himself to breathe slowly as Morrigan stalked forward, but he could do nothing about the fear sweat that slid down his back as she came to stand over Jane.

'You will invite me in, in your mind.'

She pushed back the swags of that hip-length fall of nightshade hair. It was hard to tell in the dim light, but Aidan thought he saw blotches blossoming along her hairline like a handful of dark fingerprints as though blood from unseen haemorrhages was pooling beneath that exquisite alabaster skin. In that moment her features seemed to blur and shift until they formed neither Gwyn's face nor Morrigan's but something else entirely, something far less human, gaunt and sunken like a death's head skull. Was this Gwyn's body failing under the strain of containing Morrigan's energy? Aidan thought it must be, and an anxious cocktail of hope and guilt kicked through his system. *Just a little longer,* he willed his girlfriend. *Just keep her talking for a little longer.* He couldn't tell if the changes in Morrigan's appearance had been visible to Jane – certainly she gave no indication that they had been – and as the goddess leaned forward her face had reverted to the other-worldly beauty of her glamour.

Jane licked her lips. 'Okay.' She gave a soft huff of breath. 'I'm not sure I know how to do that.'

But Morrigan was not going to be delayed any longer. 'Say the words in your mind. It will be enough.'

'Right.' A small laugh accompanied the agreement as though Jane were being asked to do nothing more deadly than to try an unfamiliar karate technique. 'Here goes.'

Jane tilted her face up towards Morrigan, as innocent and natural as a flower turning towards the sun. Her eyelids slid partly closed as she offered herself up to the goddess's will. For a moment Morrigan did nothing. She stood poised above the kneeling woman and her full lips curved into a smile as though she were savouring the moment before transfer. Then slowly and deliberately she bent to take her sacrifice.

Jane's move was timed to perfection. As Morrigan leaned over her she uncoiled, driving the heel of her hand up to smash under the point of the goddess's jaw. Jane was strong and her momentum added further power to the strike. It was a devastatingly efficient attack that should have taken Morrigan down. But it didn't. At the last possible moment Morrigan swayed backwards, her body moving with a sensual, ophidian grace, and the blow that should have knocked her senseless brushed harmlessly past her face.

It seemed to Aidan as though time itself slowed. Even as he saw Morrigan slide out from beneath Jane's blow Jane reversed her strike, dropping her arm in a tight arc to hammer a tetsui into the inside of Morrigan's knee. At the same time, she pivoted her weight to her left, bringing her right leg around in a scything curve to sweep her opponent. Yet unbelievably Morrigan blocked both attacks. In a move so perfect it could have been choreographed, she dropped to one knee, her right hand coming under Jane's arm to deflect the blow while her left arm caught Jane's leg in a scooping motion, trapping it tightly against her own hip. Aidan watched in stunned amazement; he knew seniors with half a lifetime of training who wouldn't have managed such a counter and then he remembered what Eldritch had said about the entity currently possessing Gwyn's body. 'The cult of Morrigan worshipped her as a warrior goddess.'

He felt the blood drain from his face, his whole body turning cold as the implication of that statement hit him like a wave of iced water.

Dear God!

At the same time Jane gave a sharp, involuntary yelp of pain as Morrigan's fist smashed down on the top of her kneecap.

Before he had consciously realised what he was doing Aidan was lurching to his feet, stiff and awkward, his bad leg protesting the movement though he barely registered the impediment. All he could think of was that he couldn't leave Jane to fight Morrigan on her own; good though she was, he understood that she wouldn't stand a chance. He felt his power then, a ball of prickly static forming in the palm of his hand as the adrenalin-frantic hammering of his heart went into overdrive. He was aware of a flash of teal silk, a moving blur of pale skin, of blonde and black hair whipping and intertwining, then he was hurling his power like a shuriken, a bladed throwing star of energy aimed straight at Morrigan's face.

He didn't wait to see the goddess's reaction. He had no expectation of hurting her, no belief that his puny bolt could succeed when Eldritch's had failed, but if he could distract her it would give Jane a precious moment's grace that she would ruthlessly exploit. He saw the goddess throw up a warding hand, but he was already flinging himself forwards. He would just have time to—

Time ran out.

Aidan cried out as the whip of Morrigan's lightning seared across his ribs. Pain dropped him to the floor, the sickening smell of burnt flesh filling his nostrils even as blackness swamped his vision. For a moment he could only lie where he had fallen, his breath hitching in short, shallow gasps as his body reeled from the shock. He knew he needed to get up, that he had to do something to help Jane, but it was all he could manage to turn his head, his cheek scraping along the wooden floorboard. What he saw told him he needn't have bothered. It was already too late. The fight was over.

A wave of darkness washed over him and he let himself sink beneath it like a stone.

CHAPTER 49

'I need to show you something.'

'What?' Startled, Aidan looked around him. A heartbeat ago he had been lying on the floor of St Martin's Churchyard. Now he stood in the echoing vastness of what he had come to think of as his safe space, the unmistakeable grittiness of powdered stone shifting beneath his feet as he turned. And there beside him, somehow visible even though they stood in darkness, was Gwyn. A surge of panicky shock overrode his momentary delight at seeing her clearly and wholly herself. 'No! Gwyn, I don't have time for this!'

He looked down sharply at his side but though a charred hole gaped in the fabric of his polo shirt he felt no pain from the flesh underneath. Yet that did nothing to reassure him. He knew what was about to happen back in the churchyard hall. He should be doing everything in his power to stop it, not talking to a woman who – he was horribly certain – was already dead.

'None of us has much time, Aidan.' Whether a fetch or a figment of his imagination, Gwyn's tone was scathing. 'You, me, or Jane.' She gave him her best basilisk glare to drive the point home. 'But there are things you need to see.'

And before he could draw breath to argue she caught hold of his hand and in that instant they were no longer standing in that comforting darkness. Instead, they were in the small front room of Gwyn's cottage. And they weren't alone.

Gwyn – another Gwyn! – knelt on the floor beside Eldritch's supine body. Mud and leaf litter clung liberally to the wizard's normally pristine boots and smeared the damp charcoal denim of his jeans while the torn and bloodied remnants of his shirt lay discarded on the floor beside him. Shocked, Aidan turned to the woman who was still holding his hand, but she simply smiled as though amused by his reaction. The couple on the floor paid them no attention at all.

'Relax, Aidan.' Gwyn let go of his hand and moved to perch on the corner of her desk. Surprisingly, none of the piles of books and paperwork haphazardly scattered across its surface ended up on the floor as a result.

Which proves this is all in my head, Aidan thought.

Gwyn turned and her elfin brows lifted in a superior look that was quintessential Gwyn. As if she had heard his thought she said, 'Of course this is all in your head, Aidan. Where else would it be?' She looked at him as though over the rim of a pair of invisible glasses. 'But that doesn't mean that it's not real.'

And with that she turned back to the figures in front of them.

Unsure what else to do, Aidan looked at them too. He recognised the scene; this had taken place the previous autumn, the morning after he and Eldritch had encountered the avatar. Gwyn had insisted that she was more qualified to deal with Eldritch's wounds than any doctor they might see if they made the hour-plus trip to either Aberystwyth or Shrewsbury A&E. Aidan smiled ruefully at the memory; at the time he hadn't been so sure and he had had little hesitation in telling Gwyn as much. But why wasn't he part of this little scene? Then he caught the drifting ashtray smell of brewing coffee and the sound of movement coming from the kitchen.

Ah, yes.

He had been making himself useful, brewing tea for Gwyn and more coffee for himself. For a moment he was tempted to go and look, curious as to what it would be like to see himself as he had been then, but he resisted. This wasn't the time for idle curiosity. 'Why are we here, Gwyn?'

Why here when he should be back in St Martin's Churchyard?

'There's something you need to remember.'

'Okay.' Aidan didn't bother to keep the confusion from his voice. 'Why can't you just tell me?'

Gwyn pursed her lips. 'Don't you think that I would if it were that simple?' she demanded as though this should have been obvious to him. When he went to protest she added, 'I don't make the rules, Aidan.'

You could have fooled me, he thought, but he had the sense not to say it. Instead, he asked, 'So what is it that I need to remember?'

'Listen,' Gwyn instructed. 'And think.'

'You used blood to anchor the veil?'

Aidan listened as Gwyn teased out from Eldritch the details of how he had protected the hut where they had sheltered from the avatar. He had seen this, he realised. He had stood in the kitchen doorway – two steaming mugs and a packet of ginger biscuits in his hands – not wanting to interrupt that quiet exchange. He remembered how he had felt like a child eavesdropping on an adult conversation, gathering little titbits of information about this new world that was both frightening and fascinating in its strangeness.

Without thinking he flashed a glance towards the kitchen door and felt his stomach lurch in shock as he saw himself standing there.

Dear God, I look rough.

It wasn't just the mud stains on his hiking trousers – as liberally smeared as Eldritch's jeans – or the unshaven stubble along his jaw. His face had a drawn and haunted look that spoke volumes about what he and Eldritch had been through the previous night – the night his life had changed forever. With an effort Aidan tore his gaze away from his own image and focused again on Gwyn and Eldritch.

'What signs did you use to shape it?' Gwyn was asking.

Eldritch didn't respond immediately. Even the act of remembering seemed to tax what little strength he had but finally the granite and silver voice whispered, 'Keth for strength, Sho for protection and Roc for safety.'

The words had meant nothing to Aidan when he had first heard them. Now he considered those choices, interested to know that he had used two of the three sigils Eldritch had named to strengthen his own shields today.

Gwyn made a little humming noise in her throat. Her head tipped to one side as she weighed up Marcus Eldritch and his choice of wardings.

'I would have used Bel for sanctuary, Mir for silence and Serreth for stillness,' she said.

'Avoid its notice rather than confront it.' The idea seemed to intrigue Eldritch. 'I wouldn't have thought of that.'

Gwyn gave a one-sided shrug. 'You learn to work within the limits of your power.'

'Do you understand, Aidan?'

Gwyn's voice beside him brought Aidan's attention back to the present. He turned to face her but if he had hoped for an explanation of what he was meant to gain from this recollection he was to be disappointed. She put her hand on his arm.

'Just remember,' she said, cutting off any comment he might have made, and then, 'There's more.'

From his earliest childhood, Aidan had associated the smell of Gwyn's house – the mingled scents of herbs, of lavender and beeswax and incense – with comfort and safety. This next location smelled of anything but. Aidan took one breath of the antiseptic-laden air and knew exactly where he was before he had even looked around him. A hospital. His heart twisted at the thought of what he was about to be shown, but when he looked at the figure in the bed he realised that it wasn't his mother who lay there, still and fragile as a china doll against the white sheets; it was Gwyn. He and Eldritch were sitting in grim vigil on either side of the bed.

Even knowing that neither he nor the wizard were aware of his presence, still Aidan found it disconcerting to stand at the foot of the bed, so close he could have reached out and touched either one of them. Even more distressing was the sight of Gwyn. She lay motionless as death, her hair spread out across the pillow like a tidal wave of darkness, a mass of unalleviated black. There had been no skunk stripe in it then. It surprised Aidan to realise how accustomed he had become to seeing that familiar flash of white and he considered this for a moment. It was easier to focus on that than on the horror of bruising that rendered Gwyn's face all but unrecognisable or the awful, empty stillness of her body. He could remember all too readily the queasy coldness that had gripped him when he and Eldritch had been shown to her bedside. At the time he had thought he was going to lose her. And now he was on the verge of losing her again – if she wasn't gone already. Aidan felt the grief he had been trying to deny tighten its claws around his chest.

'Why, Gwyn?' A dozen questions compressed into one.

Her hand felt warm on his arm, her grip solid as she gave a reassuring squeeze, just as she would have done when he was a child. 'It will make sense, Aidan, I promise you. Watch and listen – you'll figure it out.'

'So, what are you going to do?'

Aidan did as he had been instructed, watching himself watching Eldritch, wary and anxious and not quite ready to believe that the wizard was going to agree to help Gwyn. He had known the other man for barely a week at that time and while he was already coming to view Eldritch as a friend, he also recognised that the Englishman had a complex morality in which any individual – including Eldritch himself – might justifiably be sacrificed for the greater good. In contrast to his own edginess, Eldritch seemed self-assured as he leaned back in the grey plastic chair, idly turning Gwyn's rose quartz bracelet in his fingers.

'I'm going to give her some of her power back.'

Hearing that now, Aidan couldn't help but smile at the glib response and the familiar rakish grin that accompanied it. Eldritch might have answered his question but he had done so in a way that left his audience little the wiser, a trait Aidan now knew was typical of the wizard.

He shook his head, raising his eyes heavenwards as he heard his earlier self take the bait and ask the obvious follow-up question.

'How's that going to help?'

You were showing off, he mentally chided the tall wizard as Eldritch's grin broadened.

'The one thing I do know about healing is that it takes a lot of energy. So, I'm going to give her more to draw on.'

'But why the bracelet?'

'Because, while our self-sufficient neighbourhood witch has walled herself off from the world, I can't give her power directly. But if I use this as an energy sink the power's there for her to tap into if she needs it.'

Aidan saw the understanding dawn on his own face and smiled again, this time at his inexperience.

'Just like your ring.'

He sounded like a white belt who had managed to answer one of Sensei's questions. He shook his head. All this had been so new to him back then.

'Exactly. And because the bracelet's hers she's already attuned to the crystals so it should be easier to make a link to them for her.'

Aidan turned away from the little tableau, amused but also puzzled. Power sinks were one thing, but … 'I don't understand, Gwyn. How can you be showing me this? You weren't there.'

Gwyn huffed and drew herself up to her full but unimpressive height, looking like nothing so much as a blackbird indignant at being cheeked by a worm.

'Of course I was there. Who else do you think was in that bed?' A jerk of her chin indicated the small shape – face ghastly above the incongruously cheerful mustard and blue hospital gown. If she felt any distress at the sight of her unconscious self it didn't carry into her voice. 'Just because I wasn't responding to you doesn't mean I wasn't there.'

'Oh.' Suitably chastened, Aidan was about to ask his mentor how that worked when the significance of the comment hit him. 'Oh!'

Gwyn canted an eyebrow. 'Now do you see what I'm getting at?'

Before Aidan could answer the hospital dissolved around them and they were back in the darkness.

'But I don't have any power left, Gwyn. I don't know how to do a final strike—'

Gwyn cut him off. 'And thank the Lady that you don't. That idiot,' and Aidan realised she was talking about Eldritch, 'could have killed me.'

As if her words were a cue the darkness around them thinned like morning mist lifting from the bottom of the valley, and the gritty texture of the floor changed to wooden boards under Aidan's feet. He looked down and saw they were standing beside Eldritch's unconscious form. A dozen feet away his own body lay in an abandoned sprawl while beyond that Jane and Morrigan's intertwined figures were frozen like an Oberammergau tableau.

'Time moves differently here.' Gwyn answered Aidan's unasked question with a one-sided shrug. Though part of him wanted nothing more than to run to Jane's side, Aidan stayed where he was. He couldn't see how the pieces of this puzzle fitted together, but as Gwyn had guided him to them he had to hope that she would also show him the key. He watched as she bent and gently pushed the matted strands of hair back from the wizard's face.

'Will he be alright?' He understood how much that meant to Gwyn.

Gwyn tipped her head in a way suggestive of a noncommittal hand gesture. 'That will be up to him. It's going to be a long journey. Not so much physically,' she qualified. Her fingers lingered for a moment on Eldritch's cheek. 'But his power …'

She stopped and Aidan could almost see her put away the words that she would have used and return to the matter in hand. She straightened up, brushing an invisible fleck of dust from the knee of her jeans.

'A final strike, Aidan?' Her tone was brisk. She shook her head dismissing the idea. 'I wouldn't ask that of you, not to save my life. As for saving hers,' Gwyn glanced across to the motionless figures of Jane and Morrigan, 'well, you don't need a final strike for that.'

'Then what do I need, Gwyn?'

Even with time seemingly suspended, Aidan had no patience for riddles. He wanted a clear answer, something he could act on. What he got was another question.

'Why is the final kata of a grading the best one you do?'

Huh?

But if Aidan had learned one thing during his months as Gwyn's student it was that she rarely asked a question that didn't have a point to it – whether or not he could see it at the time. So, while his initial reaction was to wonder what the hell gradings had to do with their current predicament, he bit his lip putting his impatience to one side as he did his best to formulate an answer.

'Because you put everything into it,' he said, feeling his way around what she had asked.

But there was more. 'Because you feel like you've already given everything you've got and you don't have anything left. And that's what you use. You're probably hurting.' He smiled wryly, remembering ribs cracked during his first Dan grading, courtesy of Graham 'Tigger' Tiggs, and of Sensei telling his subsequent opponents to go for his injured left side. Jane had been particularly remorseless in following that instruction. 'You're so knackered you feel you're going to throw up and you've got all the sick feelings of everything you know you got wrong, that you're sure Sensei's going to fail you on. You take all of that and you channel it into the kata – twenty or so moves.' He nodded to himself, reliving that strange sense of utter determination he knew any of the seniors would recognise. 'You condense all of that into one perfect form.'

Gwyn's smile transformed her face.

'Exactly.' Her forest-cat eyes locked on his, demanding that he understand. 'Use everything. Everything physical.' She jabbed a finger at his side. 'Everything that's in here.' She tapped her chest over her heart. 'It's time for you to wake up, Brightboy.'

Her eyes twinkled with sudden mischief as her use of his childhood nickname made Aidan scowl.

'Use it,' she whispered. 'Use it all.'

Then, like a human version of the Cheshire cat, she faded away leaving only a wicked grin behind her. He blinked and even that was gone.

CHAPTER 50

Aidan opened his eyes and did a momentary double take as the world swam back into focus. Everything was once again tilted on its side, his cheek pressed into the grubby boards of the churchyard's floor. For a moment he almost wished himself back in that comfortable darkness with Gwyn. But he knew that was futile and besides it seemed that Gwyn was right.

Time moves differently here.

The tableau in front of him hadn't changed. Morrigan's hands still gripped Jane's head and Jane was still frozen in horror as she waited helplessly for the goddess's next move – the sudden twist that would snap her neck or the kiss that would steal her body. It made little difference which it was to be – either would kill her. What mattered now was what Aidan could do about it. He clamped his teeth on another groan, automatically steeling himself to ignore the pain radiating from his side. But for once the pain was having none of it. It pushed back at him and in a voice reminiscent of an angry basilisk glare it reminded him of what he had to do.

Use it.

Aidan didn't know how he was going to do that, but he did know he had to try.

'Okay, Gwyn.'

He couldn't have said if the promise was in his head or on his tongue, but he let his eyes slip closed and with a mental shrug dismissed all thought of resistance. He took a deep in-breath and as he exhaled he let the red energies of pain fill him.

'The choice is yours now, little warrior.'

Aidan didn't think he should be able to hear the whispered murmur of Morrigan's words as she leaned close to Jane's ear, but they came to him anyway.

'Resist me and I will kill you.'

It seemed as though he could feel the desperate rigidity of Jane's body and the frantic hammering of her heart. Rather than draw back, Aidan pulled the sensations to him, wrapping them in the clammy folds of his own shivering fear. He hadn't realised how much simple feelings could hurt but if it was bad for him, how much worse must it be for Jane? And yet still she managed to reply.

'You … lose too.' A pause as she sucked in breath. 'No … vessel.'

Aidan felt a momentary rush of pride blazing like sunshine, defiant and golden and bright.

'Do you think my having no vessel will save him?'

Morrigan's words were a feral promise of pain tarnishing the brightness and turning it grey and bitter as ashes. Aidan felt her grip tighten and Jane's pulse spike in horror and panic. Sick dread drenched him followed by the leaden burn of helpless and impotent anger when Morrigan laughed. Hating himself, he clutched at the ugly, lumpen shape of it, adding its black and red coals to the messy tangle of energies building within him.

'This body will last more than long enough for me to kill him.'

Even with closed eyes Aidan could picture the sensuous curve of those full red lips as the goddess smiled.

'You think you understand pain and how he will die? Little warrior, you have no idea.'

But Aidan did. He had often thought he had too much imagination to be brave. Now he deliberately opened himself up to the fear of what Morrigan was promising, reaching out for each slippery, queasy dread and letting them wrap around him like cold and greasy tentacles slithering over his flesh.

Dear God, this has to work.

He scooped up the desperate agony of that hope and the even more hideous fear that told him what he was doing could not possibly be enough – fear for himself and for Jane and for Gwyn, if it wasn't too late to save her. There was fear for Eldritch too and for what Morrigan would go on to do if she wasn't stopped. He moulded them all together, weaving in the muddiness of bone-deep fatigue and finally, dragged up from the very core of what he held himself to be, he added in the silver-white ferocity of determination, sharp as a fine blade and burning bright as magnesium.

And then there was no more to be done.

He felt the cold fire filling the marrow of his bones like quicksilver.

He was ready. He reached inwards.

'Don't.'

The one word forced from an overextended throat broke his concentration.

What? Oh God, Jay, no!

His eyes snapped open and the power slid away from him, running from his grasp. Frantically Aidan tried to clasp his mind around it and haul it back, but all he could see was Jane's face staring up at the goddess, the winter-sky blueness of her eyes wide and overly bright against the sweat-sheened pallor of her skin.

'Leave him … alone.' The desperation in Jane's voice was another source of pain. 'I'll … give you … what you want.'

'Don't play with me, little warrior. Say the words.'

Jane's eyes didn't stray from the goddess leaning over her, but Aidan thought he heard his name in the whisper of breath as she exhaled. He felt as much as saw the rigid tension go out of her body.

'I … let … you in.'

Morrigan's head lifted, her eyes flashing jade fire, triumphant in the gloom. Then, like an eagle mantling over its prey, she arched forward.

No!

As though a dam had burst within his flesh, Aidan felt the rush of power flood through him. It rose up through his bones and poured into his hands, pooling there like phosphor and molten silver. He had thought to throw it but instead it seemed to him that he stood up, the wooden floorboards dissolving into gritty sand beneath his feet as he stepped forward. He was aware of the soot-streaked walls falling away into darkness and then all that was left was the image of his hands closing around the silver and turquoise cuff encircling Morrigan's wrist and the string of amethyst chips around Jane's.

'Come back to us, Gwyn.'

He felt as though his flesh should be glowing, lambent in the tenebrous gloom, as the energy flowed through it pouring from him into the waiting reservoir of semi-precious stone and metal.

'We need you. I need you.'

He was aware of another flow of energy moving from the amethysts under his left hand through him and into that broad cuff under his right. Everything he was seemed to join with that stream until he couldn't have said where flesh ended and crystal and metal began.

Aidan felt a strange rippling as though the fabric of the world had shivered and for a moment he was incarnate again, but now it was his hands that were gripping Jane's head, his lips that were curving open as he bent over his captive. Then the world shuddered again and he was back in his own body, chest heaving as though he had run to the point of exhaustion, watching as Morrigan's mouth closed over Jane's.

'No!'

He hurled the protest across the hall, tried to roll to his feet and failed. Dizziness swamped him even as he dragged himself up to all fours and stopped, staring at the scene in front of him. Jane now lay on the floor in front of the kneeling goddess, her body curled in on itself in a protective huddle, her arms raised to shield her head and neck. Though she didn't move the tight clamp of her muscles told Aidan she was still conscious. Given the circumstances, that was little comfort.

Morrigan herself was staring at Aidan. No, not at him, he thought, but through him as though there was nothing directing that gaze, no intelligence behind those emerald-green eyes, as if that capricious mind had already moved on to a new home.

Oh, dear God ...

A wave of cold ran through him as though his body had been doused with iced water. Even as he watched, Morrigan's eyes closed. The goddess swayed then sagged forward, catching herself on one arm to stop herself going face down on the floor but making no other move. Then very slowly she lifted her head, and it was Gwyn's face that looked blankly back at him.

Aidan didn't dare breathe, waiting for those familiar features to morph and change. For several heartbeats nothing happened and then, almost painfully, the woman in front of him blinked.

'Sweet Lady!'

The voice was Gwyn's, Morrigan's hauteur replaced by the dazed but altogether familiar tones of his ex-guardian. Moving carefully, she sat back on her heels, gingerly twisting her head from side to side as though it were she who needed to ease an overstrained neck. Then she paused, looking back at Aidan as though only just registering his presence. Her dark elfin brows drew down as she studied him. For a moment she seemed on the verge of asking him what he was doing on the floor but then she visibly dismissed any such concerns as irrelevant. Instead, she pulled herself up straight and lifted her chin.

'I could really do with a drink.'

CHAPTER 51

Even in the bright late-morning sunshine the West Cemetery at Highgate retained an air of other-worldliness. Passing between the massive black iron gates that dominated the entrance to the cemetery and into the shade of the entrance porch Aidan paused, taking in the tidy yellow brick arches of the Colonnade and the dense green of the wooded hillside beyond. There the chaotic ranks of huge Victorian headstones, mausolea and monuments could be glimpsed, crowding together amongst the trees; vast waves of carved stonework slowly subsiding back into a living shroud of ivy and equisetum, bracken and fern. In the leaf-dappled sunlight angels and crosses, broken pillars and covered urns leaned at crazy angles alongside the winding pathways, crammed between sarcophagi and chest tombs, headstones and ledger slabs. And behind each was another, pushing close as if jostling for position, ready to step forward when the front row finally collapsed.

Yet, for all the crazy profusion of gothic monuments, there was also an aura of peace about the dilapidated splendour. The gently sloping grounds lacked the neatness of the small cemetery at Llancathan with its tidy, ordered rows of headstones in black and grey marble, none over hip height and all with a carefully regimented amount of space around them, but there was something soothing about the obvious age of this place and its slow slide back into nature. No traffic sounds penetrated to disturb the cemetery or its occupants. It wasn't a Welsh hillside, but the London air here was fresh and there was a sense of timelessness that spoke to a simple part of Aidan's soul, easing some of the sadness at the task that lay ahead. He took a long, steadying breath and, with a last look at the view, went to join the tall man standing silently beside the war memorial, staring up to where the great inverted sword spilled green verdigris onto the Cross of Sacrifice, the stain spreading out across the pale stone like strange and alien blood.

Eldritch looked awful. Even as a friend, Aidan could think of no kinder word to describe him. The wolf grey eyes were red-rimmed and raw looking, as though the wizard had lain awake throughout the night, and possibly for many nights before. He had lost weight in the weeks since Aidan had last seen him, not that he had been carrying any excess before. Now, with his dark hair slicked back from his temples – a look that accentuated the sharpness of his cheekbones and the angular prominence of his nose – he looked like a displaced Lucifer still mourning the loss of heaven, or perhaps one of the Victorians' feared Resurrection Men, the grave robbers that the cemetery's high gates and fiercely spiked railings had been designed to keep out.

'Hi.' Aidan gave his friend a wry smile, as brief as the greeting. He didn't ask the older man how he was; the question was superfluous.

Still, Eldritch gave him a small, lopsided shrug – a minuscule movement, more tic than gesture – as though he had heard the question anyway and this was the best answer he could give. *I've no idea* or maybe *I'm still here.*

Aidan nodded in response, understanding. Though the circumstances had been different, he too had buried people he had loved. He knew that nothing he could say would make things easier. He had once told Eldritch that the trick to survival was to keep breathing until help arrived. The wizard looked as though making it to his next breath was an achievement that was by no means certain. And yet, Aidan thought, even with a world of hurt and grief radiating from him, Eldritch looked better than he had.

Physically, the wizard had recovered surprisingly quickly from his ordeal at the hands of the grieves and from the injuries he had received confronting Morrigan. Aidan had no doubt that that was largely due to Gwyn's fiercely attentive care, administered whether or not her patient had wanted it. But not even she had been able to get anything but a blatantly false response of 'I'm fine' to any question concerning the Englishman's mental state or to crack the wall of gallows humour he had taken refuge behind. Marcus Eldritch had retreated from the world, rebuffing all attempts at comfort as unnecessary and unwanted. He had tolerated the presence of his friends but had withdrawn so totally from any emotional engagement that Aidan had wondered if he could possibly find his way back. Painful though it was to witness, today's achingly visible grief suggested that Eldritch might be ready to let them close again.

And perhaps the best thing he could do to help Eldritch heal was to stop treating him as though he was broken. Aidan shook Eldritch's hand and then punched him on the biceps, just hard enough to make the wizard blink.

'Hang in there.'

For a moment Eldritch looked as though he would speak but perhaps, like Aidan, he was unsure what to say. In the end he nodded instead. Aidan stepped back, satisfied for now that the smallest chink had opened up in that wall of self-declared invulnerability. He glanced over his shoulder back towards the entrance. It was time for the big guns.

Jane had hung back deliberately to give Eldritch and Aidan space. Now she came to join them, the heels of her black patent leather court shoes clicking on the stone sets as she walked across the courtyard. In a black skirt suit and white blouse, with her hair brushed back into a sleek ponytail, she looked smart and efficient and worlds away from the fierce-eyed fighter who had faced off against a warrior goddess in the burned-out gloom of St Martin's Churchyard. Aidan smiled inwardly. It was surprising how deceptive appearances could be.

To be honest, we both scrub up well, he thought.

Bruises had faded and battered bodies recovered. Even the burn over his ribs was healing well, reduced to a puckered red weal that was now more itchy than it was painful. He would carry the scar for life, but it could have been so much worse. No, neither of them would be taken for fighters today.

Typical of Jane though – she looked a lot more comfortable in her suit than he felt in his, but then she didn't have to spend the morning with a noose around her neck. Aidan resisted the urge to run a finger around the inside of his collar and took a moment to appreciate the rare spectacle of his girlfriend's stocking-clad legs instead. From the corner of his eye he caught Eldritch's puzzled look and then his almost comical double take as he suddenly registered who this unfamiliar career woman was. Aidan realised Eldritch had never been exposed to the phenomenon that was Jane in a business suit and smothered a proprietary smirk along with several more inappropriate thoughts before either could get him into trouble.

Fortunately, Jane missed the smirk or perhaps, given the circumstances, chose to pretend that she had. Nor did she waste time with meaningless platitudes. Without any preamble she caught Eldritch in a swift, strong hug that was more like the prelude to an aikido throw than an embrace – encircle, grip, unbalance your opponent – except that in the middle of that sequence she kissed Eldritch's cheek, looked him straight in the eyes, and said something in a voice pitched too softly to carry to anyone else's ears. Then, before Eldritch had time to do more than stare at her in surprise, she stepped away, giving him back his personal space after having so comprehensively violated it. Looking slightly overwhelmed, Eldritch managed the faintest twitch of his lips in response. He was still off balance when Gwyn joined them.

Like Jane, she had abandoned her more familiar uniform of bright shirt and faded jeans for a black skirt and jacket, albeit ones that could best be described as neat rather than stylish. Aidan noted that she had opted for a pair of flat ballet pumps rather than Jane's choice of killer heels, but then Gwyn had never needed heels to make her presence felt. Still, her wild hair was swept back and tamed in a classic French plait and even her jewellery showed an uncharacteristic level of restraint, being limited to a heavy silver cuff inlaid with opal and jet on her right wrist and just the one strand of amethyst chips alongside the watch on her left. The only thing about her that wasn't pared back was the oversized black leather handbag she carried on one shoulder. Aidan could only guess at what was concealed in its depths and Gwyn's cryptic response of 'Nothing for you to worry about' when he had asked her that morning had left him none the wiser.

But Eldritch knew. As the tall wizard eyed the bag and its bearer, Aidan saw something – acknowledgement? gratitude? – flicker in the back of those grief-shadowed eyes. Whatever it was he was sure that Gwyn was acting with the wizard's approval. That belief became certainty as Eldritch stepped forward, closing the distance between himself and the Welsh witch. He inclined his head slightly, somehow managing to give the impression of an old-fashioned courtier bowing over her hand.

'Gwynyfa.' The deep voice sounded rusty and underused.

'Marcus.' Gwyn returned his formality with her own.

For a moment she held his gaze, solemn and reserved as the occasion demanded. She had changed too, Aidan thought, since that afternoon in St Martin's Churchyard. Not in a way that he could give voice to – she still seemed like the Gwyn of old – but sometimes he wondered if she was being too Gwyn, as though she was trying to deny that the act of channelling Morrigan had altered something deep within her. She had said very little about what she had done while possessed of the goddess's energy, and would not be drawn at all on what had happened after that capricious entity had manifested fully, something she claimed to have no clear memory of. Aidan wasn't brave – or foolhardy – enough to challenge her on that, but he wondered if she did recall the power that had blazed through her and was mourning for the time when her own magic had burned as bright.

He thought he sensed that sadness in her now as she stood facing the wizard, but then she smiled and it was like the sun breaking through the clouds after a summer storm. She looked the wizard up and down, her head cocked to one side as she studied him, for all the world like a small blackbird assessing the suitability of a well-dressed but not overly padded scarecrow as a potential nesting site.

'You look very smart.' There was neither appraisal nor judgement in her comment; it was simply a statement of fact.

Eldritch glanced down as though he had momentarily forgotten what he was wearing. A little self-consciously he straightened the immaculate silk waistcoat just visible under the tailored wool of his suit jacket. Both fitted him well, Aidan noted, despite his weight loss.

'Yes.' The soft breath of sound was almost apologetic as though the wizard was worried they might think that being smartly dressed was somehow inappropriate for his wife's funeral. Gwyn offered him a curiously gentle smile in return. Rising up on tiptoe, she reached out and picked a fleck of lint from his shoulder. Her hand closed briefly on his arm in a wordless gesture of comfort.

'I think she'd be pleased.' There was no need to ask who she was referring to.

Grief momentarily tightened the network of fine lines around Eldritch's eyes, like an imprint of physical pain. He turned away, long fingers pinching the bridge of his nose, his eyes screwing shut, but when he turned back moments later his face was composed once more.

'Thank you.' The words were shaky, but the sentiment was sincere.

There was a moment of awkward silence. Eldritch checked his watch then self-consciously squared his shoulders. He cleared his throat. 'Perhaps we should go.'

The grave lay just a short walk from the Colonnade along the curving shingle and tarmac path. Shaded by the branches of a mature hornbeam and with the rising hillside forming a backdrop the ground dipped slightly to form a small dell. A tall granite chest tomb, adorned with bas relief anchors twined around with curling strands of ivy, guarded the approach while on the far side a serene-faced angel pointed the way to heaven with one outstretched finger. All around the two tombs the ground was thick with the glossy green spears of bluebell leaves and the broader blades of wild garlic pushing up through the leaf litter. There were wood anemones there too, Aidan noted. The flowers themselves were long since over but in spring this whole area would be a profusion of blue and white petals. He pictured the wooded hillsides around Caeglas and, like an unexpected treasure pulled from a conjurer's pocket, the memory came back to him of his mother's delight each year when their slopes softened beneath a sweet-smelling violet-blue carpet. He gave a little huff of breath, bemused that a recollection could be both sad and happy at the same time and wondered if Eldritch had felt a similar dichotomy in choosing this spot. It was a beautiful last resting place for the woman he had loved.

A tug on his arm jerked Aidan out of his reverie. 'Hmm?'

He turned to Jane, adjusting his pace to match hers as she slowed and almost stopped. 'Where is everyone? Surely we can't be the only people who've bothered to turn up?'

She kept her voice soft in deference to their surroundings, but the look she shot him was anything but. In her heels she stood as tall as he did and there was no missing the little kink that anger carved between her brows. Because he knew her Aidan also recognised the concern that underpinned that emotion.

He looked again at the burial plot – the dark cut of the grave surrounded by protective green matting to keep the mourners' shoes out of the newly turned soil, the coffin on its trestles positioned to one side and the small group of people waiting on the path – and he realised what Jane meant. There were six pallbearers in their uniform black suits, their faces schooled into professional solemnity, their backs soldier straight. At the head of their line was the undertaker distinguishable by the silk top hat and silver-headed cane held respectfully in his gloved hands, and beside him a tall, regal-looking woman whose cap of peroxide-blonde hair belied the smooth ebony of her skin. Aidan marked her out as the celebrant, although her simple black shift gave no indication as to which faith or doctrine she might represent. He bit his lip unhappily. Eight people and each one of them had been paid to attend. Where were Helen's friends and family, the people who had known and loved the living woman? He glanced around but there were no latecomers following behind him and Jane and no sign of anyone else congregating on the path beyond the grave site. No one else had come; not Carol nor any of the other neighbours; not even the cousin whose insistence on medical intervention had kept Helen's body alive. Aidan glanced at the tall figure in front of them. Even with Gwyn walking beside him Eldritch seemed remote and somehow distant, as though an invisible wall separated him from them, rendering him unreachable.

'I think we're the only ones he asked.' Aidan shook his head, bemused and uncomfortable with the idea that there had been no one else Eldritch had wanted to attend, that the three of them were perhaps the only people he trusted to be with him today. His heart ached at the thought and at the responsibility such trust entailed.

'Maybe because we were there, because we know what really happened …' He searched for the words or the reasoning that would make such a thing alright and failed to find them. 'I don't think he could face anyone else.' Not their questions and the sideways, inquisitive glances, nor the need to give answers that would match the reported circumstances of Helen's death while avoiding the truth. 'I don't know.' Aidan shrugged helplessly.

Truth be told, he had been surprised when Gwyn had called to pass on the details of the funeral. In the weeks since the events in St Martin's Churchyard, Eldritch had stayed in London, dealing with the questions and the inevitable speculation. Every time he had passed the empty house on Caeglas Terrace, Aidan had wondered if the wizard would come back. As time had passed it had seemed increasingly unlikely. Even now, Aidan wasn't sure what Eldritch would decide to do. The man was city born and bred; you could tell it by looking at him. Though he had given every appearance of settling into rural life, Eldritch belonged in the city in a way that Aidan knew he himself never would – not that he could imagine ever wanting to. He eyed the black-clad wizard unhappily, not caring to think of how much he would miss the Englishman if he decided not to return to Caeglas.

He turned back to Jane. 'Gwyn said she thought there'd be a memorial service later.'

The cyber ninja considered this. The kink between her eyebrows softened, her expression now more sad than angry. 'Perhaps once they've added her name to the headstone?' she suggested.

The existing lettering, pale gold and elegant against the dove grey marble, spelled out only the name Paul James Asher and the dates that bounded his life. Helen was being laid to rest beside her brother.

'Yeah, maybe.'

But somehow it was difficult to imagine Eldritch having planned anything beyond today's funeral.

'Come on, we don't want to hold things up.'

If Eldritch was upset by the lack of mourners, his face showed no sign of it. Then again, save for the physical signs of grief, which nothing but the passage of time would erase, Eldritch's face wasn't showing very much at all. Aidan watched his friend as he responded to the celebrant's greeting. Her words were met with the slightest of nods to show that they had been understood, but at no point did Eldritch look as though the words meant anything to him. The aching vulnerability that the tall man had shown as they stood in the Colonnade was gone, locked away behind a stoic's mask. Perhaps the wall he had retreated behind wasn't as strong as the barrier he had erected in the immediate aftermath of their defeat of the grieves, but it was there nonetheless. No wonder he had seemed so remote as they walked to the grave site; he had been withdrawing from them even then, contracting back into the safety of that self-imposed exile. The realisation troubled Aidan, but he knew there was nothing he could do about it now. He could only hope that this was a temporary retreat, an act of self-preservation that was the only way Eldritch knew to get through what lay ahead. Mentally Aidan acknowledged his friend's coping strategy while making a silent promise that he would be around to help pick up the pieces when that protective wall shattered, or to help to break it down should that prove to be necessary.

Jane's hand tightened around his own as if she had felt his tension and was offering her unspoken support. He returned the pressure, grateful beyond words that she was there, a pragmatic, no-nonsense ally. He glanced at Gwyn and she turned her head towards him as though she had felt the weight of his gaze. Her expression didn't change but he felt the nudge of her power against his shields, like a cat bumping its head against his arm. Like the squeeze of Jane's fingers, there was reassurance and agreement in that simple gesture. Aidan allowed himself to relax a little. If Eldritch decided he was going to descend into hell he was going to have to go through the three of them to do so.

'I'd like to take a moment first, if I may.'

Eldritch's voice was like the whisper of wind across a granite tor, bleak and desolate. But though he phrased the words as a request there was no suggestion that he was seeking anyone's consent.

Now it was the celebrant's turn to nod in understanding. Her smile was sympathetic as she stepped aside. 'Of course. Take all the time you need.'

Eldritch approached his wife's coffin like a priest drawing near to an altar, silently, almost reverently, each step measured and restrained. His gaze was fixed as though everything else around him had ceased to register, as though he stood alone outside time and space and the only thing that was real to him was that one wooden casket.

Like the woman herself, Helen's coffin had an understated elegance. The sides were made of contrasting panels of blond and honey-coloured woods, seamlessly blending together, with an inlaid brass trim running just below the lid. The smooth, rounded curves of the brass handles were almost voluptuous, inviting the hand to caress them like the swell of a woman's breast. Whether deliberately or not, Eldritch had captured some of the essence of his wife in the choices he had made for her interment.

A large, pillowed spray decorated the top of the coffin, a mass of cream and pink roses, woven through with a scattering of deep raspberry stargazer lilies and the crisp white of carnations. Their perfume rose and mingled with the green scent of the trees and the dark smell of freshly turned soil.

Eldritch's fingers brushed over them, a flicker of pain breaching the mask of his face as he inhaled, breathing in that evocative mix of scents. He went very still and Aidan tensed, waiting for the tidal wave of grief he felt sure was about to follow, but Eldritch only swallowed heavily and the moment passed. Slowly, carefully, the wizard placed his hands on either side of the cascade of flowers, pressing his palms flat to the coffin lid as though he might somehow feel Helen's presence beneath it. His eyes closed as he leaned forward, his expression achingly tender as he bent his head, his cheek against the wood just as he might once have rested it against the flesh of the woman within. Was he listening for one last message from her or whispering a final goodbye? Feeling like a voyeur, Aidan dropped his eyes to his shoes, not wishing to intrude in this most private of communions. He kept his head bowed until he heard the soft slur of movement that signalled Eldritch's return to the little knot of mourners.

The celebrant stepped forward, her expression gently querying. 'Should I start?'

For a second Eldritch stared at her, like a prisoner nonplussed by his torturer asking his permission to tighten the thumbscrews. Ingrained politeness took over. 'Please.'

The words *get this over with* hung unspoken in the air between them.

'We are gathered here today to commit the body of our friend and loved one, Helen Lydia Eldritch, to the earth. Beloved wife, sister and friend ...'

Aidan listened as the celebrant outlined the details of Helen's life. How long, he wondered, had it taken her to perfect that gently solemn tone? Her voice held a trace of accent that he couldn't place but the overall effect was rich and smooth, like the taste of rum-laced coffee drunk from a flask after a day out in the hills. It was an odd image to conjure with, standing in a London cemetery in the bright heat of a summer morning, but somehow comforting. He glanced at Eldritch, standing rigid and remote, for all that he was physically close, bearing his grief with a terrible, private dignity, and hoped that some small measure of that sense of solace might reach him.

Even if he does decide to stay in London, at least let him be happy with that choice.

'We do not know what lies beyond this earthly plane, but we lay Helen's body to rest in this place in a spirit of gratitude for her life and in sadness for her loss.

'It is only natural that we feel such sadness. We should not try to mask it for to do so is to deny Helen's importance to us and the depth of our feelings for her. Yet, while we acknowledge those painful feelings, we should not focus on the fact that Helen is gone. Instead, we should be joyful for the time that she was with us. For this is the truth each of us must find the courage to remember – the world was blessed by Helen's living presence. That blessing is not undone now that she has moved beyond us. Helen would be the first to tell us that this is so.'

The celebrant's dark eyes locked on to Eldritch's as if willing him to accept this and be comforted by it. For a moment he met her gaze and then he lifted his head, staring off into the green canopy of the trees as though he could not quite bring himself to do what she asked, not yet. His lips tightened, holding firm against the emotions churning inside him, but the freshness of tears brightened his eyes. He didn't look as the celebrant turned to the undertaker. She said nothing, but he must have been waiting for this moment for he handed his hat and cane to the nearest pallbearer and walked to the coffin, pausing at its foot to bow stiffly. But as he moved to grasp the casket spray Eldritch spoke.

'Leave it.' The granite and silver voice was sharp, as though those were the only words the wizard could manage. The undertaker froze for a second then stepped back empty-handed. In dignified silence he retrieved his hat and cane and, taking this as their cue, the six pallbearers arranged themselves around the coffin and with quiet efficiency lifted it from its trestles and into position over the grave.

'As we commit Helen's body to the earth, to rest beside her brother Paul, I ask you to remember both the pleasure that Helen brought to this world and the joy that she herself experienced from it. In doing this we honour her memory, and we can be certain that she will live on within our hearts.'

Slowly the pallbearers lowered the coffin and its cascade of flowers into the grave. Aidan swallowed to ease the knot that tightened unexpectedly in his throat as he watched it sink downwards. He hadn't known the woman the celebrant had described but he realised now he would have liked to have done so. He watched as the earth seemed to rise up around the pale wood as though the grave were reaching out and embracing it. The soil reached the level of the brass trim and then the lid. For a solitary moment the flowers themselves seemed suspended above that hungry void and then, in the space between one heartbeat and the next, they too were gone from sight. Aidan shuddered; dear God, he hated funerals.

Wishing that the whole thing could be over he watched the pallbearers withdraw and the celebrant take her place once more beside the grave. She looked back at the mourners but then turned and her next words were spoken not to them but to the woman they had come to inter.

'Helen Lydia Eldritch, we will hold your memory forever in our hearts but now we set you free to continue your journey. May you ride on the winds and dance among the stars. May the sun caress you at dawn and the earth comfort you at night. Lay your body down and be at peace.'

She bowed once to the grave and the woman within it and then she straightened and, though she still moved with the innate dignity of her office, Aidan realised that the ceremony was over.

'Thank you.' Framed in the slicked-back wings of his hair Eldritch's face looked paler than ever, but from somewhere he dragged up the wreck of a smile as the celebrant came over to join him. 'That was a beautiful service, Tanith.'

Tanith's own smile bloomed in response, open and unforced. It wiped the gravity from her face and with it the years that her air of solemn composure had lent her. Her eyes sparkled with genuine pleasure and Aidan realised she was younger than he had assumed.

'I'm glad you thought so.' Her smile widened to encompass all four of them before she focused back on Eldritch. 'We'll leave you now,' a brief glance acknowledged the undertaker and pallbearers patiently waiting a discreet distance away along the path, 'but you can stay as long as you wish. There's no rush.'

'Thank you.' The twitch of Eldritch's lips was little more than a reflex of politeness as brief as his words.

Tanith paused, studying him for a moment and then reached for his hand. 'Will you be alright?' The professional gravitas was back, mantling her like a cloak, but it did nothing to hide the natural compassion that had provoked her question.

Eldritch looked down, contemplating the fingers clasping his own as though to give himself time to consider his answer. The silence stretched as he took a deep breath then exhaled it in a slow sigh like a man refamiliarizing himself with the art of breathing. 'Yes.'

And just possibly, Aidan thought, the tall man was telling the truth.

'We'll stay for a few minutes.'

'Alright.' Tanith rubbed her thumb over Eldritch's knuckles in a gesture at once familiar and yet oddly formal, then let his hand go. 'You have my number. Call me if you need to, any time.'

Eldritch stood silently, watching the black-clad figures walk away, heading back towards the Colonnade and the cemetery entrance, their duty done. Only once the curve of the path had taken them out of sight did he turn and address the woman standing patiently beside him. 'Would you?'

Gwyn tilted her head, looking up at him with the calm composure of someone who had been waiting for that exact invitation. 'Of course.'

For a second something flickered in the back of the wizard's eyes, an odd mix of emotions, and it seemed as though he might make some additional comment but then he swallowed, his expression closing back in on itself and the moment passed. Wordlessly he gestured with his hand: *go ahead.* It was as though he didn't quite trust himself to speak.

Whatever reticence Eldritch might feel regarding what was about to take place it was clear that Gwyn did not share it. She stepped towards the grave purposefully, as though it was the most natural thing for her to do. After a moment Eldritch followed her, walking round to the far end of the grave to stand beside his brother-in-law's headstone. Like the wordless squeeze of a hand on a comrade's shoulder his long fingers curled briefly around the chamfered stone and Aidan wondered what words his friend would have shared with the deceased man and what message he might have hoped for in return.

'Now what?' Jane's hair brushed against Aidan's cheek as she leaned her head close to his, her voice pitched for his ears alone.

'God knows.'

Whatever Gwyn and Eldritch had planned he wasn't privy to it, but as Gwyn started pulling items from her oversized handbag and laying them out on the green matting Aidan realised he did know what his mentor was about to do.

Oh.

'Is she …?' Jane spoke as though she too had guessed the answer and didn't much care for it.

'Yes.'

Aidan heard the sharpness in his reply and grimaced, surprised by his own discomfort. It wasn't as though he considered the casting of a circle to be sacrilegious, yet it felt inappropriate here, even if it was being done with Eldritch's blessing.

And why would Eldritch need—?

He got no further with that thought.

'The first sign she's going dark side on us and I'm pushing her in that grave.' Jane's tone was matter of fact but Aidan didn't think she was joking.

Having survived one encounter with rogue magic – and, given the hours she was spending with Sensei practising neck locks and chokeholds and the best ways to break them, Aidan knew his girlfriend was still processing that experience – of course she wouldn't stand by and let any future HPS get out of control. Equally, being Jane, she would have no qualms about letting both their resident magicians know that that was the case. She certainly wasn't keeping her voice down.

Still, it was a moot point whether Eldritch got the warning. The tall Englishman didn't react to Jane's words although he must surely have heard her. But Gwyn turned her head, her gaze fierce as she studied the younger woman.

'I appreciate the sentiment, Jane,' she said in a voice that suggested appreciate might not be an accurate description of her feelings, 'and you'd be entitled to do so. Indeed, I believe I said as much to you last time, in the event of anything going wrong.' Gwyn's winged brows quirked as if inviting the younger woman's recollection. 'However, I promise you that won't be necessary today.'

Jane's response was a huff of breath that suggested she was reserving judgement. 'Just so you know.'

Gwyn tipped her head in acknowledgement.

'Now that we've got that out of the way I propose we continue,' she said dryly.

With that the older woman turned away from the grave and, with a half bow to the angel guarding the neighbouring tomb, she dropped her bag beside the celestial being's feet. Moments later her shoes joined the bag and Gwyn stepped back to Helen's graveside unselfconsciously barefoot, wriggling her toes as though she would push them down through the matting and root them in the soil underneath. It was such a Gwyn thing to do that Aidan found himself smiling. Nevertheless, apprehension prickled the hairs on the back of his neck as she raised her face to the sky and spoke.

'Gatherer of Souls, Watcher on the far horizon. You who stand against the darkness, I ask your help.'

In the gloomy confines of St Martin's Churchyard Gwyn's invocation of Morrigan had brought power seething around her, but today there was no such answering surge of energy. Her words had power certainly – Aidan could feel the intent behind them – but generated no obvious effect. Here, in the green-scented sunlight, Gwyn might be nothing more than a small middle-aged woman adding a New Age litany to a funeral. He allowed himself to relax as he watched her pick the first of the packages from the matting, nodding in recognition as she tipped a small heap of salt crystals into the palm of her hand. This was familiar. His fingers twitched as she sketched the pentagram glyph for Earth over it with neat, economical moves, just as when she had first drawn it for him in her kitchen. But instead of pouring the salt into the grave as he had expected, she held out her hand as though displaying the little pile of crystals to a waiting crowd.

'Spirits of the Earth, Guardians of the North, I ask your protection.'

Eldritch, who had remained unmoved by Jane's outburst, turned his head sharply. On the one occasion Aidan had witnessed the English wizard casting a circle the process had been a silent one – if there had been any dedications Eldritch had made them in the privacy of his own mind. Watching how his lips tightened now, Aidan gathered that Eldritch didn't necessarily approve of Gwyn's way of doing things. Yet the salt went into the grave in a neat cascade and Eldritch's expression softened as if the Englishman had reminded himself that this was Gwyn's ritual, not his.

With the north cardinal point dealt with Gwyn picked up her remaining markers. Two cloth-wrapped bundles – one red, one black – went into her suit pockets along with the plastic bag that had contained the salt. She kept a little packet of yellow crystals in her hand as she moved to the foot of the grave.

On the Day of Judgement the dead were meant to sit up in their graves, their faces to the sunrise and to the glory of the second coming. Or at least, Aidan thought, that was what Gwyn had told him was the reasoning behind the once traditional Christian burial alignment. His teacher had an eclectic knowledge of the world's religions and, though she had her own beliefs, she would pepper such facts through her lessons when the fancy took her. Aidan could still recall the mischief in her voice as she pointed out that the practice could equally be viewed as an act of homage to the Morning Star and to the Guardians of the East. He guessed it was those latter entities that Gwyn would entreat for their protection now.

Gwyn's deft fingers duly sketched the swirling lines of the glyph for Air over the palmful of yellow crystals she held up to the sky. Flowers of sulphur, Aidan thought, and recalled she had spoken of mixing them with incense or with pollen grains although he couldn't remember what governed that choice. He wondered which she had used and whether Eldritch would have done the same, but a glance at the wizard gave no indication of approval or disapproval and Gwyn made her invocation without interruption. Then, with a steady breath she blew across her outstretched palm sending the crystals aloft in a canary-bright stream that showered down into the grave.

So far so good, but as Gwyn moved to stand on the left side of the grave Aidan felt a surge of discomfort as he realised which direction came next. There were two ways to mark the south, but the transient brightness of fire was only suitable for a power working that had to last no more than a few hours. Every instinct was telling him that Gwyn intended the wards of this circle to be permanent – and that would require a very different marker indeed.

He licked his lips, making himself breathe slowly as Gwyn withdrew the red silk bundle from her pocket. He understood the principle of what she would do, but his heart still lurched with the swift surge of adrenalin as she unwrapped the stiletto shape of a small bone-handled knife.

It's Gwyn. She wouldn't hurt you, he told himself, swallowing against the sudden dryness in his mouth and trying not to think of her incarnation as Morrigan. Beside him Jane made a low sound like the disapproving rumble of Sula's warning growl. Strangely his awareness of her fear calmed Aidan.

'It's okay,' he murmured even as she pulled her hand free of his, getting ready to fight. His fingers found hers again and gave them a reassuring squeeze. 'This is normal HPS.'

He could almost laugh at the words, remembering the first time he had seen this done amidst the lamplight and shadows of a forest hut. He had known nothing of casting circles then and Eldritch had made a lame joke about virgin blood to ease the tension. The wizard didn't look up to joking now; there was a rigidity in his stance that hadn't been there previously and he was staring fixedly down at the edge of the grave just inches beyond his feet. Still, Aidan thought it wasn't so much that Eldritch was afraid of what Gwyn was about to do. It was more the case that he simply didn't want to watch it. Aidan could sympathise with that. He didn't want to see this either, but he made himself keep looking.

Perhaps Gwyn could sense their unease because, for all her flamboyance working with the first two directions, she made no drama out of what she did next. In a small, precise movement she sliced the point of the knife across the ball of her thumb. Jane's breath hissed – in protest or sympathy, Aidan wasn't sure which – as blood welled up behind the blade. Gwyn herself ignored both the blood and her audience's reaction, deftly rewrapping the knife one handed and tucking it back into her pocket. Only then did she look at the cut she had made, drawing the Fire glyph over the dribble of red collecting in her cupped palm.

'Spirits of the Fire, Guardians of the South I ask your protection.'

Her voice was as strong and level as it had been for the other directions, but then Gwyn wasn't one to wobble at the sight of blood, not even when it was her own. As she finished, she turned her palm and let that most personal of offerings drip into the waiting earth.

The colour of the west was black and Gwyn's final marker was a long shard of obsidian, the glassy, volcanic rock that ran in seams as dark as the Styx. She held it between her fingers as she stood at the head of the grave, careful not to contaminate its surface with any trace of her blood. On the other side of Paul's headstone Eldritch watched her, his expression unreadable as, dainty as one of her cats, she licked a fingertip and drew the glyph for Water onto the shining surface. The vitreous stone glittered in the sunlight as she raised it in front of her like a sacrificial dagger.

'Spirits of the Water, Guardians of the West, I ask your protection.'

Gwyn opened her hand and the final marker slid from her fingers and dropped into the earth.

And so, it was done.

With the four cardinal directions named and physically bound to the working, Aidan thought that Gwyn would close the circle but instead she turned and looked expectantly at Eldritch. She said nothing but for a moment something beyond grief tightened the lines around Eldritch's eyes. The hand resting on Paul's headstone stiffened, the knuckles showing white below the dark wool of his suit cuff. Then the hand relaxed and Eldritch nodded.

'Of course.' There was no hint of mockery in the deep voice as he returned Gwyn's earlier words to her.

For her own part the smile Gwyn gave him in response held nothing of the sandpaper edge that so often marked their exchanges. Instead, there was only encouragement as though she knew that what she was asking would be hard for him. Not knowing what that might be, Aidan was surprised when Eldritch reached into the breast pocket of his suit and pulled out his grandmother's ring.

Aidan had last seen the ring when Gwyn had picked it off the floor just before they had left St Martin's Churchyard. There had been so much going on in the aftermath of that day that he had given it little thought. Now he wondered just when Gwyn had returned the ring to the wizard and how Eldritch felt about having it, given what was imprisoned in its central stone. Aidan shivered remembering the twisting wraiths of oily black smoke that had been sucked into the sapphire and how the stone itself had seemed to change as a result. Just the idea of having it in his possession made his skin creep. He shuddered again.

Yet, if Eldritch had any such reservations about the ring he showed no sign of them. If anything his expression turned slightly wistful as he held it in front of him, the thin gold band gripped carefully between thumb and forefinger. The central sapphire might be dark but the diamonds surrounding it still glittered in the sunlight, throwing back tiny rainbows with the movement of Eldritch's hand. For much of his adult life Eldritch had carried the ring as a tool, as a power sink. Now, watching the way he gazed at its delicate antique shape, Aidan realised that the wizard had valued it just as much as a keepsake of the woman who had been his teacher but also his much-loved grandmother.

Slowly and deliberately Eldritch raised the ring to his lips although Aidan noted that the wizard turned his hand at the last moment, smothering the ring in his fist so that his lips touched only his fingers and not the ring itself.

'Look after her for me, Grandma.' The gravelly voice shook just a little. 'You too, Paul.' His other hand tightened on the stone above his brother-in-law's name as he leaned forward. 'Keep us all safe.'

Then, like a gambler throwing a dice across a table, Eldritch cast the ring into the grave. The tiny chink of sound as it struck the coffin lid was just audible in the quiet of the cemetery and Eldritch's lips tightened as he stared down into the earth.

'To pay for the crossing,' he said as if addressing someone or something only he could see. He didn't look up as, on the other side of the headstone, Gwyn lifted her face once more to the sky.

'Guardians of the four directions, elemental spirits, we place the grave of our sister Helen in your protection. Hold it within the circle of your light this day and every day.'

Aidan tensed but he felt no change in the atmosphere, no other-worldly presence coming to join them. Unsure whether to be disappointed or relieved he looked at Gwyn, but she seemed blithely unconcerned that her ritual had generated no tangible result.

And then Aidan felt it, a sudden change in pressure as the temperature dropped and a breeze sprang up out of nowhere. It brushed his skin, cool and welcome, until he realised that none of the leaves on the hornbeam were moving. In that same instant he thought he saw a foxfire gleam shimmer across the grave, columns of coloured flame – black, white, yellow and red – burning in the air at each of the cardinal points and gone even as he tried to look at them. Once more the air moved and then the breeze dropped as suddenly as it had sprung into being. Gwyn turned to look across the headstone at Eldritch and Aidan caught her smug, cat-got-the-cream expression as the wizard slowly raised his head to meet her gaze. 'Amen,' she said.

Eldritch's head inclined fractionally, the merest suggestion of a nod acknowledging what she had done just as his own whispered 'Amen' acknowledged the end of the ceremony. The wizard offered Gwyn a tenuous smile but his gaze was already returning to the grave as though what lay within held more relevance for him than anything beyond it.

The look of triumph faded from Gwyn's face. With lips pursed she studied the wizard as, almost unconsciously, he crossed his arms over his chest, hugging himself as if despite the warmth of the late-morning sunshine he had grown chilled. He looked as though, with the ritual over, he didn't know what to do next; that, having come so far, he had no idea how to take the first step into the rest of his life.

It was Gwyn who moved first. Rather than reach out to Eldritch she left him to his brooding, opting instead to retrieve her belongings from the angel's plinth. She hitched her bag over one shoulder, brushed off the soles of her feet and then slipped on her shoes as unselfconscious as though she stood in her own garden. Then, respectable once more, she walked back to where Eldritch was still staring into the grave.

Without any preamble, she linked her arm with his. 'Come on,' she said.

The top of her head might have barely come level with his shoulder but when Gwyn had decided something she was akin to a force of nature. With a none-too-gentle tug she started Eldritch towards the path. As the pair of them reached it she jerked her head at Aidan and Jane, indicating that they should follow.

'Let's go home.'

AUTHOR'S NOTE

I would like to thank all the people who read my first two books and contacted me to say they wanted more of Gwyn, Aidan and Eldritch's adventures. I hope you think this latest outing was worth the wait.

Thank you to Lesley Jones for her line edit, her detailed commentary and her positive feedback. The finished book is much tighter as a result - and I hope she'll forgive the occasional external point of view I've left in. Any errors that have crept in during the final writing are down to me. Thanks also to Sanja Gombar for her striking cover design and to the ever-helpful team at Matador for their work formatting the book you have before you now.

Llancathan is a figment of my imagination. London was created by far stranger minds than mine.

To find out more about my writing visit my website:
www.kimgravell.com.

If you enjoyed this book please consider leaving a review on Amazon or Goodreads.

This book is printed on paper from sustainable sources managed under the Forest Stewardship Council (FSC) scheme.

It has been printed in the UK to reduce transportation miles and their impact upon the environment.

For every new title that Matador publishes, we plant a tree to offset CO_2, partnering with the More Trees scheme.

MORE TREES
LET'S PLANT A BILLION TREES

For more about how Matador offsets its environmental impact, see www.troubador.co.uk/about/